GRAF SPEE'S RAIDERS

GRAF SPEE'S RAIDERS

Challenge to the Royal Navy, 1914–1915

Keith Yates

Naval Institute Press   Annapolis, Maryland

All photos used by permission of Wilhelm Heyne Verlag are taken from R. R. Lochner,
Die Kapernfahrten des Kleinen Kreuzers Emden, © Wilhelm Heyne Verlag, München, 1982.

Library of Congress Cataloging-in-Publication Data

Yates, Keith, 1928–
    Graf Spee's raiders: challenge to the Royal Navy, 1914–1915 / Keith Yates.
        p.   cm.
    Includes bibliographical references and index.
    ISBN 1-55750-977-8
    1. World War, 1914–1918—Naval operations, German. 2. Spee, Maximilian, Graf von,
1861–1914. 3. Müller, Karl von, 1873–1923. 4. Germany. Kriegsmarine—History—
World War, 1914–1918.
I. Title.
D581.Y37   1994
940.4'5943—dc20   94-29959
                                                                                          CIP

Printed in the United States of America on acid-free paper ∞

9 8 7 6 5 4 3 2

First printing

To June

Old and young, we are all on our last cruise.

—*Robert Louis Stevenson*
"Crabbed Age and Youth"

Contents

Illustrations

MAPS

Preface

I t is now about fifty years since I first read about the exploits of Graf Spee and Karl von Müller, and I have never forgotten those stirring tales of courageous and chivalrous sailors. My interest in things nautical was reawakened during my brief career as a seaman in the Royal Navy, and I read all the books I could find about the German cruisers in the Pacific in World War I. Although my naval service was in peacetime, I felt I had gained a fair appreciation of what it must have been like for the men on board those hunted ships and those of their relentless pursuers. A common thread weaves its way through the experiences of those opposing men and ships, even though their areas of operation and fates were quite different. I have now tried to link all their stories together in one narrative, keeping to the chronology of events as best I could.

In researching this book I found such a wealth of published material that I've had to be selective to keep it to a digestible length for the average reader with an interest in military history, like myself. (The book is not aimed at academic historians; it would have been presumptuous of me to try to write such a book.) My use of the references listed in the bibliography has been highly subjective, and I make no apologies for this. I have not used any footnotes because these tend to distract the attention of the lay reader from the flow of the narrative. I have striven for accuracy, however, inventing nothing and staying clear of the "faction" approach to the narration of historical events. Any errors or omissions are solely my responsibility.

I have generally followed the practice of previous authors of giving abridged versions of direct quotes since the abridgments did not significantly affect the sense or context. But in a few cases I have given the complete quotation to convey the full flavor or impact.

I have relied heavily on the excellent books of Hirst, Hough, and Irving for information about the Battles of Coronel and the Falklands and on the equally enjoyable accounts of Keble-Chatterton, Hohenzollern, Hoyt, Lochner, McClement, Parker de Bassi, and Van der Vat for details of the careers of individual raiders. For general information on naval operations in 1914–1918 I found the authoritative series of Corbett, Marder, Raeder, and Scheer invaluable. Two other less comprehensive accounts that are remarkable nonetheless for their readability are Bennett's *Naval Battles of the First World War* and Hough's *The Great War at Sea,* and I made extensive use of both of these excellent texts. For general background on the Europe of 1914 the books of Falls, Gilbert, Hough, and Morton were especially useful.

I have tried to give a fair and balanced account of the activities of both sides, but because of the nature of the topic, I have tended to write more from the German perspective than from the Allied viewpoint.

One minor but persistent problem I encountered was the spelling of certain place names. In some cases I found so many variants that it seemed that every source I read used a different spelling. The island of Simeuluë, for example, appeared in at least half a dozen different versions. I decided in most cases to adopt the spelling given by the authoritative *Times' Atlas of the World.* Exceptions to this are the spellings of Chinese place names. It seemed historically more appropriate to use the English transliterations of Chinese characters that were common in 1914 rather than the new system in widespread use today. Tsingtao, for instance, seemed preferable to Qingdao, since this was the way all the English-speaking authors spelled it.

Another problem area was South American place names. Many of those given in historical accounts were the English versions of Spanish names, and in most instances I have stuck to the names given in those sources. For example, I have used Last Hope Inlet rather than Seno Ultima Esperanza. Other places have been renamed by the Chileans and Argentines since 1914. Más á Fuera is now Más Afuera, and Vallenar Roads appears to be the mouth of the Gulf of Corcovado. In a few cases it was difficult to identify with certainty the locations of some of the more obscure bays, channels, and inlets in Tierra del Fuego and Patagonia that are mentioned in historical accounts. In these cases I have identified their location with reference to the nearest important landmark.

Ship names were less of a problem, except for Russian vessels. I found that the name of the first Russian merchantman captured in the war was spelled in at least five different ways, depending on the author's transliteration of the Cyrillic characters. Since the ship was obviously named after the city of Ryazan, I adopted the spelling given in the *Times' Atlas*. The variants of the name of the Russian cruiser sunk at Penang were even more numerous. I consulted a Russian colleague who assured me that the best equivalents of the Cyrillic letters led to the spelling *Zhemchug*. My spellings of the several German cruisers named *Cormoran* or *Kormoran* may seem whimsical, but they are based on the two German spellings of the word cormorant that were in use in 1914 and 1939, respectively.

For technical details of warships I have relied on the nonpareil *Jane's Fighting Ships* in its various editions, or the authoritative Conway series *All the World's Fighting Ships*. Occasionally these sources differ, but not to a great degree. For details of merchant vessels, including correct names, I have relied mainly on the compilations of Jung and Stevens for German and British vessels, respectively.

Finally, I want to acknowledge the help and encouragement I have received from many people. I sincerely hope I have not missed any of them in what follows. If I have, I can only put it down to failing memory and not deliberate intent.

I greatly appreciate the comments and suggestions of those who read the manuscript in draft form: Ivan Pojarlieff, Jack Edward, Jeremy Edward, Arnold Gatzke, and particularly Alexander Finlayson. I would also like to thank my friends and colleagues Bill Nelson and Bill Callahan for encouraging me to venture into their territory—history—which, after working in a totally disparate field for so long, I did with some trepidation. I thank Beverley Slopen for her interest, invariable kindness, and patience in making suggestions for the improvement of the manuscript, and Ian Montagnes and George Burns for useful comments.

To the librarians at the Universities of Toronto, McGill, and Victoria I would like to express my appreciation of their help in tracking down source material, and I offer particular thanks to Warren Holder, Head of Circulation at the Robarts' Library, for his liberal interpretation of borrowing regulations.

Special thanks are due to Rae Pemberton-Billing for her excellent typing of the first draft and, together with my daughter Nicola Fillier, for leading me through the intricacies of WordPerfect. I also thank Frank Safian for his excellent drawings of maps and Deidre Reid and Bill

Hayward for their help with the illustrations.

I would also like to express my sincere appreciation to Anne Collier and Linda O'Doughda of the Naval Institute Press for their encouragement and valuable editorial experience.

Last, but far from least, I thank my wife, June, for her constant support and patience.

Keith Yates
Mayne Island, British Columbia

Prologue

He was a cut flower in a vase. Fair to see yet bound to die.
—Winston Churchill, First Lord of the Admiralty

I f you ask them, most people who lived during the Second World War will have heard of the *Graf Spee* and the Battle of the River Plate. Those who saw the newsreels in December 1939 will remember the dramatic sinking of the German pocket battleship off Montevideo, after she had been torn apart by the internal explosions set off by her own crew. But few of them will know anything about the man who gave his name to this unfortunate vessel, or what he did to be so remembered by the German navy.

In the incredibly short span of the twenty years before the First World War, Adm. Alfred von Tirpitz built a navy that by 1914 was ready to challenge the Royal Navy for its long-held supremacy at sea. With the powerful support and influence of his master, Kaiser Wilhelm II, he transformed the negligible Prussian navy—really no more than a coastal defense force—into a modern oceangoing battle fleet. The Germans, especially their emperor, were justifiably proud of the new *Kaiserliche Marine*. It was now the second biggest navy in the world.

But when it came to naming its mightiest warships, the Imperial German Navy had no traditional or honored names of its own to give them. They usually named their battleships after federal states—Nassau, Westfalen, Ostfriesland—or gave them royal titles such as Kronprinz, König, or Kaiserin. The Germans' rivals in the Royal Navy, on the other hand, had no shortage of time-honored names like *Warspite* and *Revenge,* or the names of famous admirals such as Nelson, Collingwood, and St. Vincent.

A few of the German navy's newest ships, the battle cruisers, were named after heroes, but these were Prussian generals and field-marshals— Moltke, Lützow, Seydlitz—not naval men. That they should name warships after soldiers, not sailors, was hardly surprising. Germany had become a world power because of its army, not its navy. The German army was the most powerful military machine in the world in 1914, and its generals considered the navy a mere adjunct to their land forces. Even as late as 1900, the overall direction of German naval policy was in the hands of the army general staff.

All this changed in November 1914, when a largely unknown and junior admiral named Graf Maximilian von Spee shattered the myth of British naval invincibility once and for all.

As they prepared for the Second World War, the high command of Hitler's *Kriegsmarine* were determined to commemorate both the admiral and the ships that had given Germany its first-ever victory at sea. They called one of their new pocket battleships *Graf Spee;* two other battleships were named *Scharnhorst* and *Gneisenau.* The earlier versions of the latter two had been named after famous Prussian generals, but there is no doubt that when the new battleships were launched in 1936, it was Graf Spee's armored cruisers that were being venerated.

Still other ship names from the First World War were carried on by the Kriegsmarine. The most famous of these was the *Emden,* also a member of the Graf Spee squadron. This elusive little cruiser and her gallant captain, Karl von Müller, all but paralyzed merchant shipping in the Indian Ocean in 1914 by carrying out daring attacks on Allied trade routes and shore installations. The *Emden* led dozens of British, French, Russian, and Japanese warships on a merry dance for more than three months until she was finally cornered and destroyed by a greatly superior enemy.

Several other light cruisers distinguished themselves in 1914, and their names were also borne by German ships in 1939. The *Karlsruhe, Königsberg, Nürnberg, Leipzig,* and *Dresden,* though less famous than the *Emden,* all played their part in building a tradition and esprit de corps in the German navy.

Graf Spee and his cruisers accomplished a great deal in 1914–1915 in addition to the damage they inflicted on Allied warships and merchant ships. They gave Tirpitz's young navy the self-confidence it had badly lacked in the years leading up to the war. The men of the Imperial German Navy had for a long time harbored deep feelings of inferiority when they compared themselves to the Royal Navy, with its enduring and glorious roll of great sea victories and naval heroes. Graf Spee and his men changed all that. The brilliant exploits of these ships, and the courageous and often chivalrous behavior of their officers and men, belong to an earlier and less ruthless era of naval warfare. They richly deserve the acclaim they received, from their enemies and fellow countrymen alike.

This book is an attempt to tell the story of Graf Spee and his gallant men in an interrelated and more-or-less chronological narrative covering the period from August 1914 to June 1915. It is a tale of courage, minor successes, occasional triumphs, and, ultimately, tragedy.

Table of Equivalent Ranks

KRIEGSMARINE	UNITED STATES NAVY	ROYAL NAVY
Admiral	Admiral	Admiral
Vizeadmiral	Vice Admiral	Vice-Admiral
Konteradmiral	Rear Admiral	Rear-Admiral
Kommodore	Commodore	Commodore
Kapitän zur See	Captain	Captain
Fregattenkapitän	——	——
Korvettenkapitän	Commander	Commander
Kapitänleutnant	Lieutenant Commander	Lieutenant-Commander
Oberleutnant zur See	Lieutenant	Lieutenant
Leutnant zur See	Ensign	Sub-Lieutenant
Oberfähnrich zur See	——	——
Fähnrich zur See	Midshipman	Midshipman Cadet

GRAF SPEE'S RAIDERS

1

Prelude to War

We had . . . a kind of subconscious feeling that we were approaching a difficult time.

—Hans Pochhammer, first officer of the *Gneisenau*

D uring the morning of June 12, 1914, a large gray four-funneled warship steamed into Kiaochow Bay, her White Ensign and admiral's pennant waving gently in the offshore breeze. She was HMS *Minotaur,* the flagship of Vice-Adm. Sir Martyn Jerram, commander in chief of the Royal Navy's China Station. The *Minotaur* was making a friendly visit to the German naval base of Tsingtao. No less than the harbormaster himself came out in the pilot boat to help steer the fifteen-thousand-ton armored cruiser safely to the dockside. She slowly made her way past two white-hulled German warships anchored in the roadstead and headed toward the inner harbor, where a smaller ship, the light cruiser *Emden,* was tied up. When the *Minotaur* had finished docking, the two larger ships—Seine Majestäts Schiff *Scharnhorst* and her sister ship *Gneisenau*—moved from their customary deep-water anchorage to tie up alongside the *Minotaur.* Both protocol and convenience demanded that all the ships lie close together during the British visit.

The armored cruiser *Scharnhorst* was the flagship of Adm. Graf Maximilian von Spee's East Asia squadron, which the Germans simply called the *Kreuzergeschwader* because it was the only cruiser squadron they had. (Most of their other cruisers were attached to the High Seas Fleet to act as scouts for the battleships in the North Sea.)

At full strength there were five ships in Graf Spee's squadron, but two of them were away from Tsingtao. The light cruiser *Leipzig* had left a few days before the *Minotaur*'s arrival. She was now docked at Yokohama,

1

taking on coal and provisions before starting the first leg of her long journey across the Pacific to relieve the fifth member of the squadron, the *Nürnberg*. Graf Spee had sent the *Nürnberg* to Mexico to try to protect German businesses and civilians during the civil war that had been raging on and off for more than a year. At the time, she was at Mazatlán waiting for the *Leipzig* to arrive.

Graf Spee was not pleased with the timing of Admiral Jerram's visit. The relief ship *Patricia* had only just left Tsingtao, and the hundreds of fresh crew members she had brought from the naval barracks at Kiel and Wilhelmshaven needed training at sea. It was the squadron's practice to replace up to one half of the crew on each ship every two years, and Graf Spee needed time to bring his cruisers back to their normal level of efficiency. The admiral and his captains were eager to get on with the job of coaling, loading ammunition and supplies, and dozens of other last-minute tasks before they took their ships to sea for the annual summer cruise to the Pacific islands. They didn't want to carry out their preparations under the eyes of the visitors, given the developing tension in Europe and the strong possibility of war against these same guests.

The British were naturally keen to observe the German ships and their state of readiness and to glean any information they could about Graf Spee's plans for his squadron that summer. It was Jerram's responsibility to keep a close eye on the so-called German East Asiatic Squadron because at the outbreak of war, it would be his job to hunt down its ships and destroy them. The timing of his visit was hardly accidental.

All the same, relations between the Germans and the British on the China Station had been cordial for a long time. They had fought together during the Boxer Rebellion in 1900 and had cooperated in the European relief expedition to Peking. More recently, they had joined forces to protect expanding European interests in China against both the Chinese government and the rebel warlords. The *Emden* and her captain, Karl von Müller, had already distinguished themselves in attacking rebel forts on the Yangtse River in the previous year, fighting alongside British and American warships.

During this period it wasn't unusual for German and British officers to dine together on board ship or for their crews to go carousing with each other on shore leave. It was natural that the Germans would try to show their guests the greatest hospitality that Tsingtao and the squadron could offer. Anything less would reflect badly on the honor of the Kaiserliche Marine and the German empire. Preparations for the summer cruise would simply have to wait.

After the *Scharnhorst* and *Gneisenau* had docked, the day began formally with an exchange of visits by the two admirals and their staffs. Less formal visits took place between the captains and officers of the *Minotaur* and the three German cruisers. That evening, Admiral von Spee gave a dinner on board the *Scharnhorst* for the senior officers of the *Minotaur,* and the next night the governor of Tsingtao, Alfred Meyer-Waldeck, himself a navy captain, gave a grand ball for the ships' officers and local dignitaries and their families at his official residence.

On the last evening of the *Minotaur*'s visit the officers of the *Gneisenau* held an open house and dancing party for the British visitors and distinguished residents of the German colony. There was a lavish buffet in the officers' mess and dancing on the quarterdeck to the music of the ship's band. The dance floor lay directly beneath the muzzles of the 8.2-inch guns of the *Gneisenau*'s aftermost turret.

Like most people in Europe, the party goers realized that war between Germany and Britain was probably inevitable. None of them had any idea how imminent it was. The remoteness of the colony from Berlin and London lent the occasion a sense of detachment from such concerns. After all, not much had happened in Europe that summer.

The days were also filled with festivity, on shore as well as on board ship. Naturally, a football match was arranged between the German and British crews; the British sailors won, five goals to two in overtime. There were boxing matches, a whaleboat race, track-and-field events, and a tug-of-war, which the German seamen won, thus satisfying the honor of both sides. After an enjoyable four days, it was time to get back to more serious matters.

The *Minotaur* cast off on June 16 and headed out of the harbor toward her secondary base at Weihaiwai, two hundred miles to the north of Tsingtao. It was no accident that Britain had established a second treaty port so near to Tsingtao. Its main naval base at Hong Kong was more than a thousand miles to the south, too far away for the Royal Navy to keep a close watch on the movements of Graf Spee's squadron.

After the *Minotaur* had left, the squadron went back to its preparations for the summer cruise. Life in the German enclave of Kiaochow—two hundred square miles of territory along the south coast of Shantung province—returned to normal. The Germans had moved inland because they needed a naval base on the Chinese mainland from where they could oversee their Pacific empire. They had chosen Kiaochow because of the excellent ice-free harbor at Tsingtao, to say nothing of the valuable mineral resources inland, especially the excellent Shantung coal, which they needed as fuel for their warships. Rich deposits of gold, copper, and kaolin were also mined in the area, and the Germans built a railway to bring these to port at Tsingtao.

Germany had been determined to join the other European powers in their exploitation of China in the late nineteenth century, even though it was slow off the mark compared with Britain, France, and Portugal. In 1897 it made an offer to the Chinese government to buy the Kiaochow territory. The only government response this provoked was a movement of troops into the area. Soon afterward, the murder of two Lutheran missionaries provided Germany with a convenient pretext to send in three warships and a squadron of cavalry, under the command of Prince Heinrich of Prussia. In the words of his elder brother, Kaiser Wilhelm II, "We must take advantage of this excellent opportunity before another great power either dismembers China or comes to her help! Now or never!"

Backed up by the threat of naval bombardment, German troops landed at Tsingtao without meeting resistance and occupied the entire enclave. In 1898 Germany pressured a weak Chinese government into signing a treaty that leased Kiaochow to Germany for ninety-nine years, in much the same way that Hong Kong was leased to Britain.

Within fifteen years the Germans had turned a small fishing village into the bustling seaport and commercial center of Tsingtao. They spent in excess of 50 million marks—a huge sum in 1900—to create a naval dockyard and separate harbors for warships and merchant vessels. The city was made to look like a German provincial town, with tree-lined streets, a railway station, theaters, hotels, cafés, and spacious parks and gardens. There was even a racecourse, a concert hall, and, as in any German town, a beer garden. Its patrons drank the locally brewed Tsingtao Beer, which is still popular in China today.

The Germans set up barracks, infantry works, and gun batteries on the hills east of the city. Some of the guns faced inland, ready to repel an invader; others faced out to sea, guarding the entrance to Kiaochow Bay against a naval attack.

By 1914 Tsingtao had become the centerpiece of Germany's Pacific possessions, which stretched from the Marianas in the north to New Guinea in the south. They had other harbors at Truk, Apia, and Rabaul, but none of these had the well-defended naval facilities of Tsingtao. Germany needed a strong squadron of warships to guard its eastern empire, and Tsingtao was its only secure base in the Pacific.

Germany's colonial adventures began in the 1880s after the expanding trade of merchants from Bremen and Hamburg had reached as far as Samoa and New Guinea. This was a period of European expansion, and

Germany didn't want to fall even further behind Britain as an imperial power. The Kaiser's dictum was, "If anyone dare to interfere with our good right, ride in with the mailed fist!"

Germany had already seized Southwest Africa in 1883, and in 1885 it annexed Togoland, the Cameroons, and the part of East Africa later known as Tanganyika. But it had no Pacific territories. The British had moved into the Pacific by making treaties with native rulers, and Bismarck decided it was time for Germany to consider "how she can secure for her trade the larger and yet unexhausted portion of the South Sea Islands."

He sent one colonizing expedition to the New Guinea area, "leaving a trail of German flags behind them until their supply was exhausted." To the added annoyance of the British, place names, as well as colonial rulers, were changed. New Britain became Neu Pommern, New Ireland became Neu Mecklenburg, and the group of islands off the northern coast of New Guinea was renamed the Bismarck archipelago. The Kaiser found there was prestige as well as profit to be gained from his eastern empire, and when the northern part of New Guinea was annexed, it was called Kaiser Wilhelmsland.

Nor was Germany idle elsewhere. By 1890 it had occupied Western Samoa, and in the next few years it annexed the Marianas, Carolines, Marshalls, and part of the Solomons. In the many natural harbors in this vast array of islands and atolls, the cruiser squadron could anchor and take on coal, fresh water, and provisions. The Germans also set up a network of cable stations and high-powered wireless transmitters: at Yap in the Carolines, Apia in Samoa, and Herbertshöhe in New Guinea. This enabled Graf Spee's cruisers to keep in touch with the *Admiralstab* (naval staff), but even so, it often took a day or more for messages to be relayed from Berlin.

All of these island possessions needed protection, and it was the squadron's duty to visit them periodically to show the flag. According to Admiral von Tirpitz, the role of the squadron was "to represent the German navy abroad . . . and to gather the fruits which have ripened as a result of the naval strength of the Reich . . . embodied in the Home Battle Fleet."

Sometimes it was necessary to put down uprisings by reluctant members of the new imperial domain. The cruisers were called upon to shell rebel strongholds into submission so that armed landing parties could go ashore on punitive raids. The Germans captured the insurgent leaders, executing some and transporting others to more remote islands where they would cause less trouble.

But by 1914 the cruisers' visits had for the most part become peaceful affairs, and their crews looked forward to pleasant trips ashore. Local

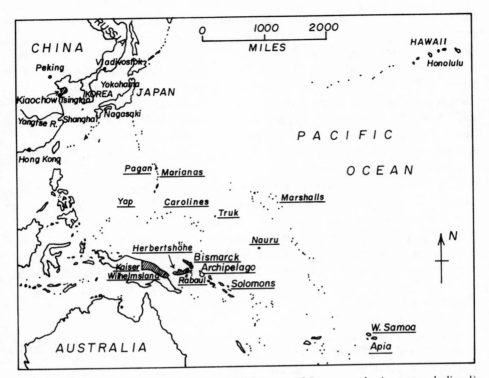

Germany's Pacific colonies in 1914 (Names of German colonies are underlined)

chieftains often entertained them by giving sumptuous banquets, usually accompanied by music and native dancers.

Unlike his men, Graf Spee preferred to spend his time ashore exploring the natural vegetation of the islands, collecting samples of exotic plants and making notes of the wildlife. Sometimes he went on these trips with his son Heinrich, from the *Gneisenau,* or with her captain, Gustav Maerker, who shared the admiral's keen interest in natural history.

But Graf Spee had a more pressing need in the summer of 1914. He was eager to bring each ship's company back to peak efficiency as soon as possible, in case war broke out, so this was going to be a training cruise, especially for the new officers and men. Most important were gunnery and torpedo practice, which were to be carried out at sea, with each ship taking a turn at towing a target for the others. The Germans stressed gunnery above all else because they knew their ships were likely to be overmatched by the bigger fleet of the Royal Navy. Their best chance of survival, let alone victory, was to outshoot their opponents.

Nearly as important, the crews needed practice in coaling at sea. This was every bit as laborious and filthy a job as coaling in harbor, but difficulties were magnified when transferring coal from another ship, particularly in any kind of rough weather. Yet this would often be necessary in the coming weeks if they were to have any chance of surviving as fighting ships. Failure to coal frequently and efficiently could mean their destruction. If they ran low on coal and were unable to outmaneuver or run away from a superior enemy force, their only alternatives were to scuttle their ships or face dreary internment in some neutral port.

After the delay caused by the *Minotaur*'s visit, it was more urgent than ever to prepare quickly to leave Tsingtao for the summer cruise. The *Gneisenau* was the first to take on provisions and coal for the lengthy voyage. Graf Spee ordered Captain Maerker to go to Nagasaki before meeting the *Scharnhorst* at Truk in the Caroline Islands, to see if any important messages from Berlin were waiting for him at the German consulate.

It took two full days to complete the filthy, backbreaking task of taking on board two thousand tons of clean-burning Shantung coal, which would give the *Gneisenau* twenty days' steaming at her most economical speed of ten knots. The Germans normally hired coolies to do all the work when they coaled in harbor, but this time the admiral was in such a hurry to get things under way that the *Gneisenau*'s crew were pressed into service as well.

Men on shore in the coal sheds had to shovel the coal into two-hundred-pound sacks, which dockside cranes then hoisted on board the cruiser in cargo nets. The bulging nets were dumped on the ship's deck near the coal chutes, where seamen waited to empty the heavy sacks by hand. The stokers below kept trimming the growing piles of coal at the bottom of each chute by shoveling it into the corners of the bunker. It was grueling work for all concerned because of the choking dust and stifling heat, especially below decks. The crew's mood was not improved by the sure knowledge that the procedure would have to be repeated in another two weeks. The German sailors sardonically referred to the whole business as a *Kohlenfest* (coaling festival).

By the time the job was finished, coal dust was everywhere, and a dark haze hung over the ship. After the men had washed the black grime from their eyes, hair, and bodies, their next task was to clean the ship. It took almost as long as coaling itself to remove every trace of coal dust from the guns, machinery, decks, and living quarters.

The cleanup was still going on when the *Gneisenau* sailed out of Tsingtao harbor on the morning of June 20 to the stirring music of the favorite "Die Wacht am Rhein" (The Watch on the Rhine), played by the *Scharnhorst*'s band. The men of the departing cruiser responded by singing the folksong popular among German seafarers "Wem Gott will rechte Gunst erweisen, den schickt er in die weite Welt" (Whom God holds in special favor, so sends he into the wide world). This was to be their last view of Tsingtao.

Graf Spee was busy with last-minute details and discussions with the captain of the *Emden,* and so he delayed the *Scharnhorst's* departure. He had decided to leave the *Emden* on the China coast for the summer, not only to guard Tsingtao but also to visit Shanghai and travel up the Yangtse River to check on the activities of the rebel warlords.

After two days of taking on coal and provisions, the *Scharnhorst* also sailed from Tsingtao for the last time, heading for Truk. By this time the *Leipzig* had reached Honolulu, on her way to meet the *Nürnberg* at Mazatlán. So, in the last days of June 1914, Graf Spee's ships were scattered all over the Pacific. It would be several weeks before they were reunited as a squadron.

While the German cruisers were engaged in these peacetime duties in the Pacific, several thousand miles away another warship was making her stately way down the Adriatic coast. The Austrian battleship *Viribus Unitis* carried the crown prince on a state visit to Bosnia, for the governor of the province had invited the Archduke Franz Ferdinand and his wife, the Duchess Sophie of Hohenberg, to visit Sarajevo.

On the morning of June 28 the archduke and his procession of cars entered Sarajevo, on their way to an official reception at the city hall. Stationed along the route to be followed by the motorcade were five young Bosnian nationalists, led by an eighteen-year-old schoolboy named Gavrilo Princip. His group had been supported with money and weapons by the Serbian secret organization called the Black Hand, led by the shadowy figure of Col. Dragutin Dimitrijevic, head of Serbian military intelligence. Their plan was to assassinate the heir apparent to the Emperor Franz Josef and strike a blow for Bosnian independence from the Austro-Hungarian empire.

Before the motorcade arrived at the city hall, one of the conspirators threw a bomb at the archduke's car, but it bounced harmlessly off and exploded near the next car. Choking from the cyanide pellet he had tried to swallow, the would-be assassin was immediately seized by police. The only harm done was by a bomb splinter, which wounded the archduke's aide-de-camp. The archduke and his wife proceeded to the reception shaken but unscathed.

After the reception, the archduke ordered his car to take him to visit his wounded aide. This unforeseen departure from the official route led the car to stop and turn around exactly at the point where Gavrilo Princip was standing. With a few quick steps he reached the open car and fired two shots from his Browning pistol. The first bullet hit Franz Ferdinand in the throat, severing his jugular vein. The second hit Sophie in the stomach. The duchess died within ten minutes, and the archduke, who kept murmuring, "It is nothing. It is nothing," bled to death before the car could get him to a hospital.

The young assassin tried to shoot himself, but he was seized too quickly by police. The other conspirators were soon arrested because they were all known associates of Princip. Prolonged interrogation could get no details out of them about the assassination plot, but they did let slip that it had been planned while they were in Belgrade. This was all the Austrians needed to know.

Graf Spee didn't find out about Sarajevo until the evening of June 29 because the *Scharnhorst* was at sea, heading toward the rendezvous at Truk. Captain von Müller was the first to hear of the assassination—via the telegraph station at Tsingtao—and he relayed the news to his admiral by wireless. Captain Maerker learned about it from the wireless station at Pagan, where the *Gneisenau* was anchored en route to Truk. The *Leipzig* picked up a broadcast from a Honolulu station, and the *Nürnberg* heard the news from the German consulate at Mazatlán.

None of the captains realized the full implications of the incident because so few details were available. They were all aware, though, that the situation in Europe had suddenly become more tense and that their summer cruise had taken on a different character. In the words of one executive officer, "Now into our fight drill, which we had zealously been carrying out all the time, was imparted a more serious flavor, and a kind of subconscious feeling that we were approaching a difficult time."

Graf Spee was Germany's senior naval officer overseas at the time of the assassination in Sarajevo. In addition to his cruiser squadron in the Pacific, the light cruiser *Königsberg* was on detached duty in German East Africa. Another light cruiser, the *Dresden,* was in the Caribbean. She was due to be relieved by the brand-new *Karlsruhe,* which was then preparing to sail from Wilhelmshaven. Apart from a few old gunboats and armed merchant ships, these eight ships represented the whole of Germany's overseas naval strength in the event of war.

It wasn't clear exactly who their enemies would be if war broke out, but it seemed likely that, at the very least, the Triple Entente of Russia, France, and Britain would be ranged against Germany and its ally,

Austria-Hungary. This meant that the Royal Navy would be Graf Spee's main opposition. The German cruisers were an obvious threat to shipping routes vital to Britain—no other country was so dependent on its maritime trade—and the Allies had a seemingly formidable array of warships stationed in foreign waters in 1914.

Jerram's cruiser squadron on the China Station was supported by the French armored cruisers *Dupleix* and *Montcalm*. To cover the South Pacific, the more powerful squadron of Rear-Adm. Sir George Patey was operating in Australian and New Zealand waters. His flagship, the new battle cruiser HMAS *Australia,* was so well armed and armored, and so fast in comparison to Graf Spee's cruisers, that even by herself she was more than a match for the entire German squadron.

To guard against any move by Graf Spee's ships into the Indian Ocean, Rear-Adm. Sir Richard Peirse was in charge of the East Indies Station, with his flagship, the predreadnought battleship *Swiftsure,* and a cruiser squadron based on Singapore. Peirse could also count on the Russian cruisers *Askold* and *Zhemchug,* which had been detached from the Siberian flotilla and placed at his disposal by the Russian navy. In the western half of the Indian Ocean, to counter the lone threat of the *Königsberg,* was the Cape of Good Hope squadron. This was based at Simonstown and commanded by Rear-Adm. Herbert King-Hall.

To meet the threat of the *Dresden* and *Karlsruhe* in Caribbean waters, the Royal Navy had stationed the Fourth Cruiser Squadron, led by Rear-Adm. Sir Christopher Cradock in the armored cruiser *Suffolk.* The French heavy cruisers *Descartes* and *Condé* were also in the West Indies.

In case Graf Spee's squadron crossed the Pacific and went around the Horn to threaten the Atlantic trade routes, or it tried to get back to its home base at Wilhelmshaven, Rear-Adm. Archibald Stoddart was patrolling the Cape Verde area with his flagship *Carnarvon* and four other armored cruisers. The weakest spot in the steel net around Graf Spee was the South American Station. It had only one light cruiser, HMS *Glasgow.*

In retrospect, the Allied naval forces overseas in 1914 seemed so overwhelming that Graf Spee was scarcely a serious challenge to their control of the Pacific, or indeed any other ocean. To make matters worse for the German admiral, Japan was likely to join the Allied side if war was declared. It had signed a mutual nonaggression treaty with Britain in 1902 and had obvious territorial designs on German possessions in the Pacific, especially Tsingtao. By 1914 the Imperial Japanese Navy had a formidable war fleet that was even stronger than it had been in 1905 when it annihilated the Russian fleet at Tsushima. In the Allied view, if Japan did enter the war, its ships would soon put a stop to any German naval operations in the northern Pacific. This was bound to strengthen the Allies' commerce protection in other parts of the Pacific Ocean, as well as in the Indian Ocean.

In spite of the apparently insuperable odds against him, Graf Spee had several advantages. The sheer vastness of the Pacific would make it difficult for even a well-coordinated search to track down an enemy squadron, let alone an individual raider. The Allied commanders had no radar to help them detect enemy warships and no aircraft to search them out. The few naval aircraft in service in 1914 had an extremely short flying range, and there were no aircraft carriers. (The Royal Navy had two seaplane tenders in 1914, but they were attached to the Home Fleet.) The searchers had little to rely on other than their binoculars and telescopes. Since they could see no farther than the horizon, they would need a combination of good luck and good communications to find their quarry in an area as immense as the Pacific Ocean.

Communications were primitive by present-day standards. The most powerful seaborne wireless transmitters had a range of only several hundred miles, even under ideal conditions, and most ships carried equipment of much shorter range. Wireless telegraphy (W/T) communications were also subject to interference from bad weather and high mountains. Cable transmissions were of much longer range, but cable stations were few and far between, and, in the end, cable messages had to be relayed to ships at sea by means of wireless. It frequently took two days or more for a signal from Europe to reach a ship in the Pacific. If the ship was at sea and out of range of a wireless station—which was often the case—the delay could be as long as a week, until she put into a port where there was a consulate and collected any messages waiting for her.

Even when a signal from a powerful shore-based station did reach a warship directly, the captain would often be unable either to acknowledge that he had received it or to send a reply with his low-powered transmitter because of atmospheric conditions or the distance involved.

Another problem was that most warships in 1914 carried spark transmitters whose signals were easy to intercept by any ship in the vicinity. Thus, the use of W/T would reveal their presence to an enemy. Though the intercepting ship could not determine the bearing, she could estimate from the signal strength how near the vessel was and, from the signal's characteristic note, whether the ship was British or German. For this reason the German cruisers maintained strict radio silence, unless signaling their supply ships was unavoidable.

Many islands and atolls with sheltered harbors were accessible to the German cruisers; here, they could hide either for minor repairs or to take on supplies from their transport ships. Many of these islands were uninhabited. Even those that were populated usually had no wireless to report the presence of a German ship to Allied patrols.

But Graf Spee's main advantage was that once war was declared, his enemy's ships would have other duties in the Pacific and Indian Oceans, and those duties would keep the Allies from concentrating their efforts on tracking him down. Allied vessels were needed to patrol trade routes and escort troopships to Europe from Australia, New Zealand, and India. They also had to provide support for planned invasions of Germany's Pacific territories in China, New Guinea, and Samoa. These distractions made it impossible for the Royal Navy to be strong enough everywhere Graf Spee might strike; they could never be confident of bringing a superior force against him. Apart from HMAS *Australia*, Graf Spee's armored cruisers had little to fear from any British, French, or Russian warship they were likely to meet.

The *Scharnhorst* and *Gneisenau* were both fast, modern ships manned with highly professional officers and seasoned crews. Even the new crew members taken on board at Tsingtao had been in the service a long time. Graf Spee's flagship had competed against all the ships in the German fleet to win the coveted Kaiser's Cup for gunnery in each of the previous two years. The whole squadron was respected in foreign naval circles, as well as in the Imperial German Navy, for the quality of its gunnery. Several British commentators referred to it as that "crack German squadron," even before it had gone into action and shown that its reputation was well deserved.

Graf Spee had several options in deploying his squadron if war broke out. He could use it exclusively to attack merchant shipping in a single area, hoping that the resulting panic and disruption of commerce and troop convoys would seriously impinge on Britain's war effort. Or he could break up the squadron by detaching individual raiders to prey on shipping in widely separated areas, in addition to those threatened by the *Königsberg, Dresden,* and *Karlsruhe*. Finally, and most to his personal inclination, Graf Spee could maintain the cruiser squadron as a "fleet-in-being," an ever present threat to Allied ships and shore installations wherever it might show up to make hit-and-run attacks.

This strategy would force Britain to keep major naval forces in overseas waters, which, in turn, would weaken the Grand Fleet's ability to blockade Germany and repel raids by the High Seas Fleet from its bases in the river Jade or the Kiel canal. By 1914 the Royal Navy's numerical superiority over the German battle fleet was no longer so great that it could afford to divert capital ships from home waters to deal with the distant threat of the German cruisers.

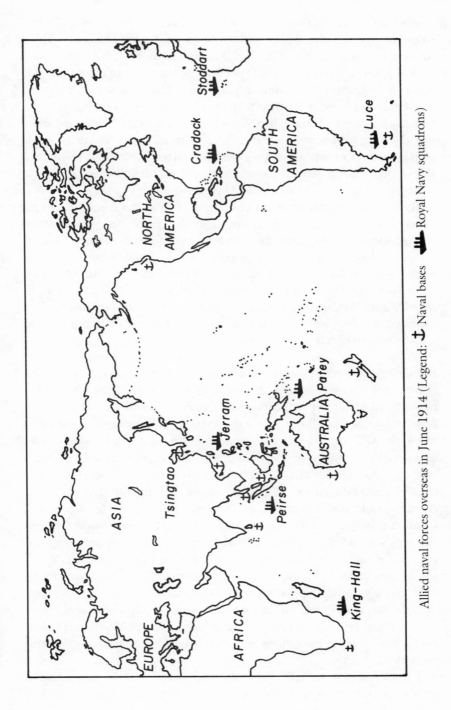

Allied naval forces overseas in June 1914 (Legend: ⚓ Naval bases ⚓ Royal Navy squadrons)

Also in Graf Spee's favor was the fact that his choice of targets and tactics would be completely unknown to the Allies, at least at the beginning. This is the one natural advantage of the hunted over a more powerful hunter. Such decisions were entirely up to Graf Spee because the policy of the Admiralstab was to leave them to their admiral on the spot. The naval staff in Berlin felt that Graf Spee knew more than they did about the local conditions where his squadron was to operate. In addition, wireless and cable communications in 1914 were neither swift nor sure. The Admiralstab realized there would be long periods of time when they were completely out of touch with their ships, and once war seemed imminent, they were content to issue only the most general orders to Graf Spee and his captains.

By contrast, the Admiralty in London, with Winston Churchill as First Lord, was not inclined to leave much to the discretion of its overseas commanders. Despite being thousands of miles from the scene of action, the Admiralty issued all the important orders, which were sometimes vague or were based on unrealistic evaluations of the strengths of opposing forces. In a few cases it sent signals that didn't reach the local commander until they were too late to be of any use. In another instance the intended recipient was killed in action two days before an important signal was sent to him from London.

But Graf Spee was not without serious problems of his own. These mainly concerned his supply lines. All of his ships were coal burning, and the difficulty of obtaining adequate coal supplies would be a constant worry both to him and to all of his cruiser captains. In the years leading up to 1914, the Germans had used considerable foresight and planning to set up a series of *Etappen,* or communications and supply bases. These were scattered throughout the Pacific, South Atlantic, and Indian Oceans, mainly in neutral countries. Each one was run by a middle-rank naval officer who could obtain without question any help he needed from local German banks or businesses. The Etappen were there to supply German warships with intelligence (and Allied ships with misinformation) and to arrange for coal, provisions, and fresh water to be stored in merchant vessels docked in neutral ports. These ships were ready to sail at any time to rendezvous with warships at sea or in remote harbors.

Although it was efficient, this system was not foolproof. Supply ships were liable to be intercepted by Allied warships, and neutral patrol vessels would limit coaling operations inside their territorial waters to one visit every three months.

The Germans were well aware that their Pacific islands were going to be hard to defend for very long against inevitable Allied invasions. Their warships would soon be without friendly, well-defended harbors—except for Tsingtao—where they could make repairs, which might be needed because of mechanical faults or battle damage.

Also, whether they were powered by the new steam-turbine engines or the older, less reliable reciprocating engines, the warships still needed regular overhaul. Boilers and steam condensers had to be cleaned periodically, or the ship's speed would suffer. Some of these problems could be dealt with at sea, but more serious defects could prove critical. Neutral dockyards were open to the warships of combatant nations, but only for the minimum time needed to make them seaworthy. Repairs of a military nature would not be permitted.

In the event of a sea battle, whether successful or not, another crucial problem would be a shortage of ammunition. German-chartered merchant ships carrying coal or provisions might pass the scrutiny of Allied naval patrols by feigning neutrality, but if they were carrying naval ordnance, it would be seized as contraband. Whenever Graf Spee's captains fired their guns, they had to bear in mind that there was little or no prospect of replacing their shells.

None of these factors was a problem for Graf Spee's adversaries. The Royal Navy had secure, well-equipped naval bases and dockyards at Hong Kong, Singapore, Colombo, and Simonstown, as well as those in Australia and New Zealand. Because the Allies would effectively control all major sea routes from the outset, supplies or repairs of any kind were readily available to their warships.

The story of Graf Spee's squadron and the detached cruisers operating as lone raiders is a remarkable one. When war broke out, these eight ships were thousands of miles from a safe harbor. They had no secure lines of supply, and they were hemmed in on all sides by powerful and relentless enemies. They could expect no reinforcements from the High Seas Fleet, whose ships would be bottled up in the North Sea by the British blockade.

Theirs is a tale of courage, skill, and determination in the face of staggering odds. The material and psychological impact that these ships made in the opening stages of the war was out of all proportion to their numbers and strength.

2
A State of
Uneasy Peace

*If there is ever another war in Europe, it will come out of some damned foolish
thing in the Balkans.*

—Prince Otto von Bismarck

The kingdom of Serbia was a focal point for pan-Slavic movements in the Balkans and a thorn in the southern side of the Austro-Hungarian empire. The Austrian General Staff, supported by the Foreign Office, were determined to crush Serbia by military force, hoping this would put an end to any moves toward a Slavic confederacy. They were right to fear this possibility, largely because of the activities of the Serbian Black Hand society, whose motto was "Union or Death."

Ironically, the Archduke Franz Ferdinand had always argued at court against any military intervention in Serbia. He also favored a greater degree of autonomy for the Slavic provinces of the Hapsburg empire. Sadly for him, this was not widely known, and it was his assassination that gave Gen. Franz von Hötzendorf, Chief of the General Staff, and Foreign Minister Count Leopold von Berchtold the pretext they needed. They worked hard to convince Emperor Franz Josef that war with Serbia was now inevitable.

In 1914 the Austro-Hungarian empire was in a state of elegant decay, led by an eighty-three-year-old ruler who was more interested in past glories (and a platonic affair with the famous actress Katharina Schratt) than he was in military adventures. Berchtold and Hötzendorf had to tread carefully. They needed to test their alliances, particularly with Kaiser Wilhelm II of Germany, and assess potential adversaries. They knew that Tsar Nicholas II would oppose an attack on his Slavic cousins in Belgrade and that Franco-Russian treaties would inevitably draw France into any general conflict.

Britain's reaction was less predictable, but it seemed likely that as a member of the Triple Entente, it would side with France and Russia.

While the Austrians were cautiously making preparations for war against Serbia, and deciding how to use Sarajevo in justifying it to the world, they took no overt action for several weeks. During the month of July 1914, Europe was lulled into a state of uneasy peace.

Far away in the Pacific, there was neither definite news of the European situation nor fresh instructions from Berlin. All Graf Spee and his captains could do for the moment was to carry on with their summer plans. The *Gneisenau* arrived at Saipan on the last day of June, but there was still no further news about the crisis developing in Europe. Captain Maerker had brief visits with the governor of the Marianas colony, German dignitaries, and local native groups. The cruiser then left Saipan on July 2, and after stopping briefly at the island of Rota, ran into a typhoon. The *Scharnhorst,* which had been steaming directly toward Truk to catch up with her sister ship, ran into the same typhoon. Luckily, both ships were far from its center, although they had to reduce speed and finally heave to until the storm blew itself out.

The weather was still bad when the *Gneisenau* reached Truk on July 5, and she had to ride at anchor off the atoll, pitching and rolling in the heavy swell. Captain Maerker dared not try the narrow entrance through the coral reef. The following day it became calm enough for him to anchor in the lagoon, where Graf Spee joined him in the *Scharnhorst* on the morning of July 7. A few hours later the chartered Japanese collier *Fukoku Maru* arrived on schedule, escorted by the *Titania,* a lightly armed German merchant vessel that served as the squadron's dispatch ship. Japan's attitude toward Germany was at best ambivalent, and Graf Spee was determined to dispense with the services of the *Fukoku Maru* and her Japanese crew as soon as he had used up all her coal.

Coaling began the next day because the cruisers had burned a huge amount of fuel to cover the three thousand miles from Tsingtao. Their bunkers were exceedingly low, particularly in the *Scharnhorst,* which had steamed faster than usual to catch up with the *Gneisenau.* This time no Chinese coolies were there to help with the drudgery, and the coaling would have to be done under a blazing tropical sun. Those who could avoid the Kohlenfest, such as the admiral and senior officers, went ashore. So did any junior officers who could find an excuse to join them. The work began before daylight—to try to avoid the worst of the afternoon sun—but it had not even been completed by nightfall. Between them the two big ships needed more than four thousand tons to fill their bunkers, and the work went on by searchlight until it was finished.

Graf Spee had received a message from Berlin on his arrival at Truk. "Political situation not altogether satisfactory, await developments at Truk or Ponapé. Expect situation to become more clear in eight or ten days." Two days later, when they had finished cleaning their ships, both officers and men were given welcome shore leave. This was to be their last peacetime visit ashore. Parties of natives came out to the flagship in their canoes to exchange gifts, and some went on board "to dance before the great German chief." An observer commented, "The squadron chief was visibly pleased."

That night Graf Spee received another telegram from Berlin. "Hostile developments between Austria and Serbia possible, and not impossible that Triple Alliance will be drawn into it."

Graf Spee signaled Captain von Müller to cancel his visit to Shanghai and keep the *Emden* at Tsingtao until the situation in Europe became clearer. In the meantime, Müller was to take charge of the harbor defenses and do what he could to strengthen them.

The admiral decided to wait at Truk for further news. On July 11 he received yet another telegram. "England probably hostile in case it comes to war; situation otherwise unchanged. English China Squadron at Hakodate and Vladivostok."

This message put Graf Spee on the alert, but the British ships were far enough away that he could afford to continue night training and maneuvers at Truk for a few days.

On July 15 the two armored cruisers left Truk with the *Titania* and *Fukoku Maru* and headed for Ponapé, capital of the Caroline Islands colony. On the way they stopped off at the uninhabited Oroluk atoll, where Graf Spee intended to explore the island, which was noted for its rare species of tortoises. He sent the two cruisers out to sea to practice gunnery while he made for shore in the admiral's launch. When he arrived inside the lagoon he was disconcerted to find a Japanese schooner, ostensibly engaged in fishing. It was likely that Japan would join Graf Spee's growing list of adversaries, and he was sure that a report of his whereabouts would soon reach Tokyo. He took the launch back to the flagship and cut short the visit to Oroluk.

Early the next morning the four ships left for Ponapé, where they anchored on July 17. The Carolines were Germany's most recent colonial acquisition, having been bought from an impoverished Spain after the Spanish-American War of 1898 for the princely sum of 17 million marks. The native inhabitants didn't like their new masters any better than the old ones, as they showed in 1910, when a bloody uprising took place at Ponapé

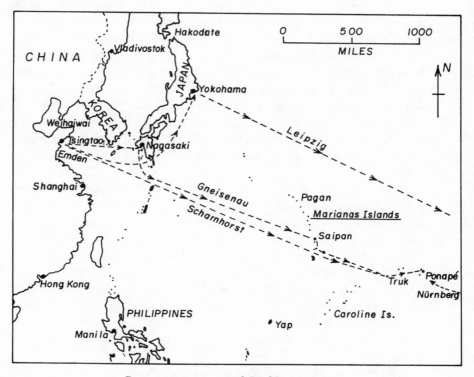

Prewar movements of Graf Spee's cruisers

in which a number of Germans were killed. Local troops were unable to put down the rebellion, and the governor had been obliged to call on the cruiser squadron for help. Four warships, including the *Emden* and *Nürnberg*, came from Tsingtao and bombarded the rebel stronghold until it surrendered. On the present visit, Graf Spee had brought a stone memorial to the German soldiers and civilians killed in the 1910 uprising. This was erected in the churchyard at Ponapé with suitable ceremony.

Meanwhile, the other two members of the squadron were seven thousand miles away in Mexican waters. The *Leipzig* had completed her long voyage from Honolulu and anchored off Mazatlán on July 7. The *Nürnberg* had just returned from a brief visit to Panama and was ready to be relieved on the Mexican Station. The Admiralstab had decided that one warship should stay on station as long as the civil war lasted, to try to protect German businesses and civilians.

Captain von Schönberg of the *Nürnberg* brought Captain Haun of the *Leipzig* up to date on the local situation. A civil war had been raging on and off in Mexico since 1910. The long dictatorship of Gen. Porfirio Diaz had been overthrown by Francisco Madero, who had tried to establish representative government. He, in turn, had been arrested and murdered by Gen. Victoriano Huerta, who reestablished a military dictatorship. Soon after this, civil war broke out again with yet another general, Venustiano Carranza, challenging Huerta for supremacy. The picture was even further complicated by Madero's former allies, with Pancho Villa's insurgents fighting in the north and those of Emiliano Zapata in the south.

What all this meant for Captain Haun was that coal supplies would be uncertain, no matter where he docked in Mexico. With their usual foresight, the Germans had arranged for coal to be stored at several west coast ports, but the problem was how to get it safely out to the anchored *Leipzig*. The rebel factions were opposed to the European presence in Mexico and would fire on any lighter loading coal at the docks. In the end, it seemed preferable to obtain coal from the United States. The *Nürnberg* had already chartered a decrepit British collier, the *Citriana*, to bring coal from San Francisco for the *Leipzig*. She was fired on by the rebels when she came too close to land but still managed to get her coal to the cruiser.

On July 8 the *Nürnberg* sailed for San Francisco to take on coal herself before heading west to rejoin Graf Spee. She took with her one of the *Leipzig*'s officers whose job was to stay in the United States to order more coal to be sent to Mazatlán and to arrange for colliers to meet the *Leipzig* at sea when needed.

On the east coast of Mexico, the U.S. Marines had occupied Vera Cruz, nominally to protect American lives and property during the civil war. Besides several U.S. and British cruisers lying off Vera Cruz, the *Dresden* was anchored there, ready to take off German civilians, if necessary, as she waited to be relieved by the *Karlsruhe*. Partly due to the U.S. intervention, which included an arms embargo, the Huerta government collapsed on July 15, and the general abdicated the next day. Germany was sympathetic to Huerta and, in fact, had been trying to ship arms to him in spite of the U.S. embargo. So when he wisely decided to leave Mexico on July 17, the *Dresden* was ordered to go into Vera Cruz to ferry the general and his entourage to safety in Kingston, Jamaica. The *Karlsruhe*'s orders were changed. She was to meet the *Dresden* later at Havana or Port au Prince.

* * *

While the ships of the squadron were busy with their peacetime duties in the Western Hemisphere, the Austria-Serbia situation, which had been quietly simmering ever since Sarajevo, was now coming to the boil. Within twenty-four hours of the assassination, the Serbian government telegraphed its condolences to Vienna and declared that it would "certainly, most loyally do everything to prove that it would not tolerate within its borders the fostering of any agitation . . . calculated to disturb our already delicate relations with Austria-Hungary."

These sentiments were less than sincere. The Serbian foreign office had been fully aware of the activities of Colonel Dimitrijevic and the Black Hand. They couldn't control them, but they had tried to warn the Austrians obliquely of possible danger in Sarajevo by suggesting that the archduke's visit be postponed until after Serbia's national holiday in honor of St. Vitus. This had been a singularly unfortunate date to pick for a state visit.

The Serbians made further conciliatory gestures during the following week, but it made no difference. Berchtold and Hötzendorf were determined to "crush the Serbian skull." Over the next three weeks the Austrian Foreign Office set the stage for giving an ultimatum to Belgrade that the Serbs would never be able to accept. But they had to secure German support. This was lukewarm at first but grew more definite as a result of machinations by ministers on both sides. They had to convince the two "All Highest"—Franz Josef and Wilhelm II—that war on Serbia was the only acceptable response to Sarajevo.

On July 20 Berchtold took his "jewel," the final polished draft of the ultimatum, to show it to the emperor and obtain his approval. Although it was couched in polite diplomatic French, it provoked this exchange.

"The note is pretty sharp."

"It has to be, Your Majesty."

"It has to be indeed. You will join us for lunch."

Thus, given the imperial seal of approval, the note was ready for Belgrade, where it was sent on July 23. It demanded an end to all anti-Austrian propaganda in Serbia and the arrest of officials alleged to be involved in conspiracy against Austria. Most important, it insisted on the direct participation of the Austrian police in the investigation and suppression of anti-Austrian activity inside Serbia.

Winston Churchill received a copy from the British Foreign Office and commented: "This note was clearly an ultimatum; but it was an ultimatum such had never been penned in modern times. As the reading proceeded, it seemed absolutely impossible that any State in the world could accept it, or that any acceptance, however abject, would satisfy the aggressor."

This was precisely what the Austrians hoped, and they gave Belgrade just forty-eight hours to reply.

The Serbian response was conciliatory, almost abject. They meekly accepted all the Austrian demands except the involvement of Austrian police on Serbian soil, which no sovereign state could tolerate. When the message reached Vienna—"Serbia rejects essential demand"—the emperor began to have second thoughts. "But the rupture of relations needn't necessarily mean war!" So too did a nervous Kaiser, who said of the Serbian reply: "More than one could have expected! A great moral success for Vienna! All reason for war is gone!" It was too late for second thoughts.

Under pressure, Franz Josef yielded and gave permission for general mobilization. Austria broke off diplomatic relations with Serbia, and on July 28, one month to the day after the assassination, declared war. Curiously, this was done by telegram, the first time a declaration of war had taken place in this fashion. The next day Austrian artillery began a bombardment of the Serbian capital. In 1914 Belgrade was less than twenty miles from the border, and the Austrians were able to attack Serbia without even crossing the frontier. This started a chain of events that gathered momentum each successive day.

On July 30 Russia ordered general mobilization. The Serbs had already appealed to the Tsar for support, and, in fact, the Russians had helped them construct their reply to the Austrian ultimatum. This mobilization provoked the Germans into an ultimatum of their own. On July 31 they demanded Russian demobilization within twelve hours and asked St. Petersburg to "make us a distinct declaration to that effect." Naturally, the Russians could not accept such a peremptory demand, and on August 1 Germany declared war on them. The French, who had also been consulted every step of the way by Serbia, agreed to honor their treaty with Russia. France would certainly come to Russia's aid if the Germans attacked. This caused Germany to declare war on France on August 3.

Britain was not legally bound by its treaties with Russia and France to enter the war, even though it had an unwritten obligation to support France if it was attacked by Germany. But it did have a formal treaty with Belgium, and the British government sent the Germans an ultimatum that demanded assurance that Belgian neutrality would be respected. Its deadline was 11:00 P.M. Greenwich mean time on August 4, 1914. When the Germans made no reply, Britain signaled its forces to "commence hostilities against Germany."

Thus, the Great War had begun, and as Bismarck had predicted, it was started by "some damned foolish thing in the Balkans."

* * *

While these momentous events were taking place in the chanceries of Europe, preparations for the war at sea were under way at the Admiralstab in Berlin and at the Admiralty in London. These two were quite different in their organization and strategies, although they shared an overriding preoccupation with the number of battleships in home waters. A battleship race had been going on ever since the launching of the revolutionary HMS *Dreadnought* in 1906, and it had become the major cause of enmity between the two nations. Every time the Germans laid down a new battleship, public cries were heard in Britain such as "Two keels to one" or "We want eight and we won't wait."

In Germany the Admiralstab was in charge of operations and strategy. In addition, the *Reichsmarineamt* (imperial navy office) was responsible for general policy, and the *Marinekabinett* (naval cabinet) took care of personnel matters. These bodies were all directly answerable to the Kaiser and dared not take any major step without his approval.

Wilhelm II, who once described himself as the "Admiral of the Atlantic," enjoyed nothing better than cruising in the imperial yacht *Hohenzollern* and reviewing his fleet. His envy of his grandmother Queen Victoria, his uncle King Edward VII, and their Royal Navy had led him to develop the Kaiserliche Marine into the second most powerful navy in the world. He accomplished this by giving free rein to his secretary of state for the navy, Admiral von Tirpitz, the "Father of the German Navy." In the short space of twenty years, Tirpitz had transformed a negligible coastal defense force into a modern oceangoing battle fleet.

By 1914 the Kaiser was ready to challenge Britain for its long-held command of the seas. But despite his pretensions to naval leadership, he at least had enough common sense to leave operational decisions to the Admiralstab. In turn, the naval staff gave their ship commanders a free hand by issuing only the most general instructions. For example, when the crisis developed, they had wired Graf Spee: "Samoan cruise will probably have to be abandoned. *Nürnberg* has been ordered to proceed to Tsingtau [*sic*]. Everything else is left to you."

By contrast, the Admiralty was ruled by its First Lord, Winston Churchill, and its First Sea Lord, Prince Louis of Battenberg. In principle, the role of the First Lord of the Admiralty was a political and strategic one, leaving all operational and tactical decisions to the First Sea Lord.

With Churchill at the helm this was far from the case. He had a great affection for the Royal Navy although, to put it mildly, this feeling was not reciprocated. He had a consuming interest in all aspects of naval operations, no matter how technical or detailed. Not content to leave things in more experienced hands, he involved himself in day-to-day operational decisions. But despite his complete lack of firsthand experience in naval matters, he had great intelligence and intuition; thus he sometimes made judgments that were superior to those of his admirals.

Battenberg was one of the navy's most experienced and respected admirals, with a brilliant sea career behind him, but he couldn't stand up to the dynamic and persuasive Churchill. He so frequently added the comment "quite concur" to Churchill's memos that this eventually became his nickname in Whitehall circles.

The problem with Churchill was that, unlike his counterparts in the Admiralstab, he tried to take personal control of events that were taking place thousands of miles from Whitehall. He was "entranced by the prospect of moving fleets and squadrons, and even individual men-of-war about the oceans of the world: and then matching their cabled orders by shifting miniature replicas on the huge map in the War Room at the Admiralty."

Admiral Beatty remarked, "Winston I hear does practically everything and some more besides."

The First Lord was also inclined to make assessments of the relative strengths of British and German naval forces that were based more on paper than in reality, and on occasion he issued orders to his admirals that were less than clear in their intent.

Just as the direction of naval operations was different in the two countries, so were their plans for overseas warfare. The Germans had a relatively simple task because they had only one cruiser squadron and three detached cruisers to worry about, and only one major objective: the disruption of Britain's commerce by surface raiders.

Fortunately for the Allies, the unrestricted use of mines and submarines was not seriously contemplated by the Germans in 1914. Mines were mainly used in coastal European waters, and then not in any widespread fashion. Minelayers were too vulnerable to British naval patrols because the Royal Navy would control the Channel and North Sea from the outset. Tirpitz was strongly against the use of submarines, which he regarded as experimental and unproven. As he put it in his memoirs, "The question as to how far our submarines were capable of rendering material assistance in the war had not been settled in July 1914."

German overseas naval plans can be summed up by the general orders issued to Graf Spee and the cruiser captains during the period of strained relations, or *Kriegsgefahr*. They were told: "[C]arry on cruiser warfare against enemy merchant vessels and against contraband carried in neutral vessels, raid the enemy's coasts, bombard military establishments, and destroy cable and wireless stations . . . and . . . by engaging equal or inferior enemy forces, the conduct of the war in home waters would be assisted by holding many of the enemy's forces overseas."

The Admiralstab had no illusions about their cruisers' chances of carrying out these orders for very long. Their ships had no secure bases in the Atlantic or Indian Oceans, and only Tsingtao in the Pacific. If Tsingtao fell to the Allies, their next nearest naval base was Wilhelmshaven, but their chances of breaking through the inevitable North Sea blockade were slim.

The Germans had known for a long time that their overseas warships would be in a precarious position when war broke out, and they had tried to offset the lack of naval bases by setting up their network of Etappen. Many German colliers and transports were at sea in every part of the world, but even with the full cooperation of the merchant marine, the cruisers' supply lines would be undependable—particularly their sources of coal, a warship's lifeblood.

It wasn't just the amount of coal available that was important but also its quality. Allied warships had access to superior coals such as Welsh anthracite and bituminous black coal from New South Wales. The slower burning rate and higher heating value of these coals gave the greatest steaming range per ton. But after the Germans had burned up the excellent Shantung coal they had taken aboard at Tsingtao, they would have to take what they could get. The use of lower quality fuel such as Indian sub-bituminous, or brown coal, could easily cut their cruisers' steaming range in half.

The *Kohlenfrage* (question of coal supplies) would remain a nagging problem for all Graf Spee's captains. The eight cruisers were in a hopeless predicament in the long run. Their crews knew this as well as the Admiralstab. All they could hope to do was survive for as long as they could, do as much damage as they could, and tie up as many enemy warships as possible while they were doing it.

Unlike the Germans, the Royal Navy ships had many secure bases overseas and plentiful supplies, but they also had wider responsibilities at the outbreak of war, particularly in the Pacific and Indian Oceans. They not only had to guard the commerce routes vital to Britain's survival, they also had to escort troopships to Europe from India, Australia, and New Zealand. The traditional convoy system used by the navy in previous wars had fallen into disfavor as a means of protecting trade, although it was still used for troopships. As far as general commerce was concerned, the navy's strategy was to use its forces more economically by concentrating them at focal points on the trade routes where raiders would be most likely to attack.

The Allies planned to invade all major German possessions in Africa and the Pacific. This meant that the navy would be called on to escort landing forces and provide support by shelling shore installations. In addition, they would be required to destroy enemy cable and W/T stations, even before the invasions were under way, to curtail enemy communications.

Added to all of this was the need to seek out and destroy the German cruisers, particularly Graf Spee's dangerous squadron, before they could do any serious harm to Britain's war effort. To succeed in these many tasks called for coordinated effort by several squadrons, clear decisions on priorities, and an adequate supply of fast modern cruisers. Unfortunately, none of these conditions were met in August 1914.

The admirals commanding the cruiser squadrons in the Pacific and Indian Oceans were given their orders separately, and although they did communicate with each other, there was little or no cohesive effort on their part. Priorities were poorly established. Given the threat posed by Graf Spee's squadron, the highest priority should have been to find and destroy it. Because of the huge distances to be covered, and the many islands and atolls where the squadron could hide, this would need a determined and well-coordinated effort.

Raids on the German colonies and W/T stations could wait, since these were almost certain to fall to Allied forces whenever they were attacked. The Germans had no illusions about their vulnerability in this area. Except for Tsingtao, their possessions in the Pacific were not heavily fortified. Even the troopships to Europe could wait until Graf Spee's ships had been located and destroyed, or at least until they had been driven away from the routes the convoys planned to take.

Another problem was the number and quality of the Allied ships serving abroad. The Royal Navy had almost as many cruisers afloat in 1914 as the rest of the world's major navies combined, but its most modern ships were usually attached to the Home Fleet to act as scouts for the battleships. Except for the *Australia,* the most heavily armed British, French, and Russian warships in overseas waters were older vessels, often manned by reservists. Most of these ships weren't fast enough to catch Graf Spee's cruisers even if they were lucky enough to spot them. Also, in spite of the total number of Allied warships assigned to cover them, which on paper seems overwhelming when matched against only eight cruisers, the Allies were thinly spread in view of the vast territory they had to patrol. What at first sight might have appeared to be an impenetrable steel net around the German ships was, in reality, far from that.

* * *

By contrast, the German cruisers were all fast modern ships, none more than eight years old. The two big armored cruisers, *Scharnhorst* and *Gneisenau,* carried 8.2-inch guns that could propel a 240-pound shell a distance of thirteen thousand yards. They also had a secondary armament of 5.9-inch guns, which fired one-hundred-pound shells. These were more effective weapons than the 6-inch guns carried by most British cruisers. The two ships were heavily protected with an armor belt up to six inches thick, but in spite of the extra weight, they were reasonably fast. Both had exceeded their designed speed of twenty-three knots, and they were a match for any enemy warship smaller than a battleship, which they could easily outrun. The only serious threats to these armored cruisers were the new battle cruisers, which were both faster and more heavily armed. In August 1914 only one such ship was cruising in the whole of the Pacific Ocean: HMAS *Australia.*

The light cruisers *Emden, Nürnberg, Leipzig, Dresden, Karlsruhe,* and *Königsberg* were armed with rapid-firing 4.1-inch guns. Their shells weighed only thirty-eight pounds, but they could be projected a distance of nearly six miles with great accuracy. The quality of the gunnery in all these German cruisers was remarkable for its precision, discipline, and rapid fire. The squadron's reputation was as well known in the Royal Navy as it was in the Imperial German Navy.

Equally important was their ship construction. Admiral von Tirpitz had stated as his doctrine: "The supreme quality of a ship is that it should remain afloat. . . . so long as a ship is afloat it retains a certain fighting value and can afterwards be easily repaired."

The ability to remain afloat after withstanding tremendous punishment was characteristic of all modern German warships in 1914, and it remained so in 1939. Even the light cruisers, with their thin armor plating, could stay afloat and could fire after a severe pounding from heavier guns because of the German system of hull construction that was based on subdivision into many watertight compartments.

The officers of these ships were of the highest caliber, handpicked by Tirpitz himself. The crews, also handpicked, were fanatically loyal to their captains, their admiral, and the Fatherland. A British naval correspondent wrote: "The German Squadron . . . was like no other in the Kaiser's navy. It was commanded by professional officers and manned by long-service ratings."

The cruiser squadron was not only the largest group of German warships outside of European waters, it was also probably the strongest force of its kind anywhere in the world. No wonder that command of this squadron was one of the most prized assignments in the Imperial German

Vice Adm. Graf Maximilian von Spee *(Imperial War Museum)*

Navy. It was to this post that Graf Spee was appointed, taking command at Tsingtao in December 1912.

Maximilian Johannes Maria Hubertus Reichsgraf von Spee was born in 1861, fifth son of a family that could trace its roots back to the twelfth century and had been raised to the status of nobility by Charles VI in the early eighteenth century. Graf Spee was educated privately at the family castle in Rhineland until he was old enough to attend Gymnasium. He joined the navy as a cadet at the age of eighteen, and as a young lieutenant he served in the Cameroons and Togoland during the rapid expansion of Germany's African colonies in the 1880s. He was invalided home with rheumatic fever, however, which troubled him sporadically for the rest of his life.

In later years Graf Spee became a gunnery specialist. In 1897 he served as flag-lieutenant on the cruiser *Deutschland* and took part in Prince Heinrich's colonizing expedition to Kiaochow and Tsingtao. Promoted to commander that same year, Graf Spee saw action on the Yangtse River during the Boxer Rebellion. In 1910 he reached flag rank when, at the unusually early age of forty-nine, he was made rear admiral.

Graf Spee's last, and most important, assignment was command of the cruiser squadron at Tsingtao, where he was promoted to vice admiral in 1913. He brought to this position more than thirty-five years of naval experience, including several years in the German colonies. His rapid rise from cadet to vice admiral in many ways paralleled that of both the German navy and the empire. The navy had changed over the same period from a motley collection of old frigates and gunboats to become the second biggest fleet in the world, and the empire now occupied an area several times that of Germany itself. Graf Spee was probably privileged in his opportunities because of his noble birth and rank, but there can be no doubt of his ability. His service record was flawless, and he had that rare capacity to inspire loyalty and confidence in all those who served under him.

He married the young baroness Margarete von der Osten-Sacken in 1889, and she bore him a daughter, Huberta, and two sons, Otto and Heinrich. The boys followed their father into the navy and served with him in the cruiser squadron as junior lieutenants: Otto on the *Nürnberg* and Heinrich on the *Gneisenau.*

Graf Spee was a tall, erect figure who "looked as if he had swallowed a broomstick." He had a pointed beard, bushy eyebrows, and calm blue eyes. In photographs he appears stern, but this impression is belied by a glint of good-natured amusement in his eyes. Opinions vary as to his personality. Some found him austere, distant, and somewhat shy. To others he had a simple, kindly, and unpretentious nature. It is likely that in his lofty and remote position as admiral it was hard for him to show his true personality. One of his early colleagues wrote of him: "He was . . . a favourite in the wardroom. He made everybody his friend by his invariable kindness, his unaffected and engaging nature and his dry sense of humour. I sat next to him for eighteen months and during that time I got to know him and appreciate him more every day. . . ."

He had a deep interest in natural history, enjoyed a game of bridge, and detested formal social occasions, especially when he was the guest of honor. He once wrote to his wife: "To my shame, I lied at least eight hundred times. You say, 'It is my greatest pleasure to meet you,' while you are thinking how much better it would have been if they had stayed home." With so many guests, he wrote, "This handshaking is no joke."

By all reports, Graf Spee didn't fit the then-popular picture of the typical German militarist. He was a devout Catholic and an affectionate family man, and he had keen interests outside the military sphere. But because of his ability and experience he would be a determined and dangerous adversary.

Graf Spee and his men were in an unenviable position at the outbreak of war. They were thousands of miles from a safe harbor, faced with uncertain supply lines, and surrounded by hostile forces. But things could have been much worse. Their careers would have been shorter and less spectacular if the Allies had immediately taken determined countermeasures against them.

Each cruiser captain had been told by his emperor that when war broke out:

> From that moment he must make his own decisions. . . . Above all [he] must bear in mind that his chief duty is to damage the enemy as severely as possible. . . . The constant strain will exhaust the energy of his crew; the heavy responsibility of the officer in command will be increased by the isolated position of his ship; rumours of all kinds and the advice of apparently well-meaning people will sometimes make the situation appear hopeless. But he must never show one moment of weakness. He must constantly bear in mind that the efficiency of the crew and their capacity to endure privations and dangers depend chiefly on his personality, his energy and the manner in which he does his duty. The more difficult and desperate the position, the more strictly the officer must adhere to the laws of military honour. . . . If an officer in command succeeds in winning for his ship an honourable place in the history of the German Navy, I assure him of my Imperial favour. . . .

3

Rendezvous in the Marianas

I intend to sail with the remaining formation to the west coast of America.
—Adm. Maximilian Graf von Spee

O n August 4, Graf Spee was still at Ponapé with the *Scharnhorst* and *Gneisenau*. The news that Britain was now in the war didn't reach him until the next afternoon because the telegram from Berlin had to be relayed by wireless from Tsingtao. The German naval staff had considered a series of war scenarios of increasing seriousness, depending on which combination of enemies they would have to fight. The signal to Graf Spee meant that the so-called "Plan C" was now in effect, with all three of the Triple Entente against them. When he heard the news, one of the *Gneisenau*'s officers commented, "Against France and Russia it would have been a merry war, for which we were perfectly ready, even in these remote parts."

But with the Royal Navy as their chief opposition, the prospect wasn't so appealing. The cruiser squadron now had to face the threat of Admiral Jerram's China squadron to the north and Admiral Patey's Australia and New Zealand squadron to the south, to say nothing of the Russian and French cruisers, whose location was unknown to the Germans. Although Jerram's squadron, with the armored cruisers *Minotaur* and *Hampshire,* was probably no stronger than his own, Graf Spee knew that he must at all costs stay away from Patey and the huge 12-inch guns of the battle cruiser *Australia.*

Graf Spee wanted to raid the rich commerce routes in the South China Sea, which would draw Jerram's ships away from Tsingtao and allow the German ships docked there enough time to escape. He had received the advice from Berlin, "The best means of affording relief to Tsingtao is for the ships of the Cruiser Squadron to retain their freedom of movement as long as possible."

He was determined not to let his cruisers be trapped and attacked while they were in port, as the Japanese had done to the Russians at Port Arthur in 1904. In any case, he didn't believe that Tsingtao could hold out for long against a determined attack, especially if Japan decided to join the Allies. Tsingtao's fate would be decided with or without his help.

When Berlin signaled him on August 5, "Chili [*sic*] neutral and friendly. Japan neutral, providing no attack directed against British East Asia district," Graf Spee was forced to give up the idea of operating off the China coast, at least until the Japanese position became clear. He expected that Japan would sooner or later declare war on Germany, but there was no point in hastening this. If its formidable fleet entered the conflict, it would immediately bar his ships from the northern Pacific.

The admiral was not comfortable having his ships stay at Ponapé any longer than necessary. Their presence in the Carolines was bound to be known to the Allies by now because of the Japanese schooner that had seen them at Oroluk atoll on July 15. Graf Spee's immediate priorities were to get his ships ready for action and assemble the squadron in some more remote German harbor where he could meet with all his captains to discuss their next move. The *Nürnberg* was on her way to join Graf Spee from Honolulu, where she had stopped to take on coal, and the *Emden*'s captain had been given orders to contact the main squadron as soon as he had done his best to make Tsingtao secure.

While Graf Spee was making plans to leave the Caroline Islands, Admiral Jerram was considering how to deploy his China squadron to guard against the German threat to Allied trade routes. Britain's overseas trade in 1914 was not only vital to its ability to wage war but also to its very survival as a nation. Roughly two-thirds of its supplies had to be imported. A commission of enquiry had estimated that if shipping was seriously disrupted, food reserves in Britain were only sufficient to last for six weeks.

At the outbreak of war, Jerram's squadron consisted of the armored cruisers *Minotaur* and *Hampshire* and the light cruisers *Newcastle* and *Yarmouth*. (The old French cruisers *Dupleix* and *Montcalm* were supposed to come under Jerram's command, but their admiral had not been told this, and at the start of the war even the French admiralty didn't know where the *Montcalm* was.) Jerram's forces were barely sufficient to deal with the German cruiser squadron, even if they could find it. They

were certainly insufficient for the immense area they had to cover to protect Allied shipping routes.

On Churchill's instructions, Battenberg signaled Jerram to strengthen
his squadron by having the battleship *Triumph* mobilized as soon as possible. This was a predreadnought that had been laid up in reserve at Hong
Kong. Churchill believed this ship would give Jerram clear superiority
over Graf Spee's squadron. This may have looked good on paper in the
Admiralty war room six thousand miles away, but the *Triumph* was an old
ship with a skeleton crew, and there weren't enough naval personnel
available in Hong Kong to man her properly. In the end, naval reservists
and even a hundred soldiers from the Duke of Cornwall's Light Infantry
had to be pressed into service to bring her up to fighting complement.
The Lords of the Admiralty placed too much reliance on a poorly manned
and obsolescent battleship to counter Graf Spee's modern cruisers with
their crews of highly trained professionals. It would not be the last time
they made this mistake.

Jerram's war plan was to concentrate his ships off Shanghai and cut
Graf Spee off from his only secure base at Tsingtao. He believed this
would prevent any southward thrusts against Allied shipping. Churchill
and Battenberg had different ideas. They sent Jerram a signal ordering
him to concentrate his forces at Hong Kong. The admiral had no choice
but to obey, although as he wrote later, "[This] placed me 900 miles from
my correct strategical position." With admirable restraint he commented
that he "assumed Their Lordships had good reason for sending me
there."

The seriousness of the Admiralty's interference with the judgment of
its admiral on the spot was compounded by faulty intelligence about the
location of Graf Spee's forces. The Allies knew that the *Scharnhorst* was
in the Carolines at the outbreak of war, but they believed that the
Gneisenau was in the Singapore area. This was due to an error in deciphering a signal, which, in reality, referred to the harmless old gunboat
Geier, which had just left Singapore and was scurrying to find a safe harbor in some German possession. The Allies also believed that both the
Leipzig and *Nürnberg* were still in Mexican waters, when, in fact, the latter was well on her way to join Graf Spee in the Carolines. The *Emden*
was known to be at Tsingtao at the end of July, and the Allies thought she
was still there. But she had left as soon as Germany declared war on
Russia, narrowly missing detection by two of Jerram's ships.

While he waited impatiently for the *Nürnberg* to arrive at Ponapé, Graf
Spee ordered his captains to strip their vessels of all unnecessary trim-

mings, such as the draperies, wood paneling, and pictures in the officers' quarters. (Portraits of the Kaiser were exempted from this order.) Any furniture that could be spared had to go because it would be a fire hazard in a sea battle. (The *Gneisenau*'s prized piano was apparently not considered a fire hazard.) The crews of both ships were told to pack up their treasured mementos of the Far East and any other nonessential personal belongings. These were going to be stored with a local German trading company for recovery after the war.

The ships were completely blacked out at night. From dawn to dusk the lookouts in the crows' nests anxiously scanned the horizon for any sign of smoke or mastheads that might tell the approach of enemy ships. Instead of standing watch once every twenty-four hours, each ship's company was divided into two watches that served four hours on and four hours off. Hands were mustered for battle drill every afternoon, until loading and training the guns became almost automatic.

Most of the ships' boats, including the admiral's launch, were taken ashore for storage. Lifeboats were impractical in wartime; in any battle serious enough to cause abandoning ship, they would almost certainly have been damaged beyond use. And they were a fire hazard. Boats that were retained were always filled with seawater before the ship went into action.

The *Nürnberg* was sighted off Ponapé at dawn on August 6 and entered the lagoon soon after. She was stripped for action and ordered to take on fresh water, provisions, and coal as quickly as possible. Her bunkers and tanks were nearly empty after steaming more than three thousand miles, nonstop, from Honolulu. The admiral was anxious to get away from Ponapé, and he ordered the *Nürnberg* to be ready to leave by nightfall. This meant that the crews of all three cruisers had to turn to and help with the grimy business of coaling the *Nürnberg*. Coaling from another ship was even harder work than coaling in harbor, because no dockside cranes were there to lift the heavy coal sacks. When the men in the collier had filled them, the sacks were swung across to the cruiser using loading booms and winches. The sailors working on deck dressed in their oldest clothes, but the stokers trimming the coal in the bunkers were practically naked because of the high temperatures below decks. In the tropical heat the work was even more unpleasant than usual because all the deck awnings had been removed as fire hazards.

The ship's band played lively music to spur the men on, and tubs of lemonade and ice were kept handy for when they took a break. They could only work for short periods at a time because of the heat, and a junior officer stood by to record how much coal they had just shifted.

German officers and men at Tsingtao after coaling *(Wilhelm Heyne Verlag)*

Every fifteen minutes he would chalk up the watch totals on a slate so that the new men would see how much coal their rivals from the other watch had moved; they were determined not to be outdone.

In the early afternoon Graf Spee took one of the remaining gigs across to the *Nürnberg* to pick up Otto, then to the *Gneisenau* for Heinrich. The admiral and his two lieutenant sons went ashore to the Catholic mission to make their confessions. They received the holy sacrament from Salvator Walleser, the apostolic vicar of the Marianas and Carolines, who commented, "Their marvellous example made a deep impression on everybody." When coaling the *Nürnberg* was finished, priests from the Capuana mission were asked to go on board each cruiser to hear the confessions of the other Catholic officers and men.

By late afternoon the German ships were ready to sail, and the little *Titania* was given the honor of leading the squadron out to sea. She was followed by the *Scharnhorst,* then the *Gneisenau,* and finally the *Nürnberg,* which had just finished her hasty loading of fresh water and provisions. Once outside the coral reef the squadron lined up, the flagship leading the way, and headed north into the quickly gathering dusk.

The chartered collier *Fukoku Maru* and her Japanese crew were left behind. She had no wireless, and it would be a long time before her captain could reach Tokyo with the news that Graf Spee had left Ponapé. Even then, the Japanese didn't know the squadron's destination because Graf Spee had told only his captains of their next port of call. As a precaution, he ordered the *Fukoku Maru* to go to Samoa the next day to find more coal and bring it back to Ponapé as soon as possible. This was a fool's errand since Graf Spee had no intention of returning to Ponapé. Not trusting the Japanese captain, he sent a German official with the collier to make sure he kept to the charter agreement. The information the captain eventually gave the Allies was not only out-of-date, but misleading.

The admiral had decided to take his ships to the isolated atoll of Pagan. This lies at the northern end of the Marianas chain, twelve hundred miles to the northwest of Ponapé. According to official German reports, "Hidden fitting out places had . . . been established in the decades of peacetime employment by our foreign service cruisers and their utility tested repeatedly from time to time."

Pagan was one of these secret bases.

This was a bold move by Graf Spee because it took his squadron in the last direction the Allies would expect him to go—toward Japan. It also made it easier for the *Emden* and the other ships from Tsingtao to rendezvous with the rest of the squadron. Pagan kept them near to the major shipping routes, which they could attack if Japan remained neutral. Most important, the move took them well away from Patey's squadron to the south.

Pagan was, of course, nearer to Hong Kong and Weihaiwai, where Jerram's cruisers were believed to be, but Graf Spee was not overly concerned about the chances of running into the *Minotaur* or the *Hampshire*. What he needed was a friendly, isolated harbor where he could take some time to meet with his captains and plan how and where they were going to strike at enemy shipping and shore installations. Best of all, his enemies would have no idea where he was until he actually did attack.

Since the admiral's departure in June, Captain von Müller of the *Emden* had been senior naval officer at Tsingtao. Left in his charge was a motley collection of ships, most of them quite useless for action at sea. In addition to the *Emden* were the old cruisers *Cormoran* and the Austrian *Kaiserin Elisabeth,* whose captain had wisely sought refuge at Tsingtao when the crisis in Europe deepened. These two would be helpless against any of Jerram's cruisers. There were also four old gunboats and a destroyer, but these were only useful for operations in coastal waters. The German merchant vessels in the harbor came under Müller's command,

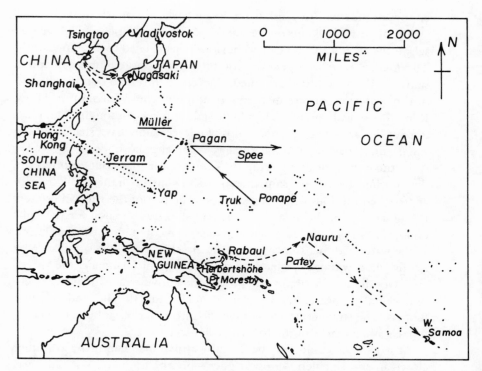

Opening moves in the Pacific, August 1914

because once war was declared, the entire merchant fleet was at the disposal of the Kaiserliche Marine. Of these, the colliers and merchant ships were to be used to supply the cruiser squadron, and the passenger ships were to be converted into armed merchant cruisers by transferring deck guns from the old gunboats and cruisers.

Müller's orders were clear. "In the event of strained relations *Emden* is to protect colliers leaving Tsingtao, but must not allow herself to be blockaded there. Colliers to proceed to Pagan. *Emden* will endeavour to join squadron."

On July 31, when war with Russia seemed imminent, Müller took the *Emden* out to sea, accompanied by the chartered collier *Elsbeth*. He didn't want to run the risk of being trapped in Tsingtao by Jerram's ships if Britain entered the war, and he decided to await developments while at sea. The next day he received the signal that Germany had declared war on Russia. He detached the *Elsbeth* to go to Yap and wait for instructions, then headed toward the straits of Tsushima to look for Russian merchant ships.

On August 1 lookouts on the *Emden* saw the wakes of several large vessels in the calm water. They had obviously just passed by heading south. The *Emden*'s wireless operators also picked up a large number of coded signals in the area. Müller assumed, correctly as it turned out, that he had just missed some of Jerram's cruisers heading from Weihaiwai to Hong Kong. He must have breathed a huge sigh of relief. Although Britain had not yet declared war, Jerram's ships would certainly have shadowed the *Emden* until they received the signal to commence hostilities.

In the early morning of August 4 the cruiser's lookouts spotted the dim outline of a large ship that was showing no lights. The *Emden* approached cautiously at first—she might be one of the Russian cruisers thought to be in the area. The German ship was a match for the light cruiser *Zhemchug*, but the heavy cruiser *Askold* could blow the *Emden* out of the water with her 6-inch guns. The *Askold* was easily recognizable by her five narrow funnels, which led the British to nickname her the "packet of Woodbines." Visibility was poor, with a driving rain and heavy swell, but as they got nearer, the Germans could see that the ship had only two funnels. The stranger was soon identified from her black hull and yellow funnels as a member of the Russian Volunteer Fleet.

At worst, she could only be a lightly armed merchantman, so Müller closed in and signaled, "Stop at once—do not use wireless." This was ignored, and the Russian ship headed toward Japanese territorial waters at high speed. The cruiser's operators could hear her sending out frantic wireless requests for help. The *Emden* fired two blank shells across her bow, but these were ignored as well. When the *Emden* began firing live shells, the chase ended as the Russian ship heaved to.

Captain von Müller sent ex-merchant marine captain Julius Lauterbach across in a cutter with an armed boarding party to seize the ship and act as prize officer. The portly and jovial Lauterbach was a lieutenant in the naval reserve and was to become a valuable member of the *Emden*'s crew. He signaled back that the captured vessel was the seven-thousand-ton mail steamer *Ryazan*, with eighty passengers but little cargo on board, en route from Nagasaki to Vladivostok. At first Captain Ausan of the *Ryazan* claimed not to understand German, until Lauterbach laughingly reminded him that they had been drinking together in a Tsingtao bar only a month before, and Ausan had been able to speak German then. The Russian explained that he had hoped to escape, but his passengers had become so terrified by the shelling that he had been forced to stop. Thus, the *Emden* had the honor of taking the first German prize of the war.

Although it was risky, since he had just received the news of Britain's declaration of war, Müller decided to take the *Ryazan* back to Tsingtao and arm her as a merchant cruiser before setting out for Pagan. That evening, a lookout saw the smoke of several ships that turned out to be, from their uncoded wireless signals, French warships. Müller's good fortune continued because the enemy ships turned away when they sighted the *Emden*'s smoke. The *Emden* learned from their signals that she had been wrongly identified as an armored cruiser and that the French believed they were running into the whole German squadron. The next morning, August 5, the *Emden* made a triumphant return to Tsingtao harbor, followed by her prize.

In Müller's absence the North German Lloyd Line's *Yorck* and *Prinz Eitel Friedrich* had already been converted into armed merchant cruisers by transferring guns from the old gunboats. He now gave orders to remove the eight 4-inch guns from the *Cormoran* and mount them on the *Ryazan,* which took over both the old cruiser's name and her crew. The *Kaiserin Elisabeth* was anchored in shallow water near the harbor mouth where she could easily be scuttled to act as a block ship. Her guns were taken off and set up in one of the shore batteries.

The *Emden*'s captain had done all he could for Tsingtao, and it was time to leave. On the evening of August 6 the *Emden* sailed from Tsingtao for the last time, accompanied by the *Prinz Eitel Friedrich* and the collier *Markomannia.* Müller set a course for Pagan. According to the first officer of the *Emden,* Lt. Comdr. Hellmuth von Mücke: "There was great enthusiasm, the band playing the 'Wacht am Rhein.' There was a general feeling: 'We shall manage it all right.'"

The next morning Müller sent the collier ahead, with orders to rendezvous with the two warships later, while they carried out a search for Allied merchantmen. This proved fruitless; the only ships they saw were Japanese, and the Germans were obliged to let them pass. Japan was still neutral, and they had no wish to provoke it by capturing one of its merchant ships, whether she was carrying contraband or not. Müller knew that one of these ships would be bound to signal the news of his whereabouts to Tokyo, so he gave up the search and headed directly for Pagan.

Meanwhile, Jerram had sent the *Yarmouth* and the French cruiser *Dupleix* to blockade Tsingtao, and he took the rest of his ships to the Carolines to see if any of Graf Spee's cruisers were still there. When the *Yarmouth* and *Dupleix* arrived at Tsingtao, they learned that only old cruisers and gunboats were left in the harbor. Jerram was equally unlucky; there were no warships at Yap. He found only the fully loaded collier

Elsbeth, which Müller had sent there to await further orders. After evacuating her crew, Jerram promptly sank her. He also warned the civilian staff on shore to get clear, then destroyed the powerful W/T station by gunfire, hoping to disrupt German communications.

The next day Jerram had to abandon his search of the Carolines; the *Hampshire* was running low on coal. This meant the squadron had to go all the way back to Hong Kong. The *Hampshire* could certainly have used the *Elsbeth's* coal, but Jerram later justified sinking the collier by claiming that the sea was too rough to coal and besides, he couldn't spare men for a prize crew. ("A helpless performance," in the words of one naval expert.)

On August 11, while the German squadron was converging on Pagan almost a thousand miles away in the Marianas, the Admiralty sent Jerram new instructions. "Practically certain Japan declares war on 12th. You may now leave protection of British trade north of Hong Kong to Japanese, concentrating your attention in concert with Australian squadron on destroying German cruisers. Send one light cruiser to close *Rainbow* at Vancouver."

Jerram ordered the *Newcastle* to go to the west coast of Canada to support the obsolescent cruiser *Rainbow* (donated by the Royal Navy to the fledgling Royal Canadian Navy). This was the only warship at the naval base of Esquimalt, and the Admiralty wanted to calm the growing public concern about the presence of a dangerous German raider in the coastal waters of British Columbia. It was also important to counter rumors that the *Leipzig* planned to attack unprotected Canadian Pacific liners off the North American coast.

The Admiralty signal was overoptimistic. Japan had, in fact, sent only an ultimatum to Germany on August 12, demanding that it give up its Kiaochow territories to Japanese forces without opposition. This was not due to expire for ten days. Japan didn't actually enter the war until August 23, when its forces attacked Tsingtao. Jerram was then ordered to send the *Triumph* to assist them in the siege. In return, he received the modern battle cruiser *Ibuki* and the light cruiser *Chikuma* to help with shipping protection, a good exchange from Jerram's point of view.

Due to the Japanese delay in entering the war, Jerram had to keep the rest of his squadron at Hong Kong for another two weeks, by which time Graf Spee's ships were thousands of miles away. But at least he had the satisfaction of knowing that the German cruisers would now have to abandon the western Pacific.

Farther south, Admiral Patey's Australian squadron was fully occupied in supporting Allied invasions of German New Guinea. On August 9 he assembled his ships off Port Moresby before attacking the German bases at Rabaul and Herbertshöhe. The expeditionary forces met no serious opposition when they reached shore, and they easily occupied the two bases. Then Patey received a report from the Australian Naval Board saying that Graf Spee's ships had been seen off the Solomon Islands, heading southeast. (He had no way of knowing this information was incorrect.) He signaled Jerram, suggesting they join forces to make a sweep through the area between northern Australia and New Guinea to trap the German squadron. Jerram didn't reply. He was maintaining strict radio silence during his own futile sweep through the Carolines.

When Patey found no sign of German warships in the New Guinea area, he concluded that Graf Spee would decide to head east across the Pacific, now that Japan was about to enter the war. But on the night of August 12–13, before Graf Spee had left Pagan, Patey received a telegram from the government of New Zealand saying that the expeditions against Nauru and Samoa were now ready to begin. The signal asked if the route could be made safe from Graf Spee's cruisers. Patey was obliged to escort the New Zealand invasion forces, an action that deflected him from any immediate attempt to cut Graf Spee off.

Thus, while Graf Spee was bringing his forces together in the Marianas, the two Allied squadrons were nearly a thousand miles to the southeast and southwest of him. They were engaged in anything but "concentrating . . . attention in concert . . . on destroying German cruisers." This gave the Germans ample breathing space to plan their next move.

It took Graf Spee's ships more than four days to steam the thousand miles from Ponapé before they saw the twin volcanic peaks of Pagan. They arrived on the morning of August 11. The North German Lloyd steamer *Yorck* was already in the harbor. German merchant ships in the Far East had been ordered to rendezvous there with Graf Spee, and all day long ships of the North German Lloyd and Hamburg America Lines steamed into the harbor. By nightfall the lagoon was crowded with the *Prinz Waldemar, Holsatia, Longmoon, Mark, Staatssekretär Krätke,* and *Gouverneur Jäschke,* which had managed to elude Allied patrols off the China coast. The *Titania* was left outside the coral reef as sentry.

Besides the *Elsbeth,* several other expected merchantmen didn't make it to Pagan, but Graf Spee now had enough colliers and supply ships to keep his squadron going for months. The crews spent the next two days coaling and transferring food and fresh water to the three cruisers.

On the afternoon of August 12 the *Titania*'s lookouts spotted the smoke of two vessels approaching from the north. After initially being alarmed, they recognized the *Emden* and *Prinz Eitel Friedrich.* The latecomers were escorted through the gap in the coral reef. The collier *Markomannia* was not with them, and Müller reported to the admiral that she had failed to meet them two days before, as arranged. This was bad news because she was carrying five thousand tons of coal, enough to keep a light cruiser like the *Emden* supplied for months. Fortunately, she showed up the next morning. Her captain had simply misunderstood his instructions about where to meet the *Emden*.

The same day, Graf Spee called a conference of all the cruiser captains in his suite on board the *Scharnhorst*. He outlined the options for the squadron to get the reactions of his captains and staff officers before he came to a final decision on where to attack. German strategy was simple. "In any war in which England is Germany's adversary the destruction of English trade . . . is of paramount importance. Ships on foreign stations are to wage a cruiser commerce-war."

The choices were to take the squadron west through the East Indies into the Indian Ocean or to head east toward the coast of South America. The Germans knew that the Allies had weak squadrons in these two areas. Graf Spee thought his ships would be able to inflict considerable damage along the shipping lanes before the Allies could send out strong reinforcements. When they did, the squadron could evade them by heading into the Atlantic, either by going around the Cape of Good Hope or through the Strait of Magellan. Graf Spee knew his ships had only a slim chance of getting back to Germany, but if they could run the Allied blockade, it would be a great moral victory.

The problem with heading west lay in securing coal supplies. Few Etappen operated in the East Indies and Indian Ocean, and these would be reduced even further once the Allies began their attacks on German possessions. The Indian Ocean would, in effect, become "a British lake." Also, the Dutch were unfriendly neutrals who would strictly enforce the rule of staying twenty-four hours only in any of their possessions in the East Indies. This rule allowed warships just one visit every three months and permitted them to take on only coal, water, and food supplies.

A more attractive proposition was to head for South America, where there were trade routes vital to Britain. Argentina and Chile were Britain's major suppliers of beef, grain, and nitrates, but they were also pro-German and could be expected to ignore infringements of their neutrality, if these were not too blatant. Many Etappen were located in South American countries, and there would be no difficulty obtaining coal supplies or provisions when the squadron reached Chilean waters. Another advantage was that Graf Spee would more easily be able to reestablish contact with the naval staff in Berlin through the German consulates in South American countries.

The next question was whether to keep all the ships of the squadron together as a powerful unit or to detach some of them as lone commerce raiders. Graf Spee was in favor of the fleet-in-being philosophy, since the Allies would then have to try to match him in strength in all areas where the squadron was likely to strike. This would tie up a large number of their warships overseas and help even up the naval situation in European waters. Graf Spee was personally more inclined to use his strength to destroy enemy shore installations or to force a battle with their warships rather than attack such easy prey as unarmed merchant vessels.

After presenting the options to his senior officers, he asked for their opinions. Whether from conviction or awe, most of them agreed with the admiral that it would be best to keep the squadron together. Capt. Felix Schultz, who commanded the *Scharnhorst,* proposed that they make a massive attack on some enemy port in order to panic shipping in its area. This idea received little support.

When it was Karl von Müller's turn to speak, he suggested that one cruiser be detached to go into the Indian Ocean and raid shipping there. He pointed out that coaling would be less of a problem for a single ship, especially for a light cruiser whose daily coal consumption was much lower than that of the big armored cruisers. Given a collier to accompany her, a light cruiser might expect to capture other colliers when her supply ran low and to survive as a raider for several months. If things became desperate, she could always be scuttled or interned in a neutral port. Graf Spee's Chief of Staff, Captain Fielitz, supported Müller's proposal. The admiral said he would consider the matter.

The meeting was adjourned. Graf Spee gave orders for all ships to be ready to sail at 1730. He was anxious to leave because the wireless station at Yap had suddenly stopped broadcasting the previous day. Also, the *Elsbeth,* which had been ordered from Yap to Pagan, had failed to show up. The Germans guessed that Yap had been attacked by Jerram. Because this island was only seven hundred miles away, it was too dangerous to stay at Pagan any longer. Graf Spee had no wish to have his ships surprised by Jerram's squadron while at anchor. The outcome would be disastrous because of the time it would take for ten ships to get up steam and pass through the narrow entrance one at a time. If one of his ships was sunk in the mouth of the lagoon, the rest might be trapped.

Late that afternoon Graf Spee made his decision. He sent a written order to Müller by way of the *Scharnhorst*'s cutter:

PAGAN, AUGUST 13, 1914.

Accompanied by the steamship *Markomannia,* you are to be detached for deployment in the Indian Ocean, there to wage a vigorous cruiser war to the best of your ability.

Enclosed is a copy of telegraphic communications with our southern supply network during the last few weeks. It lists the amount of coal ordered for the future, an amount that will be turned over to you.

Tonight you will remain with the squadron. Tomorrow morning, this order will be set in motion by the signal "Detached."

I intend to sail with the remaining formation to the west coast of America.

Signed, Graf Spee

Precisely at 1730 on August 13, the ships of what was now a small fleet weighed anchor and started to move out of the calm waters of Pagan harbor. The *Scharnhorst* led the cruiser squadron in a line consisting of the *Gneisenau, Nürnberg, Emden,* and the patrol vessel *Titania.* The *Prinz Eitel Friedrich* led out the eight merchant ships in a second line. The two lines formed up outside the harbor, with the merchant vessels trailing the cruiser squadron on its starboard quarter, and set a course to the east at ten knots.

"Dawn light," wrote an observer on the *Emden,* "revealed a shambles. The warships were still in line ahead, but no vestige of organization could be seen in the second line." The merchant ship captains had never practiced formation steaming, and some of their ships were out of sight of the main squadron. Graf Spee sent the *Nürnberg* to round up the stragglers and shepherd them back into line.

The fleet was back in close formation by 0800. The flagship ran up the signal "*Emden* detached. Good luck." This came as a surprise to most people in the squadron, even to many of the *Emden*'s crew. Müller signaled back: "My dutiful thanks for the confidence placed in me. Success to the squadron and bon voyage." The flagship sent another signal, this time to Captain Faass of the *Markomannia.* "Follow *Emden.*" The little cruiser pulled out of line to starboard, followed by the collier, and set a course south-southwest at twelve knots. The rest of the squadron kept on its eastward course.

So on August 14, 1914, ten days after war had been declared, the Royal Navy still had no idea where Graf Spee's squadron was or where it planned to strike. They were to remain in the dark for several more weeks as far as the squadron was concerned, but it wasn't long before they heard from one of the cruisers. By the end of September the names of the *Emden* and her captain would be household words in most parts of the world.

4

Karl von Müller's Adventure

Our false fourth funnel was hoisted, sharp war watches were set, and special lookouts were posted.
— Prince Franz Josef von Hohenzollern, torpedo officer on the *Emden*

Karl von Müller had been granted his wish to be a lone wolf. He had a fast ship, a well-trained crew, his own collier, and a whole ocean before him. But he still had several rendezvous to keep before he could begin raiding Allied shipping. Transports and colliers had been assigned to meet him at out-of-the-way harbors in the East Indies because he had no base in the Indian Ocean closer than Dar es Salaam, a distance of more than four thousand miles. His only reliable sources of food, fresh water, and coal would be these German supply ships.

The *Emden* and her collier headed southwest toward their first rendezvous. This was in the Palau Islands, which lie at the western end of the Caroline chain. They were scheduled to meet the collier *Choising* at Angaur because the cruiser would need coal after covering the eleven hundred miles from Pagan. The *Markomannia* carried five thousand tons of good quality coal, but Müller wanted to keep this in reserve until he reached the Indian Ocean, where there would be no more German ships to supply him. He couldn't rely entirely on capturing Allied colliers, which might not oblige him by showing up when he most needed them.

The first five days of the voyage were uneventful. The cruiser was far from the usual trade routes, and there were few islands to see in this lonely stretch of the Pacific. The *Emden* steered well clear of Yap, which by now might have been occupied by Allied forces. Müller passed most of his time on the bridge and even slept there. He pored over charts and handbooks and read all the old newspapers he could find, looking for information about shipping routes and schedules. He spent long hours thinking about what he was going to do when he reached the Indian Ocean. His crew passed their days much as they had in peacetime, except that extra lookouts were posted, and the torpedo tubes and guns were kept ready at a minute's notice. The gunners also slept at their stations, a pleasant change from their cramped quarters below decks.

German cruisers had a reputation for "keine Bequemlichkeit, kein Platz"—they were neither comfortable nor roomy. Most German warships had not been designed for long overseas voyages but for service in the North Sea, where the crews lived ashore in barracks except for brief periods when the ships were actually at sea. The slim four-hundred-foot hulls of the light cruisers had to pack in engine rooms, boiler rooms, magazines, torpedo tubes, coal bunkers, fresh water tanks, and stores. This didn't leave much living space for the three to four hundred men of their crews.

As the *Emden* approached the Palaus on the evening of August 19, Müller decided to reduce speed so they would arrive at Angaur just before daybreak the next morning. The island had been leased to a German company that was mining its rich deposits of phosphates, but for all Müller knew, it might be in Allied hands by now. The last thing he wanted was to run into one of Jerram's cruisers before he had a chance to attack Allied shipping. As dawn broke he scouted the island cautiously before entering the harbor.

The crew were relieved to see that the German flag was still flying over several buildings at Angaur, but there was no sign of the *Choising*. The manager of the phosphate company and his officials came out to the *Emden* for a social visit in the wardroom. Over glasses of *Sekt* (champagne) or whiskey they told Müller that a British freighter, loaded with seven thousand tons of phosphates, had left Angaur three days previously. Her captain had tried to reach Yap by wireless for news of the war situation. When he received no response, he became suspicious. Believing that a German warship would soon come looking for him, he left in a hurry before his ship was fully loaded. The *Emden* was unlucky to have missed this valuable war prize.

Müller couldn't afford to wait around for the *Choising* and so had to take coal from the *Markomannia*. While this was going on, the lookouts spotted smoke clouds to the north. The *Emden* was in a vulnerable position while she was tied up to the collier, but as the newcomer drew nearer, the lookouts recognized the black hull and buff funnels of the North German Lloyd Line. She was the eleven-thousand-ton mail steamer *Prinzessin Alice,* coming from Manila under orders to meet the *Emden* to deliver messages and to transfer provisions.

Captain Bortfeld and the pursers of the steamer turned out to be sticklers for regulations and demanded that all requisition forms be filled out in detail and in triplicate before they would transfer any provisions. In the words of one of the *Emden*'s exasperated officers: "The celebration of St. Bureaucratius bordered on the orgiastic. The mail steamer's pursers lacked common sense, insisting that peacetime procedures should be maintained in a war!"

The *Emden*'s captain had no time to fool around and gave orders for all three ships to sail that evening. He told the captain of the *Prinzessin Alice* to follow the cruiser. By the morning of August 21, however, only the faithful *Markomannia* remained in sight. Müller was reluctant to use his wireless because his signal might be intercepted by an Allied ship. Even though the message would be in code, it was easy for the enemy to recognize the high pitch of Telefunken transmissions. But both the *Emden* and her collier were badly in need of fresh provisions and he had no choice. He signaled the *Prinzessin Alice* to meet him the next day to transfer her supplies at sea. Bortfeld's answer came back that he was short of coal and having boiler trouble; he could not meet the *Emden* at all.

Müller was angry, but he had to accept the excuse. He ordered the steamer to go back to the Philippines and avoid capture by seeking internment. The behavior of the captain of the *Prinzessin Alice* was later severely criticized, but this was one of the few occasions when German merchantmen didn't cooperate fully with the Kaiserliche Marine.

The captain's displeasure was shared by a crew tired of "a maddeningly monotonous diet of corned beef, rice and a few dried vegetables." An officer wrote in his diary, "Though officers' cook Schultz became a master at dressing the stuff in different ways, corned beef and rice remained what they were: boring."

Later that day, the *Emden* received a surprise wireless message from the gunboat *Geier*, which had left Singapore just before war broke out to seek refuge in some German possession. Müller arranged to meet the gunboat and her collier *Bochum* at a point south of Angaur. The *Geier* was old, slow, and armed with antiquated guns. Her status had recently been downgraded from "cruiser" to "gunboat." Despite her name, which means vulture, she was easy prey for an Allied warship, even one as small as a destroyer. Since she could neither run away from enemy warships nor catch merchant ships, Müller ordered her captain to head for Yap. He told him to approach the island cautiously and find out whether it had been occupied by the Allies, then try to contact Graf Spee for further orders. He had heard nothing from his admiral since he left Pagan, and all he could tell the captain of the *Geier* was that the squadron was heading toward South America. This was the *Emden*'s last encounter with a friendly warship.

Müller set a course for the Molucca Straits, planning to meet the Hansa Line's collier *Tannenfels* at the eastern end of Timor. On August 22 the *Emden* crossed the equator, but there was no time for the fun and games of traditional crossing-the-line ceremonies. The two ships were in an area with many islands from which they could be spotted, and Müller was eager to get through it as quickly as possible.

The next morning they passed a Japanese steamer but had to be content with a polite exchange of flag signals. The Japanese ultimatum to Germany had expired the previous day, but Müller had no way of knowing whether Japan had actually entered the war. The *Emden* hoisted the White Ensign of the Royal Navy, hoping to be mistaken for a British cruiser.

The *Emden* and *Markomannia* arrived at the rendezvous a day early and waited off the coast until daybreak on August 25. They approached the island of Leti, where they were supposed to meet the *Tannenfels,* but there was no collier in the bay. Once again they had to use the *Markomannia*'s coal reserves to bring the cruiser's bunkers up to a full load. After coaling, a landing party went ashore to get fresh fodder for the *Emden*'s livestock. These animals, including pigs, cattle, lambs, hens, and geese, were kept in pens that the ship's carpenters had built on the cruiser's deck. The idea was not to slaughter them until it was necessary. In the meantime, they were used to supply fresh milk and eggs.

Müller thought it was too risky to wait for the *Tannenfels.* (It was later discovered that she had arrived at Leti before the *Emden* but had been ordered to leave by a Dutch warship. Soon after this the *Tannenfels* was captured by a British patrol.) He decided to stay well north of Timor and headed through the Lesser Sunda Straits into the Flores Sea. This would keep them away from the Australian coast—where Patey's ships might be patrolling—until they were ready to cross over to the southern side of the Dutch East Indies by way of the little-used Lombok Strait.

The Germans didn't know it, but Admiral Jerram had just moved his headquarters to Singapore, now that the Japanese navy was taking care of the South China coast. The route Müller had chosen was taking the *Emden* straight into the area being patrolled by the *Yarmouth,* *Hampshire,* and *Minotaur.* Any of these ships could easily outgun the German cruiser.

The *Emden*'s next rendezvous was at the island of Tanahjampea, midway between the Celebes and Sunda Islands, where the collier *Offenbach* had been instructed to wait. After their experiences at the last two ren-

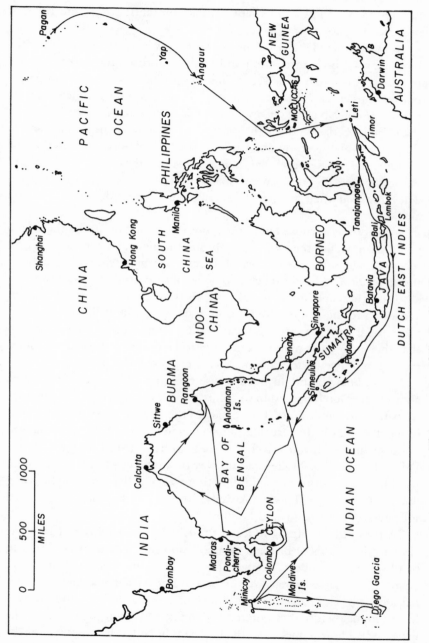

The war cruise of the *Emden*—Pagan to Penang

dezvous, the crew weren't optimistic about seeing her there. Timing their arrival again for daybreak, they approached the harbor slowly but could not tell if any ships were there because the entrance to the bay was obscured by a low spit of land.

As they rounded the point they saw a large warship steaming out of the bay. She was about three thousand yards away, heading directly toward them. Her mainmast flags were flying—a sign she was prepared for battle. Because of her head-on approach, the Germans couldn't tell whether she was a neutral ship or an enemy. The *Emden*'s captain gave orders to clear the ship for action and for the battle flag to be hoisted. When the two ships were only two thousand yards apart, the lookouts reported that the ship was flying the Dutch flag. She was identified as the coastal defense battleship *Tromp*. The crew on board the *Emden* were greatly relieved. They lowered their flag, and the two ships entered the harbor and anchored.

A collier was anchored in the bay, but she turned out to be the Dutch vessel *Batavia,* not the *Offenbach.* During the inevitable exchange of protocol visits between the officers of the two warships, Müller learned that the *Offenbach* had arrived at the rendezvous on time but had been sent away by the captain of the *Tromp.* He reminded the Germans that, according to the Hague Convention, warships of the belligerent nations were not allowed to set up regular coaling points in neutral harbors and that they were only permitted to stop to coal in territorial waters for a maximum of twenty-four hours, once every three months.

Müller knew he might need to use this rule in an emergency, so he allowed the Dutch battleship to escort the *Emden* out of Tanahjampea as far as the three-mile limit. The captain of the *Tromp* was sympathetic, but his government had instructed him to maintain the strictest neutrality to avoid giving offense to the Japanese, who had obvious designs on the Dutch East Indies. Müller had no way of knowing whether the Dutch would report his position and direction to the Allies, so he kept going due north until the *Tromp* was well out of sight, then he changed to a southwesterly course toward Lombok.

To pass into the Indian Ocean the two German ships had to come close to the islands of Bali and Lombok, and their passage was bound to be observed from shore. It was even possible that enemy warships were guarding the narrow straits. Although it is not certain who had the original idea, the Germans decided to disguise the *Emden* by mounting a fourth funnel before they entered the straits. Most British cruisers in the Far East had four funnels, and the Germans hoped to be mistaken for the *Yarmouth,* whose hull was not much longer than the *Emden*'s. They constructed a dummy funnel out of laths, bamboo poles, and sailcloth and arranged it so that it could be raised and lowered quickly. At first the funnel was two dimensional, which only looked authentic at a long distance. Later the crew made refinements and changed its shape to round, and eventually to oval, as in British cruisers. They even added a boiler to give the appearance of smoke coming out of all four funnels. The *Markomannia,* which was a British-built ship, was also disguised by repainting her hull and upper works to make her look like a ship of the Blue Funnel Line.

The cruiser and her collier reached Lombok on August 28 and increased speed to thirteen knots, all that the *Markomannia* could manage. In his memoir, Prinz Franz Josef von Hohenzollern, the junior torpedo officer on the *Emden* (and the Kaiser's nephew), gives a graphic account of the passage into the Indian Ocean.

> Toward midday, we sighted the mountains of the islands of Lombok to the east and Bali to westward, guarding the flanks of the Lombok Straits. Sunset was magnificent: the dark rim of the mountains against a red-gold sky, reflected in the sea, was truly worthy of a Master's brush. Night fell quickly, as it always does in the tropics. Our false fourth funnel was hoisted, sharp war-watches were set, and special lookouts were posted. Soon we sighted some sailing ships and began the passage of the straits at about 2200. Many eyes strained into the night. We met a steamship; then some sailing vessels. But no hostile warship was to be seen, and nothing could be missed in the bright moonlight. Shortly after midnight we were safely through.
>
> Our captain must have offered a prayer for reaching our objective unseen.

In spite of all that has been written about his exploits, the man who commanded the *Emden* remains a somewhat enigmatic figure. Unlike his colorful brother officers Julius Lauterbach and Hellmuth von Mücke, he had no penchant for publicity or self-glorification. He left no memoirs, and his official reports were models of brevity.

Karl Friedrich Max von Müller was born in Hannover in 1873, the son of an army colonel. After attending Gymnasium in Hannover and Kiel, he enrolled at the army's *Kadettenanstalt* (officers training school) in Plön in 1888. His father wanted his son to continue in his footsteps but reluctantly allowed him to transfer to the less glamorous naval service in 1891, when Karl became a midshipman on the training ship *Stosch.* After a cruise to the Americas in 1892 in the old frigate *Gneisenau,* Müller became an ensign in 1894 and served on the battleships *Baden* and *Sachsen.* He was promoted to lieutenant in 1897 and did a tour of duty in

Capt. Karl von Müller *(Wilhelm Heyne Verlag)*

German East Africa, where he contracted malaria. This illness forced him to return to Germany in 1900 and was to trouble him throughout the rest of his life.

Promotion came slowly for Karl von Müller. After twelve years of service he was still only a lieutenant commander. But his next assignment was as a staff officer to Prinz Heinrich von Preussen, the Kaiser's younger brother, who commanded the battleship *Deutschland*. Müller's conscientious performance helped advance his career. Promoted to commander in 1908, he got his big chance the following year when he was transferred to the Reichsmarineamt in Berlin. Here he served for three years under no less a figure than Grand Admiral von Tirpitz. The great man wrote of

Müller: "First-class, completely reliable officer. Warmly recommended to future superiors."

This was good enough for Müller to achieve every officer's dream—his own command. Appointed to the *Emden* in 1913, he didn't disappoint Tirpitz. As a result of his daring and resolute performance against the Chinese rebel forts on the Yangtse River, Müller was decorated and promoted in 1914 to the rank of captain (junior).

On a personal level Müller was reserved, even withdrawn, and, according to his peers, "not pushy at all." To his subordinates he was fair and good-natured and always earnest. He did not often join his officers in the wardroom on social occasions. A former superior commended him in a backhanded way for his "painful conscientiousness." Nevertheless, he was to prove himself an imaginative and adventurous raider who gained the respect of friends and enemies alike.

Now that he was safely into the Indian Ocean, Müller had one more rendezvous to keep before he struck at the busy trade routes off the coast of India. The last German merchantman that had been ordered to supply the *Emden* was the *Ulm,* of the German-Australia Line. A meeting had been arranged at the small island of Simeuluë, which lies seventy miles off the coast of Sumatra, near its northern tip.

Staying out of sight of land, the *Emden* and *Markomannia* kept parallel to the southern coast of Java, past the Greater Sunda Straits, then followed the coastline of Sumatra. They must have been spotted because they picked up a news broadcast from the Batavia radio station that an unidentified four-funneled warship had been sighted in the straits area. The dummy funnel was obviously doing its job, but not quite as they had planned. The British also heard the Batavia broadcast. They knew they had no such ship in that area, so Jerram sent the *Hampshire* to investigate. During the next few days the *Emden*'s wireless operators picked up a lot of coded messages, often coming from a ship with the call sign "QMD." They suspected this was a British warship because it was transmitting on the six-hundred-meter band normally used by the Royal Navy.

When the *Emden* arrived at Langini harbor, Simeuluë, on the morning of September 4, the Germans were disappointed once again. The expected freighter was nowhere in sight. This was bad news because the *Ulm* was carrying supplies as well as coal. Provisions were sorely needed by the *Emden*'s hardworking crew, even though the men were given priority over the officers when food became scarce. The supply of fresh food had long since run out, except for milk and eggs from the livestock. Tinned food, even pâté de foie gras from the wardroom, was beginning to pall as

The "Swan of the East," SMS *Emden* (*Wilhelm Heyne Verlag*)

a staple diet. The ship's officers traded with the natives who paddled out to the ship from Langini, but the medical officer, Stabsarzt Johannes Luther, would permit only fresh fish and coconuts to be brought on board. Even so, these made a welcome change from corned beef and rice.

The *Ulm* was also carrying soap, which was in short supply due to an ordering error in Tsingtao. The laundrymen, in particular, were having great difficulty, and the white tropical uniforms were approaching a uniform gray. When the *Emden* left Tsingtao for Pagan, three Chinese laundrymen were on board. Originally there had been four, but their leader, Joseph, deserted at Tsingtao as soon as war was declared. When they reached Pagan, the other three refused to go any farther because of the danger the cruiser might be involved in, and they asked to be taken back to Tsingtao. The Germans pointed out that none of their ships was going there. They praised their skills as laundrymen, begged them to stay on, and offered them greatly increased wages. The three civilians finally agreed to serve during the rest of the *Emden*'s cruise, even though they knew they were taking a grave risk. Their names were never known, and the crew simply called them "One," "Two," and "Three," in Chinese.

The usually efficient German supply system had let Müller down again, so once more the *Emden* had to coal from the *Markomannia*. The work had not been finished by 0700 on the morning of September 5 when a small steam yacht flying the Dutch flag appeared and drew alongside the *Emden*. The Dutch captain reminded Müller of the twenty-four-hour rule. The German replied that he had not arrived until 0900 the previous day and, therefore, still had two hours to go. But the Dutchman told him that his ships had been seen entering the harbor at 0700, and it was now time for them to leave. Müller then claimed it would take at least two hours to get up steam. In truth, the Germans had kept full steam up the whole time they had been at Langini, in case they had to leave in a hurry. The Dutch captain good-naturedly accepted the excuse and a glass or two of whiskey in Müller's cabin as coaling went on.

By 1100 the *Emden* and *Markomannia* were ready to leave and were escorted out to the open sea by the little patrol vessel. The Germans again set a false course to the southeast until their escort was far out of sight, then they reversed direction toward Madras.

The captain of the Dutch vessel maintained strict neutrality and did not inform the Allies of the *Emden*'s visit. Neither did he tell Müller that the *Hampshire* had visited Langini only twenty-four hours before the *Emden* showed up. In fact, the British heavy cruiser had been anchored on the other side of the island, barely ten miles away from the *Emden,* the whole time she had been coaling. The Germans would have had no chance at all against the *Hampshire*'s battery of 6- and 7.5-inch guns if they had been caught motionless, tied up to the *Markomannia* as they were. This was another narrow escape for Müller. Capt. H. W. Grant was truly unlucky to have missed his quarry by so little a margin.

By the evening of September 9 the *Emden* and her consort had crossed the widest part of the Bay of Bengal and entered the Colombo-Calcutta shipping lanes. At 2300 the lookouts saw the lights of a ship to the north, and the *Emden* turned and increased speed to twenty-three knots, leaving the *Markomannia* to follow. As they drew near, they could tell from her silhouette that the vessel was a merchantman. They flashed the signal "Stop engines. Do not use wireless."

This was followed by two blank rounds from the forward 4.1-inch gun. The merchant ship stopped her engines and heaved to, rolling gently in the light sea swell.

Müller sent Lauterbach across to her by cutter. He took an armed boarding party that included a signalman and wireless operator. The *Emden*'s searchlights were trained on the vessel, but it wasn't possible to tell her nationality. Finally, Lauterbach signaled back, "Greek steamship *Pontoporos.*"

At first Müller was disappointed that the captured vessel was a neutral, but after Lauterbach had examined the ship's manifest, he continued: "Carrying 6,500 tons of coal for the English government. Bound from Calcutta to Bombay."

Since she was carrying contraband, the Germans could then legally confiscate her cargo, according to the Hague Convention, but not the ship herself.

The *Markomannia* was now down to about half her original load, so the *Pontoporos*'s coal was more than welcome. The problem was what to do with it. Müller signaled Lauterbach to ask the Greek captain if he would agree to have his ship serve as a German charter vessel, if he was paid adequately. The answer came back: Captain Polemis would be glad to do so. He may have believed that if he refused, the Germans would take his ship anyway, rules or no rules. The *Emden* resumed her course, with the *Markomannia* and *Pontoporos* on either side of her.

The following morning, September 10, the three ships were about 250 miles southeast of Madras, heading toward Calcutta. The lookouts sighted more smoke on the northern horizon. The *Emden* hoisted her fourth funnel and increased speed. As she approached the strange vessel, the lookouts identified her as a large steamship with unusual superstructures. From a distance these looked like gun emplacements, and the Germans feared she might be an armed merchant cruiser. As they drew nearer, they saw she was flying the Blue Ensign of the merchant marine and decided she must be an unarmed merchantman. The other vessel steamed toward the *Emden* without apparent concern, taking her to be a British cruiser. A warning shot and the international flag signal "Stop. Do not use wireless." soon corrected this impression.

Lieutenant von Levetzow took a boarding party across to the steamer, and after examining the ship's papers he signaled back: "Steamship *Indus*, 3,413 tons, en route from Calcutta to Bombay for Indian government. Equipped to carry troops and horses."

The curious structures on her deck proved to be horse stalls. The Indian government had chartered the ship to transport cavalry from Bombay to Europe.

Although the *Indus* was traveling in ballast, she was well supplied for her trip to Europe. She carried a large quantity of soap, as well as fresh provisions. (Because of his experience in the merchant marine, Lauterbach was sent over to supervise the unloading.) It was mid-afternoon before all these spoils had been transferred to the cruiser. According to an eyewitness: "Our upper deck looked like a colossal warehouse. There were towels, soap, linen, tinned foods, fresh meat, live hens and ducks, drinks, nautical instruments, charts, pencils, and some very welcome oilskins for the cutters' crews and the watches."

After the crew of the *Indus* had been taken to the *Markomannia*, a scuttling party went over to the British ship. They opened the sea-cocks and the connecting doors between the lower compartments so that the holds would flood more quickly. The *Emden*'s gunners fired six shells into the freighter's hull near the waterline to speed up the process, but the *Indus* took an hour before she began to settle in the water. This was the first time the *Emden*'s crew had witnessed the death of a ship, and they watched silently as she went down. So did the captain and crew of the freighter. One of the *Emden*'s officers wrote: "The bows went under, and all at once *Indus* rushed gurgling into the depths. The spectacle was eerie. Escaping air made a loud bang, throwing up masses of débris, while the masts sprang several meters out of the water before splashing back audibly. Some of *Indus*'s boats remained afloat, but they could neither be taken in nor easily destroyed. This was unfortunate . . . as they might betray to the enemy that *Emden* had been waging war on merchant shipping in these particular waters."

The Germans were always concerned about leaving traces of their presence that might give useful information to the enemy. They had even painted all of the *Emden*'s life belts and life rafts with the name *Nagato Maru,* in case the cruiser was sunk by accident. If this happened, they wanted the Allies to keep searching for them and waste valuable ships. (Later that year, the Germans managed to conceal the accidental loss of one of their cruisers, and Allied patrols went on searching for her for several months before the news leaked out.)

Müller decided to keep going toward Calcutta, hoping to capture as many vessels as he could before the Allies detected his presence. He knew it might be days, or even weeks, before the failure of captured merchantmen to reach their next port of call would be reported to the naval authorities. Most merchant ships didn't carry long-range Marconi transmitters in 1914 and wouldn't be expected to signal to shore until they were close to their destination.

The next afternoon, while the spoils from the *Indus* were still being distributed among the *Emden*'s divisions, the lookouts sighted another ship. The cruiser increased speed to twenty knots and soon caught up with her new victim. She signaled the freighter to stop, and her captain obeyed without the need for a shot across his bow. When Lauterbach went across, he reported that she was another British vessel equipped as a troopship, on her way to Bombay to embark Indian troops for Europe. This time it was the *Lovat,* a ship of 6,102 tons, and, like the *Indus,* she carried plenty of supplies. But the Germans now had all the provisions they had space for and decided to sink the steamer with her cargo.

Müller told Lauterbach to confiscate all the newspapers he could find on board the *Lovat* for he eagerly wanted information about the progress of the war and local shipping news. The Germans discovered from sailing reports in the papers that several merchant ships were headed in their direction. Such information from captured ships was extremely useful to the *Emden*. In spite of it being wartime, Indian newspapers continued to publish shipping news for months until they were finally censored.

The crew of the *Lovat,* along with their personal belongings, were taken over to the *Markomannia,* and the steamer's sea-cocks were opened. Müller wanted to give his gunnery officer, Lt. Ernst Gaede, some target practice, and Gaede fired several shells into her at the water-line. The vessel was slow to sink, and as darkness fell, the *Emden* left her to her fate.

Four hours later the Germans saw the lights of another ship, dead ahead. This time there was no need to increase speed because the vessel was fully lit and oblivious to any danger. As she approached the *Emden,* the usual signal was made, accompanied by blasts on the cruiser's siren. The merchantman stopped and made no attempt to use her wireless. Lauterbach went over with a prize crew and reported back: "English ship *Kabinga,* 4,657 tons, with cargo of piece goods. From Calcutta to Bombay, Port Said, Mediterranean and New York."

Her cargo was valuable, but most of it was American owned, under consignment to New York. The *Emden* could legitimately have sunk the *Kabinga* because she was British registered, but under international law Germany would then have been required to recompense the United States for the loss of its property.

Another complication was the presence of the master's wife and children on board the *Kabinga.* The *Emden*'s captain didn't think it acceptable to displace them from their quarters and house them on the crowded *Markomannia* with all the other prisoners, so he decided to spare the *Kabinga* and convert her into a *Lumpensammler,* or junk collector. The crews of the captured vessels now numbered in excess of one hundred. They were rowed across to the *Kabinga* the following morning because it was too dangerous to attempt this in darkness. Müller decided to retain the new prize as a prison ship until such time as he could safely release her. Because of her neutral cargo, the *Kabinga* was ideal for this purpose. Otherwise, he would have had to use another captured British vessel to house prisoners instead of sinking her.

During the night, the *Emden* encountered another fully lighted ship and ordered her to stop, using the siren and megaphone. This time Lieutenant von Levetzow went to board her and reported, "English collier *Killin,* with 6,000 tons of Indian coal, from Calcutta to Bombay, speed eight to nine knots."

It was too dark to transfer the crew or scuttle the *Killin,* and the little flotilla steamed on toward Calcutta. The *Emden* led the way, followed by the *Kabinga* and *Markomannia* on one quarter and the *Pontoporos* and *Killin* on the other.

The morning of September 13 was the start of an even busier day for the *Emden*'s crew. Seamen rowed the crews of the *Indus* and *Lovat* from the *Markomannia* over to the *Kabinga* and also transferred the crew of the *Killin* to the Lumpensammler. The demolition party, who by now were becoming old hands at the game, went across to the *Killin* to sink her. Her coal would have been useful, but she was too slow to keep with them as a collier, and it was risky to take the coal from her in their present location. In any case, the *Pontoporos* and *Markomannia* still had plenty left.

After the crews had been transferred, the *Killin* was scuttled. The cruiser and her consorts steamed on, and within a few hours the smoke of yet another ship appeared on the horizon. The *Emden* headed for her at full speed, leaving the others to catch up. It was a large vessel flying the Red Ensign, and after she was stopped, Lauterbach and his party boarded her. He signaled back, "English steamship *Diplomat,* 7,615 tons, with ten thousand tons of tea, from Calcutta to England."

Müller decided to sink her right away, and after her ship's company had been taken off by boat to wait for the *Kabinga,* he sent Lt. Robert Witthoeft over with his demolition party.

No sooner had the charges exploded when more smoke was sighted on the southern horizon. The *Emden* went racing off to investigate. The Germans were disappointed to find that the ship was flying the flag of the Italian merchant marine. Lieutenants von Levetzow and von Hohenzollern went over to examine her cargo and papers. Italy was neutral at the time, but she had been a member of the prewar Triple Alliance with Germany and Austria. The Germans presumed that the Italians were friendly neutrals, unlike the Dutch. Still, they had to check whether the ship was carrying any contraband.

The two young officers found the Italian captain distinctly unfriendly and uncooperative. He disclaimed any knowledge of German, which was probably true, or of English, which was unlikely in view of his destination. Discussions took place in halting French, and Levetzow eventually signaled the *Emden,* "Italian steamer *Loredano,* en route for Calcutta."

When Müller learned that her cargo was mainly crude wool and contained no contraband material, he had little choice but to release her. He signaled Levetzow to find out whether the Italian captain would agree to take the crews of the British ships to Calcutta, since he was going there anyway. The prisoners were now more than two hundred strong, and they couldn't be fed and kept under guard on the *Kabinga* indefinitely. The Germans offered Captain Giacopolo payment and adequate food supplies if he would take the seamen, but he refused point blank.

Müller couldn't force him to take the prisoners on board his ship, so there was nothing to be done but release the *Loredano* on condition that her captain would give his word of honor that he would remain neutral and give no assistance to the Allies that might endanger the *Emden*. Captain Giacopolo swore that he would behave correctly as a neutral, and after picking up a few cases of tea still floating where the *Diplomat* had sunk, the *Loredano* headed for Calcutta. The *Emden*'s captain was not at all confident that the Italian would keep his word. After steering a false course away from the *Loredano,* he decided to leave the Colombo-Calcutta route and head for the Madras-Calcutta sea-lanes.

Despite his vow of neutrality, the captain of the Italian steamer broke his word the first chance he had. As he approached the mouth of the Hooghly River, he met the brand-new British freighter *City of Rangoon,* which had just left Calcutta bound for Colombo. Captain Giacopolo warned her that the *Emden,* with four captured ships, lay directly in his path. The *City of Rangoon* was equipped with a long-range Marconi transmitter, and her captain wasted no time in signaling all shipping in the area of the danger, as he turned back toward the safety of Calcutta.

A grateful Indian government later presented Captain Giacopolo with a gold watch and chain for his services. His behavior may seem a bit odd for a supposedly friendly neutral, but once the war began, the Italians were at best ambivalent toward their former allies, as they demonstrated by declaring war on Austria in May 1915.

The cat was now truly out of the bag. The news that the *Emden* had been sinking merchant ships in the Bay of Bengal came as a nasty shock and all but paralyzed Allied shipping in the Indian Ocean. Nothing had been heard of the raider since war broke out, and when Jerram's cruisers found that she had left Tsingtao in August, they had safely assumed that she must have joined Graf Spee's squadron, which had just been sighted off Samoa. The Bay of Bengal was considered so secure that merchant ships leaving Indian ports had taken no war precautions whatever. In spite of Admiralty instructions, they kept to their usual tracks and carried full lights at night. None of the *Emden*'s victims had made any attempt to flee when they sighted the cruiser. Their captains were confident that she must be a British warship patrolling their sea-lanes.

The shock waves quickly reached the Admiralty. How on earth had the *Emden* managed to slip through Jerram's net? They postponed all troopship sailings until strong escorts could be guaranteed. The Admiralty did not have enough ships available to protect both the Australian and New Zealand troop convoys, so they decided to combine them in one great convoy.

Public opinion in the two countries was so aroused by the news of the *Emden*'s raids that when the great Anzac convoy finally did sail, it would have an escort strong enough to take care of any attack by Müller, or Graf Spee for that matter. The Australians and New Zealanders expected that if they were going to send their men halfway around the globe to fight in Europe, the most powerful navy in the world should at least make sure they got there safely.

Jerram's ships had been searching the Dutch East Indies for a German cruiser ever since the end of August, when they had picked up the Batavia broadcast about an unidentified four-funneled warship. But they didn't know it was the *Emden* they had been looking for. The *Königsberg* had not been seen since August 4, when she had eluded three British cruisers off Dar es Salaam, and it was feared she had crossed the Indian Ocean to raid shipping in the Bay of Bengal.

Jerram was at Singapore on September 15 when he received the news of the *Emden*'s exploits. He immediately sent the *Hampshire* and the Japanese cruiser *Chikuma* to the Bay of Bengal, and the *Yarmouth* followed the next day. The French *Dupleix* was at Penang, and the *Minotaur* and *Ibuki* went to cover areas where the *Emden* might be expected to coal—off the west coast of Sumatra and at the Cocos Islands. The admiral put Captain Grant of the *Hampshire* in charge of the hunt for the *Emden*.

Meanwhile, Müller had captured two more British merchantmen on the Madras-to-Calcutta route. On the night of September 14 he seized the 4,028-ton collier *Trabboch*. She proved to be empty, on her way to Calcutta to load coal. Her ship's company was transferred to the *Kabinga*. The prison ship was already severely overcrowded with British seamen, and Müller decided to send her to Calcutta. To the Germans' great surprise, the released prisoners lined the deck of the *Kabinga* as she steamed away and gave three parting cheers for the *Emden* because of the considerate way they had been treated.

The demolition party set timed charges in the *Trabboch,* which led to a spectacular explosion. The mixture of air and coal dust in her empty holds ignited "to provide a wonderful display of fireworks against the blackness of the night." Thirty minutes later a light was reported to starboard, and the *Emden* raced toward the ship at twenty-three knots. The captain of this merchant ship had obviously seen the explosion of the *Trabboch,* and he was making a run for safety at full steam.

The cruiser's top speed was twice that of the steamer, and she soon caught up with her prey. The merchantman ignored a signal to heave to, as well as several rounds of blank shell. It took a live shell across her bow to convince her captain to stop. The following terse exchange of signals took place.

"What ship?"

"*Clan Matheson.*"

"English?"

"British!"

When Lauterbach and his men boarded her they discovered that she was a 4,775-ton vessel registered in Glasgow. Her captain also came from Scotland. The *Clan Matheson* was carrying a mixed cargo from Liverpool to Calcutta, consisting mainly of locomotives, machinery, and cars. Among the cars were several Rolls Royces, on consignment to Indian princes. There was also a thoroughbred racehorse, which had been entered in the Calcutta Sweepstakes. Because the fireworks display from the *Trabboch* might have alerted other ships, it was important to get rid of the *Clan Matheson* without delay. The Germans quickly transferred her crew to the *Markomannia,* which had taken over from the *Kabinga* in the role of Lumpensammler, and they set large explosive charges in the freighter's hold. There was nothing to be done about the racehorse, so one of the *Emden*'s officers shot it rather than leaving it to drown. This was the first and only fatality inflicted by the *Emden* in all her captures of merchant ships. The explosives blew off the bow of the *Clan Matheson,* and she sank within a few minutes.

The release of the *Kabinga* meant that it wasn't safe for the *Emden* to stay near Calcutta, and Müller decided to head southwest toward Rangoon. This was a wise decision, because the *Emden*'s wireless operators picked up this message from the Calcutta lightship. "According to Italian vessel *Loredano,* German cruiser *Emden* sank steamships *Diplomat, Kabinga,* and *Pontoporos,* 86°24'E, 18°1'N."

Although it was inaccurate, the report meant that the Germans' presence had been known ever since they released their Italian "ally" two days previously. When the *Kabinga*'s ex-prisoners arrived in port, the full extent of the *Emden*'s raids would be world news, and the search for her was sure to focus on the Calcutta area.

The cruiser's bunkers were half empty, and she made for the northern end of the Andaman Islands with her two colliers, hoping to find a secluded harbor where it was safe to transfer coal. By September 16 they had reached the Preparis channel, where the weather was so calm that they were able to coal at sea without difficulty. This made them less vulnerable than coaling in harbor, where they might be trapped by a hostile warship. The Germans forced the lascars (or East Indian seamen) from the *Clan Matheson* to help coal the *Emden,* but they paid them for their labors.

After coaling, Müller sent the *Pontoporos* to Simeuluë with orders to wait there for the *Markomannia.* The Greek collier was too slow to keep up with them in an area they might have to leave in a hurry. To make sure Captain Polemis stuck to the charter agreement, he was accompanied by a German officer and fourteen armed men. Müller told the Greek captain that he would not be paid, or have his ship released, until he had transferred the rest of his coal to the *Markomannia* at some later date.

For the next two days the *Emden* and *Markomannia* kept on toward Rangoon but didn't sight any more ships. The crews enjoyed a well-earned rest. This interlude ended in the late afternoon of September 18 when smoke appeared on the southern horizon. The vessel was clearly heading for Rangoon, and the *Emden* simply kept on course to cut her off. As darkness approached, the steamer was stopped, and Lauterbach went aboard her with his search party. It was another neutral, this time the small Norwegian freighter *Dovre,* en route from Penang.

Her captain spoke fluent German and was quite friendly. He agreed to take the crew of the *Clan Matheson* off Müller's hands. He didn't ask to be paid for this service, but the Germans gave him one hundred Mexican silver dollars, which Graf Spee's cruisers had brought back from one of their trips to Mexico. The Norwegian also agreed to steam slowly during the night to delay his arrival in Rangoon. This gave the *Emden* plenty of time to get well away from the area before the captain of the *Clan Matheson* could report his experiences to the naval authorities.

The *Emden*'s crew had a chance to hear up-to-date war news and read about their exploits in the newspapers carried by the *Dovre.* The papers were full of praise for their daring and for their humane treatment of prisoners. More important, they learned from the Norwegians that when their ship left Penang, the French cruisers *Montcalm* and *Dupleix* had been docked there. This gave Müller the idea of making a surprise attack on the Penang naval base (following a suggestion by Lieutenant Witthoeft).

He also learned from the *Dovre*'s newspapers that shipping in the Bay of Bengal was being drastically curtailed in spite of assurances of protection by the British government and the War Risk Insurance scheme they had set up to counter the skyrocketing rates of commercial insurers.

There wasn't much point in the raiders staying where they were; in three days' steaming they had seen only the *Dovre*. The *Emden*'s captain decided to head back toward Madras. This was a bold move. It was too dangerous to stay near Rangoon, but Allied patrols would hardly expect him to go back to his previous hunting grounds.

The Germans had also picked up an uncoded wireless message from a shore station asking which ship had the call sign QMD, and the obliging reply, "'QMD' is *Hampshire*." The *Emden*'s wireless operators had intercepted several coded messages from QMD two days prior, and from the signal strength, they estimated that the *Hampshire* could be as close as fifty miles away. It was time to leave the Rangoon area.

Fortunately for the *Emden*, Captain Grant had just received a report of gunfire being heard off Sittwe, some three hundred miles to the north of Rangoon. Although the report was unconfirmed, Grant had no choice but to go there and investigate. It turned out to be a tropical thunderstorm. The Germans weren't aware of it, but this diversion gave them time to coal safely on September 19 before starting their three-day voyage across the Bay of Bengal toward Madras.

Müller decided to change tactics and strike at an enemy shore installation. Madras was the most important city on the east coast of India and its third largest port. It was also the seat of government of the Madras presidency. This made it an attractive target for the Germans, whose fond hope it was that the Indians would rise against the British if the opportunity presented itself. An attack on Madras would not only cause material damage, it would also lower British prestige and might lead to native discontent, perhaps insurrection.

One of the *Emden*'s crew had worked in Madras before the war and was able to give his captain valuable information about the layout of the port. The beach at Madras is long and straight, with the city in the middle, and the harbor at that time consisted of a pier and a long curved mole. At the shore end of the mole lay the oil storage tanks of the Anglo-Persian and Burmah Oil Companies. The harbor and city were defended by Fort St. George, which had batteries of 6-inch guns. These were old weapons, but they fired much bigger shells than the *Emden*'s 4.1-inch naval guns. Because Müller suspected warships might also be in the harbor, surprise was essential. So when the cruiser approached Madras on September 22, she lay well off the coast until nightfall.

The captain ordered the officers and crew to bathe and put on clean underclothes to avoid infection (wounds easily became infected in the tropics). The few lifeboats still on board were filled with seawater to reduce fire hazard. Müller sent the *Markomannia* south to a rendezvous off the French enclave of Pondicherry, telling Captain Faass that if the *Emden* didn't show up by the following morning, he was to take the collier to Simeuluë and wait.

As soon as it was dark the *Emden* steamed toward the lights of Madras. Then the engines were stopped, and she slowly came to a halt broadside to the city at a range of about three thousand yards. At 2145 the cruiser turned on her four powerful searchlights and opened fire. The first few salvoes from the starboard battery found their main target: the oil storage tanks erupted in flames. Dense clouds of smoke rose over the city. After a few minutes the searchlights were turned off because the harbor was well lit by the burning oil.

The bombardment continued for ten minutes. During this time the *Emden* pumped 125 shells into the port area. By the time Fort St. George replied, it was too dark to get the range on the *Emden*. The cruiser's men saw three splashes from the fort's 6-inch shells, all wide of the mark. Shortly after 2200 the *Emden* ceased fire. She turned around and showed her port lights and left the area at high speed, heading north. When she was out of sight of land, the lights were turned off, and she reversed course and went to meet her collier. The crew could still see the orange glow over Madras when they were sixty miles away.

Müller had instructed his gunnery officer, Lieutenant Gaede, to try not to land any shells in the city itself, to avoid civilian casualties. It is a tribute to the accuracy of the German gunners that no one was killed and only twelve people were injured outside of the harbor district. In the port itself, where most of the shells had landed, it was a different story. Several oil tanks and many of the port installations were destroyed, and 350,000 gallons of fuel oil burned. The damage to the oil storage area alone was estimated at 20 million gold marks.

But casualties were very light considering the number of shells that landed in the harbor. One of them hit the docked steamship *Chupra*. The shrapnel from the exploding shell killed a cadet and wounded four others who had been chatting on deck when the attack started. Cadet Joseph Fletcher had the unhappy distinction of being the only merchant seaman to lose his life because of the *Emden*. In the oil storage area three policemen and a night watchman were killed. Next day, the pall of smoke over Madras was visible for fifty miles.

The raid had a tremendous psychological effect. Many people fled the city, fearing a repeat of the cruiser's attack. British prestige was lowered, and government assurances of future protection were met with skepti-

One of the oil-storage tanks at Madras, the day after the raid *(The Robert Hunt Picture Library)*

cism. The local economy suffered for weeks because many merchants and moneylenders left for other Indian cities where they felt safer. Allied shipping was again brought to a halt, only two days after it had resumed. Exports from one of India's largest ports were cut in half.

The activities of the *Emden* gave the so-called "mystery cruiser" an almost mythical reputation in the bazaars along the Indian coast. For a long time after the raid the word "emden" was a synonym in the local Tamil dialect for a clever, resourceful person.

The impact in London was nearly as great. Churchill fired off a note to the Naval Staff at the Admiralty.

> The escape of the *Emden* from the Bay of Bengal is most unsatisfactory, and I do not understand on what principle the operations of the four cruisers *Hampshire, Yarmouth, Dupleix,* and *Chikuma* have been concerned. From the chart, they appear to be working entirely disconnected and with total lack of direction. Who is the senior captain of these four ships? Is he a good man? If so, he should be told to hoist a commodore's broad pennant and take command of the squadron . . . and should devote itself exclusively to hunting the *Emden. . . .*

These typically colorful and combative remarks by Churchill were not very helpful. With only four ships to cover an ocean, Captain Grant was doing his best. When he was sidetracked by the report of gunfire near

Sittwe, he dispatched the *Chikuma* to Madras because he guessed that the *Emden* might go there next. But the Japanese cruiser ran low on coal and was forced to stop at Colombo on the way. This was again Müller's good fortune, because otherwise the *Chikuma* would have been at Madras in time to greet him. Grant also deployed the *Yarmouth* and *Dupleix* in the southern part of the Bay of Bengal, but their chances of running into the *Emden* were slight because of the vast area they had to patrol.

British newspapers gave full recognition to the daring of the *Emden*'s captain and crew, particularly in view of their inescapable realization that sooner or later their ship would be caught and destroyed by superior forces. To the British, "Müller and *Emden* seemed romantic survivals in a world sliding rapidly into the ruthless realities of total war."

The *Daily Chronicle* captured Britain's mixed feelings about the German raider. "*Emden* has had a momentous cruise. The ship's company have proved their gallantry. We admire the sportsmanship shown in their exploits as much as we heartily wish that the ship may soon be taken."

Despite the wishes expressed by British newspapers, the *Emden*'s career was far from over. She steamed south during the night and met her collier the next morning off Pondicherry. (The Germans didn't know it, but the *Hampshire* was only 300 miles to the north of them at the time, and the *Chikuma* 350 miles to the south.) The *Emden* and *Markomannia* stayed twenty miles off the Indian coast, where their hulls would be below the horizon to an observer on shore, but the lookouts in the crows' nests could still scan the coast with binoculars for signs of enemy warships.

After two uneventful days they turned southeast, and on the morning of September 25 the high mountains of southern Ceylon came into view. (Unknown to the Germans, their eastward turn had saved them from being caught by the *Chikuma*, which was steaming up the west side of Ceylon at the time.) The two ships moved sixty miles off the coast and transferred coal from the *Markomannia*, whose stocks were now dangerously low. If they didn't intercept a collier soon, they would have to go all the way back to Simeulué to meet the *Pontoporos*—a distance of at least a thousand miles.

Colombo was the focal point of important shipping routes from Suez and Aden in the east and from Penang and Singapore in the west. The *Emden*'s crew hoped for a rich haul of prizes. Later that day they intercepted and sank the British freighter *King Lud*, a ship of 3,650 tons in ballast, en route from Suez to Calcutta. Her welcome provisions, including fresh meat and potatoes, were taken to the *Emden,* and her crew went to the *Markomannia.*

Because Colombo was a major naval base it was sure to be well defended, and the German ships slowed down so that they would pass by it after dark. They kept thirty miles offshore, from where the lookouts could see searchlights continually sweeping the horizon. The Germans knew that the harbor area would be heavily guarded. The British certainly didn't want another Madras.

The *Emden* turned to port, away from the coast, and two hours later sighted a merchant ship sailing with full lights. She had obviously just left Colombo. The latest victim was the British ship *Tymeric,* loaded with four thousand tons of sugar bound for Falmouth. Müller didn't want to sink her so near to Colombo, so he told Lauterbach to order her captain to follow the *Emden.* The captain of the steamer was so angry at being captured as soon as he had left harbor that he refused to cooperate with "the damned Germans," as did his chief engineer. The port authorities in Colombo had assured them there was "absolutely no danger" in the area.

Lauterbach had no time to argue. He signaled the *Emden* to explain the situation and asked if he could sink the freighter immediately. Müller told him to go ahead. The crew of the *Tymeric* had to be evacuated quickly, leaving them no time to gather their personal belongings and treasured souvenirs of the Far East. After they were taken over to the *Markomannia* and learned the reason for the haste, they became irate as well—but with their captain, not the Germans.

This was the only time that officers of a captured British vessel refused orders from the *Emden*'s boarding party. Lauterbach pointed out to the captain and chief engineer of the *Tymeric* that, according to the rules of war, they were now under German martial law. They were taken to the *Emden* under armed guard and locked in a cramped compartment that was used for storing minesweeping gear. The charges on the *Tymeric* were detonated, and the *Emden* left without waiting to see her sink. (The loss of four thousand tons of sugar on the *Tymeric* and ten thousand tons of tea on the *Diplomat* meant the *Emden* had deprived the British people of untold millions of cups of sweetened tea.)

The *Emden*'s captain now set a course for Minicoy Island, which lies at the southern end of the Laccadive chain. On the way, the crew enjoyed reading the Indian newspapers taken from the *Tymeric.* These reported their exploits at Madras with admiration. The papers estimated the damage to the oil tanks at well over 2 million pounds—a huge sum of money in 1914. An amusing advertisement also appeared in the Calcutta *Empire.*

"There is no doubt that the German cruiser *Emden* had knowledge that the *Indus* was carrying 150 cases of North-West Soap Company's celebrated Elysium Soap, and hence the pursuit. The men on the *Emden* and their clothes are now clean and sweet, thanks to Elysium Soap. Try it!"

The same night, another ship was sighted ahead of the cruiser. The new victim was the *Gryfevale,* a ship of 4,437 tons bound from Aden to Colombo in ballast. Müller decided to use this vessel to house all the captured seamen, because he planned to send the near empty *Markomannia* to Simeuluë to pick up the remainder of the coal from the *Pontoporos.* These plans were interrupted at dawn on September 26 when the lookouts saw a Dutch ship in the distance.

The Germans waited and hoped she had not spotted the *Emden* and her two consorts. The ship had a wireless aerial and could easily report the cruiser's position and direction to Colombo. Soon after she had passed out of sight, the *Emden* intercepted a signal to her from a British ship. It asked the Dutch if they had seen any sign of the *Emden*. The Germans were relieved to hear the reply, "For reasons of neutrality, answer refused." Whether he had seen the *Emden* or not, the Dutch captain had behaved correctly as a neutral.

In the early hours of September 27 the lights of another ship were seen dead ahead. After she was stopped, Lieutenant von Levetzow went aboard and signaled back, "English steamship *Buresk,* 4,350 tons, cargo 6,600 tons first-class Cardiff coal, chartered by British Admiralty from England to Hong Kong." The crew on board the *Emden* were both overjoyed and relieved at this great stroke of luck. They now had more good quality coal than the *Markomannia* had started out with—enough to last for several weeks. Their delight became even greater as they realized that the *Buresk*'s coal had almost certainly been destined for the Royal Navy ships that were hunting them.

Müller decided to use the *Buresk* as his *Hilfsschiff,* or supply vessel, and to send the *Markomannia* to Simeuluë as soon as her coal was exhausted. The British crew members of the *Buresk* went to the *Gryfevale,* except for the captain and two engineering officers, who asked if they could remain on board their ship, even though it meant they would be prisoners of war indefinitely. They were permitted to stay, and so were the officers' steward and cook. These five posed no serious threat, but Müller sent Lieutenant Commander Klöpper, two officers, and eight men to help run the ship. The Arab and Chinese crew members also stayed on board the *Buresk*. As long as they were paid, they cared little whether the ship was under British or German control.

September 27 was a Sunday, and after breakfast and church services the men of the *Emden* looked forward to a restful day. The weather was beautiful, their coal supply was assured, and the quality of their food had improved. But the peaceful Sunday morning was interrupted by a signal from Lauterbach in the *Gryfevale*. "Captured ships' companies are making trouble through drunkenness. Some fighting. Have put several men in irons. Urgently request reinforcement."

The *Emden* pulled alongside the freighter; an armed party went aboard with orders to confiscate all liquor. It turned out there had been an argument between a drunken British seaman and a Chinese cook. The cook had dumped a tureen of soup over the seaman's head. This had led to blows, then a free-for-all. Knives were drawn, but no one was seriously injured. The British captains managed to calm things down and apologized to the German officers for the behavior of their men.

The incident was instantly forgotten when smoke was sighted on the horizon. As the *Emden* raced toward it, the lookouts identified the vessel as a British merchantman. She was the thirty-five-hundred-ton steamship *Ribera,* bound from Aden to Batavia. She carried no cargo, but some of her provisions and her signal book were transferred to the *Emden.* The crew and the rest of the provisions went to the *Gryfevale.* The *Ribera* was sunk by gunfire after her valves had been opened, and she went down quickly.

Müller knew that some of the ships he had captured would soon be missed, and he resumed his course for Minicoy Island. This was close to five hundred miles from Colombo and a safer place to coal. That night a ship's lights appeared off the starboard bow. She was obviously bound for Colombo, and the *Emden* waited until she came near, then sent over the usual boarding party. They signaled back that she was a British ship, the *Foyle,* of 4,147 tons, en route from Aden in ballast. Before they could sink her, yet another brightly lit ship was sighted. She was obviously not a warship, so the cruiser and her coterie of merchantmen went to intercept her. The *Emden*'s crew hoped she was a mail packet, which would mean a large sum in prize money, but they were sadly disappointed. The ship was a mail steamer, but she was the Dutch vessel *Djocja* of the Batavia Line. A search party went over to make sure she wasn't carrying any contraband. All they came back with was a small but welcome supply of cigarettes that they had bought from the Dutch.

Next morning, the *Foyle* was sent to the bottom with blasting charges. Her crew were transferred to the *Gryfevale,* along with the captain and chief engineer of the *Tymeric.* These two promised to obey orders and cause no more trouble. In the afternoon Müller released the *Gryfevale* with all her captives, and she set off for Colombo.

This time the Germans were even more amazed than they had been when they released the *Kabinga*. The British seamen lined the railings of the *Gryfevale* as she steamed away and gave nine cheers: three each for the captain, officers, and crew of the *Emden*.

As soon as the *Gryfevale* was out of sight, the *Emden* altered course to the south, toward the Maldive Islands. Müller had changed his mind about going to Minicoy, deciding instead to coal in the Maldives before heading for the isolated Chagos archipelago. The *Emden* was badly in need of maintenance: the ship's bottom had not been scraped for months, and its condition was beginning to affect her speed.

All day long on September 29—at Miladunmadulu atoll—the *Emden* coaled from the *Markomannia* for the last time. The collier's holds were nearly empty, and it was getting more and more difficult to shift the coal from the corners of the bunkers to where the winches could lift it. The next day the *Markomannia* left for Simeuluë to meet the *Pontoporos* and pick up the rest of her coal. Müller told Captain Faass to pay off the Greek captain for his services and retrieve the armed party he had put on board the *Pontoporos*.

As the *Markomannia* pulled away, the crew of the *Emden* watched her departure with mixed feelings. They were naturally sad to lose their faithful and dependable collier after cruising together for such a long time, but there was a happy side to the parting. She was scheduled to go to a neutral port after she had met the *Pontoporos,* and this would give Captain Faass an opportunity to mail letters to Germany. The crew of the *Emden* had not been able to write home since they left Tsingtao almost three months earlier. The sailors' letters were naturally censored by the officers, who derived some good-natured amusement from the occasional gaffe. But they were pleased to report to their captain that from the tone of the letters, morale remained high.

Captain Faass also took £50 sterling to purchase such welcome items as cigarettes and tobacco when he got to Sumatra. These were to be distributed among the *Emden*'s smokers at the next rendezvous. The small supply bought from the Dutch mail boat had not lasted very long.

For the next week the *Emden* and *Buresk* steamed slowly past the chain of atolls that make up the Maldives without sighting any more merchant ships. Müller knew that his recent activities would have caused the Allies to intensify their search around Colombo. It was a good time to explore the south for possible prey before laying up at Diego Garcia, more than a thousand miles from Colombo. He had learned from the *Ribera*'s signal log that troopships from Australia and New Zealand were being routed through the Maldives. He knew these ships would be heavily escorted, but he hoped some of them might pass by on their way back from Europe to pick up more Anzac troops. Empty troopships were almost sure to be unescorted.

This turned out to be a vain hope. The Germans saw no ships at all during the rest of the voyage to Diego Garcia and spent their time on repairs and training. The ship's two main engines needed an overhaul, and the engine room staff carried out running repairs by stopping each engine alternately. They had to replace boiler tubes, scrape the salt from the steam condensers, and repair glands and bearings.

Just as important, the cruiser's stokers were trained in gun-laying and ammunition handling. When the inevitable sea battle took place, the gun crews would be the ones most exposed to enemy fire and most likely to sustain heavy casualties. It was vitally important to have trained replacements from the stoker branch to keep the guns firing.

The two ships arrived at Diego Garcia at dawn on October 9. After scouting the atoll for enemy warships, the *Emden* entered the harbor, followed soon after by the *Buresk*. The island must have looked like paradise to the ships' companies, with its swaying palm trees, white coral beach, and clear blue water, but there was work to be done before any shore leave could be granted.

Before the war the *Emden* had earned the nickname "Swan of the East" because of her lean, graceful lines, white hull, and buff-colored upper works. Now she looked much the worse for wear: the color of her hull had deteriorated to a coal-streaked dismal gray; her paint was chipped in many places; and rust was beginning to show through. Due to frequent coaling, her railings had been twisted and bent, and the linoleum deck coverings had long since been ripped to shreds. This made the iron deck terribly slippery to walk on when wet. As soon as the eternal burden of coaling had been finished, the crew would have to repair these blemishes as best they could.

The state of the hull was a much more serious matter. It was heavily encrusted with marine life—mainly barnacles—and if these were not scraped off soon, they would drastically reduce the *Emden*'s speed, vital for catching her prey and escaping her hunters. Diego Garcia had no dock, so the ship had to be heeled over by flooding the storage tanks to allow the crew to get at as much of the hull as possible. The *Emden* was far too big a vessel to be careened on shore, like an old-time pirate ship. But what took place in the lagoon at Diego Garcia was the nearest thing to it for this twentieth-century corsair.

Shortly after the work had begun, the *Emden* had a visitor. It was the assistant manager of the local coconut plantation, a seventy-year-old Madagascan who spoke very little English. A British newspaper was to describe what followed as "high comedy on the high seas." While the visitor was being regaled with the usual whiskey and soda in the *Emden*'s wardroom, he expressed surprise at seeing the Kaiser's portrait hanging there. He had at first assumed he was on board a British cruiser, but remarked then that this must be a German ship. This was freely admitted by the *Emden*'s officers, who were equally surprised when their visitor asked them about the European situation. Was the world at peace, or had war been declared? Quickly dissembling, the Germans told him they had been on a long cruise, but as far as they knew, war had not yet been declared.

Things proved more awkward when the English plantation manager came on board. Mr. Spender asked many more questions, such as what was a German warship doing in this isolated area, and how had she come to be in such a sorry state? The Germans explained that the *Emden* had been on a training cruise, as part of international maneuvers with British and French ships, but had been driven off course and battered by a tropical storm. They were not sure what Mr. Spender thought about this explanation, but it was accompanied by such generous helpings of whiskey that, according to one of the German officers, "presently he gave up thinking at all."

Once the Germans realized there had been no news from Europe for a long time, they were careful to embroider all their replies. Probably the only reliable piece of world news they gave the two plantation officials was that Pope Pius X had died on August 20.

The Chagos archipelago was a British protectorate. It lies nearly a thousand miles south of India, and Diego Garcia is at its southern tip. Practically nothing lies south of the island until Antarctica. In 1914 its only contact with the rest of the world was a trading schooner that visited every three months from Mauritius to deliver mail and supplies and to pick up copra and coconut oil from the island's only industry. There was no wireless or cable station, and the inhabitants had not seen a current newspaper since the beginning of July.

Any lingering doubts Mr. Spender might have had as Britain's ex-officio representative were assuaged by the Germans' liberal hospitality and by their offer to repair the engine of his official motor launch, which had broken down six months previously. Müller sent his machinist's mate ashore, and he soon had the launch working. Mr. Spender was delighted and sent the *Emden* a live pig and a boatload of fruit and fresh fish. Not to be outdone, Müller sent him a box of cigars and some bottles of Sekt and whiskey.

The next day, after an altogether pleasant visit for all concerned, the *Emden* and *Buresk* went on their way. After five days of steaming north along the west side of the Maldives, they arrived back at Miladunmadulu atoll and made a brief stop in the lee of the island to transfer coal. Müller wanted the *Emden*'s bunkers filled before he began his next set of attacks on shipping. He decided to make for Minicoy Island again because its lighthouse was used as a beacon by ships approaching Colombo from the west.

At 2230 on October 15 the beacon came into view. Within two hours the Germans were rewarded with the sight of a steamship, incredibly still carrying lights in spite of all the publicity about the *Emden*'s captures. She was ordered to stop, and Lauterbach and Fikentscher boarded her. They reported that she was the British vessel *Clan Grant*, carrying a mixed cargo from Liverpool to Calcutta. Among the items on board were provisions, beer, and cigarettes. The news delighted the *Emden*'s smokers, whose supply had run out again. It was too dark to transfer these treasures, and the *Clan Grant* was ordered to follow the *Emden*.

When he left Diego Garcia, Müller chose to stay on the west side of the Maldives as he made his way north to Minicoy. Captain Grant of the *Hampshire* guessed that the *Emden* might go to the Chagos archipelago because it had been used as a coaling station by ships in the Australian meat trade. He set off to investigate. Unfortunately for him, Grant took the direct route from Colombo to Diego Garcia, which kept him on the east side of the Maldive chain. He must have missed his quarry by just a few hundred miles.

When Grant arrived at Diego Garcia, an embarrassed Mr. Spender had to tell him all about the Germans' visit and that the *Emden* had left five days earlier. Grant immediately headed back to the Colombo area, but by the time he got there, Müller was at Minicoy.

There, on October 16, the *Clan Grant*'s crew were being rowed over to the *Buresk,* and the *Emden*'s officers were dividing up her spoils, when the lookouts reported smoke to the west. The cruiser left her supply ships and small boats and sped toward the new victim. There was some concern as they drew near, because the ship's mast and superstructure didn't look like a freighter's. At first the Germans thought it was a monitor or some other small warship. Their captain was about to sound "Clear for action" when, to everyone's relief and amusement, the vessel was identified as a deep-sea dredger. She was ordered to follow the *Emden* back to the other ships, and she complied, rolling heavily in the sea swell.

The little ship was the *Ponrabbel*, with a displacement of only 473 tons. Her crew were so pleased to see the *Emden* that they were packed and ready to leave long before Lauterbach's party reached them. The captain explained that this was the second dredger his company had sent out from the Clyde to Tasmania: the first one had been lost with all hands in bad weather. Dredgers were not meant to be oceangoing vessels, and the *Ponrabbel*'s crew had demanded their pay in advance to compensate for the danger of having to navigate such a small ship across the Indian Ocean. They told the German seamen that their voyage so far had been dreadful because of the dredger's rolling and pitching. On several occasions they had been quite sure they were going to join their predecessors at the bottom of the ocean.

All the British seamen were put aboard the *Buresk*, and the *Clan Grant* and *Ponrabbel* were sunk by gunfire. The dredger capsized after the third hit, but because of air trapped in her hull, she kept "floating bottom upward, like a great whale." Several more hits released the air and down she went, to the heartfelt cheers of her ex-crew members.

That same evening more lights appeared in the distance. The next victim was the British ship *Benmohr*, of 4,806 tons, bound from London to Penang with a cargo of cars, locomotives, bicycles, and machinery. Her cargo was valuable, but none of it was of any use to the *Emden*, so she was scuttled.

Lieutenant Klöpper, commanding the *Buresk*, was becoming worried about the overcrowding on the Lumpensammler with the addition of the crews of the *Ponrabbel* and *Benmohr*. It wasn't easy to provide adequate food and sanitation for several hundred men, to say nothing of keeping the peace in their confined quarters. At the rate the *Emden* was capturing merchant ships, something would have to be done about the prisoners very soon.

During the night of October 17–18, the *Emden* was still cruising in the vicinity of Minicoy. Next morning, after church services, a large vessel of the Blue Funnel Line was sighted. After she was stopped in the usual fashion, Lieutenants von Guérard and Lauterbach went over with a boarding party to seize the ship. She was the 7,562-ton vessel *Troilus*, carrying a valuable cargo of copper, tin, and rubber from Yokohama and Colombo to London. She was on her maiden voyage.

The *Troilus* also carried passengers. Among them was a lady from Hong Kong who recognized Lauterbach from his days as captain of the *Staatssekretär Krätke*. Their reacquaintance was no doubt accompanied by remarks about it being a small world. The lady, who remains unidentified, was apparently quite amused by her experience of being captured.

Not so the captain of the *Troilus*. He was extremely annoyed with the naval authorities in Colombo, who were advising ships to stay well to the north of the usual shipping lane because this was "absolutely safe." The irate captain couldn't restrain himself from blurting out this interesting piece of information. Müller decided to stay where he was.

This paid off. In the next two days the *Emden* captured three more British steamships—the *St. Egbert, Exford,* and *Chilkana*—whose fates were as different as their cargoes. The *St. Egbert* had an American-owned cargo of sugar and piece goods bound for New York. Because of her neutral cargo, all of the previously captured seamen were shuttled over to her. Müller released the *St. Egbert* and ordered her captain to go to any port but Madras or Colombo. He wanted to give the Allies the impression that his activities were spreading to other parts of the Indian coast when, in fact, he planned to leave immediately for the Malay peninsula. (The captain of the *St. Egbert* actually complied with Müller's order and took his ship to Cochin.)

The *Exford* was laden with fifty-five hundred tons of Welsh steam coal, a welcome addition to Müller's collection. The *Emden* now had enough coal to last for months. The *Chilkana* was carrying a mixed cargo, and, like the *Troilus,* she was on her maiden voyage from England. These two unlucky ships were scuttled.

The *Emden* left the area accompanied by her colliers *Buresk* and *Exford*. Müller knew he was approaching the point of diminishing returns by continuing to raid commerce in the Minicoy region. As soon as the *St. Egbert* arrived in port with her ex-prisoners, the news of the *Emden*'s fresh captures was bound to divert shipping away from the usual routes and lead to increased Allied patrols off southern India. He also realized that his crew were exhausted from their activities of the past few days. It was time to move on.

This led to another narrow escape by Müller. In the early morning of October 21, the *Emden* and her colliers were heading southeast from Felidu atoll to avoid going near Ceylon. Captain Grant, with the *Hampshire* and the armed merchant cruiser *Empress of Asia,* was going in the same direction, only about ten or twenty minutes ahead of them. If it had not been for the slow speed of his colliers, Müller would almost certainly have caught up with his hunters. As it was, it was a dark, overcast morning and the two enemy groups did not sight each other.

The *Emden*'s captain decided to change tactics again. Ever since he had learned from the captain of the *Dovre* that French warships were docked at Penang, he had been thinking about a surprise attack on this naval base. He planned to cross the widest and emptiest part of the Bay of Bengal while his pursuers were fruitlessly searching for him off the coast of southern India and Ceylon.

At this stage in the war the Allies had not only lost track of the *Emden,* they were even more in the dark about the location of Graf Spee and his dangerous squadron. There had been no definite news of its whereabouts for more than a month.

5

The Long Voyage

At any rate for several weeks we need not worry about their ships.
—Winston Churchill, First Lord of the Admiralty

Graf Spee was not optimistic about his future as the cruiser squadron crossed the vast emptiness of ocean between the Marianas and the Marshall Islands. He was later to confide to a friend: "I am quite homeless. I cannot reach Germany. We possess no other secure harbour. I must plough the seas of the world doing as much mischief as I can, until my ammunition is exhausted, or a foe far superior in power succeeds in catching me."

The naval staff in Berlin were just as gloomy about his prospects. They could not contact Graf Spee by either wireless or cable until he reached South America, and they had heard no news of the squadron since it left Ponapé on August 5. Two weeks after war was declared, they made this bleak assessment of its chances. "It may be that the Cruiser Squadron is in East Asiatic waters. Japan's impending entry into the war makes its position hopeless. It is impossible to judge from here whether the squadron will be able to choose against which enemy it will deal its dying blows."

After the squadron parted company with the *Emden* on August 13, Graf Spee altered course to the southeast and headed toward the isolated atoll of Eniwetok in the Marshall Islands. His plan was to make for Easter Island, where he hoped to join up with the *Leipzig* and *Dresden* before he began attacking the busy commerce routes off the coast of Chile. This meant he would have to cross nearly eight thousand miles of ocean without running into Allied patrols.

To cover this distance, the squadron needed to make a coaling stop every eight or nine days. A cruiser's range at her most economical speed was about four thousand miles, or eighteen days' steaming, but it was too risky to let the bunkers get low before refilling them. If the ships were spotted by superior Allied forces, they might have to steam at high speed for hours or possibly days to lose their pursuers. This would burn up enormous amounts of coal. It was safer to keep the bunkers at least half full at all times.

The British didn't believe that a whole squadron could operate for very long without secure coaling bases, but Graf Spee had no choice. His men had to learn how to coal from another ship, preferably in secluded lagoons but, if necessary, at sea. In addition to the difficulty of transferring hundreds of tons of coal between two rolling and pitching ships, there was always the danger of being surprised by enemy warships. A cruiser was in a terribly vulnerable position when she was tied up to a collier—motionless and unable to train her guns freely. All the time coaling was going on, extra lookouts were posted to scan the horizon for telltale signs of smoke or mastheads.

But if Graf Spee could make it safely to Easter Island, the addition of the *Leipzig* and the *Dresden* would bring his cruiser strength back to five, providing these two managed to dodge the many Allied warships searching for them. Graf Spee thought his forces would then be strong enough to deal with any squadron the Admiralty was likely to send out to protect its South American trade with Peru and Chile, or to prevent him from moving into the Atlantic to attack the even more important Argentine sea traffic.

He knew he had no hope of keeping his whereabouts a secret indefinitely. With Japan's entry into the war, the British would surely conclude, as he had himself, that his best chance of ever reaching Germany was to take the southern route into the Atlantic. But they would not know whether he planned to go around Cape Horn or through the Strait of Magellan.

The Panama Canal had just been opened, but this wasn't a realistic alternative because the United States imposed strict limitations on the number of belligerent warships allowed to pass through it at any one time. Graf Spee knew that if he took his ships into the canal, the inevitable delays and publicity would ensure that by the time he reached the other end, the Royal Navy would be waiting for him in force. (As a precaution, the British later sent the battle cruiser *Princess Royal* to the Caribbean Station to guard against any German use of the canal.)

On August 19 the squadron made its first stop after steaming fifteen hundred miles. The ships dropped anchor in the spacious lagoon at Eniwetok, and for three days the men of the *Scharnhorst, Gneisenau,* and *Nürnberg* transferred coal and supplies from their train of merchant ships. This took much longer than Graf Spee had hoped because of a freak storm that struck the atoll with torrential rain and a heavy swell even inside the lagoon. When the *Longmoon* and *Prinz Waldemar* had finally been emptied of coal, Graf Spee sent them to Honolulu to get more. The *Staatssekretär Krätke* and *Gouverneur Jäschke* were drained of fresh water and provisions and also dispatched to Hawaii.

Ever since Admiral Jerram had destroyed the cable station at Yap, the Germans in the South Pacific had been unable to relay messages to Berlin through their network of cable and W/T stations. Yet it was vital for Graf Spee to inform the Admiralstab of his plans so they could make arrangements to have colliers waiting for him at the Juan Fernández Islands off the coast of Chile and to supply him with provisions when he reached Valparaíso. So on August 22, before leaving Eniwetok, he sent the *Nürnberg* to Hawaii with messages to be forwarded to Berlin by the German consulate in Honolulu. The cruiser was more likely to succeed in this mission than the four supply ships he had just detached because they were slow and unarmed and easy for Allied patrols to intercept. Captain von Schönberg was ordered to rejoin the squadron at Christmas Island in two weeks' time.

The two big cruisers and the remaining supply ships moved on to the more remote atoll of Majuro, which lies at the eastern end of the Marshalls. The armed merchant cruiser *Cormoran* (the *ex-Ryazan,* captured by Müller) and the supply vessels *O.J.D. Ahlers* and *Göttingen* had been ordered to meet Graf Spee there on August 27–28. The unfortunate *Geier* was also supposed to join the squadron at Majuro, but because of her faulty engines she didn't arrive until two weeks after the squadron had left. Her captain had no alternative but to seek internment in Honolulu.

After he arrived at Majuro, Graf Spee received two important pieces of news. First, the captain of the *Cormoran* told him that Japan had declared war on Germany and was preparing to besiege Tsingtao. This absolutely ruled out any move to the west. If Tsingtao fell to the Japanese, which Graf Spee thought was inevitable, Germany's last base in the Pacific was gone, and he would have no alternative but to head for the Atlantic.

Second, the *Nürnberg* wirelessed on August 29 that she had intercepted coded signals between Allied warships when she was in the region north of the Marshalls. Her captain, Karl von Schönberg, believed one of these ships to be HMAS *Australia.* In case this turned out to be correct,

Graf Spee decided to leave Majuro that evening. The squadron sailed for Christmas Island, approximately twenty-three hundred miles to the east. (The Germans need not have worried; the *Australia* was well on her way to Samoa, about two thousand miles to the southeast of Graf Spee's ships. The *Nürnberg*'s operators had misjudged the direction of the signals and grossly underestimated the power of the battle cruiser's transmitter.)

The next day, Graf Spee detached the armed merchant cruisers *Cormoran* and *Prinz Eitel Friedrich,* with the *Mark* as their supply vessel, and ordered them to raid shipping in Australian waters. He didn't expect them to have any great success, but he hoped their attacks would draw Admiral Patey's squadron southward and keep it away from his route to Christmas Island. Graf Spee had chosen this remote speck of land as the next coaling point because it would give him the opportunity of destroying the Australia-Canada cable station at nearby Fanning Island, while keeping the squadron on a fairly direct course for Valparaíso.

That same day—August 30—Admiral Patey's squadron and a New Zealand expeditionary force attacked German Samoa. They occupied the islands after meeting only token resistance. Graf Spee was about seventeen hundred miles to the north of Samoa at the time, and it was almost a week before he heard the news. Ironically, the fall of Samoa took place barely fourteen years after Captain Emsmann of the original *Cormoran* had told the crowd at a flag-raising ceremony in Apia, "Where the German eagle has stuck his talons into a land, the land is German and German shall remain."

The slowest of Graf Spee's remaining supply ships could make only ten knots, and it took the squadron a week to reach Christmas Island, where it anchored on September 6. The *Nürnberg* was already there, after completing her mission to Honolulu.

Captain von Schönberg reported that he had only just managed to elude the Japanese battle cruiser *Kongo* off Hawaii. The port authorities in Honolulu had made coaling difficult, which had delayed his departure. Schönberg had claimed that he was entitled to take on sufficient coal to get him to his home base at Tsingtao, but the Americans would not permit this. After long arguments with the German consul, the American port commandant finally relented, but he would allow the *Nürnberg* to load only enough coal to take her to the nearest German possession, which at the time was Samoa. On his way back to join Graf Spee, Schönberg learned from intercepted wireless messages that Samoa had just fallen to the New Zealanders.

The admiral was upset to hear that the governor of Samoa had been

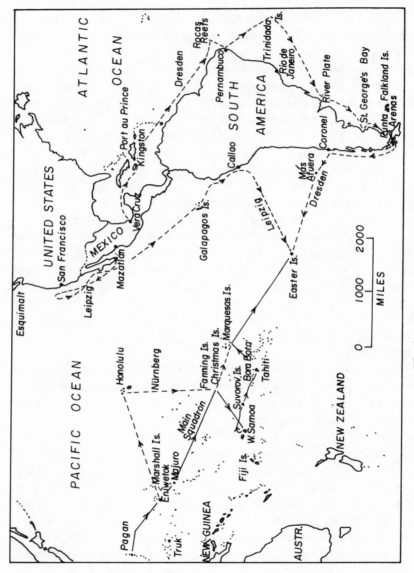

The long voyage to Easter Island

taken prisoner because the two men had become friends during the *Scharnhorst*'s summer visits to the colony. Graf Spee wanted to strike back at the Allies for humiliating his friend. He reasoned that Admiral Patey's main force would leave for other duties after the invasion was over but that the New Zealand occupation forces "would require constant supplies from steamships which must be covered: it is therefore to be supposed that warships and train are lying off Apia. An attack upon the ships lying at anchor at dawn promises success."

Graf Spee thought there was little chance that Admiral Patey and the *Australia* would remain at Samoa merely to guard transports, and he decided to attack Apia as soon as possible. He wrote in his war journal: "Moreover, a military undertaking in which the burning desire of the crews of the Squadron, after weeks spent underway, with frequent periods of coaling, to get in touch with the enemy would be fulfilled and could but have a favorable effect on the morale of the men. There was of course no idea of recovering the Samoa Islands."

After the inevitable coaling operations at Christmas Island, Graf Spee sent the *Nürnberg* to destroy the cable station at Fanning Island, just over a hundred miles to the north. He wanted to disrupt the Allies' communications and make it more difficult for them to track him down. The *Titania* went with the cruiser because she carried cable-cutting equipment. The two ships arrived at Fanning at dawn on September 7, and the *Nürnberg* sent an armed landing party ashore. The British staff watched helplessly as the Germans tore down their wireless mast and destroyed the telegraph station with hand grenades. The crew of the *Titania* traced the cable back into the sea and cut it in several places, while the *Nürnberg*'s landing party blew up its shore terminal, killing large numbers of fish in the process. After they had finished their demolition work, the German ships left and rejoined the squadron at Christmas Island the following day.

Graf Spee decided to use only the two armored cruisers for the raid on Samoa. He sent the *Nürnberg* and supply ships ahead to wait for him in the Marquesas Islands. Just before dawn on September 14, the *Scharnhorst* and *Gneisenau* arrived off Apia, cleared for action. The lookouts could see the dark mass of Mount Vaea behind the town. (As an oddly appropriate sidelight, this mountain was where Robert Louis Stevenson, author of the line "Old and young, we are all on our last cruise," had been buried twenty years before, having spent his final years in Samoa.)

Daylight revealed that no warships were anchored in the harbor at Apia, nor were there any transports. Only a three-masted American schooner and a small sailing vessel were anchored there. As they moved in closer to land, the Germans could see the Union Jack flying over several buildings, but no targets seemed worth the use of valuable ammunition. The island of Western Samoa is more than twenty miles wide at this point, and the masts of the wireless station were too far inland to be within easy range of the cruisers' guns. The raiders turned away in disappointment.

Graf Spee could not have been pleased with his visit to Samoa. He had given away his squadron's position for no gain. Although the Germans jammed the warning signals being sent out by Radio Apia as they left, they knew it wouldn't be long before their presence was reported to Allied warships. Graf Spee feinted northwest until Samoa was out of sight before returning to an easterly course toward the Marquesas. Later that day he was relieved to hear that Allied wireless stations were reporting his squadron to be proceeding northwest.

Graf Spee's next stop was at the isolated Suvorov atoll. Although this was a British possession, the small island had no defenses or wireless. The *Scharnhorst* and *Gneisenau* were met there by the collier *O.J.D. Ahlers,* which had been sent from the main supply train, but the sea was too rough to allow them to coal. They went on to Bora Bora in the Society Islands, which offered a more sheltered anchorage in its large lagoon. The two cruisers coaled from the *Ahlers* while armed parties went ashore to commandeer provisions. The few French inhabitants at Bora Bora were in no position to offer any resistance. They couldn't even warn other French possessions that a German squadron was in the vicinity because they had no wireless.

Instead of heading directly to the Marquesas to meet the *Nürnberg*, Graf Spee wanted to salvage something from his detour, and so he decided to raid Papeeté. Tahiti was only 150 miles away and an easy target. He hoped the raid would raise his mens' morale and show the Allies that their Pacific possessions were not immune to attack. He intended "to engage any enemy ships encountered at Tahiti and to requisition coal and provisions."

When the two big cruisers arrived off Papeeté harbor at dawn on September 22, it was obvious that the French had heard about Graf Spee's visit to Apia. The fort immediately opened fire on the German ships. The guns of the dismantled French gunboat *Zelée* had been mounted ashore, and they joined in the attack. Graf Spee gave the order to return fire. The cruisers' 8.2-inch guns quickly silenced the fort and the shore batteries from the *Zelée* before they could do any damage.

The German merchant ship *Walküre* was also in the harbor, having been seized by the French as a prize as soon as war broke out. The guns of the *Scharnhorst* scored several direct hits on the *Zelée* and *Walküre*, which sank at their moorings.

At this point the governor of Tahiti ordered the island's coal stocks to be set on fire and storehouses to be blown up. He was determined to prevent the Germans from using them. When Graf Spee saw this, he realized it was not worth continuing the raid. The French had also removed the harbor entrance markers, and he knew it would be disastrous if one of his ships ran aground.

The Germans again withdrew in disappointment and headed for their rendezvous in the Marquesas. They had not achieved much more than they had at Apia, and once again they had revealed their position to the Allies.

From the known facts that the squadron had started off in the Carolines, then appeared at Samoa, and now at Tahiti, it was pretty clear that Admiral Patey had been right when he guessed that Graf Spee would head toward South America. Yet in spite of all the evidence, the Admiralty signaled him: "It is very probable that *Gneisenau* and *Scharnhorst* may repeat attacks similar to one at Papeeté; they may be expected to return towards Samoa, Fiji and even New Zealand. Making Suva your base, search in these waters."

This order sent Admiral Patey in the opposite direction from Graf Spee.

The reason the Admiralty chose to ignore the mounting evidence that Graf Spee's squadron was steadily moving east was its concern for the safety of Anzac troop convoys. Sailings were postponed once more, as they had been by the news of the *Emden*'s raids in the Indian Ocean. It was important, especially politically, to guard against any westward movement by Graf Spee. The orders to Admiral Patey would help to ensure the safety of the convoys when they eventually did sail.

Even if the Germans did keep on an eastward course, then, as Churchill said, "At any rate for several weeks we need not worry about their ships." But by the same token, Graf Spee would have plenty of time to reach the South American coast without interference from Allied warships.

The *Scharnhorst* and *Gneisenau* reached the Marquesas on September 26. They joined the *Nürnberg* and the four remaining supply ships at Nuku Hiva. The French authorities could do nothing to prevent the Germans from landing because the islands had no defenses. They couldn't even inform the outside world because their only contact with it was by ship.

The Germans stayed in the lush, tropical Marquesas for a week. They bought coal, fresh food, and live pigs, mainly from two German-owned firms long established in the South Sea islands. The money they used to pay for their supplies came from the Allies because Graf Spee's captains had emptied the government coffers in every British and French possession where they had landed. All this was meticulously recorded in Graf Spee's official log, with such comically precise entries as, "Fanning Island £720 2s. 6d; Hakapeki 9,862 fr. 20 centimes."

The Germans even confiscated postage stamps and money orders, although just what they intended to do with them wasn't clear.

The ships' engines were given a rest after their long hard steaming, and the crews were allowed ashore to stretch their legs. For most of them it was their first time on land in almost two months. Graf Spee wrote his wife that the crews were able "to enjoy a little recreation together with bathing, excursions and so forth in Nukuhiva Island, so marvelously endowed by nature." The admiral enjoyed himself in his own way, paying a courtesy visit to the Roman Catholic mission, then exploring the island to take notes and samples of its tropical plants.

During the relaxing stay in the Marquesas, Graf Spee decided to reduce his train of merchant ships, some of which were slowing him down. He was keen on getting to South America and to start doing some real damage. When the *Holsatia* and *O.J.D. Ahlers* had been stripped of their supplies, he sent them to Honolulu. He gave each captain one of a duplicate set of messages to be forwarded to Berlin. These reported on Graf Spee's activities and his plans to stop at Easter Island, then the Juan Fernández Islands, and finally to reach Valparaíso. Also included were instructions to be sent to the German consulate in San Francisco, detailing Graf Spee's coal requirements at Juan Fernández and Valparaíso. Graf Spee sent the *Titania* ahead to make sure that Easter Island was clear of enemy warships. The squadron now had only the *Yorck* and *Göttingen* left as its supply ships. These were both capable of better than fourteen knots.

Before the squadron left the Marquesas on October 3, the *Scharnhorst*'s wireless operators heard faint signals between the *Leipzig* and the *Dresden*. This meant that both cruisers had so far eluded Allied patrols and reached the South Pacific, and they were probably on their way to meet Graf Spee at Easter Island as arranged. This was confirmed two days later when the *Scharnhorst* was near enough to the *Dresden* to contact her directly by wireless.

When war was declared, Capt. Johannes Haun of the *Leipzig* planned to leave Mexican waters and operate as a commerce raider off the West Coast of North America. The Admiralstab especially wanted him to prey on the vulnerable Canadian Pacific "Empress" liners traveling between San Francisco and Vancouver. The plan failed, for two reasons. The

Americans made it difficult for Haun to get coal in their West Coast ports, and the British ordered all their merchant ships in the area to remain in harbor until further notice.

The only Allied warships available to protect shipping on the West Coast were the small Canadian sloops *Algerine* and *Shearwater* and the cruiser *Rainbow.* HMCS *Rainbow* had just come to San Francisco from her base at Esquimalt. She was about the same size as the *Leipzig* and slightly better armed, but she had been launched in 1893 and was no match for the modern *Leipzig.* The *Rainbow* was instructed to escort the weakly armed sloops back to safety in Esquimalt, which she did in the second week of August. The *Leipzig* was cruising in the Golden Gate area from August 11–18, and if she had intercepted the three Canadian warships, the outcome would have been a foregone conclusion.

In peacetime the *Leipzig* and the two sloops had been "chummy ships," and, according to one report: "It was the unanimous view of the *Shearwater*'s crew that the *Leipzig* deliberately let her pass because they had been friends for a long time. Indeed the two crews used to go around together looking for fights with American sailors who were so unfortunate as to be ashore at the same time."

Haun's coal supplies in U.S. ports were uncertain, and he had just received a report that the *Newcastle* was on her way from Hong Kong to Esquimalt. He also knew that the Japanese heavy cruiser *Idzumo* was in the San Francisco area, and he had no wish to run across her when Japan entered the war. He prudently decided to head south. After coaling from the German-chartered *Mazatlan* and *Marie* in an isolated bay in Baja California, on August 27, the *Leipzig* set sail for the Galápagos Islands.

Haun's decision to move south was approved by the Admiralstab, who signaled him on September 3, "Transfer cruiser warfare to southwest America and the Atlantic."

On her way to the Galápagos Islands, the *Leipzig* captured the brand-new 6,542-ton British steamer *Elsinore,* en route to Panama. The *Elsinore* was scuttled and her crew transferred to the *Marie.* On September 18 the Germans arrived at the islands, where the supply ship *Amasis* was waiting. The crew of the *Elsinore* were marooned there. The Germans thought it would be a long time before they were able to report the *Leipzig*'s position.

After leaving the Galápagos Islands, the next capture was the *Bankfields,* carrying five thousand tons of Peruvian sugar cane to Britain via Panama. She was sunk and her crew sent to the *Marie.* By September 28 the *Leipzig* had arrived off the Peruvian coast but found no more prizes because British ships were still being detained in port.

Haun sent the *Marie* to Callao, where the crew of the *Bankfields* duly reported the *Leipzig*'s last known position. By this time the crew of the *Elsinore* had managed to escape from the Galápagos Islands in a small boat and reach Guayaquil, so it was well known that the *Leipzig* was heading for the South Pacific.

On October 1 Berlin signaled Haun to tell him to operate with the *Dresden,* which was on her way to the Pacific. Rather than continue his fruitless search off Peru, he decided to go to Easter Island and wait for the *Dresden.* Haun had no idea that the main squadron was also making for Easter Island because he had heard nothing from Graf Spee for almost two months. He was pleased to hear from the *Dresden* by W/T on the night of October 2–3. "My position Más á Fuera Island. Intend to proceed to Easter Island to get in touch with the Cruiser Squadron."

This was one of the signals that had been heard faintly by the *Scharnhorst.*

Before war was declared the *Dresden* was scheduled to return to Germany for a refit, and the brand-new, larger, and more heavily armed *Karlsruhe* was sent out to replace her on the Caribbean Station. Her commanding officer, Fritz Emil Lüdecke, a captain (junior) in the navy, had been given the task of ferrying the *Karlsruhe* across the Atlantic, with orders to turn his ship over to Capt. Erich Köhler, then to return to Wilhelmshaven with the *Dresden.* Lüdecke had just finished a three-year stint as a staff officer and was not one of the Kaiserliche Marine's first line sea captains. Köhler, on the other hand, was an experienced seagoing officer who had served overseas longer than any of the other cruiser commanders. After the *Dresden* had taken General Huerta to sanctuary in Jamaica in mid-July, she met the *Karlsruhe* at Port au Prince, where the two ships exchanged captains.

The plan was for the *Karlsruhe* to stay on station to monitor the Mexican situation, but if war broke out in Europe, she was to act as a commerce raider in the Caribbean and North Atlantic. Köhler was ideally suited for this assignment, as he was to demonstrate in the first few months of the war.

Lüdecke's orders were to take the *Dresden* to the Danish Virgin Islands to pick up coal and provisions before starting back for Germany. St. Thomas was the overseas headquarters of the powerful Hamburg-Amerika Line and, in effect, a German naval base. On the last day of July the *Dresden* was only three hours out from St. Thomas on her way to Wilhelmshaven when Lüdecke received a signal from the Admiralstab, relayed to him by the German consulate in San Juan, Puerto Rico. His previous orders were canceled, and he was told to stay in the Caribbean during the period of Kriegsgefahr and to be ready to act as a commerce raider off South America as soon as war was declared.

The British were becoming worried about the threat to their vital Atlantic shipping routes posed by the *Dresden* and *Karlsruhe*. At about the same time as Lüdecke received his new orders, the Admiralty signaled their senior officer in the Caribbean—Rear Admiral Cradock, in command of the Fourth Cruiser Squadron—to "shadow unostentatiously enemy warships." The squadron consisted of the armored cruisers *Suffolk, Berwick, Lancaster,* and *Essex* and the light cruiser *Bristol*. Cradock also had under his command the French armored cruisers *Condé* and *Descartes*.

This seems an overwhelming force when set against two German light cruisers, but Cradock's responsibilities to protect trade stretched from Halifax, Nova Scotia, to Pernambuco, Brazil, a distance of nearly four thousand miles. It is not surprising that he lost track of the *Dresden* for the first two weeks of the war.

As soon as war was declared, Lüdecke took the *Dresden* to the Rocas reefs, 150 miles off the northern coast of Brazil, where he met the supply tenders *Corrientes* and *Prussia* and the collier *Baden,* which had just slipped out of Pernambuco with twelve thousand tons of coal. Lüdecke's idea was to attack Allied shipping, first in the Pernambuco area until his presence was detected, then to plunder the busy trading routes off the mouth of the River Plate. After coaling and transferring provisions from his supply ships, he headed toward the mouth of the Amazon.

Lüdecke, better supplied than any other German raider, was assigned to an area with rich pickings, but he wasted his opportunities in the first few weeks of the war. On August 6 he stopped the *Hostilius, Drumcliffe,* and *Lynton Grange,* all British registered, but because none of them carried war materials, he released them. The only precaution he took was to remove any wireless equipment before turning them loose. But within a few days, all three ships had reached port and reported the *Dresden*'s location to the nearest British consulate.

When Allied merchant captains in the area learned that the *Dresden* was merely stopping British freighters and not sinking them, their confidence was restored. This was further reinforced when the *Dresden* sighted the British steamer *Dunstan* and the Brazilian *Bahia* on August 8 and let them pass unmolested. Both captains recognized the *Dresden* and wirelessed her position to the authorities in Brazil.

Lüdecke was obviously not from the same mold as Karl von Müller, apparently viewing only enemy ships carrying war materials as legitimate prey. Not until August 15 did the *Dresden* finally capture and sink a

British ship, the *Hyades*. She was carrying a cargo of corn, hardly a war material, but for some reason Lüdecke decided to scuttle her anyway. The crew of the *Hyades* were put on board the tender *Prussia* and sent into Rio de Janeiro, where they reported their experiences. The next day the *Dresden* stopped the *Siamese Prince,* also British, but because she carried a neutral-owned cargo bound for a neutral port, Lüdecke let her go. Once again, he had revealed his position to no advantage.

When reports of the *Dresden*'s activities came to Cradock's attention, he dispatched the *Bristol* to the Abrolhos rocks region to block any move by the German cruiser toward the River Plate area. The *Glasgow* was the sole British cruiser on duty south of the Plate, so Cradock sent the armored cruiser *Monmouth* from Stoddart's squadron and the armed merchant cruiser *Otranto* as reinforcements. He also wanted to prevent the *Dresden* from heading for the Strait of Magellan to join up with Graf Spee in the Pacific.

Lüdecke's next move was to rendezvous at the isolated island called Trinidade, five hundred miles off the Brazilian coast, with the collier *Santa Isabel,* which had left Buenos Aires and managed to dodge Allied patrols. Using the island as a base, he planned to raid shipping off the mouth of the Plate. The only success he had came on August 26 when he captured the *Holmwood,* which was carrying six thousand tons of Welsh coal to Bahia Blanca.

The *Dresden* was so well supplied by the *Baden* and *Santa Isabel* that she had no need of this prize haul, and the Germans decided to sink her. They sent the crew of the *Holmwood* to the *Katherine Park,* another British ship that Lüdecke had stopped. Because she was carrying a neutral cargo, he released her, and she promptly went into Rio to report his position.

It was now obvious to everyone that the *Dresden* was steadily working her way south. It is hard to avoid the conclusion that Lüdecke was simply not cut out to be a corsair. Müller may have been called "the last gentleman of war," but it seems that Lüdecke was too much of a gentleman to be a successful raider.

The River Plate area was an attractive target, but the weather turned bad. Frequent gales buffeted the cruiser and her two consorts. The *Dresden* was getting low on coal, but heavy swell and strong winds frustrated all attempts to coal at sea. The cruiser had suffered damage to her plating and superstructure when she was tied up to the *Santa Isabel,* so Lüdecke decided to move farther south. The coast of Patagonia had many sheltered bays where Lüdecke could coal more easily. Argentina was a friendly neutral, and the Germans thought its patrol vessels wouldn't strictly enforce the twenty-four-hour rule if they came upon them coaling. By the end of August the three ships had reached St. George's Bay, where the *Dresden* transferred coal from the *Santa Isabel*.

By early September they had met no more merchant ships, and after being battered by a severe storm, the *Dresden* and her tenders entered the Strait of Magellan. It was still spring in the South Atlantic, and it was a relief to escape the miserable conditions at sea and take shelter in the calmer waters of the strait. Lüdecke sent the *Santa Isabel* to Punta Arenas to buy more stores, while he took the *Baden* to the landlocked Orange Bay on Hoste Island for four days of coaling and carrying out repairs.

The crews went ashore, which was a welcome change in spite of the barren surroundings of glaciers and snow-covered mountains. Some of the men left the usual sort of memento of their visit—"X was here, September 11, 1914"—carved on pieces of wood or marked on rocks. As previous sailors had done, they added the name of their ship. Captain Lüdecke was furious when he heard about this and sent a party ashore to remove all traces of the *Dresden*'s visit. They were not very thorough, however.

The *Santa Isabel* rejoined the *Dresden* on September 12, bringing a message from Berlin that had been relayed to the consulate in Punta Arenas. "It is advisable to operate with the *Leipzig*."

Coupled with a false report that British ships had been sighted off the eastern entrance to the strait, this signal convinced Lüdecke it was time to make for the Pacific, which he did on September 18.

Within hours the *Dresden* came upon the British freighter *Ortega*, bound from Valparaíso to Europe. The Germans fired two blank shells across her bow, but Capt. Douglas Kinnier was not about to surrender meekly. He took the eight-thousand-ton *Ortega* at full speed into the uncharted Nelson Strait. This was a courageous move since he could easily have driven his ship onto the rocks, but he knew that the cruiser wouldn't dare follow him. Captain Kinnier was soon able to give a report of the *Dresden*'s location. His bravery was recognized by a grateful Royal Navy, which gave him a temporary commission as a lieutenant in the Royal Naval Reserve so that he could be awarded the Distinguished Service Cross.

Lüdecke abandoned the chase and headed north up the Chilean coast as far as Coronel, but he found no more merchant ships. He turned west toward the Juan Fernández Islands and coaled from the *Baden* at Más Afuera before making for Easter Island. The *Dresden* and her collier arrived at the rendezvous on October 10, after an undistinguished cruise. She had achieved little and had advertised her route so plainly that it was obvious to the Allies she had gone to join forces with Graf Spee somewhere in the Pacific.

* * *

Graf Spee's main squadron and supply ships arrived at Easter Island two days after the *Dresden*. The *Leipzig* showed up on October 14 with the collier *Amasis* and the supply ships *Anubis, Abyssinia,* and *Karnak.* The five cruisers were now well supplied with provisions. The Kohlenfrage was no longer a source of anxiety because the *Baden* and *Amasis* had brought a large supply of coal to add to the dwindling stocks of the *Yorck* and *Göttingen.* The squadron now had in excess of fifteen thousand tons on hand.

Graf Spee was pleased with events to date. His ships had managed to steam almost ten thousand miles without sustaining any serious damage or mechanical faults. After being scattered and in a weak position at the outbreak of war, the squadron was reunited and back to its original strength of five cruisers. This had been achieved without much interference from the Allies, in spite of their overall command of the seas. The crews were well fed and in good health. Their morale was excellent, particularly in view of the constant uncertainty and strain they were under, knowing they had no secure base and little prospect of reaching a friendly harbor.

Nevertheless, more than three months had passed since the war began, and apart from the *Emden,* the German cruisers hadn't had much of an impact on Allied sea traffic. Graf Spee had certainly caused his enemies great concern and tied up a large number of valuable warships searching for him, and he had also delayed the sailings of important troop convoys. But he hadn't inflicted any real damage.

All this was to change soon after the squadron reached the coast of South America. But before Graf Spee got there, Müller and the *Emden* would strike again.

6

Emden at Penang!

Numbers are everything; and the extirpation of these pests is a most important object.

—Winston Churchill, First Lord of the Admiralty

While Graf Spee's squadron was at Easter Island, thousands of miles away in the Indian Ocean no less than fourteen major warships from five navies were now engaged in hunting the *Emden*. Winston Churchill had long since grown impatient at their lack of success. At the beginning of October he sent a long memo to the First Sea Lord and the chief of naval staff marked "Urgent" in his own hand. He wrote: "I am quite at a loss to understand the operations of *Hampshire*'s captain to catch *Emden*. He has apparently started eastward from Colombo on the 26th, and is now marked on the chart nearly opposite the Andamans. *Emden* was, however, reported on the 27th near the Laccadives. Did *Hampshire* get this information? If so, what did she do? What has happened to *Yarmouth*? Her movements appear to be entirely disjointed and purposeless. . . ."

In fact, the astute but unlucky Captain Grant was now on his way to the Minicoy area. When he had found no sign of the German cruiser near Colombo, he guessed that Müller might have headed back to Minicoy. Once again he arrived on the scene just too late to trap the *Emden*.

Churchill went on to make proposals for deploying even more Allied cruisers in an organized search for the *Emden* because, as he said, "Numbers are everything; and the extirpation of these pests is a most important object."

After the *Emden* and her two colliers left Minicoy, they headed eastward

93

across the Bay of Bengal. They had to cruise slowly because the *Exford*'s tired engines could manage only nine knots. This gave Müller plenty of time to work out a plan of attack on Penang and to discuss it with his officers. The crews enjoyed some well-earned relaxation after the strain of the previous week.

Several ships were seen hull down on the horizon on October 20 and 21; Müller ignored them. He didn't want to take any chance of giving away his position or direction. Because the *Exford*'s boilers were giving him trouble, he sent the collier away with orders to wait at a rendezvous north of the Cocos Islands until after the attack on Penang.

October 22 was the Kaiserin's birthday. The event was celebrated in the wardroom with a toast to Her Majesty, using one of the few remaining bottles of Sekt. The captain made a short patriotic speech and ordered the *Emden*'s gunners to fire a twenty-one-gun salute to the empress. It was quite safe to do this; there was no one to hear them. The next day he ordered a battle practice, and the *Buresk* towed a target for the cruiser's already highly proficient gunners.

The Nicobar Islands came into view on the morning of October 26. The *Buresk* anchored in a secluded bay, and the *Emden* came alongside to fill her bunkers with five hundred tons of coal. Müller knew that even if the surprise attack were to succeed, he would have to leave Penang in a hurry and get well away from the area before the Allies had time to react. After coaling, the *Buresk*'s name and port of registry were painted out, and she was sent to a rendezvous west of Sumatra to wait for the *Emden*.

By the afternoon of the twenty-seventh the cruiser had reached the entrance to the Straits of Malacca. Müller gathered his officers to go over the final plan of the raid, then he assembled all hands aft to explain what was expected of them the next day. That evening the men were fed and ordered to bathe and put on clean clothes.

Müller wanted to enter the straits after dark, so he timed his attack for dawn on October 28. The Penang lighthouse came into view at 0200. The night watch on the *Emden* could see the lights of a ship approaching the harbor mouth. Because there was bright moonlight Müller ordered speed reduced, and the *Emden* moved slowly toward Penang until the moon became partly obscured by cloud.

The harbor at George Town is on the island of Pulau-Penang, which forms a narrow channel with the mainland. Lauterbach claimed to know the port like the back of his hand because he had docked there many times when he was captain of the *Staatssekretär Krätke*. He was given the helm and steered the ship safely around a small island in the harbor mouth, but then he almost ran down a fishing boat.

The ship they had seen entering the harbor was waiting for the pilot. As they passed by her, the pilot boat came directly toward the *Emden*. The cruiser had been painted gray at Diego Garcia, and the dummy fourth funnel was in place. Since she was also flying the White Ensign, the people on the pilot boat thought she was a British cruiser and went past her toward the merchant ship without signaling. (To enter an enemy harbor under false colors was questionable conduct according to the terms of the Hague Convention and out of character for the *Emden*'s usually chivalrous captain.)

Because Müller didn't know what to expect at Penang, he had ordered the torpedo officers to load both tubes. If the French armored cruisers *Dupleix* and *Montcalm* were in port, it would be vital to disable them quickly before their 7.6-inch and 6.5-inch guns could overwhelm the light cruiser. The lookouts anxiously scanned the darkened harbor, lit only by the moon and the riding lights of the ships at anchor. But as it happened, only one warship could be seen among the forest of ships' masts. She had a lower silhouette than the other vessels, and all she carried were stern lights. As they drew nearer, the Germans were able to tell from their warship identification books that she was the light cruiser *Zhemchug* (one of the few Russian ships to escape destruction at Tsushima). She was about the same size as the *Emden* and just as heavily armed.

As far as the men on the *Emden* could tell, nobody was on her deck keeping watch. The darkened cruiser moved slowly and undetected into the heart of the enemy harbor.

At 0505 Lieutenant Witthoeft cleared the torpedo tubes for action. The German naval ensign was run up the foremast, and at 0518, when they were merely four hundred yards from the *Zhemchug*, Müller gave Witthoeft the order to fire the starboard tube. It was impossible to miss at this range. The torpedo didn't even have time to rise to the surface before it hit the target. It struck the Russian cruiser well below the waterline, just aft of the second funnel. A dull explosion lifted the stern of the *Zhemchug* out of the water.

With a deafening roar five of the *Emden*'s 4.1-inch guns opened fire at point-blank range. The gunners aimed their broadsides at the forward part of the *Zhemchug*, where most of the crew were quartered. Men suddenly appeared on deck, and the Germans could see them scattering, running about in a panic or jumping overboard to get away from the exploding shells and the deadly hail of splinters.

A brief lull in the action came when the *Emden* turned away to port to bring the other torpedo tube to bear. By this time the Russian cruiser was wrapped in clouds of steam and yellow smoke. The glow of fires blazing inside the ship was visible through her portholes and the gaping holes torn in her side by the German shells.

Some of the *Zhemchug*'s gun crews bravely manned the only two 4.7-inch guns bearing on the *Emden* and opened fire. Their aim was wild. The Germans could hear the whine of the Russian shells passing overhead. After a few minutes, the Russians stopped firing because they had run out of ammunition.

At 0528 the *Emden* launched her port torpedo at a range of eight hundred yards. It struck the *Zhemchug* near the bridge, causing a tremendous explosion that broke the Russian ship in half. The Germans watched the two sections of the ship begin to sink. When the smoke cleared, all they could see above water were the two masts. The devastating attack had taken just fifteen minutes.

The *Emden* didn't stop to pick up survivors. Müller had no wish to be trapped deep inside an enemy port. In any case, several small boats were now heading out from the dockside toward the sunken Russian ship. As the Germans made for the harbor mouth at top speed, a small vessel came toward them. Fearing it might be a torpedo boat, Müller gave the order to open fire. After one salvo the Germans realized it was an unarmed government patrol vessel, and they ceased fire. Fortunately, only one hit was registered on the harmless *Sea Gull*, which damaged the ship's funnel but luckily caused no casualties.

Soon after this a much bigger vessel loomed out of the darkness—it was still not fully daylight—and she seemed to be blocking the *Emden*'s way out of the narrow channel. It turned out to be a freighter that was flying the yellow flag of a vessel carrying explosives. Despite being in the middle of an enemy naval base, Müller had the audacity to order her to stop. Lauterbach and his boarding party went by cutter to take her over as a prize, but they had no sooner arrived on board the ship, the *Glenturret*, when Müller signaled them to return immediately. He told Lauterbach to ask the ship's captain to pass on his deep apologies to the port authorities for firing on the defenseless *Sea Gull* and for not stopping to pick up survivors from the *Zhemchug*.

The reason for the sudden recall was that a warship had just entered the narrow mouth of the harbor and was blocking the *Emden*'s escape route. The cutter was quickly hoisted on board, with Lauterbach's men still in it, and the *Emden* made for the stranger at full speed. The cruiser turned to port to bring her full starboard broadside to bear and opened fire at a range of forty-five hundred yards. In the moonlight the Germans were able to identify the newcomer as a destroyer.

The *Emden*'s first two ranging salvoes missed the target. Unfortunately for the French ship *Mousquet,* she turned away to try to escape, realizing the danger she was in. This presented her whole length to the *Emden* just as the third salvo arrived. Two of the shells struck the destroyer. One of them exploded in the boiler room, and clouds of steam poured out of her. She managed to fire a torpedo at the *Emden,* but it missed. The French gamely opened fire with their forward gun, which was only a nine-pounder.

The *Emden* now had the range on the *Mousquet.* Nine more salvoes reduced the destroyer to a floating wreck. She was completely obscured by billowing steam and yellowish smoke. Müller gave the order to cease fire. He approached the French destroyer cautiously from the rear, because he didn't want to risk being torpedoed by his crippled enemy. When the smoke cleared, the destroyer was still afloat. Her flags were flying and she gave no sign of surrender.

Müller reluctantly gave the order to open fire on her again. After several more direct hits, she began to sink. The *Emden* lowered her second cutter, as well as Lauterbach's boat, to try to rescue survivors. It was chivalrous of Müller to stop, because he was still inside an enemy harbor and every minute counted. For all he knew, the *Dupleix* or *Montcalm* might be in the area and on her way to trap him. More than half of the *Mousquet*'s crew had been killed or drowned. The *Emden*'s boats managed to pick up thirty-six men: most were wounded, and several were badly mutilated.

But the gunboat *D'Iberville* and the destroyer *Fronde,* a sister ship of the *Mousquet,* were the only other French ships in Penang at the time. They were anchored at the far end of the island undergoing boiler repairs, and neither of them had steam up. It would have been suicidal if they had fired at the *Emden* with their puny guns and drawn attention to themselves.

Another sister ship of the *Mousquet,* however, was on patrol duty in the Malacca Straits. The sound of gunfire brought her racing toward the harbor mouth to investigate what was going on at Penang. This was the *Pistolet,* and when the *Emden* moved out of Penang into the straits, she swung around and kept at a respectful distance, shadowing the German cruiser.

Müller thought it would be unwise to turn back and deal with her because his operators were picking up frantic signals from the local wireless station. "*Emden* at Penang! *Emden* at Penang!" He increased speed to twenty-three knots and steered northwest. The *Pistolet* was just as fast as the *Emden* and continually signaled her position and course. The Germans tried to jam her transmissions but didn't succeed.

Müller knew that the small destroyer's coal supply wouldn't allow her to keep shadowing him for very long. Fortunately, a rain squall blew up, and after it had cleared, the *Pistolet* was nowhere in sight. The *Emden* headed for the northern tip of Sumatra, planning to turn southwest to meet her two colliers at the rendezvous.

The consequences of the *Emden*'s dramatic attack were far-reaching. The Germans could be well pleased with their daring performance. They had penetrated an Allied naval base, sunk a cruiser and a destroyer, and come out completely unscathed. Much more important than these minor material losses was the profound psychological impact of the raid. Coming so soon after the attack on Madras, it caused Allied naval prestige in the region to reach a new low. Shipowners lost confidence in the ability of the navy to protect their vessels, and all shipping on the Singapore-to-Calcutta trade route came to a standstill.

The raid had exposed glaring weaknesses in the Royal Navy's allies. The *Mousquet*'s survivors reported that they had seen the *Emden* entering the harbor, but they had not challenged her to identify herself because they thought she was the *Yarmouth*. The French still believed she was a British cruiser when they steamed directly toward her after they heard the explosions inside the harbor. Their complete lack of caution sealed their fate.

The incompetence of the Russians was far worse. The *Zhemchug* had just finished cruising through the Andaman and Nicobar Islands searching for the *Emden*. The Russian captain, Baron Cherkassov, was well aware of the danger she posed if she appeared in the area. Admiral Jerram had reluctantly given him permission to spend a whole week in Penang for boiler repairs, but Cherkassov had neglected to take any precautions whatsoever while he was in the harbor. Both Commander McIntyre, the harbormaster at Penang, and Lt. Guy Maund, the British liaison officer attached to the *Zhemchug*, had told Cherkassov that he should always keep his ship anchored broadside to the harbor mouth, as British cruisers did, and have all his guns ready to fire. In fact, only twelve rounds of ammunition were available on deck for all the guns' crews. Once these had been fired, the *Zhemchug* was defenseless.

Lieutenant Maund had despaired of the Russians' incorrigibly sloppy lookout system. He had warned Cherkassov to post a sharp lookout at all times, but as far as is known, the only people awake when the *Emden* opened fire were the ship's cooks, who had risen early to go to market. The captain wasn't even on board the ship; he had gone to George Town to spend the night with a woman he had met. But the clearest indication of the state-of-war readiness on board the *Zhemchug* was that in addition to the heavy casualties among the crew, reportedly sixty Chinese prostitutes went down with the ship.

All but 133 men out of a crew of 341 were killed or wounded, many of those horribly mutilated. Ten of the fourteen officers escaped injury, probably because the *Emden*'s fire had been concentrated on the *Zhemchug*'s forecastle.

Baron Cherkassov and his first officer Lieutenant Kulibin were later found guilty of gross negligence at a court-martial in Vladivostok. They were both reduced in rank to seamen. In addition, the baron was stripped of his title and sentenced to three and a half years in prison, and Kulibin received an eighteen-month sentence.

The raid had an even bigger impact in Australia and New Zealand. The great Anzac troop convoy, which had originally been due to leave Wellington on September 22 bound for Europe via Fremantle, had already been held up twice: once by the news of the *Emden*'s attacks on shipping in the Bay of Bengal and once by the threat of Graf Spee's big cruisers after they had appeared off Samoa. Sailing was postponed again. Public fears in New Zealand about the danger to troopships ran so high that at one point the prime minister threatened to withdraw his troops from the war.

In the end, the convoy sailed with a heavy escort consisting of the Japanese battle cruiser *Ibuki,* the armored cruiser *Minotaur,* and the Australian cruisers *Melbourne* and *Sydney.* Any one of these was easily capable of overpowering the *Emden* if she dared to attack the convoy.

The *Emden*'s captain was completely unaware of all this. He had other ideas. Buoyed by the success of his raid on Penang, Müller was now planning another attack on an enemy shore installation, and he had chosen the important cable and wireless station on the Cocos Islands as his next target. His direct route from Penang to Cocos was bound to cross the path to be taken by the Anzac troop convoy.

Meanwhile, another lone raider was giving the Allies nearly as much trouble in the Atlantic as the *Emden* was causing in the Indian Ocean.

7

The Mystery of
the *Karlsruhe*

. . . return home: your work is done.
— Final order from Admiralstab to Captain, SMS *Karlsruhe*

As the *Emden* was heading for the Cocos Islands, and Graf Spee was steadily working his way across the Pacific, another German cruiser was lost at sea somewhere in the Caribbean. Although she sank in November 1914, it wasn't until March 1915 that the Admiralty learned of her fate. This lone raider was not uppermost in their minds at the time for they had a much more pressing problem: what to do about the menace of the Graf Spee squadron. Even the Admiralstab were in the dark about the loss of their cruiser until December 1914. They were still sending wireless messages to her captain six weeks after she went down.

The *Karlsruhe* was the newest addition to the German light cruiser fleet. She was longer, bigger, and more heavily armed than her predecessors in the city-named class, and she was faster. Her top speed of twenty-seven knots gave her a three-to-four-knot advantage over any other light cruiser, German or British, and an even bigger advantage over an armored cruiser. Since her launching at Danzig three months before the war, she had been commanded by Capt. Fritz Emil Lüdecke. He had taken her through her training period and sea trials before she left the Jade River to relieve the *Dresden* on the Caribbean Station, when Capt. Erich Köhler of the *Dresden* was scheduled to take over command.

After crossing the Atlantic the *Karlsruhe* made a brief stop for coal at St. Thomas on July 1 and reached Port au Prince during the period of Kriegsgefahr. Lüdecke had originally been ordered to meet the *Dresden* at Havana, but because of a revolution taking place in Haiti he was sent to Port au Prince to try to protect German businesses and civilians. When he arrived there, he found only the USS *South Carolina* in the harbor, also keeping a watchful eye on national interests. The *Dresden* didn't arrive until July 25, after she had taken General Huerta to sanctuary in Kingston, Jamaica.

The German captains had already received warnings from Berlin that war was likely within the next few weeks, and they knew there was no time for the usual formalities. The two cruisers exchanged captains quickly and without ceremony. The next day Lüdecke left for St. Thomas with the *Dresden,* and the more experienced Köhler took the *Karlsruhe* to Havana to pick up messages and take on coal.

Köhler had intended to go to Vera Cruz to monitor the situation in Mexico, but on July 29 he heard the news that Austria had declared war on Serbia, and he changed his mind. He postponed coaling and left Havana the next day to await developments while at sea off the coast of Cuba. The following morning he received a Warning Telegram from the Admiralstab, relayed to him by the shore station in Havana. (This was a prearranged signal that war was expected at any time.)

He abandoned the idea of going to Mexico because he knew there were Allied cruisers patrolling off Vera Cruz. He headed back along the coast of Cuba and turned north to wait in the Bahamas, among the Plana Cays. These islets were far off the usual steamer tracks, and Köhler planned to hide there for a few days until he received his War Telegram.

In the meantime, Admiral Cradock was aware of the *Karlsruhe's* arrival on the Caribbean Station, and he knew she could prove to be a serious threat to North American sea traffic. It has been estimated that in 1914 almost half of Britain's food supplies came from Canada and the United States. It was important for Cradock to catch the *Karlsruhe* quickly when war broke out, or at least to drive her southward, away from the North Atlantic sea routes.

One of Cradock's squadron, HMS *Berwick,* had actually passed within hailing distance of the *Karlsruhe* when she was on her way to Haiti to meet the *Dresden,* and the two captains had exchanged friendly greetings. Since that time, the German cruiser had been reported to be docked at Havana. Cradock sent the *Berwick* there with orders to shadow her until war broke out. When the *Berwick* arrived, it was too late; Köhler had left the day before for an unknown destination.

Cradock deployed his squadron to try to encircle the German cruiser. He left Vera Cruz hurriedly and stationed his flagship, *Suffolk,* off

Jamaica. He ordered the *Bristol* to head north toward the mouth of the St. Lawrence, to help the Canadian cruiser *Niobe* protect troop convoys leaving Halifax. The *Lancaster* and *Essex* were already at Bermuda, ready to begin patrolling the main Atlantic routes out of U.S. ports. When he failed to find the *Karlsruhe* at Havana, Capt. Lewis Clinton-Baker of the *Berwick* suggested to Cradock that the Germans would probably head for the Florida channel, a likely spot for a raider to use as a base to strike at ships coming out of U.S. ports. The admiral told him to take the *Berwick* there and search the channel.

On August 4 the British and German captains received their respective War Telegrams. Köhler opened his sealed orders from the Admiralstab that directed him to wage war on North American sea trade, attack enemy shore installations, and sink enemy warships. Only the first of these was a practical proposition for a single cruiser in the middle of a hostile environment like the Caribbean. Every one of Cradock's ships was superior in armament to the *Karlsruhe*. Even against the weakest of them— the light cruiser *Bristol*—Köhler knew he would stand little chance. His only advantage was speed.

Köhler's first move was to arrange a rendezvous with the twenty-seven-thousand-ton North German Lloyd liner *Kronprinz Wilhelm,* which had just sailed from New York. He wanted to transfer the guns and ammunition that the *Karlsruhe* had brought her from Germany. The British blockaded all American ports as soon as war was declared, and the *Kronprinz Wilhelm* was one of the few German ships that managed to dodge the blockade. The Germans planned to convert the huge passenger ship into an armed merchant cruiser by mounting 3.4-inch guns on her upper deck. (With their usual foresight, they had installed gun mountings on the *Kronprinz Wilhelm* before the war.) In return, the liner was bringing Köhler supplies and coal from the United States.

The *Karlsruhe* met the *Kronprinz Wilhelm* 120 miles north of Watling Island on the morning of August 6 and began transferring the guns and ammunition. The site arranged for the rendezvous was rather an unfortunate choice. Cradock had decided to take the *Suffolk* north from Jamaica and search the Windward Passage area. He was heading directly toward the meeting point from the south. When Clinton-Baker found no sign of the *Karlsruhe* in the Florida channel, he decided to move east with the *Berwick*. He picked up signals between the *Karlsruhe* and an unidentified German ship and headed toward them as fast as he could steam. By this time the *Bristol,* on her way to Canadian waters, had reached a point just four hundred miles north of the rendezvous.

Thus, unknown to the Germans, two of Cradock's squadron were

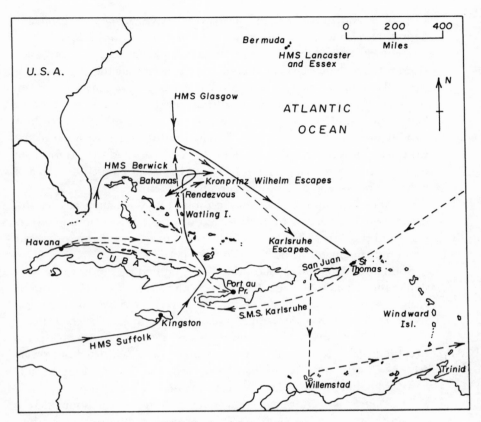

The *Karlsruhe*'s narrow escape

converging on their rendezvous from the south and east, and a third blocked any escape route to the north. There was no easy way out to the west because of the Bahamas and the Florida coast.

By 1100 on August 6 the *Karlsruhe* had transferred all of the guns and half of the ammunition to the *Kronprinz Wilhelm*. The transfer of coal and supplies to the cruiser had just started when smoke appeared on the southern horizon. The lookouts identified the ship as a British heavy cruiser, and the two German ships hastily cast off from each other and separated. The *Karlsruhe* headed due north at full speed, and the *Kronprinz Wilhelm* fled in a northeasterly direction.

As soon as he sighted the two ships, Cradock ordered full speed ahead. The fleeing Germans could see dense black smoke begin to pour from the *Suffolk*'s funnels as she picked up speed. Cradock signaled the *Bristol* to turn back and gave Captain Fanshawe the *Karlsruhe*'s position and course. He also wirelessed the news to Clinton-Baker in the *Berwick*.

Cradock ignored the *Kronprinz Wilhelm* and kept after the *Karlsruhe*. A grim stern chase began that continued throughout the afternoon, as the stokers on both ships worked tirelessly to achieve maximum steam pressure. But the *Suffolk* had a rated top speed of less than twenty-four knots, and Köhler was able to use his three-knot advantage to draw steadily away from his pursuer. All he could do was run, because the British ship was nearly twice as big as the *Karlsruhe* and carried fourteen 6-inch guns to his own twelve 4.1-inch. If he had attempted to turn and fight, the result would have been certain destruction.

Cradock kept up the chase—even though he was falling farther and farther behind—because he knew he was driving the German ship directly toward the *Bristol*. He lost sight of his quarry when darkness fell but kept on doggedly to the north at his best speed.

Soon after dark, lookouts on the *Bristol* sighted the outline of a warship in the distance. She was showing no lights, but it was a clear moonlit night and there could be no doubt that it was the *Karlsruhe*. She was about six miles away and steaming directly toward them. They had apparently not been spotted themselves, because the Germans made no attempt to alter course. By 2015 the range had closed to about seven thousand yards, and Captain Fanshawe turned to port to bring his full starboard battery to bear. He then gave the order to open fire.

The Germans were taken completely by surprise and immediately swung ninety degrees to starboard. It took a few minutes before they opened fire themselves. The *Bristol* changed direction to bring the two ships onto parallel courses, and firing continued. Both sides were using their full broadsides. Fanshawe signaled Cradock that he was engaging the *Karlsruhe*. The admiral replied, "Stick to it— I am coming."

The range was too great for accurate shooting at night, even with a full moon. Neither side scored any hits. Once again the *Karlsruhe*'s superior speed allowed her to pull ahead, and she altered course to southeast. The *Bristol* followed this change of direction, and another stern chase began.

The British cruiser had a rated top speed of twenty-five knots. This should have been enough to keep the enemy in sight, but her boilers were badly in need of cleaning, and so the *Bristol*'s speed gradually fell to eighteen knots, and the Germans pulled farther and farther ahead. By 2230 Fanshawe had lost sight of the *Karlsruhe*. But the Germans weren't out of danger yet.

The *Karlsruhe*'s bunkers were getting low because her coaling from the *Kronprinz Wilhelm* had been interrupted by Cradock's arrival. An anxious

Captain Köhler consulted his chief engineer as to which neutral ports they could reach, in darkness if possible. After careful calculations the engineer concluded that if speed was reduced to the most economical, namely twelve knots, they might just reach St. Thomas, but not until the morning of August 9. This meant they would have to steam slowly in broad daylight all of the following day. The Germans nervously monitored the cruiser's coal consumption during the night, and further calculations showed that it was safer to head for San Juan, Puerto Rico, which was about fifty miles nearer than St. Thomas on the course they were taking.

By this time the *Suffolk* had turned eastward after receiving wireless reports from the *Bristol* about the *Karlsruhe*'s position. If she kept to her last reported course, Cradock should cut her off some time during the following morning. The *Berwick* was also heading directly toward the German cruiser's path.

When daylight came the crew of the *Karlsruhe* were greatly relieved to find no sign of smoke in any direction. Köhler could do nothing but keep on course at his present speed and pray that he was not spotted by any of the British ships. He no longer had enough coal to run away or to outmaneuver them. If one of his pursuers spotted him, he would be trapped. All day long his anxious lookouts scanned the horizon in every direction for signs of smoke or mastheads.

Unknown to Köhler, the *Suffolk* had crossed his path shortly after daybreak. She was about twenty miles astern, just out of sight. As the morning wore on, the worried Germans heard wireless signals from the *Berwick* that were getting louder and louder. But just after noon the signals began to grow faint. Once again the crew breathed a collective sigh of relief. When he had seen no sign of the *Karlsruhe* all morning, Captain Clinton-Baker decided to turn back and search the Windward Passage. He thought the Germans might have headed for one of their previous anchorages in Haiti or Cuba. If he had kept on to the east for another hour, he would probably have spotted the *Karlsruhe*.

The *Karlsruhe* steamed slowly toward Puerto Rico during the night of August 8. Next morning, at daybreak, she arrived in San Juan with only twelve tons of coal left in her bunkers. This was barely enough for another four hours of steaming. Köhler had just had the narrowest of escapes.

Of the ships chasing the *Karlsruhe*, only the *Bristol* had kept on toward the south. She was now patrolling off the Danish Virgin Islands. Fanshawe guessed that the *Karlsruhe* would head for St. Thomas—an unfortunate but reasonable guess—because St. Thomas was known to be a German supply base. Köhler was awfully lucky when he decided to change his destination to San Juan, otherwise he would have been trapped in the harbor at St. Thomas. This would have forced him to choose between internment or certain defeat at the hands of the *Bristol*.

The escape of the *Karlsruhe* was a source of great frustration to all the captains of the Fourth Cruiser Squadron, but it had the most profound effect on the admiral. Cradock fully realized that his superior firepower was utterly useless without the speed necessary to keep up with his enemy. When the hastily recommissioned *Good Hope* was sent out to join his command, he made the fateful decision to transfer his flag to this ship, simply because she was faster than the *Suffolk*. But the *Good Hope* was of 1899 vintage and manned by a green crew of reservists and cadets, some of them as young as fifteen.

The day the *Karlsruhe* arrived in San Juan was a Sunday. The crew gratefully attended church services on the quarterdeck, probably seeing their providential escape as an affirmation of their credo, "Gott mit uns" (God with us). The captain was more preoccupied with coaling as quickly as possible, because he wanted to leave San Juan before any of Cradock's squadron could show up. He knew the British consul would waste no time in reporting his arrival.

The Germans found it wasn't easy to buy coal on a weekend. They also had trouble hiring boatmen to ferry the coal to the ship, which was anchored well out in the roadstead, ready to fly at the first sign of an enemy warship. In addition, Köhler had to contend with delaying tactics by the French and British consuls, who protested to the port authorities that the Germans were infringing the rules of neutrality by trying to buy a full load of thirteen hundred tons of coal. Köhler claimed that this much coal was needed to get his ship to the nearest German port, which was in West Africa. The Allied diplomats said that, in reality, the *Karlsruhe* was going to use the coal to prey on Allied shipping in the Caribbean. Finally, with the help of the German consul, Wilhelm Hepp, Köhler managed to buy five hundred tons of coal, but it was of poor quality.

As soon as the coal was loaded on board, the *Karlsruhe* left San Juan; it was 2000 on the same day she had arrived. The ancient German collier *Patagonia* was in the harbor at the time, and Köhler instructed her captain to go to St. Thomas to pick up some decent coal and meet him later off Barbados. He dared not go near St. Thomas himself and decided to make for Curaçao where he hoped for a less hostile reception to his efforts to obtain a full load of coal.

The *Karlsruhe* arrived at Willemstad on August 11, having used half of the poor, fast-burning coal to get there. The Germans were relieved to find that no warships were in the harbor except for the Dutch coastal defense vessels *Jacob van Heemskerck* and *Kortenaer.* These two were certainly capable of enforcing the rules of neutrality, if necessary, but Köhler was able to buy eleven hundred tons of good coal, as well as supplies and fresh water, and leave within the prescribed twenty-four-hour limit.

After his narrow escape in the Caribbean, Köhler gave up on the idea of raiding North American trade routes or shore installations in the West Indies, at least for the time being. He decided it was safer to make for the coast of Brazil and raid shipping in the Pernambuco area. Thus, in a real sense, Cradock had succeeded in his most important duty. He may have failed to catch the *Karlsruhe,* but he had driven her away from the vital North Atlantic shipping area. On August 14 the Admiralty was able to report: "The passage across the Atlantic is safe. British Trade is running as usual."

After leaving Curaçao the *Karlsruhe* hugged the coast of Venezuela and headed for her rendezvous with the *Patagonia.* Since his ship now had plenty of coal, Köhler was in no hurry to get there. He hoped to capture Allied merchantmen along the normally busy sea-lanes, but for three days the Germans saw nothing. They didn't know that sailings had been delayed by nervous shipping agents because of the menace of the *Dresden* and *Karlsruhe,* which were both believed to be somewhere in those waters.

They finally saw a ship on August 16, but she was hull down on the horizon and headed due north, directly away from them. They set off in hot pursuit and heard the ship frantically signaling that they were being chased by a German cruiser. Köhler decided it was too risky to continue a long chase back into the heart of the Caribbean. He gave the order to reduce speed to conserve coal and turned away to the east.

The *Karlsruhe* passed between the Windward Islands and Trinidad and met the *Patagonia* south of Barbados the following day. Köhler was delighted to discover that she had obtained two thousand tons of good-quality coal at St. Thomas. This would be enough to keep the cruiser going for weeks. The two ships had turned toward the Brazilian coast to look for a safe spot to transfer coal when, on August 18, they came upon the British freighter *Bowes Castle.* The Germans ordered her to stop and found that she was a 4,650-ton vessel loaded with nitrates from Antofagasta. Her captain protested that his cargo was U.S. owned, but because it was obviously a war material, Köhler decided to sink the freighter.

Her crew were transferred by cutter to the *Patagonia.* Then the boarding party from the *Karlsruhe* opened the connecting doors between the boiler room and engine room and the engine room tubes to the sea. They set timed blasting charges to open still more holes in the hull. The two large compartments filled quickly as the sea rushed in, and the *Bowes Castle* began to settle in the water. The ship sank by the head, and she stayed upright for a few seconds before plunging into the depths. A loud hiss of escaping steam and compressed air was heard. Afterwards, there was nothing to be seen but scattered bits of wreckage and a swirl of oily water.

In their official reports after the war the Germans made futile attempts to conceal their sinking of the *Bowes Castle*. She carried a neutral-owned cargo, and they hoped to avoid paying the United States for the loss of its property.

On August 21 the cruiser and her collier arrived at the island of Maracá, just off the coast of Brazil, where they spent the next three days coaling. This stretch of coast offered many secluded bays where the Germans could set up secret coaling bases without much fear of detection. The cruiser took on thirteen hundred tons, which meant that not only were her bunkers full, even her decks were piled high with coal sacks.

The two vessels headed toward their next rendezvous at São João Island, where they met the collier *Stadt Schleswig,* which had been ordered to wait there. Because she had only eight hundred tons of coal on board, it was transferred to the *Patagonia*. In return, the *Stadt Schleswig* received the crew of the *Bowes Castle* and took them to the Brazilian port of São Luís. Köhler knew that when the *Stadt Schleswig* arrived in harbor, his position would be signaled to Cradock, and he immediately left the area, accompanied by the *Patagonia,* to make for the islands of Fernando de Noronha.

These islands were at the focal point of most sea traffic between South American ports and Europe. They also had the advantage that the uninhabited Rocas rocks were nearby, where the *Karlsruhe* could hide her supply ships. The *Asuncion* and *Rio Negro* of the Hamburg-South Amerika Line and the North German Lloyd vessel *Crefeld* had been instructed to meet her there, if they could evade Allied patrols.

When Köhler arrived at the rendezvous on August 28, he was pleased to find all three supply ships waiting for him, but he wasn't aware that he had just had another narrow escape. Less than forty-eight hours before the *Asuncion* and *Rio Negro* arrived, Captain Luce of the *Glasgow* had searched the Rocas reefs area because of reports that German ships had been seen in the vicinity. Cradock had ordered the *Glasgow* to move north from the River Plate area and meet the *Monmouth* and *Otranto* coming south. If these three ships had arrived at Rocas two days later, they would have trapped Köhler's supply ships and been waiting at the rendezvous to overwhelm the *Karlsruhe* with their greatly superior armament.

Köhler took the *Patagonia* with him, leaving the other colliers at Rocas, and set out to raid the South American trade routes. On August 31 he captured the steamer *Strathroy,* carrying a full load of five thousand tons of Welsh coal from Barry to Buenos Aires. This "splendid windfall" was sent with a prize crew to join the others at Rocas reefs. Three days later the *Karlsruhe* stopped the 4,338-ton freighter *Maple Branch,* also British registered, with a general cargo including some welcome livestock and marine stores. These were taken on board the cruiser, her crew were taken by the *Patagonia,* and the merchantman was sent to the bottom with explosive charges.

While all this was going on, Cradock passed by in the *Good Hope,* barely fifty miles away. He had now been given the task of finding the *Dresden* and the Graf Spee squadron, and he had stopped to search the Fernando de Noronha region on his way south to Port Stanley. The fortunate Captain Köhler wasn't aware that he had just narrowly escaped destruction again.

Nevertheless, after one month of war Köhler had achieved surprisingly little. He had spent most of his time dodging Allied patrols and securing coal supplies. Apart from the thrilling escape from Cradock's squadron, the first month of war had meant long days of boring inactivity for his men. The monotony had been relieved only by the three captures and by yet another Kohlenfest.

To keep up the crew's morale, the ship's band gave concerts on the forward deck every evening after dinner. They played such crew favorites as "Snuten und Poten" and "Es war in Schöneburg im Schöner Monat Mai." They invariably concluded the concerts with "Die Wacht am Rhein."

Despite Köhler's lack of success to date, his presence was a continued source of anxiety to merchant ship captains and owners and an irritation to the Royal Navy. But at his present rate of captures he would soon cease to be regarded as a serious threat. Either his fortunes would have to improve or he would need to change his tactics.

After returning to his supply ships Köhler left the Rocas reefs on September 10, this time with the *Crefeld* and *Rio Negro.* He had decided on a new approach. He stationed the two fast auxiliaries abreast of the cruiser about twenty miles away on either side, to act as a screen. This broadened his range of search to about eighty miles. If any merchantman was sighted, the flag signal "Ship in sight" could be made to the

Karlsruhe. She would then speed up and chase the unsuspecting victim, who would at first see only the apparently harmless *Crefeld* or *Rio Negro*.

The screen also prevented Köhler from being as badly surprised by enemy warships as he had been in the Bahamas. His range of vision would be far greater than that of an enemy approaching from any direction other than dead ahead or astern. This was a clever idea of Köhler's. It may now seem a fairly obvious tactic, but he was the only surface raider to use this approach during the period of the Great War.

Even so, it took another four fruitless days, with the lookouts on all three vessels constantly scanning the horizon for smoke, before the tactic paid off. On September 14 they captured the frozen meat ship *Highland Hope*, which was traveling in ballast from Liverpool to Buenos Aires. Although she was empty of cargo, she did have fifteen hundred tons of coal in her bunkers that Köhler decided to take before sinking her.

Before he could do this, the Spanish steamer *Reina Victoria Elena* chanced upon the little group of ships. She wirelessed to ask who they were and what they were doing. The *Karlsruhe* signaled back, "Convoy of British ships." One hundred miles to the north, the old battleship *Canopus* was laboring her way south to join up with Cradock's forces in the Falklands, and she intercepted these signals. Capt. Heathcote Grant was highly suspicious; he had not been told of any such convoy in the area. He wirelessed the Spanish ship to ask for her position.

The *Karlsruhe* heard Grant's request. It was too dangerous to stay any longer. The Germans couldn't tell how close the *Canopus* might be, so they abandoned the *Highland Hope*'s coal and sank her immediately. Because he believed the *Canopus* was somewhere to the north, Köhler left the area at full speed and headed west. He arrived off the shoulder of Brazil the next day, well away from regular sea-lanes.

In spite of the isolated area, he surprised the collier *Indrani* just after dawn on September 17. Her captain had been running under full lights because he felt safe steaming so far off the usual track. The *Karlsruhe* had spotted the lights before daybreak and hurried toward them. The Germans were overjoyed to discover that the *Indrani* was carrying seven thousand tons of coal from Virginia to Rio via Pernambuco. Two days later their pleasure was somewhat dampened by a signal from the German consul in Pernambuco, asking if the *Karlsruhe* had seen any sign of the *Indrani*. The consul had recently bought its shipment of coal to supply German raiders and was worried because the collier was overdue. Köhler didn't respond in case his signal was intercepted. He kept the *Indrani* as a collier until the end of his cruise, optimistically renaming her the *Hoffnung* (hope).

Unknown to Köhler, he had just had another narrow escape. Rear-Admiral Stoddart had brought his squadron over from Cape Verde to cover the Pernambuco region now that Cradock was headed south to hunt for the *Dresden*. His flagship, the *Carnarvon*, searched the area where the *Karlsruhe* was operating. Unaccountably, Stoddart decided to turn back just as he was near to intercepting Köhler's ship.

The *Karlsruhe* needed coal again—which she took from the *Asuncion* at the secret coaling base—and then returned to her cruise pattern with the *Crefeld* and *Rio Negro*. After several fruitless days she captured the *Maria* on September 21 and the *Cornish City* and *Rio Iguassu* the following day. The *Maria* was a Dutch vessel with a load of wheat destined for a neutral port, and her captain protested vigorously that wheat had not yet been declared a contraband material. The Germans sank the *Maria* just the same. The other two ships were both British, loaded with coal bound for Brazil. Their coal was of inferior quality, and Köhler now had plenty in the *Indrani-Hoffnung*, so he sank the two colliers as well.

That same day, the *Karlsruhe* stopped another ship, this time the Italian vessel *Ascaro*. She was allowed to proceed because the grain she was carrying was destined for an Italian port. The Germans appear to have been convinced of Italy's neutrality, yet when the *Ascaro* arrived at St. Vincent in the Cape Verde Islands on September 28, her captain promptly reported the *Karlsruhe*'s position to the authorities. This was the first definite news of the German cruiser for almost a month. Ever since the crew of the *Bowes Castle* had been put ashore in São Luís, the *Karlsruhe* had acquired the reputation of a ghost ship.

All the same, most of September was a barren period for Köhler. He had only six more captures to show for all his efforts and new tactics. The main reason for his lack of success was that Allied shipping had been diverted from its usual routes and was now moving well to the east of regular sea-lanes. Also, the cruiser needed a boiler overhaul and more coal, and these tasks took most of the last week of September. By the time they were finished, the decks of the cruiser were so congested with coal sacks that most of the guns couldn't be trained properly. This placed the Germans in a disagreeably unprotected position. They were lucky that Cradock's ships were far away on their southern sweep looking for the *Dresden*, and Stoddart's squadron was now patrolling to the north of Cape San Roque.

Köhler returned to his previous hunting ground on October 1. After several days without seeing any ships, it became obvious that South American sea traffic was not following its usual routes, so he sent the

Crefeld forty miles to the east. This move met with immediate success.

In the next week the *Karlsruhe* captured as many merchantmen as she had in the entire previous month. On October 5 the *Crefeld* sighted smoke and signaled Köhler. The *Karlsruhe* went after the British collier *Farn* and caught her after a two-hour chase. This ship was loaded with six thousand tons of high-quality Welsh coal—the last thing Köhler needed at the moment, with his decks piled high with coal sacks. So he sent the *Farn* away with a prize crew, with orders to rendezvous with the *Asuncion*.

Köhler was not far from the track that merchant ships were now taking, and Allied patrols unwittingly drove him right onto it. When Cradock moved his main squadron south, he left the *Bristol, Cornwall*, and *Macedonia* behind to search the area where the *Karlsruhe* was believed to be operating. (In fact, the *Cornwall* passed over the spot where the *Farn* was captured, but forty-eight hours too late.) For the two previous days, the *Karlsruhe*'s operators had been picking up coded wireless messages between British warships that had been growing in signal strength. Consequently, Köhler decided it was prudent to move farther east and accidentally stumbled onto the new trade route.

Between October 6 and 9 he captured the *Niceto di Larrinaga, Lynrowan, Cervantes*, and *Pruth* on successive days. These were all British vessels, the first two loaded with grain from Argentina and the other two with grain and nitrates from Chile. The Germans transferred their useful stores to the cruiser and their crews to the auxiliaries. Then they scuttled all four of the ships.

Following this brief spell of success, Köhler moved west toward a rendezvous with the *Asuncion* and *Farn*. He needed coal, and the two prison ships *Rio Negro* and *Crefeld* were becoming seriously overcrowded. The latter alone had more than four hundred merchant seamen on board. Apart from the obvious problems of feeding them and providing adequate sanitation, the prisoners were from at least twenty different nationalities. In their confined quarters trouble often broke out, in spite of German efforts to control fighting. They would soon have to send the prisoners in one of the auxiliaries to a neutral port.

As he approached the rendezvous on October 11, Köhler was surprised to find three ships there instead of two. He was even more surprised when one of them started to flee at high speed. This was the *Farn*, whose prize crew at first took the *Karlsruhe* for a British cruiser and panicked. When they realized their mistake, they returned sheepishly to the rendezvous. The mystery of the third ship was soon explained. While waiting for the *Karlsruhe*, the *Farn* and *Asuncion* had induced the British freighter *Condor* to approach them by hoisting the Red Ensign, and they had succeeded in boarding and capturing her. Her captain had decided it would be safer to keep well away from the usual steamer track. Unfortunately for him, this course brought him to the isolated area chosen for the rendezvous. The *Condor* was loaded with provisions, engine oil, and dynamite—just what the Germans needed. After they had stripped this prize of her cargo, they sent her to the bottom using some of her own explosives.

Even with these new provisions, Köhler knew he couldn't keep feeding his prisoners for much longer. On October 13 he reluctantly decided to put them all on board the *Crefeld* and send her to a neutral port. This would give away his position and the full extent of his activities. As a precaution, he ordered the captain of the *Crefeld* to go to the Canary Islands, approximately two thousand miles away, and told him not to put into Tenerife before October 22.

Once he had released the *Crefeld,* Köhler hoped he would have ten days of relative safety before she reached port. The Allies were aware that several of their merchant ships were overdue, but they didn't realize how much damage the *Karlsruhe* had done, or where. Once the *Crefeld* arrived at Tenerife, they would be bound to focus their search on the region north of Fernando de Noronha.

By October 18 Köhler was back on the previous route and captured the British collier *Glanton,* loaded with the best Welsh coal, en route from Barry to Montevideo. Since he was already so well supplied with coal and couldn't spare any more men for a prize crew, he sank the collier with her valuable cargo.

After Cradock's squadron moved south to try to catch the *Dresden* before she could join up with Graf Spee, Admiral Stoddart was appointed "Senior Naval Officer north of Montevideo." He was made responsible for the Pernambuco region and for putting an end to the *Karlsruhe*'s activities. He meant to search the area with his flagship *Carnarvon,* supported by the *Albion, Marmora,* and *Empress of Britain,* but he received fresh orders from the Admiralty. It told him to proceed down the trade routes to Montevideo and take under his command the *Cornwall, Bristol, Macedonia,* and *Orama.* The armored cruiser *Defence* was also on her way to join his squadron from the Mediterranean. The Admiralty ordered Stoddart "to keep sufficient force ready to concentrate in case the Graf Spee squadron from the Pacific escapes past Admiral Cradock."

Had it not been for the Admiralty's preoccupation with Graf Spee, it is highly likely that Stoddart's planned sweep of the Fernando de Noronha area would have trapped the *Karlsruhe*. As it was, Stoddart's flagship passed the place where the *Glanton* had been sunk less than forty-eight hours earlier.

Köhler knew from frequent interceptions of W/T signals between Stoddart's ships that Royal Navy patrols had intensified. It was dangerous to stay where he was for much longer. He had seen mostly neutral ships in the past few days and concluded that Allied shipping was being rerouted again. He stopped the Spanish ship *Cadiz*, the Norwegian *Bergenhus*, and the Argentine *Chaco*, and after inspection of their cargoes, let them pass. He did capture one British vessel, the *Hurstdale*, which carried forty-six hundred tons of maize bound from Rosario to Bristol. She was sunk on October 23. That same day Köhler stopped the Swedish vessel *Annie Johnson* but let her go because she had no contraband on board. She went directly to Pernambuco and reported his presence to the authorities on the twenty-sixth.

Köhler realized that at least one of the neutrals he had released would soon give away his location, and he reverted to his original plan of attacking shore installations in the Caribbean. He had been forced to abandon this idea after his narrow escape from Cradock's squadron in the Bahamas. He hoped that by now most of the Royal Navy patrols had been drawn to the Pernambuco region. He suspected that Barbados and Martinique were not strongly guarded, which would give him an opportunity to emulate Karl von Müller and strike at Allied seaports. Köhler knew all about the *Emden*'s raid on Madras from newspapers taken from captured merchantmen. He sent the *Rio Negro*, *Asuncion*, and *Indrani-Hoffnung* away, with orders to meet him later, and took the *Farn* with him toward the West Indies.

Rumors circulated in Allied shipping communities that the *Karlsruhe* had left the Brazilian coast and was now operating off the Canary Islands. These rumors were strengthened by the arrival of the German collier *Walhalla* at Las Palmas, for the Allies believed she was waiting there to supply the *Karlsruhe*. This was not true, but the *Walhalla*'s presence was a lucky break for the *Crefeld*. HMS *Victorian* had been ordered from Gibraltar to Las Palmas to investigate, but when she arrived, the *Walhalla* had already put to sea. There were reports of signal lights off the island, and when she left Las Palmas to chase the *Walhalla*, the *Victorian* missed the *Crefeld* in the darkness. The prison ship arrived safely in Tenerife on October 22, exactly as Köhler had ordered.

For some inexplicable reason the Spanish authorities concealed the news from the world for longer than twenty-four hours. It came as a bombshell that the *Crefeld* had on board the crews of no less than thirteen Allied merchant ships that the *Karlsruhe* had captured or sunk between August 31 and October 11. The Allies had heard nothing definite about the German raider for weeks. They knew that a few of their ships were overdue, but the true extent of the *Karlsruhe*'s haul came as a nasty shock.

Largely because of rumors previously fueled by the presence of the *Walhalla* and then by the arrival of the *Crefeld* in Tenerife, the Allies concluded that the *Karlsruhe* had moved her area of operations to the Cape Verde-Azores-Canary Islands triangle. They increased their patrols in the triangle to protect shipping, especially convoys of troopships from South Africa.

The supposed danger from the *Karlsruhe* helped the British cabinet decide that it would be safer to route the great Anzac convoy through the Suez Canal, not around the Cape of Good Hope as originally planned. Thus, unwittingly, Köhler was partly responsible for sending this convoy across the path that the *Emden* was to take for her raid on the Cocos Islands.

On his way north on October 26 Köhler was fortunate to capture the new ten-thousand-ton liner *Van Dyck,* which was on her way from Buenos Aires to New York with mails, bullion, frozen meat, and general cargo. It was pure chance that she ran into the *Karlsruhe*, because her captain had stayed away from regular shipping lanes and used no lights or wireless. This was the most splendid prize the *Karlsruhe* had ever taken. The liner also carried in excess of two hundred passengers, mostly Americans, although she was a British-owned ship.

The crew and passengers were taken off and put on the *Asuncion*, along with the crews of the *Glanton* and *Hurstdale*. Köhler sent the collier to Para, with orders not to dock there before November 1. The provisions and stores were stripped from the *Van Dyck* and she was sunk. News of this latest sinking brought more protests from insurers and shipowners and angry demands that the Royal Navy do something about the aggressive *Karlsruhe*.

During the night of October 27–28 the *Karlsruhe* captured the fully lit *Royal Sceptre*, an old worn-out ship with a neutral-owned cargo of £200,000 worth of Brazilian coffee. This was hardly a strategic material, and Köhler decided to let her go.

By now, Köhler had captured seventeen British ships and one Dutch vessel under British charter. He had sunk sixteen of them and kept two as supply ships. In total, he had been responsible for destroying 76,500 tons of Allied shipping, to say nothing of the almost equal tonnage of their cargoes, which were of great strategic value. Coincidentally, the damage he had done was about the same as that inflicted by the *Emden,* but Köhler had received much less publicity and acclaim than Müller because of the more shadowy nature of his exploits. Müller's raids on Madras and Penang had placed him squarely in the limelight. Perhaps a raid or two in the Caribbean would do the same for Köhler.

On November 1 the *Karlsruhe* coaled from the *Farn,* and the near empty collier was detached with her prize crew. She eventually put into San Juan, Puerto Rico, where she was interned. The cruiser steamed on to the north, with the *Rio Negro* on one side of her and the *Indrani-Hoffnung* on the other. These two supply ships had joined up with the *Karlsruhe* the previous day and were once again being used as a screen for the cruiser.

They were not as spread out as when Köhler had been looking for merchant ships. Now he was more intent on raiding shore installations, first at Barbados, then at Martinique. Köhler thought that Allied patrols would have been sidetracked by the arrival of the *Crefeld* in the Canaries and by the news of the capture of the *Van Dyck* in the Pernambuco region. He was confident that the West Indies area was not being heavily guarded by Allied warships.

He hoped to steam into Bridgetown harbor unmolested and strike a blow at British morale and prestige in the West Indies. He planned to sink any ships in port and shell the shore installations, just as Müller had done at Madras and Penang. Köhler had heard about the *Emden*'s exploits at Penang from radio broadcasts, and he was keen to match them by attacking Barbados and Martinique. The Allies considered the West Indies area so secure that they were in for another nasty shock if he succeeded in destroying the harbor installations at Bridgetown and Fort de France.

Köhler chose Barbados as his first target because there was a chance that the French cruiser *Condé* might still be at Martinique.

The *Karlsruhe* and her two consorts crossed the equator on November 3, and by the following evening they had reached a point 11°7'N and 55°25'W, about three hundred miles southwest of Barbados. Köhler planned to begin his raid at dawn on November 5. That evening, he and Lieutenant Althaus were the only officers on the bridge. Most of the crew were relaxing after dinner on the forward deck, listening to the ship's band. At 1830 a terrific explosion occurred in the area just ahead of the funnels, blowing the cruiser's bow section completely off. In the after part of the ship panicked cries, "We've been torpedoed!" were heard.

After the smoke had cleared, the surviving crew members could see that the bridge and forward part of the ship had disappeared entirely, taking with them Captain Köhler, Lieutenant Althaus, and 259 petty officers and men. They must have been killed instantly by the force of the explosion, or drowned when the bow section sank like a stone.

Lieutenant Commander Studt realized that he was now senior officer. He quickly gave orders for all remaining boats and rafts to be lowered. The after part of the ship was taking water fast and listing to port. The sea around the ship was covered with oil from ruptured tanks, and there was a grave danger that this would be ignited by the burning wreckage in the floating section of hull. Studt ordered the crew to abandon ship.

As soon as the explosion occurred, the *Rio Negro* and *Indrani-Hoffnung* raced toward the stricken cruiser and lowered their lifeboats. Within twenty minutes they had taken aboard Studt and 17 other officers, along with 112 petty officers and men. The survivors watched grimly as the *Karlsruhe* sank by the bow, or what was left of it. At 1857, only twenty-seven minutes after the explosion, the stern section of the cruiser plunged into the depths.

The cause of the explosion has never been determined, and the end of the *Karlsruhe* is likely to remain a mystery forever. It was certainly not due to a torpedo attack since no Allied submarines were in the vicinity at the time. It has been suggested that the cruiser may have struck a floating mine. Whereas this cannot be discounted, it does seem improbable. The mine would have had to drift more than three thousand miles from European waters, because neither side had laid any mines in the Caribbean in 1914.

The most probable explanation is that some of the *Karlsruhe*'s ammunition had become unstable after three months of tropical heat, and it caused a spontaneous detonation of the forward magazine. This would account for the extreme force of the explosion, which broke the six-thousand-ton ship cleanly in two. (If a ship of this size had merely struck a mine, this would not have been expected to happen.) A similar explosion, which sank the British cruiser *Natal* in Cromarty Firth on New Year's Day 1915, was also believed to have resulted from unstable ammunition.

Studt took command of the *Rio Negro,* ordering the *Karlsruhe*'s survivors to go on board this ship, without exception. He told them to remove all traces of the *Karlsruhe* from their uniforms, especially their cap ribbons. He also ordered them to stay below decks if another ship came in sight. Studt was determined to conceal the loss of the *Karlsruhe* from the Allies for as long as he could.

The *Indrani-Hoffnung*'s coal was transferred to the *Rio Negro,* and all the captured merchant seamen were put on board this ship as well. Studt dared not let them go to a neutral port to tell of their experiences. He sent the *Indrani-Hoffnung* away with a prize crew, who were all Germans. Studt ordered them to sink the ship in deep water as soon as the *Rio Negro* was out of sight, then to take to the ship's boats and head for a neutral port. They were under strict orders to give no information whatsoever to the port authorities.

Studt decided to run the Allied blockade by going north to Iceland, then heading for Norwegian coastal waters, eventually reaching Germany. The *Rio Negro* finally arrived in Hamburg in early December. When Studt and the survivors of the *Karlsruhe* showed up, the Admiralstab were flabbergasted. They had just sent Köhler a signal that ended, ". . . return home: your work is done."

The Germans managed to conceal the loss of their cruiser until March 1915. The Allies kept up a futile search for the mystery ship for four months, until some wreckage from the *Karlsruhe* washed up on the beach at St. Vincent, close to five hundred miles from the scene of the explosion.

Captain Köhler and his men had served their country well, with courage and skill and without much fanfare. Köhler's good luck undoubtedly contributed to his success as a raider, but even when his luck finally ran out, his ghost continued to serve the Fatherland.

A few days before the mysterious explosion on board the *Karlsruhe,* Graf Spee's squadron had made their own dramatic appearance off the coast of South America.

8

The Battle of Coronel

I will take care I do not suffer the fate of poor Troubridge.
—Adm. Sir Christopher Cradock

Easter Island was a Chilean possession, and in 1914 the bleak volcanic island's only nonnative residents were the English manager of a sheep and cattle ranch, a French carpenter, and a German tobacco planter. There were also a few hundred Polynesian natives and the members of a British scientific expedition who were visiting the island to study its mysterious stone statues. The latter had arrived in May in a ninety-ton schooner.

Apart from the schooner, the islanders' only contact with the outside world was a Chilean sailing ship that came twice a year to pick up beef and the wool crop. The island had no wireless. So, when a fleet of warships and merchantmen visited their remote colony in the fall of 1914, the inhabitants were amazed, and they watched in astonishment as ship after ship steamed into the bay and dropped anchor. Within five days the anchorage was crowded with more than a dozen German ships. The *Dresden* and her collier, *Baden,* were the first to reach the rendezvous, on October 10. Two days later the *Scharnhorst, Gneisenau,* and *Nürnberg* arrived with the *Titania* and the supply ships *Yorck* and *Göttingen.* Finally, the *Leipzig* steamed in on the fourteenth with her coterie of colliers.

The residents of Easter Island had no idea that Germany was at war with Britain, and the visitors didn't enlighten them. Even if they had known about the war, the inhabitants couldn't have done anything about the Germans' arrival because there was no representative of the Chilean government to insist on the rules of neutrality. Graf Spee knew that his squadron's visit would remain a secret for several weeks because it would take that long for the British schooner to reach the mainland.

His officers bought beef and lamb from the English rancher, Percy Edmonds, with a bank draft. (The meat was examined thoroughly by the ships' doctors before being taken on board ship.) Edmonds was dubious about this method of payment because he began to suspect that war had broken out. The draft was later honored by a German bank in Valparaíso, "vastly to his astonishment and relief." The Germans also traded with the island's Polynesian natives for fresh fruit, vegetables, and eggs. All these purchases were thoroughly examined before they were allowed on board.

While his cruisers loaded coal and provisions, Graf Spee went ashore with his two sons and Captain Maerker. They explored the island but found its plant life disappointingly sparse. The only part of the trip they enjoyed was their visit to the huge stone idols that had been discovered by the Dutch admiral Roggeveen in 1722.

Coaling operations at Easter Island were the most unpleasant the squadron had ever experienced. The only decent anchorage was in the unsheltered Mataveri Bay. The weather conditions became so bad, with high winds and driving rain, that the cruisers were in danger of dragging their anchors and drifting onto the rocky shore. They had to put to sea to finish coaling.

But there was a pleasant side to the visit, once the *Leipzig* had arrived. Her officers and men were able to renew old acquaintances in the other ships and exchange experiences since the squadron had left Tsingtao in June.

The *Leipzig* had brought some fairly recent newspapers from Peru, and the crews were delighted to read about the *Emden*'s brilliant success as a commerce raider and of her daring attack on Madras. They also learned that the *Königsberg* had sunk a British cruiser at Zanzibar. The islanders found some of these newspapers after the Germans had left and discovered that war had broken out months earlier. But without a wireless there was nothing useful they could do to inform anyone about the squadron's visit. By the time the schooner could get the news to the mainland, Graf Spee would have long since left the island, and his whereabouts would remain a mystery.

While the German squadron was moving steadily across the Pacific, far away in the Admiralty building Churchill, Battenberg, and the Chief of Naval Staff, Vice-Adm. Sir Doveton Sturdee, were becoming increasingly worried about the threat it presented. From all reports, Graf Spee seemed to be heading for the west coast of South America. If his squadron

Graf Spee's squadron off South America in heavy weather *(Suddeutscher Verlag)*

descended on this busy shipping area, it would create havoc. Britain had important trade with Peru and Chile in grain, lamb, nitrates, and copper and could ill afford to have it interrupted.

As Churchill put it, the problem with Graf Spee was: "He had no lack of objectives. He had only to hide and strike. The vastness of the Pacific and its multitude of islands offered him their shelter and, once he had vanished, who should say where he would reappear. So long as he lived, all the Allies' enterprises lay under the shadow of serious potential danger. We could not be strong enough every day everywhere to meet him."

Even if the Admiralty sent a squadron to try to intercept Graf Spee and to protect the trade routes from Chile and Peru, he might slip by it and reach the South Atlantic by going through the Strait of Magellan or around Cape Horn. Attacks on the River Plate traffic would be even more damaging to Britain because of its heavy dependence on Argentine beef and grain.

Four weeks before the Germans arrived at Easter Island, the Admiralty had given Rear-Admiral Cradock the task of stopping Graf Spee. Cradock had left the hunt for the *Karlsruhe* to Admiral Stoddart, and he was now doggedly working his way down the eastern side of South America searching for the *Dresden*. He planned to sink the cruiser if he could catch her. If not, he would follow her trail until it led him to Graf Spee.

On September 3 Cradock signaled the Admiralty: "*Good Hope* arrived Fernando Noronha. *Cornwall* is proceeding south. *Glasgow* is proceeding with *Monmouth* and *Otranto* to Magellan Straits, where German colliers reported, and where concentration of German cruisers from China, Pacific and Atlantic appears possible."

The Admiralty approved of these plans, but when Cradock asked, "*Gneisenau* and *Scharnhorst* reported Caroline Islands 8th August. Is there any later information?" it could only tell him, "No certain information . . . since August 8 . . . Magellan Straits and vicinity quite possible."

Two weeks later the Admiralty was a bit more definite. Cradock had reached Santa Catarina Island, four hundred miles southwest of Rio, where he received the following orders:

> There is strong possibility of *Scharnhorst* and *Gneisenau* arriving in Magellan Straits or on west coast of South America. Germans have begun to carry on trade there. Leave a sufficient force to deal with *Dresden* and *Karlsruhe*. Concentrate a squadron strong enough to meet *Scharnhorst* and *Gneisenau*, making Falkland Islands your coaling base. *Canopus* is en route to Abrolhos; *Defence* is joining you from Mediterranean. Until *Defence* joins, keep at least *Canopus* and one "County" class cruiser with your flagship. As soon as you have superior force, search Magellan Straits, being ready to return and cover Plate, or search north as far as Valparaíso. Break up German trade and destroy German cruisers.

This signal is as breathtaking in scope as it is vague on detail. How on earth was Cradock supposed to accomplish all this, even if his four ships were reinforced by the *Canopus* and *Defence*? The latter was more heavily armed than any of Cradock's ships, with four 9.2-inch guns and a secondary armament of ten 7.5-inch. She was a match for either the *Scharnhorst* or the *Gneisenau*, but it would take her at least two weeks to reach Cradock from the Mediterranean. In the meantime, did the

Rear-Adm. Sir Christopher Cradock *(Imperial War Museum)*

Admiralty believe that two old cruisers and an obsolescent battleship could stop Graf Spee's modern armored cruisers, whether they were accompanied by his light cruisers or not?

The *Canopus* was still rated as a battleship, but she was of 1897 vintage and had been ready for the scrap heap by 1914. When war came she was hastily recommissioned with a crew of reservists who were never given any practice firing her 12-inch guns. These were potent enough weapons to sink Graf Spee's ships if they could hit them, but the battleship could only manage seventeen knots at best. Graf Spee could easily steam away from the *Canopus* or simply maneuver just outside of her range and sink her with his own big guns. Although they were of the same range on paper, in reality they probably outranged the *Canopus*'s old guns by a thousand yards. The Germans were to show later that their smaller-caliber weapons could easily outrange bigger British guns.

Furthermore, it was twenty-five hundred miles from Cradock's base in

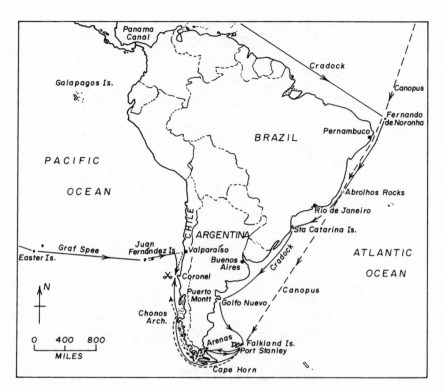

The road to Coronel

the Falklands to Valparaíso and thirty-three hundred miles to where the *Karlsruhe* was operating. How could Cradock cover all this territory with his handful of ships, and who was to know whether Graf Spee would go through the Strait of Magellan or around Cape Horn? Fortunately, the German trade referred to as one of Cradock's tasks was based more on rumor than fact. The only German merchantmen off South America at the time were Graf Spee's supply ships.

The Admiralty had originally considered sending Cradock not only the *Defence* but also no less than three armored cruisers. But because of fears of a German invasion of Britain, it decided that these ships could not be spared from their patrol duties in the English Channel. Sturdee and Battenberg proposed an alternative: Why not send Cradock some fast battle cruisers from the Grand Fleet? The fleet's admiral, Sir John Jellicoe, protested strenuously to Churchill that this would dangerously reduce his slim battle cruiser superiority over the High Seas Fleet. In the end,

Churchill gave in to Jellicoe and decided to order only the *Defence* to join Cradock. This would have been a vital addition to his squadron, but when news reached the Admiralty that Graf Spee had left Samoa in a northwesterly direction, the order was canceled and the *Defence* stayed at Malta.

Unaccountably, the Admiralty didn't see fit to tell Cradock about this change of plan. Apart from the ancient *Canopus,* he was to get no more reinforcements. It signaled him on September 16: "Situation changed. *Scharnhorst* and *Gneisenau* appeared off Samoa on 14 September . . . and left steering NW. . . . Cruisers need not be concentrated. Two cruisers and an armed liner would appear sufficient for Magellan Straits and west coast. Report what you propose about *Canopus*. . . ."

The Admiralty believed that the situation in South America was no longer urgent because the two most dangerous German ships were apparently heading toward the northern Pacific. Graf Spee's feint at Apia had worked.

By the time Cradock received this signal two days later, he had reached Montevideo. He replied that he intended to sweep south as far as the Strait of Magellan to search for German ships. Based on the Admiralty's faulty assessment of Graf Spee's movements, Cradock now believed that he was likely to meet only the *Dresden,* which he could deal with easily. He told the Admiralty he had decided to send the *Glasgow* and *Monmouth* to the west coast to destroy German trade and that he was leaving the *Canopus* in the River Plate area to guard his supply ships.

On its way to the strait, Cradock's squadron met the *Ortega* on September 25, homeward bound after her escape from the *Dresden.* Captain Kinnier told Cradock about his experiences, and the admiral immediately set out for Punta Arenas to see if the British consul had any further news of the German cruiser. Punta Arenas, like many South American ports at the time, was teeming with intelligence agents. Some were professional spies, others were talkative port officials or amateur observers. Both sides used these people to gather information, however dubious it might be.

It was rumored that the *Dresden* had been using Orange Bay as a supply base. Cradock also learned that one of the merchant ships docked in Punta Arenas had recently sailed full of livestock and provisions and returned empty a few days later. In the hope his quarry might still be in Orange Bay, Cradock left Punta Arenas on September 28 with all four of his ships, hoping to trap her before she could reach the open waters of the Pacific. Cradock deployed his ships during the night, and at dawn they entered the landlocked bay at full speed. They came in from four dif-

Cradock's flagship, HMS *Good Hope (Imperial War Museum)*

ferent directions to block any escape route, but as one of the *Glasgow*'s officers wrote in his diary, "The battle of Orange Bay was rather a farce, as the enemy didn't show up."

Cradock went back to Port Stanley because his cruisers were short on coal. He sent the *Otranto* to Punta Arenas to collect intelligence reports from the British consulate. After coaling, the *Monmouth* and *Glasgow* left Port Stanley on October 3 to meet the *Otranto* and search for the rumored German trade on the west coast. The *Good Hope* stayed at Port Stanley in case the *Dresden* doubled back into the Atlantic.

Two days later the *Otranto* intercepted coded German signals coming from somewhere off the Chilean coast and signaled Cradock. The admiral once again left Port Stanley at high speed. He ordered the *Monmouth* and *Glasgow* to meet him in Orange Bay. The same officer on the *Glasgow* wrote in his diary: "[The] second battle of Orange Bay was also a frost. Weather atrocious and it would have been quite impossible to fight our guns. Rather interesting if we met an enemy light cruiser in similar conditions."

The prophetic nature of this remark would soon be brought home to its author.

Cradock's second visit to Orange Bay was not a complete waste of time. A landing party from the *Good Hope* found a wooden sign that had been left there by the survey ship *Bremen* in 1912. Markings on it showed that the *Dresden* had been there three weeks earlier. Cradock knew that by now she must have joined up with Graf Spee's squadron in the Pacific.

Capt. John Luce of the *Glasgow* headed west, leading the *Monmouth* and *Otranto,* while the flagship returned once more to Port Stanley to wait for the *Canopus.* The weather remained "atrocious," and one of the *Glasgow*'s officers wrote: "[I]t blew, snowed, hailed and sleeted as hard as it is possible to do. . . . I thought the ship would dive under altogether at times. *Monmouth* was rather worse if anything. . . . We were rolling thirty-five degrees at times and quite useless for fighting purposes. . . . The ship was practically a submarine."

Even on board the much bigger *Otranto* conditions were bad. One of her officers commented, "We finally got past caring what would happen . . . what with the strain, the weather, and the extreme cold, we longed to find something and to have it out, one way or the other."

On October 7 Cradock was still at Port Stanley waiting for the *Canopus.* He received a message from the Admiralty, sent two days earlier. The wireless station in Fiji had intercepted a signal from the *Scharnhorst* to a German supply ship saying that she was headed for Easter Island. The message was in code, but the Royal Australian Navy had captured a German merchant ship in the Pacific at the beginning of the war,

Graf Spee's flagship, SMS *Scharnhorst (National Maritime Museum)*

with her mercantile code book intact, and the Allies were able to decipher the signal.

At this point no one doubted where Graf Spee was heading, and the Admiralty signaled Cradock: "[I]t appears that *Scharnhorst* and *Gneisenau* are working across to South America. You must be prepared to meet them in company, possibly with a 'Dresden' scouting for them. *Canopus* should accompany *Glasgow, Monmouth,* and *Otranto,* the ships to search and protect trade in combination. If you propose *Good Hope* to go, leave *Monmouth* on east coast."

Cradock received further intelligence reports that indicated "possibility of *Dresden, Leipzig, Nürnberg* joining *Scharnhorst* and *Gneisenau.*"

He signaled London: "Have ordered *Canopus* to Falklands where I intend to concentrate and avoid division of forces. Have ordered *Glasgow, Monmouth,* and *Otranto* not to go north of Valparaíso until German cruisers located. . . . does *Defence* join my command?"

The last comment shows that Cradock was still in the dark about his reinforcements.

He was becoming uneasy about his overall strength and sent another signal to London on October 11.

> Without alarming, respectfully suggest that in event of enemy's heavy cruisers and others concentrating on west coast of South America, it is necessary to have a British force on each coast strong enough to bring them to action. Otherwise, should concentrated British force sent from southeast coast be evaded in Pacific, and get behind the enemy, latter could destroy Falklands, English Bank and Abrolhos coaling bases in turn, and with British ships unable to follow up owing to want of coal, enemy might reach West Indies.

Churchill decided that Cradock's ships should stay within supporting distance of each other and postpone any forays against German trade on the west coast until the whereabouts of Graf Spee's big cruisers had been determined. He minuted his copy of Cradock's last signal and sent it to the First Sea Lord. "They and not the trade are our quarry for the moment. Above all we must not miss them." Battenberg's laconic reply was, "Settled."

On what to do about reinforcing Cradock, Churchill commented to Battenberg, "I presume Cradock is fully aware of the possibility of *Scharnhorst* and *Gneisenau* arriving on or after the 17th instant in his neighbourhood; and that if not strong enough to attack, he will do his utmost to shadow them, pending arrival of reinforcements."

This was sensible advice. It would have helped Cradock if he had received it. If he had been told that shadowing was an acceptable option in the eyes of the Admiralty, he might have deployed his forces differently. But the Admiralty's reply to both his previous signals merely stated: "Your concentration of *Good Hope, Canopus, Monmouth, Glasgow,* and *Otranto* for combined operations concurred in. Stoddart in *Carnarvon* has been ordered to Montevideo. . . . *Defence* ordered to join *Carnarvon.* He will also have *Cornwall, Bristol, Macedonia,* and *Orama* under his orders. *Essex* remains in West Indies. . . ."

This message reassured Cradock. Even if Graf Spee slipped by him and reached the Atlantic, he would have enough strength there to contain the German squadron. The signal didn't insist that Cradock concentrate his whole force on the Falklands, although it did finally inform him that the *Defence* was not on her way to join him after all. At this point he realized he would probably have to make do with his present forces.

Most important, the Admiralty still did not see fit to tell Cradock that it was alright for him to shadow Graf Spee if he felt he was not strong enough to attack.

By October 18 Graf Spee's ships had finished coaling, and everyone was glad to leave the miserable conditions at Easter Island. The squadron set sail for the Juan Fernández Islands, fifteen hundred miles to the east. The admiral intended this stage of the voyage to be a final preparation for the sea battle he thought was inevitable once he reached the South American coast. He knew that the weather off the coast would probably be bad in October and November, and he asked his staff to work out the best gunnery ranges and tactics to be used, depending on sea conditions. The ships carried out range-taking exercises and practiced different battle formations.

October 22 was the Kaiserin's birthday, and a carefully preserved case of champagne was broken out on board the flagship. In the wardroom there were toasts to Her Majesty and to victory for the Fatherland. The admiral gave a patriotic speech to the crew. The event was celebrated in much the same fashion as it was on board the *Emden* far away in the Indian Ocean.

By this time Cradock was fully aware of his precarious position. He was resigned to the fact that he would probably get no reinforcements besides the *Canopus,* which was still plodding her way toward Port Stanley. While awaiting her arrival, Cradock became quite friendly with the governor of the Falklands, Sir William Allardyce, known locally as "The King of the Penguins," and his aide-de-camp, T. N. Goddard. The latter wrote: "The Admiral was a brave old man; he knew that he was going to almost certain death in fighting these new and powerful ships and it seemed to be quite all right as far as he was concerned. . . ."

When the *Canopus* finally arrived at Port Stanley on October 18, Cradock was dismayed to learn that she would need to remain in port at least five days to clean boilers and repair an engine defect. Worse still, Captain Grant informed the admiral that even after repairs, his ship would be able to make only twelve knots. Cradock signaled the Admiralty the same day. "I fear strategically the speed of my squadron cannot exceed 12 knots, owing to *Canopus,* but shall trust circumstances will enable me to force an action."

Even without the *Canopus* to slow him down, his squadron's top speed would be held to eighteen knots by the *Otranto.* It is difficult to see how the British squadron could force an action on Graf Spee with his twenty-three-knot vessels, except on the German admiral's terms.

This was the day that Graf Spee's squadron set out for the Juan Fernández Islands, which was to be their last coaling stop before reaching the coast of Chile. On the way, Graf Spee changed his plans because of intelligence reports that British naval forces were being sent to the area. These reports mentioned only the *Good Hope* and *Monmouth.* He wrote in his war journal: "The presence of strong enemy forces on the coast makes it impossible for the present squadron to carry out its original intention of carrying on a war against commerce. This purpose is therefore renounced and the destruction of enemy forces is substituted for it."

A sea battle was much more to his liking than commerce raiding. He was confident of success now that he believed he had nothing more dangerous to face than the two old British cruisers, whose armaments and gunnery ranges he knew very well.

By October 22 Cradock decided he couldn't wait any longer for the *Canopus* to finish her refit. He signaled London: "*Good Hope* left Port Stanley via Cape Horn. *Canopus* following on 23rd via Magellan Straits with three colliers."

Before he left the Falklands he gave a letter to Governor Allardyce, with instructions to forward it to his friend, Adm. Sir Hedworth Meux. "I will give you all the warning I can if the German squadron eludes us; and only in case of my 'disappearance' will you send the letter to Meux. I mean to say, if my squadron disappears—and me too—completely. I have no intention after forty years at sea of being an unheard victim."

Although the letter has never been traced, and its contents remain a subject of speculation, one thing is clear: Cradock was very much aware of what happened to Adm. Ernest Troubridge in the Mediterranean on the first day of the war. That officer failed to press home an attack with his squadron on what he believed was a stronger enemy force. This resulted in the escape of the *Goeben* and *Breslau* to Constantinople and led indirectly to Turkey's entry into the war on the German side. Troubridge had come very close to a charge of cowardice when a court of inquiry was held. Although he was acquitted of the lesser charge of negligence at a subsequent court-martial, his career was ruined and he was never given another sea command. Cradock wrote to a friend, "I will take care I do not suffer the fate of poor Troubridge."

No one knows what was in Cradock's mind as he left the Falklands, but in the opinion of the governor's aide-de-camp: "He knew what he was up against and asked for a fast cruiser with big guns to be added to his squadron, for he had nothing very powerful and nothing very fast, but the Admiralty said he'd have to go without. So old Cradock said, 'All right; we'll do without,' and he slipped off early one morning, and left the *Canopus* to look after the colliers and transports, and picked up the *Glasgow* and *Monmouth* and set out to look for these crack Germans."

The German squadron reached the Juan Fernández Islands on October 26 and anchored at Más Afuera to coal. This island and Más a Tierra are the two main islands of the group, which lies about five hundred miles off the coast of Chile, due west of Valparaíso. Más a Tierra is now called Isla Robinson Crusoe because it was the inspiration for Daniel Defoe's novel based on the adventures of the Scottish sailor Alexander Selkirk who was marooned there in the eighteenth century. The other island, Más Afuera, is now called Isla Alejandro Selkirk.

A German officer wrote, "Here we spent several melancholy days in the shelter of this gigantic rock, which frowned on the pygmy line of our ships and was the silent witness of our laborious activity."

No shore leave was permitted, except for a few officers and, naturally, the admiral. He explored the island and took notes on its many seabirds and brought back samples of spring-blooming plants and shrubs.

While the squadron was coaling, the *Prinz Eitel Friedrich* arrived, short of coal herself. She had returned after an unsuccessful voyage as a raider off Australia and New Zealand. Her captain had decided to leave before he ran out of coal and was caught by Patey's squadron. Graf Spee had no coal to spare for a mere armed merchant cruiser and sent her into Valparaíso with the *Göttingen* to get some from one of the German colliers there. The two ships were escorted by the *Nürnberg*, which waited off the coast to collect any intelligence reports that were sent by wireless from German agents on shore.

Meanwhile, the *Good Hope* met the *Glasgow* and *Monmouth* at a secret coaling base in the Chonos Islands on October 27. (The coast of Patagonia has many tortuous channels and inlets where warships of both sides set up coaling points inside territorial waters, without much fear of being interrupted by Chilean patrol vessels.) While coaling the *Good Hope* from one of the supply ships, Cradock came to a decision about the *Canopus*. The old battleship had got only as far as Punta Arenas, and he knew he could never force an action on Graf Spee if he had to wait for her, because this would reduce his squadron's speed to twelve knots.

He wirelessed the Admiralty: "With reference to orders to search for enemy and our great desire for early success, consider it impracticable on account of *Canopus's* slow speed, to find and destroy enemy squadron. Consequently have ordered *Defence* to join me after calling at Montevideo for orders. *Canopus* will be employed convoying colliers. From experience of 6 August respectfully suggest not to oppose depredations of *Karlsruhe*. May they continue until he meets vessel of superior speed."

This message showed that Cradock still believed, or at any rate hoped, that the *Defence* was on her way to South America. His oblique reference to the *Karlsruhe* was meant to tell the Admiralty that the *Defence* was more useful to him off Chile than chasing after a German light cruiser that had already shown that she could easily outrun armored cruisers.

He had given up on the *Canopus* as a useful member of his squadron. This was the ship that Churchill believed would give Cradock protection from Graf Spee's squadron, if not superiority over it. Churchill thought the Germans would never dare challenge the 12-inch guns of the old battleship, which he described as "a citadel around which all our cruisers in those waters could find absolute security."

Yet here was Cradock relegating her to convoy duty.

Churchill was not pleased by Cradock's decision. He minuted the signal to Battenberg with the comment, "This telegram is very obscure and I do not understand what Cradock intends or wishes."

Although he claimed not to know what the admiral had in mind, he sent a further minute to the First Sea Lord. "The situation on the west coast seems safe. If *Gneisenau* and *Scharnhorst* have gone north they will meet *Idzumo*, *Newcastle*, and *Hizen*, and will be forced south on *Glasgow* and *Monmouth* who have good speed and can draw them on to *Good Hope* and *Canopus*, who should keep within supporting distance."

This woolly and overoptimistic assessment of the situation was not sent to Cradock. The chances of the *Newcastle* and the two Japanese ships running into Graf Spee in the vast expanse of the Pacific were about one in a million. What the Admiralty did tell Cradock was that it had counter-manded his orders. "*Defence* is to remain on east coast under orders of Stoddart. This will leave sufficient force on each side."

Its signal also mentioned that the *Newcastle* and the two Japanese ships were heading south from the Galápagos Islands, but they were much too far away to help Cradock. The Admiralty did not criticize or even men-tion his decision to leave the *Canopus* behind, which implied approval. In any event, this telegram, which was sent on October 28, didn't reach the squadron until November 1, when it was too late to have any effect on Cradock's deployment.

There have been suggestions that the signal never reached the admiral. This seems doubtful because Captain Luce of the *Glasgow* certainly received it that day. Even if Cradock did get the message, it can only have convinced him that the Admiralty thought he now had "sufficient force" to deal with Graf Spee, without the *Defence*. To refuse an engagement under these circumstances would place him in the unenviable predica-ment that Troubridge had faced in the Mediterranean.

The German squadron left Más Afuera on October 28, and two days later they were rewarded with a view of the Chilean coast and the distant snowcapped Andes. They had steamed twelve thousand miles to get there. Graf Spee kept his ships fifty miles offshore, out of sight of land, while he waited for the *Nürnberg* to bring intelligence reports back from ships anchored at Valparaíso. German merchant ships in Chilean ports customarily gathered intelligence and transmitted it to Graf Spee's cruis-ers in code, in flagrant violation of international rules. Ships of the bel-ligerents docked in neutral harbors were permitted to send wireless mes-sages only *en clair,* but violations were usually overlooked by the pro-German Chilean authorities.

On October 31 Graf Spee received a message from the *Göttingen* that she had picked up distant wireless signals between the *Good Hope* and *Monmouth*. The signals were coming from the south at equal strength, which indicated that the two ships were traveling together. Stronger sig-nals were heard from the *Glasgow* in the Coronel area. The next morning the collier *Santa Isabel* sent a message that the British cruiser had been anchored in Coronel Roads at 1900 the previous evening. The only news of the *Canopus* came from a German agent in Punta Arenas, fourteen hundred miles away. He reported that she had passed by on the afternoon of October 27. It wasn't likely that she was anywhere near Coronel on the thirty-first.

* * *

Meanwhile, the British squadron was moving steadily up the Chilean coast. It reached the Vallenar Roads, just south of Chiloé Island, on October 29. Cradock sent the *Glasgow* ahead to see if there were any important messages for him at the British consulate in Coronel. He also dispatched the *Otranto* to Puerto Montt to try to gather information as to the whereabouts of the German warships.

The next day the *Good Hope* and *Monmouth* headed north from Vallenar, intending to rendezvous with the other two members of the squadron after they had completed their intelligence missions. One hour after they left Vallenar Roads the *Canopus* and her convoy of supply ships arrived. Their approach had been seen in the distance by the lookouts on Cradock's ships, but the admiral had no time to wait for them.

While the *Canopus* was coaling and repairing a minor engine defect, Captain Grant discovered that his chief engineer, Comdr. William Denbow, had been mentally ill for some time and had deliberately falsified his reports about the state of the engines. According to a report by the junior engineering officer, Lt. Comdr. Sydney Start, Denbow had never left his cabin once during the whole voyage and so could not possibly have inspected the engines. It turned out that after a minor repair, the ship was capable of approaching the seventeen knots she had made on her sea trials after recommissioning. She had been restricted to twelve knots ever since the false report. The unfortunate engineer was sent back to England under medical attention. He was invalided out of the navy and never heard from again.

Captain Grant didn't want to break W/T silence to tell Cradock the news. Even with the *Canopus* capable of seventeen knots, he didn't think the admiral would slow down to let him catch up. Whether or not Cradock would have been influenced by this information can never be known, but it is most likely that he would have kept on without the old battleship.

By October 31 the *Otranto* had rejoined the squadron. She had not been able to obtain any information in Puerto Montt because the Chileans there were solidly pro-German. That same day, however, the *Glasgow* signaled from Coronel that German supply ships had been frequently sailing in and out of the port. More important, she had intercepted several transmissions between the *Leipzig* and one of her colliers.

Cradock ordered the *Glasgow* to leave Coronel immediately and meet him the next day fifty miles west of Arauco Bay. Just after noon on December 1 the squadron was reunited. The admiral signaled his ships to spread out at twenty-mile intervals and sweep north to look for the enemy.

* * *

The Admiralty and Naval Staff far away in London remained confident that their dispositions in the Pacific were perfectly adequate to deal with Graf Spee's squadron. Churchill's secretary wrote at the time, "The situation on the west coast seems safe."

The mood in the British squadron was just the opposite. Lt. Lloyd Hirst of the *Glasgow* wrote: "In the wardroom, a fight within a few days was considered inevitable, but there was not much optimism about the result; two of the Lieutenant-Commanders in *Monmouth,* both old shipmates of mine, took me aside to give me farewell messages to their wives. . . ."

The officers on the *Monmouth* were of the opinion that "*Glasgow* has got the speed, so she can get away, but we are for it."

The *Glasgow*'s officers reported that the admiral had "buried all his medals and decorations in the Governor's garden" before leaving Port Stanley, to be dug up in the event of his death and sent home after the war. It was also rumored that Cradock had given the governor "a large sealed packet to be sent home to the Admiralty as soon as his death was officially confirmed." These reports are unsubstantiated, but true or not, if these were the perceptions of his officers, they can scarcely have led to a feeling of confidence.

There was little reason for confidence. Of the four ships, only the *Good Hope* had any guns capable of inflicting serious damage on Graf Spee's armored cruisers. These were the two 9.2-inch guns of the main armament, which were mounted on the upper deck. The secondary batteries of 6-inch guns were in casemates on the main deck, close to the waterline. They were practically useless in any kind of sea swell because of the gunners' poor visibility and the danger of being flooded by high waves.

The *Monmouth* was rated as a heavy cruiser but undergunned for her size. Adm. "Jacky" Fisher had scathingly remarked, "Sir William White designed the 'County' class but forgot the guns." The cruiser carried only 6-inch guns, whose hundred-pound shells were unlikely to pierce the armor plate of the *Scharnhorst* and *Gneisenau*. Half of these guns were mounted close to the waterline. Fisher's final caustic comment on the "County" class was, "[W]ith their wretched pea-shooters, they can neither fight nor run."

These were the two major units of Cradock's squadron. They were both old ships that had been condemned as unfit for further service before the war. When war seemed imminent the Admiralty decided it was too costly to scrap them, and they were hurriedly recommissioned and manned with crews of untrained reservists, coast guardsmen, naval cadets, and boy seamen, some of them as young as fifteen. Many of those hastily recruited to serve in the *Monmouth* were Scottish crofters and fishermen who had been given little or no gunnery practice. Even some of their gunnery officers had never been inside a real gun turret before. Things weren't much better aboard the flagship. Since Cradock had taken over command of the *Good Hope* in August, her green crew "had only carried out one full calibre practice shoot."

As for the other two ships, the *Glasgow* was a fast, modern cruiser with a regular navy crew, but she was armed with only two 6-inch and ten 4-inch guns. These were more than adequate for fighting Graf Spee's light cruisers, but they were totally ineffective against his big ships. The *Otranto* was a twelve-thousand-ton liner that had been given eight 4.7-inch guns and converted into an armed merchant cruiser. Because of the thinness of her hull and her huge profile, she was known in the squadron either as the "sardine tin" or the "floating haystack." She made a splendid target for the squadron's gun-laying and range-taking practice. The *Otranto* was meant to fight other armed merchantmen, not regular warships, and she was of no value to Cradock except as a dispatch ship.

Most critically, the weight of shell that could be fired by the whole of Cradock's squadron was not much more than that of either of Graf Spee's big cruisers. This assumes that the British ships would be capable of firing full broadsides in any kind of sea conditions. In the poor weather typical of the South American coast in November, Graf Spee's advantage would be far greater because half of the British guns were mounted too low to be of any use.

Graf Spee knew from his intelligence reports that he was up against only the *Good Hope, Monmouth,* and *Glasgow,* and because the latter had been in Coronel the previous day, he hoped to cut her off before she could rejoin Cradock. Realizing the *Glasgow* would have to leave port because of the twenty-four-hour rule, he took his squadron south toward Coronel on the morning of November 1 and ordered the *Nürnberg* to leave Valparaíso and join up with him.

That same morning, Cradock's ships heard a lot of loud W/T traffic between German supply ships and the *Leipzig.* Graf Spee had been using the *Leipzig* to transmit and receive all wireless messages between the squadron and its supply ships, so as not to give away the presence of his other cruisers. Unaware of this, Cradock thought the *Leipzig* was the only German cruiser in the Coronel area. He headed north to join up with the *Glasgow* and trap the *Leipzig* before she could rejoin Graf Spee.

This led to the dramatic situation on the morning of All Saints' Day 1914, when each admiral was taking his full squadron to "cut off and gobble up" what he believed was a single enemy light cruiser. In reality, the two formations were steaming inexorably toward each other at a combined speed of almost forty knots. The admirals, who had been friends since their days on the China Station during the Boxer Rebellion, were about to meet again.

By late afternoon on November 1 Cradock's squadron was still fanning out and moving in a northerly direction. They were about thirty miles from Arauco Bay, where the small port of Coronel is situated. The flagship was the outermost ship, close to forty miles from the *Glasgow.* At 1630 the light cruiser's lookouts sighted smoke on the eastern horizon. Captain Luce gave orders to turn to starboard and increase speed. A few minutes later the *Monmouth* and *Otranto* turned east in support of the *Glasgow.*

Very soon the lookouts were able to recognize the hull and upper works of the *Leipzig.* As the *Glasgow* got closer the lookouts saw more patches of smoke on the horizon. When these were identified as coming from four-funneled cruisers, the *Glasgow* turned back and signaled, "Enemy armoured cruisers in sight."

The *Glasgow*'s wireless operators could hear the high-pitched scream in their earphones coming from German Telefunken sets trying to jam their transmissions. They weren't sure whether the flagship had received their signal. All three British ships headed at full speed toward the *Good Hope* to warn Cradock that instead of trapping a solitary light cruiser, he was running into Graf Spee's whole squadron.

The *Leipzig* had identified the *Glasgow* at about the same time and followed her. She soon saw the smoke from the rest of Cradock's squadron. Captain Haun reversed direction and signaled the news to his admiral. Graf Spee also realized that he had found the enemy squadron, not a single light cruiser. He ordered his ships to close up and form a line heading southwest. The *Scharnhorst* was in the lead, followed by the *Gneisenau, Leipzig,* and *Dresden.* The *Nürnberg* was still thirty miles to the north and had been trying to catch up with the squadron ever since she left Valparaíso.

Cradock ordered his ships to change direction to southeast by east and form a line headed by the *Good Hope,* followed by the *Monmouth, Glasgow,* and *Otranto.* They completed these maneuvers by 1745. The Germans took longer to form their line because they were more spread out and didn't have full steam up yet. The two squadrons were now about seventeen miles apart. The Germans soon changed course to southwest by west. This brought the two battle lines onto rapidly converging paths.

Both squadrons were steaming head on into a rising swell, making all the ships pitch and roll badly, especially the light cruisers, which, according to an eyewitness, were "rolling like barrels in the heavy sea." The sky was gray and overcast, and visibility was poor because of frequent rain squalls.

At this point Cradock still had time to break off contact and move south to join forces with the *Canopus,* which was then about three hundred miles away. He knew that if he did, Graf Spee would not have time to catch him before nightfall. He could always return the next morning, strengthened with the *Canopus,* to attack the German squadron, if he could find it. Even if it slipped by him, he had been assured by the Admiralty that Stoddart had strong forces waiting in the Atlantic. (But he would have been bitterly criticized if he had let this happen.)

Cradock would certainly have been justified in refusing action until he had "superior strength," as the Admiralty put it. No matter how dubious their evaluation of the *Canopus,* he would be far better off with her than he was at present.

It was simply not in Cradock's nature to make such a decision. He was well known in the fleet for his dashing, headstrong nature and had already shown great courage on several occasions. He had been decorated by King George V and even by the Kaiser, who had awarded him the Royal Order of the Crown for his services on the China Station during the Boxer Rebellion. On several occasions Cradock had been heard to express the wish that when his time came, he hoped he would be killed in action at sea or break his neck going over a fence after a fox.

A brother officer said of him, "Cradock was constitutionally incapable of refusing or ever postponing action, if there was the smallest chance of success."

Captain Luce's opinion was, "I had the feeling that Cradock had no clear plan or doctrine in his head, but was always inclined to act on the impulse of the moment."

Cradock must have known he had little or no chance against Graf Spee's superior force, but his orders were, "Destroy enemy cruisers." If he couldn't do this, he might at least damage them enough that they would have to seek internment in a Chilean port, or else face the next British squadron at a disadvantage. One or two telling hits on Graf Spee's big ships might weaken his squadron so much that it was no longer a serious threat.

Cradock resolved to attack as soon as possible, while he still had the sun behind him. Sunset was due at about 1830. As the sun got lower and lower on the horizon, its rays would be directly in the German gunners' eyes. This would make it hard for them to see Cradock's ships in the distance, while the German ships would be clearly outlined for the British gunners.

Graf Spee was aware of this, but he knew the advantage would suddenly swing in his favor when the sun went below the horizon. Then the British ships would be starkly silhouetted against the sun's afterglow, while his own would be difficult to see in the waning daylight, lit only by the moon, which, although nearly full, was obscured by storm clouds. Graf Spee's main concern was not to let the British squadron get ahead of him and cut across his bows to gain the relative safety of the coast. But Cradock had no chance of crossing Graf Spee's "T" with the eighteen-knot *Otranto* holding him back. With his superior speed Graf Spee was able to keep the distance between the two lines at fifteen thousand yards, well outside of gunnery range.

At 1804 Cradock gave the order to turn forty-five degrees to port. He desperately wanted to close the range before the sun began to set, but Graf Spee ordered a similar turn and kept his distance. At 1818 Cradock signaled the *Canopus,* "I am going to attack the enemy," although the German ships were three thousand yards beyond his range at the time. Captain Grant signaled back that he still had 250 miles to go before he could reach Cradock's position.

Graf Spee allowed the gap between the two lines of ships to close steadily. By 1900, when the sun had just dipped below the horizon, it was down to 12,300 yards. It was now two and a half hours since the initial contact between the two squadrons. The tension on both sides was almost palpable. Graf Spee gave the order for his two armored cruisers to open fire. To quote an official German record, "[W]ith that order, disaster broke over Cradock's squadron."

At this range Graf Spee's twelve 8.2-inch guns faced Cradock's two 9.2-inchers. It was as if the *Scharnhorst* was at peacetime gunnery practice. Her first salvo landed five hundred yards short of the *Good Hope* and her second five hundred yards over, according to an observer on the *Glasgow* who was watching the gun flashes and waiting for the splashes of the shells. This was the classic straddling pattern. With an awful inevitability the third salvo smashed into the *Good Hope.*

One shell struck her forward 9.2-inch turret, which erupted in flames that shot higher than a hundred feet into the air. At one stroke the gun crew were wiped out before they had fired a shot. The turret was turned into a useless, twisted mass of steel. Cradock's heavy guns were reduced to one. This was remarkable shooting—the *Scharnhorst* was aiming at a target some five hundred feet long and only seventy feet wide from a distance of seven miles.

At almost the same time, the *Gneisenau* opened fire on the *Monmouth*. She obtained a similar straddling pattern with her first three salvoes. A shell from the third salvo hit the *Monmouth*'s forward gun turret and set it ablaze. Within minutes the *Good Hope* and *Monmouth* were suffering terrible punishment, as salvo after salvo thundered at them across the water. The German gunners on each ship managed to fire a broadside of six shells every twenty seconds. Cradock's flagship replied with her lone 9.2-inch gun. The *Monmouth* could use but half of her 6-inch guns, which were at the limit of their range.

The ships were now heading into the teeth of a Force 6 wind. It was approaching gale conditions, and heavy seas were breaking over their bows and sweeping the forward decks. The British main deck guns could not be used because of the danger of flooding the casemates. In any case, their range finders had become so encrusted with salt from the sea spray that they were useless. No hits were registered on the two German cruisers, which were rapidly becoming indistinct smudges on the darkening horizon. Cradock's ships were "etched deep black in awful clarity" in the sun's afterglow. Their own targets could only be sighted momentarily from the flashes of the enemy guns.

By this time, the *Leipzig* had begun to engage the *Glasgow*, which fired back with her 6-inch guns. The *Dresden* opened fire on the *Otranto*. After one salvo, which fortunately fell short, the armed merchant cruiser pulled out of line toward the open sea. She was a large vulnerable target and could only help the Germans find an accurate range on the British line. Captain Edwards signaled Cradock, suggesting that he keep the *Otranto* out of range. The reply was never completed. "There is danger; proceed at your utmost speed. . . ."

Edwards wasn't sure what the admiral intended, so he kept on a course parallel to the squadron, just outside the *Dresden*'s range.

Ten minutes after Graf Spee's order to open fire, the Battle of Coronel was as good as over. Cradock kept closing the range until it was down to fifty-five hundred yards, where he could use some of his secondary armament of 6-inch guns. This only made the firing by the *Scharnhorst* and *Gneisenau* more devastating, because they were now able to use their 5.9-inch guns as well.

By 1930, just thirty minutes after the *Scharnhorst* had opened fire, the *Good Hope* had been hit between thirty and forty times. She was heavily damaged in the forward part of the ship, especially the bridge and foretop area where Cradock was directing his squadron. A hail of shells had smashed through her decks and started fires in the interior of the ship. The Germans could see the orange-red glow through the *Good Hope*'s portholes.

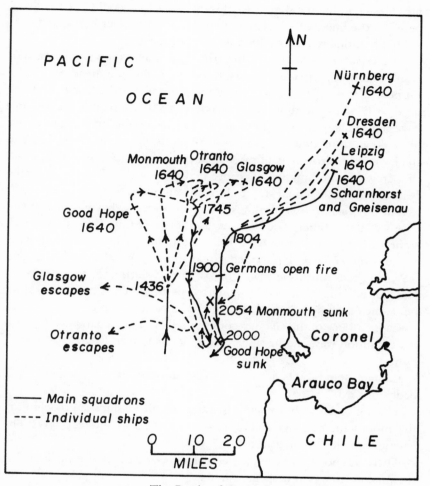

The Battle of Coronel

In what may have been a last desperate attempt to inflict some damage on her tormentors, the crippled flagship slewed out of line toward the enemy, some of her guns still firing. Graf Spee thought she was going to fire torpedoes and ordered his ships to turn away. He lost sight of the *Good Hope* in the haze that hung over the battle scene.

According to one of the *Glasgow*'s officers, "At 1950, there was a terrible explosion between her main mast and her funnel, the flames reaching a height of over 200 feet."

The forward magazine must have been ignited by one of the many fires blazing inside the ship. After this the *Good Hope* could be seen "lying between the lines, a low black hull gutted of her upperworks, and only lighted by a dull red glare which shortly disappeared."

The *Good Hope* drifted off into the gloom and smoke. She was not seen again by either side. It is not hard to imagine the dreadful carnage on board. It is likely that Cradock and his staff on the bridge were all dead or dying by this time. No one actually saw her sink, but she couldn't have stayed afloat for very long in her stricken condition and must have gone down some time around 2000. She took the admiral with her into the icy depths, drowning all those men and boys who were still alive out of a crew of nine hundred. Because the battle was still raging, no one, British or German, could stop to look for survivors.

The *Monmouth* was in almost as much distress, having been hit in excess of thirty times. The ship was ablaze and listing to port, although some of her 6-inch guns were firing sporadically. For another twenty minutes the *Gneisenau* pounded her at short range with both 8.2- and 5.9-inch shells, until she yawed out of line to starboard, away from the German onslaught. She was sinking by the head. The inrushing sea put out some of the fires, but by then she was a battered wreck.

Captain Luce of the *Glasgow* couldn't tell in the semidarkness how bad her condition was, and he signaled the *Monmouth* at 2015, "Are you all right?"

Captain Brandt replied: "I want to get stern to sea. I am making water badly forward."

Through a break in the clouds, Luce saw three ships approaching in the moonlight and signaled Brandt again: "Can you steer NW? The enemy are following us astern."

There was no reply. When the *Glasgow* drew nearer, it was obvious that the *Monmouth* was in desperate straits.

The captain of the *Glasgow* had no choice but to save his ship. The *Good Hope* and *Monmouth* were finished as fighting ships, and the *Otranto* had fled to the west at 1945 when her captain saw that the flagship was doomed. The Germans were left with the light cruiser as their only target. She had led a charmed life so far, with only four of her crew wounded, but now every time she fired her guns, the flashes lit up the darkness and attracted fire from all four German ships.

Luce knew that just one 8.2-inch salvo from the *Scharnhorst* or *Gneisenau* could blow his ship apart, and he gave the order to cease fire. He had already taken five hits from the *Leipzig* and the *Dresden*, which had concentrated on the *Glasgow* after the *Otranto* pulled out of the line. Although three of the shells had failed to explode, one had caused a large hole just above the waterline. Luce could do nothing to help the *Monmouth*, so he gave the order to head west at full speed. He wanted to find the *Otranto* and head south to warn the *Canopus* to turn back.

In the words of one of the *Glasgow*'s officers: "The *Monmouth* could neither fight nor fly. She was badly down by the bows, listing to port with the glow of her ignited interior brightening the portholes. It was essential that there should be a survivor of the action to turn *Canopus* which, if surprised alone, must have shared the fate of the other ships. . . . It was awful having to leave the *Monmouth* but I don't see what else the Skipper could have done."

The *Monmouth*'s ordeal was not over yet. The *Nürnberg* finally caught up with the German squadron at 2100 and came upon the helpless cruiser, which she identified by searchlight. The *Monmouth* was listing so badly that her guns couldn't be trained on the *Nürnberg*. Whether out of frustration at missing the main action, or from fear of being torpedoed by his crippled enemy, as claimed by the Germans, Captain von Schönberg gave the order to open fire at point-blank range.

The *Monmouth*'s White Ensign was still flying. Since she had given no sign of surrender, Schönberg was justified in sinking her. One or perhaps two torpedoes would have sufficed as a coup de grâce, but the *Nürnberg* steamed slowly from end to end of the hapless *Monmouth* and poured in a withering hail of 4.1-inch shells. The battered ship finally rolled over on her beam ends and disappeared bow first beneath the waves.

Otto von Spee wrote to his mother, "To me it was dreadful to have to fire on the poor devil no longer able to defend herself, but her flag was still flying."

A British officer remarked later, "It must have been brutal work."

No one out of a crew of approximately seven hundred survived. Because of the high seas and the wind blowing at thirty knots, it would have been dangerous and probably futile to lower boats to look for survivors in the darkness. Schönberg explained: "Unfortunately there could be no thought of saving the poor fellows; firstly I believed I still had an enemy before me, secondly the sea was so high that hardly a boat could have lived in it. . . ."

The British later agreed that the Germans could have done nothing to save any of the *Monmouth*'s crew who were still alive.

In the space of two hours the Royal Navy had suffered the loss of two heavy cruisers and nearly sixteen hundred men and boys.

Graf Spee had not had any contact with the enemy since 2000 and did not know that the *Good Hope* and *Monmouth* were both sunk. He hoped to use what little moonlight there was and signaled his forces: "Both

British cruisers severely damaged. One light cruiser fairly intact. Chase and attack with torpedoes."

Captain von Schönberg reported back that he had sunk the *Monmouth*.

The *Leipzig* steamed in the direction of a dull glow that Captain Haun took to be the *Good Hope*. By the time he reached her position nothing could be seen but some floating debris. Any survivors of the explosion could not have lasted for nearly an hour in the bone-chilling water. The *Dresden* sighted the *Glasgow* through the mist at 2030 but lost contact before she could get the British ship within range. Lüdecke was on the verge of torpedoing the *Leipzig,* which he recognized just in time.

As the *Glasgow* made her escape to the west, one of her officers, Sub-Lt. Harold Hickling, was on deck looking astern and saw the flash of a searchlight followed by rapid gunfire. He counted seventy-five flashes and knew this must have been the end of the *Monmouth*. "Utterly dispirited and sick at heart after such a crushing blow, I went down to my cabin to snatch a few hours' sleep before going on watch. . . . I threw myself on to my bunk, wet clothes and all. . . ."

The *Glasgow* managed to warn the *Canopus* of the danger ahead, in spite of German attempts to jam her signals. The old battleship was still two hundred miles away. Captain Grant immediately turned back with his supply ships to head toward Cape Horn and safety in the Falklands. This was all he could do because, as one of his officers remarked: "Our fighting value was very small—our two turrets were in charge of Royal Naval Reserve lieutenants who had never been in a turret before, and the only rounds we had fired . . . were two six-pounders to stop a merchant vessel." Some "citadel," some "security."

At 2300 Graf Spee gathered his ships together, and they spent the rest of the night steaming slowly northwest to search the battle scene for signs of the *Good Hope*. Daylight revealed that the area was clear of British ships. Graf Spee formed his squadron in line ahead and took the flagship slowly along the line, flying the signal. "By the grace of God a fine victory. My thanks and good wishes to the crews."

He stood on the bridge of the *Scharnhorst* in full dress uniform, and as the flagship steamed past them, he saluted the *Gneisenau, Leipzig, Nürnberg,* and *Dresden* in turn. To the crews who lined the decks to cheer their admiral, it was indeed a fine victory. They had met a Royal Navy squadron ship for ship in a "fair fight," for, according to the Germans, "whatever the disparity in gun power it was four ships against four ships." They had annihilated the two major enemy warships and forced the other two to flee for their lives. For them, "Coronel had destroyed the aura of British naval invincibility."

Their own ships had suffered negligible damage. The *Scharnhorst* was hit twice and the *Gneisenau* four times, and some of the shells had failed to explode. The only casualties were three wounded on the *Gneisenau*. For the first time in months the Germans didn't feel like hunted men. At least for the time being, the cruiser squadron was in full control of the Southeast Pacific.

Graf Spee took the *Scharnhorst, Gneisenau,* and *Nürnberg* into Valparaíso, where the squadron could be sure of an enthusiastic reception from the German colony and the pro-German Chileans. The admiral wanted to send the details of the glorious victory back to the Fatherland and spend some time with his two sons, however brief. For all he knew, this might be their last time together. He sent the *Leipzig* and *Dresden* to the west to search for the *Otranto* and *Glasgow.* If they couldn't find them, their orders were to go back to Más Afuera for coal and provisions and await Graf Spee's return from Valparaíso.

By now the two surviving ships from Cradock's ill-fated squadron were well out of reach to the south and heading for refuge in Port Stanley. Although they had got away unscathed, the men on these ships were in a grim mood. According to one officer: "Individually and collectively we were humiliated to the very depths of our beings. We hardly spoke to one another for the first twenty-four hours. We felt so bitterly ashamed of ourselves for we had let down the King. We had let down the Admiralty, we had let down England."

It was three days before the news of the disaster at Coronel was to reach London. On the day of the battle the Naval Staff were still considering Cradock's position.

In the week leading up to November 1, profound changes had taken place in the Admiralty. A new First Sea Lord had been appointed to replace Battenberg, who had just resigned. On October 30 Churchill spent several hours in the War Room with the new man, going over the dispositions of all Royal Navy squadrons and their responsibilities.

It was clear that the most vulnerable point was the South Pacific, and Churchill said of Cradock, "You don't suppose he would try to fight them without the *Canopus?*" The new First Sea Lord wasn't sure, but he was convinced that Cradock was in a very dangerous position if he ran into Graf Spee with his present forces, which were an ill-matched mixture of old and new, trained and untrained. To expect them to tackle a German squadron of modern ships manned by experienced professionals was a recipe for disaster.

A few days later the Admiralty received a telegram from the British consul in Valparaíso. It had been sent on November 1 and reported that Graf Spee's squadron had appeared off the coast of Chile that morning. The message didn't reach London until November 3. The Admiralty immediately signaled Cradock: "*Defence* has been ordered to join your flag with all dispatch. *Glasgow* should keep in touch with the enemy. You should keep in touch with *Glasgow*, concentrating the rest of your squadron including *Canopus*. It is important you should effect your junction with *Defence* at the earliest possible moment subject to keeping touch with the enemy."

The message came too late to help Cradock. As Churchill commented later, "We were already talking to the void."

Even if the Admiralty had acted in time, the *Defence* may not have made much difference to the outcome. This old cruiser, which had been the unfortunate Troubridge's flagship in the Mediterranean, later blew up with the loss of all hands after being hit by a single salvo of heavy shells at Jutland. The magazine explosion was believed to be due to a design fault. If the *Defence* had joined up with Cradock's squadron before he tackled Graf Spee, she may have only added to the heavy British toll of ships and men.

Unaware of the events off the coast of Chile, Karl von Müller was on his way to raid the Cocos Islands.

9

The *Emden* and the *Sydney*

I have the honour to request that in the name of humanity you now surrender your ship to me.

—Capt. John Glossop, HMAS *Sydney*

When Müller left Penang on October 28, he knew he had to do something soon about the prisoners from the ill-fated *Mousquet*. (Her captain, Lieutenant de Vaisseau Théroinne, had both of his legs shattered during the first onslaught. He had courageously had himself lashed to the bridge and continued to direct his ship until she sank, taking him down with her.) Out of thirty-six survivors, twenty-five were wounded, seven of them badly.

Dr. Luther and his assistant, Dr. Ludwig Schwabe, had so far had to face nothing more serious during the cruise than a case of pneumonia and a broken leg. In the first two days after Penang they had had to perform several amputations, as well as try to cope with the twenty-five new patients. They set up a large temporary sick bay on the cruiser's deck, but it was covered only with awnings as a protection against the blazing sun. Proper medical facilities were needed as soon as possible if the seriously wounded were going to survive. The only solution was to capture a merchant ship to take the prisoners ashore to a hospital.

Two of the most seriously wounded French sailors died during the night of October 28–29. Because of the tropical heat they had to be buried quickly, so the next morning they were given a burial at sea with full military honors. The engines were stopped, and all hands fell in on the quarterdeck in their best uniforms. They were joined by those French seamen who were able to walk. The captain conducted the burial service and read from a prayer book, first in German, then in French. He paid

147

solemn tribute to those who had given their lives for their country. The two bodies had been placed in sailcloth bags, sewn at both ends and weighted at the feet, each one draped with the French tricolor. As the bodies slid into the ocean an honor guard from the *Emden*'s crew fired three rifle volleys into the air. The crew dispersed glumly after the ceremony. It had brought home to them the one sure result of any sea battle.

The *Emden*'s bunkers were nearly full, so Müller spent the next few days searching the Rangoon-Singapore sea-lanes for a merchantman to take the prisoners to Sumatra. He also hoped to find Japanese ships, because he knew that Japan was now in the war and that her forces were laying siege to Tsingtao. After all the Japanese ships they had been obliged to let pass by unmolested in the past few months, it would boost the crew's morale to strike back at their new enemy.

But later that day another problem arose. The port engine began running hot because of a faulty bearing and had to be shut down. The *Emden* limped on one engine to find shelter in the St. George channel, which lies between the Nicobar Islands. The ship lay at anchor while the engine room staff replaced the bearing.

During the night another French sailor died. Next morning, before he could be buried, smoke was sighted on the western horizon. When the *Emden* approached and signaled the vessel to stop, she turned out to be the British freighter *Newburn*, a ship of three thousand tons, carrying a cargo of rock salt from England to Singapore. Her cargo manifest revealed that the salt was consigned to a German-owned company. This made her ideal for transporting the prisoners to the nearest port with a hospital. The *Newburn* was the thirty-second merchant ship the *Emden* had captured.

The captain of the *Newburn* gladly agreed to take the prisoners rather than have his ship scuttled. Müller asked him to steam as fast as he could to Sabang, where there was a well-equipped Dutch hospital. The French sailors agreed to sign a declaration to Müller that they would not fight against Germany if they were released. They thanked the *Emden*'s captain and his crew for their humane treatment.

The *Newburn* reached Sabang the next morning, but not in time to save a French lieutenant whose foot Dr. Luther had had to amputate. He died shortly after reaching the hospital. The rest of the men survived and, as far as is known, kept their word to Müller. The *Emden*'s wireless operators heard a local broadcast the next day, announcing the freighter's arrival in Sabang. They also heard a report that British and Japanese warships were searching for them in the straits area.

Müller decided to make for his first rendezvous and collect the *Buresk*. He certainly didn't want to run low on coal at a time when he might have to outrun Allied warships that would head for the Sabang district after the *Newburn* arrived in port.

The Germans had learned from the French prisoners that the *Markomannia* had been surprised by HMS *Yarmouth* as she was removing the last of the coal from the *Pontoporos* at Simeuluë. The *Yarmouth* escorted the Greek collier to Singapore, along with her armed guard of fourteen Germans who surrendered after throwing their weapons overboard. The *Markomannia* had tried to make a run for it, but she was stopped by a direct hit from one of the *Yarmouth*'s 6-inch guns. Captain Faass and the German crew members were taken prisoner, and the collier was sunk by gunfire.

Faass hadn't had a chance to mail the *Emden*'s letters home to Germany or to use his £50 to replenish the crew's cigarette and tobacco supply. More serious was the fact that the *Emden* now had only the *Buresk* and *Exford* to depend on for coal supplies.

The *Buresk* was waiting at the rendezvous forty miles west of Simeuluë, and the two ships headed south toward Padang, keeping well off the coast of Sumatra. On November 1, the same day that Graf Spee and his squadron were celebrating their victory at Coronel, a celebration of the success at Penang took place on board the *Emden*. Müller assembled the crew on the quarterdeck after church services and made a short patriotic speech. He also announced the promotions of forty officers and men who had distinguished themselves during the raid. Afterwards, he issued a rare invitation to his officers to come back to his cabin for a glass of Sekt.

For the next two days the *Emden* and *Buresk* steamed down the coast of Sumatra without seeing any ships and stopped near the Pagai Islands to transfer coal. A Dutch patrol vessel soon came alongside, and an officer came on board to determine whether the ships were inside the three-mile limit. He was a captain in the Dutch colonial army, and as the only government representative in the area, he had come to remind Müller that he had already spent his one permitted stay in Dutch waters when he had coaled at Simeuluë less than three months earlier. The Germans managed to convince him, with the aid of liberal amounts of whiskey and soda, that the ships were just outside territorial waters. When coaling was completed, the Dutch officer left in high spirits and wished Müller luck.

On November 7, after a three-day voyage, the *Emden* and *Buresk* reached the second rendezvous point north of the Cocos Islands. The *Exford* was nowhere in sight. The *Emden* spent the next twenty-four hours steaming in circles looking for the collier. She finally came into view on the morning of the eighth. Lauterbach explained that the delay in reaching the rendezvous was due to a navigation error caused by an incorrectly set chronometer.

Müller had originally planned the raid on Cocos for dawn on November 8, but the collier's failure to make the rendezvous on time forced him to postpone it for twenty-four hours. A day's delay didn't seem too important.

The Cocos, or Keeling Islands, are in a deserted stretch of the Indian Ocean, south of the equator and twenty-three hundred miles west of Darwin. In 1914 they were a vital communications link between Australia and Europe. The wireless and telegraph station was at the junction of three undersea cable systems. One led via Mauritius to South Africa and thence to Britain, one to Singapore via Batavia, and the other to Perth. The cable system from Australia to Britain was one of only two that passed exclusively through British territory. The *Nürnberg* had already cut the other one in its raid on Fanning Island on September 7, and it had taken almost two months to repair the damage. If Müller cut the cables at Cocos, it would mean another serious disruption of Britain's communications with Australia and New Zealand.

The raid would also upset shipping schedules and draw Allied warships to the area, which Müller intended to leave immediately after the raid. He planned to go next to the Horn of Africa and attack shipping on the Colombo-to-Suez route. On the evening of November 8 he ordered Lauterbach to take the *Exford* to a point off the island of Socotra, near the mouth of the Red Sea, and wait there for the *Emden*. If the cruiser failed to show up by the end of November, Lauterbach was to head for Sumatra and intern the *Exford*.

Meanwhile, the great Anzac troop convoy was finally on its way to Europe. It had originally been scheduled to sail on September 22, but because of Graf Spee's attack on Tahiti and Müller's raids in the Indian Ocean, there had been fears for its safety. This had led to one postponement after another. There had also been difficulties in assembling such a huge array of troops, artillery, horses, ammunition, and supplies, in addition to loading them aboard the transports. There were twenty thousand troops of the Australian Expeditionary Force, including cavalry and artillery, and more than eight thousand New Zealanders, as well as imperial troops and reservists. Altogether in excess of thirty thousand men and thirty-eight troopships were in the convoy.

Pressure from the Australian and New Zealand governments—especially the latter, who had threatened to resign en masse—forced the

Admiralty to detach four ships from Jerram's and Patey's squadrons to provide an escort strong enough to meet any possible attack by German cruisers—either the *Emden* or those of Graf Spee's squadron. The escort consisted of HMAS *Melbourne,* her sister ship HMAS *Sydney,* HMS *Minotaur,* and the Japanese battle cruiser *Ibuki.* Any one of these could easily take care of the *Emden* if she dared to attack the convoy.

It was not until October 16 that the convoy began to assemble at Albany, at the southwestern tip of Australia. Finally, on November 1, the eight-mile-long group of ships set out for Colombo at a speed of ten knots. After they reached Colombo, they were to head for Aden and the Suez Canal and then take part in the Dardanelles campaign. The original plan was to send the convoy to Europe via the Cape of Good Hope. This had been changed, partly because of fears that the *Karlsruhe* was cruising off West Africa. The direct route from Albany to Colombo would take the convoy within a hundred miles of the Cocos Islands.

It approached the islands on November 8 but didn't signal its presence to the cable station. That day Admiral Jerram wirelessed from Singapore to order the convoy commander to detach the *Minotaur.* The heavy cruiser was to proceed at high speed to the Cape of Good Hope to join Adm. Herbert King-Hall's squadron, which needed reinforcement because of General de Wet's Boer rebellion in South Africa. Jerram also feared that Graf Spee's victorious squadron might come to the support of German troops fighting in Southwest Africa. The loss of the *Minotaur* left just three escorts to look after thirty-eight troopships, but they were still more than enough to deal with an attack by the *Emden.*

During the night of November 8–9 the *Emden*'s operators picked up W/T traffic between the Cocos station and a British warship with the call sign "NC." Her identity was unknown to the Germans. They estimated from the signal strength that the ship was about two hundred miles away. The *Emden*'s captain concluded with amazing intuition that it was probably one of Jerram's ships being sent to South Africa to help quell the Boer revolt, which he had read about in newspapers taken from the *Newburn.* He considered postponing the attack on the cable station for yet another day, but when the signals from "NC" became fainter, he felt confident that the ship was too far away to come to the rescue. He decided to go ahead with the attack at dawn on November 9.

The *Minotaur,* or "NC," had not exchanged any signals with the convoy's escorts, which were maintaining strict W/T silence. Müller had no idea that the convoy was in the vicinity. It was now only about fifty miles away to the northeast. The *Emden* must have crossed its tracks sometime during the night.

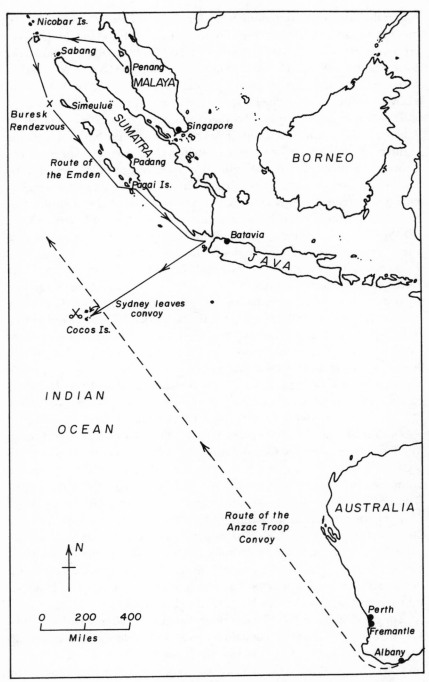

The road to Cocos

The Cocos Islands consist of two atolls, the uninhabited North Keeling Island and Direction Island, which lies about eighteen miles to its south, together with a large number of islets. William Keeling of the East India Company discovered the islands in 1609. They later passed into the hands of John Clunies-Ross, whose family was granted the islands "in perpetuity" by Queen Victoria in 1880, although they were administered by Britain. The name of the islands was later changed to Cocos by the Ross family, who developed a prosperous coconut plantation from the hundreds of thousands of palm trees that grow on the islands.

The cable and W/T station of the Eastern Extension Australasia and China Telegraph Company was on Direction Island, which has a large lagoon and a sheltered harbor at Port Refuge. The wireless station had a staff of thirty-four men, but despite their strategic importance in 1914, the islands were undefended.

The *Emden* left the *Buresk* about thirty miles north of the islands, with instructions to wait there until signaled. The cruiser approached Direction Island slowly so as to arrive at 0600, just after daybreak. The dummy fourth funnel was in place, and the ship was cleared for action when she arrived at the entrance to the lagoon.

Müller ordered the steam pinnace and two cutters to be lowered to take Lt. Comdr. Hellmuth von Mücke and his landing party into Port Refuge. The two officers and thirty-eight men were all smartly turned out in their pith helmets, with the officers in khaki uniforms and the men in white. They had been handpicked and well drilled for the attack on Cocos. The pinnace towed the two smaller boats, which carried four heavy machine guns as well as the rifles and sidearms of the officers and men.

Mücke's orders were to destroy the wireless mast and telegraph station and, if possible, to cut all the underwater cables, providing he met no armed resistance on shore. If the station was defended, he was to return immediately, and the cruiser would carry out as much destruction as possible by bombardment.

When he saw that the landing was unopposed, Müller decided it was safe to enter Port Refuge to coal. He anchored just inside the lagoon and signaled the *Buresk* to join him there. The collier did not reply, but there was an immediate response from the wireless station. "What is that code? What ship?"

The *Emden*'s operators immediately tried to jam all transmissions from the island, which by now was signaling, "Strange ship in entrance."

Unknown to the *Emden,* the station was also sending cable messages warning of a German cruiser at the island. The staff soon realized who the stranger must be and changed the cable and W/T signals to "S.O.S. *Emden* is here."

The warship with the call sign "NC" repeatedly tried to contact the island by W/T, but by then Mücke's men had sent the wireless mast crashing to the ground. On board the cruiser they estimated from the signal strength that this ship was still at least two hundred miles away. Even if she steamed at full speed it would take her about eight hours to reach Cocos. Müller was not overly concerned. He had given Mücke and his men two hours to complete their demolition work. This left plenty of time to get away before the unidentified ship could show up.

The signals were coming from the *Minotaur*. The staff at Direction Island knew she was in the area, but they didn't know about the convoy, which was still maintaining strict W/T silence. When the captain of the *Minotaur* failed to get a response from Cocos, he signaled Capt. Mortimer Silver of the *Melbourne* to tell him that an enemy ship was at the islands. Silver didn't reply because the convoy had already picked up the first alarm from the Cocos station before the Germans jammed its transmissions. At this time the tail end of the convoy was about fifty-five miles from Cocos. At full speed it would take a fast cruiser about two hours to reach the islands.

As convoy commander, Captain Silver had to decide which of the escorts to send. His first responsibility was to stay with the convoy, so the choice came down to the *Ibuki* or the *Sydney*. Captain Kato insisted that his ship be sent because she was by far the most heavily armed of the escorts. The *Ibuki* carried four 12-inch and eight 8-inch guns, and she would easily overwhelm the *Emden*. But the *Sydney* was four knots faster than the *Ibuki*, and Silver wanted to keep the big battle cruiser to protect the convoy. He decided to dispatch Capt. John Glossop with the *Sydney*, over the spirited objections of the Japanese officers. Some of them wept in frustration at Silver's decision.

The *Sydney* left the convoy at 0700 and headed southwest for Direction Island at her rated top speed of twenty-five knots. She later worked up to a remarkable twenty-seven knots.

The *Emden*'s lookouts were watching for the *Buresk*. She should have been in sight by 0900 at the latest, if she had received the recall signal. When they saw dense black smoke to the north they thought it was their collier approaching. The smoke clouds did seem too dark for the *Buresk*, which normally steamed with very little smoke, but then someone recalled that the collier had had a fire in one of her bunkers the previous day. Consequently, the lookouts were not too worried, because partly burned

HMAS *Sydney (Australian War Memorial)*

coal would be expected to give off black smoke. As the ship drew nearer, they reported that she appeared to have one funnel, which confirmed their belief that she was the *Buresk*. But as she changed direction from her head-on approach, the Germans saw to their dismay that she had four funnels and two raked masts. She could only be a British light cruiser. Since all these ships carried 6-inch guns, they knew they were in serious trouble.

The landing party had been ashore for nearly three hours. An impatient Müller had already signaled its members to speed up the demolition work. As soon as the four-funneled ship was identified as a British cruiser, he ordered a flag to be hoisted to tell Mücke to return to the *Emden* immediately. To make sure he noticed the signal, the cruiser sounded repeated blasts on her siren. But by the time the landing party reached the pier, they saw that the *Emden* was flying another flag, showing that her anchor was being raised. As they scrambled into the boats and pulled away from shore, they could see the water astern of the cruiser being churned up by the screws as she started to get under way.

Müller ordered steam up in all twelve boilers. The stokers frantically shoveled coal into the furnaces, knowing that every minute counted.

As soon as the anchor was raised, Müller gave orders for "All ahead full" and to hoist the battle flag. It was too dangerous to wait for the landing party, who were left to turn back disconsolately to Direction Island. The *Emden*'s captain had no choice but to fight. He knew that all the British light cruisers in the Far East had at least a two-knot advantage over his ship, and too many hours of daylight were left for him to have any hope of running away.

He assumed from the call sign "NC" heard earlier that his opponent was the *Newcastle*. This ship carried only two 6-inch guns, as well as ten 4-inch. If he pressed home a determined attack with his own battery of ten 4.1-inch guns and managed to score a few telling blows at the start, he might stand a chance.

Müller ordered his men, "Klar Schiff zum Gefecht (Clear the ship for action!)."

The *Emden* pulled out of the lagoon just after 0930 and headed north as fast as she could go. This was less than her rated twenty-three knots because the stokers were a long way from raising full steam in all boilers.

The *Sydney* had approached the islands obliquely in a southwesterly direction because Captain Glossop couldn't tell where the German ship had anchored or which direction she might take. As soon as the *Emden* came into view around Direction Island, he ordered a ninety-degree turn to starboard. The turn brought the *Sydney* onto a parallel course with the German cruiser at a distance of about ten thousand yards.

This was greater than the supposed maximum range of the *Emden*'s guns, but Müller gave the order to Lieutenant Gaede at 0940 to open fire with the starboard battery. Amazingly, the Germans were able to score several direct hits with their third salvo, in spite of the fact that their best gun-layers had been sent ashore with the landing party as a reward for their shooting at Penang. One of the first hits knocked out the *Sydney*'s range finder. This may explain why the Australian cruiser failed to obtain a single hit on the *Emden* with her first eight salvoes.

When the *Sydney* opened fire, the Germans could tell from the near misses that the shell splashes were tall and uniform. This could only mean that their enemy was an all 6-inch gun ship. They realized it couldn't be the *Newcastle* they were up against but must be one of the newer and more heavily armed ships of the *Chatham* or *Weymouth* classes, which mounted eight 6-inch guns. Even though Müller didn't discover his opponent's identity until after the battle, he must have known at this stage that his luck had finally run out.

The *Emden* continued to score hits on the *Sydney*, putting one gun out of commission and starting a fire in an ammunition storage area. Only the prompt action of crew members who picked up burning shell casings with their bare hands and dumped them into a tub of water saved the *Sydney* from a serious and probably fatal magazine explosion.

But by 1000 the *Sydney* had found the range. One of her first hits on the *Emden* destroyed the W/T cabin, killing or seriously wounding all the operators. Another shell put one of the forward turrets out of action and annihilated its gun crew. These were the first casualties ever suffered by the *Emden,* but they would not be the last.

Müller made a turn to starboard in an attempt to close the gap between the two ships. The most effective range of his 4.1-inch guns was about eight thousand yards. Even at that range his shells were not likely to pierce the *Sydney*'s two-inch armored belt. With his superior speed, Glossop managed to prevent the gap from closing. Hits from his 6-inch shells began to wreak severe damage on the *Emden.*

By 1020 her electrical system had been knocked out, and the steering gear was out of action. The ship had to be steered by her engines. Orders were sent down to the engine room by voice pipe because the engine room telegraph was smashed.

Lieutenant Gaede had to give his commands to the gun crews by voice pipe as well. Not surprisingly, the *Emden*'s fire became ragged. Things grew even worse when the ammunition hoists were damaged, and all shells and charges had to be brought up from the magazine by hand. After her first few successful salvoes, the *Emden* inflicted no serious damage on the *Sydney.*

The *Emden* was hit on the forward funnel. It toppled across the deck because the funnel stays had been disconnected to prepare for coaling, and there had been no time to reattach them before leaving harbor. The loss of the funnel caused spreading clouds of smoke that obscured the gunners' sighting of their target. At one stage the smoke was so dense that the men of the *Sydney* lost sight of the German ship and began to cheer, thinking they had sunk her.

The loss of the funnel also prevented proper updraft to the boilers. The *Emden*'s speed dropped to less than twenty knots. By this time the *Sydney* had reached twenty-seven knots, and Glossop was easily able to outmaneuver Müller.

Throughout the *Emden* lay dead and dying. The pitiful moans and cries for help from the wounded could be heard by their shipmates. Nothing could be done for them because every available hand was needed to run the ship and man the guns. At one time the complement of the *Emden* had swelled to almost four hundred with the volunteer reservists who had joined the ship at Tsingtao and Pagan. But now the crew had shrunk to 314 because of Mücke's landing party and the prize crews having been sent to various tenders. Only Dr. Luther and his assistant had any time to spare for the wounded.

Müller knew that his one chance was to torpedo the *Sydney.* He ordered Lieutenant Witthoeft to ready the starboard tube, and he tried to maneuver closer to the enemy ship. Captain Glossop was alert to the danger of a torpedo attack and maintained a zigzag course. With his greater speed he was able to keep the distance between the two ships from falling below seven thousand yards, knowing that German torpedoes were not effective at this range.

During the next half hour the *Sydney* almost literally shot the German cruiser to pieces. One by one the *Emden*'s guns fell silent, their crews dead or dying. Glossop closed the range to three thousand yards and tried a torpedo attack himself, but he missed. No matter how Müller tried to twist and turn, the *Sydney* continued to pour in a deadly hail of shells. After the battle it was estimated that she had scored at least a hundred direct hits on the German cruiser.

By 1100 the *Emden* was a pitiful sight. Her decks were a shambles of tangled equipment, burning debris, and gaping holes. All three funnels were down, lying at crazy angles on top of the other wreckage. The main mast had suffered a direct hit and come crashing down, killing Lieutenant von Guérard and a signalman who had been in the crow's nest spotting the fall of shot for Lieutenant Gaede, who by now was near death himself from shrapnel wounds. Lieutenant von Hohenzollern barely managed to extricate himself and his men from the damaged torpedo flat before they were asphyxiated by smoke and picric acid fumes from the lyddite shells. He later went aft to look for his friend Levetzow, who had been directing the fire of the after gun turrets. Fires from exploding ammunition had made the quarterdeck red hot in places. He was able to recognize his friend among the charred corpses only by the shape of his head and by his metal lieutenant's insignia, which hadn't yet melted.

With all his guns out of action and several holes below the waterline, Müller decided to run the ship aground before she sank. If the *Emden* went down, she would take with her all of the wounded and probably all but the fittest of the rest of the crew. Even with both engines full ahead, the *Emden* could manage merely nineteen knots, and Müller headed her for North Keeling Island, about six miles away. Steering was difficult because shouted voice commands had to be used to control the speed of each engine. As they drew near the island, Müller aimed the ship toward a small gap in the reefs.

As soon as Glossop realized what the Germans were planning, he moved in to try to cut them off. He kept up a withering barrage, hoping to sink the *Emden* before she could be beached. But as the two ships closed, he was forced to give way in case Müller tried a last desperate torpedo attack or made a sharp turn to ram him.

At 1115, barely an hour and a half after the battle had begun, Müller

ordered all hands on deck. He stopped the engines just before the battered *Emden* ran into the gap in the coral reef. Then he sent men below
to put both engines full ahead to drive the ship farther onto the reefs and
ordered them to open the sea-cocks in the after part of the ship. The
Emden settled firmly onto the reef. The fires in the boilers were drawn
and the magazines were flooded.

The *Sydney* kept firing at the wreck for five minutes after the *Emden*
ran aground, then she turned away and headed north.

Conditions on board the beached cruiser were appalling. Incinerated
and mangled bodies were strewn all over the ship. The groans of the
wounded and their pitiful cries for water could be heard everywhere.
There was no water. Some of the storage tanks had been holed, and the
rest were below decks under seawater. All that could be done was to carry
the badly wounded to the forecastle, which was less damaged than the
midships or the quarterdeck, where fires were still raging out of control.
Dr. Luther and Dr. Schwabe, who miraculously were both unharmed,
gave morphine to the most seriously wounded and the dying. A rough
count showed that there were about forty-five wounded and well over a
hundred dead. Among the dead were the three Chinese civilians, their
bodies found at their workplace in the laundry flat.

After the *Sydney* left North Keeling, Müller gave orders to destroy all
the code and signal books. He sent those men who were not wounded to
take the breech blocks from the guns and throw them overboard, to
smash the range finders and gunsights, and to destroy anything else that
might be useful to the enemy.

The few remaining lifeboats either had been burned or were too damaged to float, so he gave permission to those who were good swimmers to
head for the beach, which was about a hundred yards away. But few of them
made it because of the strong surf breaking over the reef. Most of those
who tried to reach shore were drowned or badly injured after being battered against the reef. Fortunately, any sharks that had been in the normally infested waters had been scared off by the shells exploding in the water.

One of those who did make it to shore was Dr. Schwabe, but he suffered severe head injuries on the reef. The men on the cruiser tried to get
a rope to the men who had made it safely to the beach to act as a lifeline
to get more men off the ship. They tried everything: the line-throwing
gun, floating empty ammunition crates, and even lines tied to captured
seabirds. All their attempts failed. Each time, the rope was severed by the
sharp edges of the coral reef.

At this point the tropical sun was at its highest. Because all the awnings
had been stowed below in now-flooded compartments, little could be

done to make the wounded more comfortable except to beat off the huge seabirds that swooped to peck at them. Even those who hadn't been wounded were suffering terribly from the heat and thirst.

The *Sydney* had left the wreck to chase the *Buresk,* which had been waiting five miles off the islands to watch the outcome of the battle. The collier had received the *Emden*'s recall signal at 0630 that morning but had not been able to reply because of a problem with her wireless transmitter. Lieutenant Commander Klöpper, who was in command of the collier, brought her to within sight of the islands by 0830. He saw the same dense smoke clouds that the *Emden*'s lookouts had sighted. Once he identified the ship as a British cruiser, he turned around and steamed very slowly to the north. He saw the *Emden* come out of Port Refuge to meet the *Sydney,* but there was nothing he could do except wait off North Keeling Island and watch until the battle was decided. When he saw the *Emden* being driven onto the reefs, he tried to make a run for it.

Captain Glossop had been aware of the collier's presence throughout the battle and even had one of his guns trained on her. It didn't take long for the *Sydney* to catch the fleeing *Buresk.* Glossop fired a shot across her bow and signaled her to stop. Klöpper obeyed, but by the time a boarding party arrived, he had opened the sea-cocks and smashed the Kingston valves so badly that the collier and her precious cargo of five thousand tons of coal couldn't be saved. The *Buresk*'s crew took to the lifeboats. When Glossop found the ship was sinking, he fired two shells into her to speed up the process. He towed Klöpper and his men back to North Keeling Island in the *Buresk*'s boats.

When the *Sydney* arrived back at the reef, it was obvious that the *Emden* was finished as a fighting ship, even though her flag was still flying at the after masthead. Glossop hoisted a signal flag. "Will you surrender?"

The *Emden* replied in Morse code, using her signal lamp. "What signal? No signal-book."

The *Sydney* repeated her request by wireless, also in Morse code. "Do you surrender? Have you received my signal?"

There was no reply because the *Emden*'s W/T equipment had been put out of action by a direct hit.

It is hard to understand the actions of both captains at this point. Even without a signal book, Müller must surely have realized the enemy was asking him whether he intended to keep on fighting. He may have overlooked the fact that his battle flag was still flying, which is quite possible with all the other problems he had on his mind, but it is difficult to think of what else the Australian ship could have been signaling. A few minutes later, when there was still no reply from the German ship or any attempt to haul down her flag, Glossop gave the order to open fire.

At four thousand yards it was almost point-blank range. Several salvoes hit the helpless wreck. The shells killed or wounded at least twenty more of the *Emden*'s crew. The Germans were astonished and angry at this fresh onslaught. Müller told those who were fit to jump over the lee side to protect themselves. Many of them did and clung to spars and floating wreckage. At this point the Germans must have realized their battle flag was still flying and sent a seaman up the mast to haul it down. They hoisted a white flag from what was left of the bridge. Only then did the *Sydney* cease fire.

What Captain Glossop hoped to accomplish by shelling an apparently disarmed ship is not clear. The *Emden* had not fired a gun since ten minutes before she ran aground, and she was obviously in no position to launch a torpedo attack. It may be that the Germans from the *Buresk* had told Glossop that Müller would never surrender and that the cautious Glossop was afraid of some surprise attack if he came close enough to take off survivors. The German captain had a reputation for daring and unexpected actions.

Whatever Glossop's reason for opening fire instead of simply waiting or sending a boat across under a white flag, it is plain that he was concerned at finding the German flag still flying when he returned. This concern shows in a remarkable letter he wrote to Müller.

> HMAS *Sydney*
> At sea
> 9th November 1914
>
> Sir,
>
> I have the honour to request that in the name of humanity you now surrender your ship to me. In order to show how much I appreciate your gallantry, I will recapitulate the position.
>
> (1) You are ashore, three funnels and one mast down and most guns disabled,
>
> (2) You cannot leave the island, and my ship is intact.
>
> In the event of your surrendering in which I venture to remind you is no disgrace but rather your misfortune, I will endeavour to do all I can for your sick and wounded and take them to a hospital.
>
> I have the honour to be,
>
> > Sir,
> > Your obedient servant,
> >
> > John A. Glossop
> > Captain

The letter was addressed to "Captain, His Imperial German Majesty's Ship "*Emden*." Although it was dated November 9, for some reason it was not sent to Müller that day. After Glossop gave the order to cease fire, however, he did send a message with Lieutenant Klöpper, who went across to the wreck with several seamen from the *Buresk* in one of her boats. They also took some welcome medical supplies and bandages. The *Emden*'s crew learned from these men who their nemesis had been. Glossop's message to Müller stated only that the *Sydney* was going to Direction Island to capture the German landing party and that she would return to the *Emden* the following day.

At 0630 on the morning of the battle, Mücke had assembled his men on the quarterdeck of the *Emden* and said to Müller, "Beg to report, landing party numbering three officers, six petty officers and forty-one men disembarking." (It was to be six months before the landing party officially reported again, nine thousand miles away from the Cocos Islands.)

The first thing they did when they arrived on shore was to occupy the cable and wireless station. The lone wireless operator on duty was still sending out messages warning of the *Emden*'s appearance in the harbor. His last transmission was, "They are entering the door."

The German sailors were armed with rifles and bayonets and their officers with Mauser pistols. The station manager, Mr. D.A.G. de H. Farrant, and his staff could do nothing to stop them. Their only weapons were a few twelve-bore shotguns against fifty rifles. The landing party also had four heavy machine guns, which they had mounted on shore while most of the staff were still in bed.

The Germans rounded up the staff and confiscated their weapons, and they were kept under armed guard until Mücke's men had finished their demolition work. All the equipment in the wireless station was smashed, including a seismograph that a sailor mistook for a transmitter. Generally, though, the Germans were quite considerate. They left the station's ice machine and water-condensing equipment intact, at the request of the staff. When they drilled holes for explosives at the base of the wireless mast, they arranged them so that the mast fell away from the island's tennis courts. The staff had begged that these be spared.

The landing party had trouble with the undersea cables. They finally managed to haul two of them out of the water and cut them with axes after failing to sever them with knives and saws. One of these was the cable to Perth; the other was merely a spare cable end that ran only a hundred yards out to sea. The station staff, who accepted the landing with good-natured resignation, watched with quiet amusement while the

The Cocos cable station after Mücke's visit *(Australian War Memorial)*

Germans struggled to cut it. They even provided Mücke's men with mugs of tea and slices of bread and jam.

They also had news for their captors, some of it good, some bad. They had just heard a Reuter's report that the Kaiser had awarded the Iron Cross, First and Second Class, to Müller, and the Iron Cross, Second Class, to all the *Emden*'s officers. Another fifty of these medals were to be distributed among the crew at the discretion of the captain. At this stage of the war the prestige of the Iron Cross, Second Class, had not yet been debased, and Mücke and his men were delighted. (Later in the war, awarding Iron Crosses became so widespread that some Austrians joked that the only way to avoid one was by committing suicide.)

The bad news was that the *Emden*'s base at Tsingtao had fallen to the Japanese two days previously, after a siege that had lasted seven weeks. The Germans were naturally saddened to hear this because of all the good times they had spent there in the years before the war. More important, it meant that Graf Spee's cruisers no longer had any base in the Pacific. Their only hope of survival was to get back to Germany, and the men of the landing party knew this was a slim hope.

Mücke's men collected all the wireless and cable reports, signal books, and flags they could find. Their work had not been finished by 0930, although they had already been signaled by Müller to hurry up. When the

Emden sounded her siren to recall them, Mücke quickly rounded up his men and marched them to the jetty where they loaded everything into the boats. The telegraph company staff came down to see them off. Cheerful farewells were shouted back and forth as the pinnace pulled away from shore towing the two cutters. It soon became clear that the steam pinnace would never catch up with the cruiser, which was already starting to move from her anchorage. Mücke and his men had no choice but to turn back to Port Refuge.

At first the landing party thought the *Emden* had seen a freighter and was off to capture her, but as soon as they heard the cruiser fire her first broadside, they knew she must be up against another warship. After the *Emden* moved out of sight, Mücke climbed onto the roof of the wireless station to watch the battle. When the *Emden* scored the first hits, he thought his shipmates might gain the upper hand. But when the *Sydney* found the range, and Mücke saw fires blazing on the *Emden*, he knew it was unlikely. The best he could hope for was that his ship might be able to escape to Sumatra in badly damaged condition.

When the landing party entered the harbor that morning, they had noticed a small white sailing vessel at anchor in the lagoon. Mücke planned to sink her before he left and had even gone so far as to detail a party to take explosive charges to the ship. Luckily, he decided to postpone sinking her until after he had dealt with the wireless station. The ship was the one-hundred-ton schooner *Ayesha,* owned by the Ross family. At one time she had been used to transport copra to Sumatra and to bring back supplies and provisions. Since the establishment of a regular steamship service to the islands every three months, the *Ayesha* had lain idle.

After he saw that the *Emden* was in serious trouble, Mücke changed his mind about destroying the schooner and decided to commandeer her instead. He wanted to try to escape before an Allied warship showed up. He knew this was inevitable, whatever the outcome of the battle. With but four heavy machine guns and a few rifles to defend the island, his only alternatives were to die a hero's death or surrender and spend boring months in a prisoner of war camp.

When he told the people on Direction Island what he had in mind, they did everything they could to talk him out of it. They claimed the *Ayesha* was old and unseaworthy, with defective pumps, and that she had been rotting in the harbor for years. Mücke made a trip out to the schooner to see for himself. Her condition seemed quite sound to him. The pumps were not working properly, but he was confident that his men could repair them.

The station staff on Direction Island pose beneath the German war flag. (*Wilhelm Heyne Verlag*)

The few people he found on board were Capt. J. Partridge, a seaman, and the two sons of the island's owner, Edmund and Cosmo Clunies-Ross, who were all taken off the ship and rowed back to shore. When Mücke learned from the Ross brothers that the vessel was just eight years old, his mind was made up. As he left the *Ayesha,* Captain Partridge told Mücke, "I wish you a safe journey, but her hull is rotten."

Mücke commandeered half of the island's provisions and fresh water supply and ordered his men to load everything into the pinnace and cutters. This would give them enough water for four weeks and food for eight. He took down the address of the telegraph company's office in Singapore and promised Mr. Farrant he would contact them at the first opportunity to tell them that more provisions were needed on Direction Island.

It was late afternoon by the time everything had been loaded into the boats. The Germans wanted to get through the opening in the reefs before it grew dark. There were no up-to-date charts or instruments on board the schooner, and it would be difficult enough to get away from the Cocos Islands, even in daylight.

The station staff came down to the jetty to take photographs and offer last-minute advice, good wishes, and tobacco. As the Germans cast off, the staff gave them three rousing cheers, then they watched as the pinnace towed the *Ayesha* slowly toward the entrance to the lagoon. As darkness began to fall the *Ayesha*'s sails were raised and she started to pick up speed. The *Sydney* was still at North Keeling Island, eighteen miles away.

Mücke set a course due west until the islands were out of sight (he had told the Australians he intended to head for German East Africa), then changed direction to northeast. His plan was to head for Padang, more than seven hundred miles away. He had not seen the *Emden* being driven onto the reefs and still hoped she might escape, even though badly damaged. If she did, he thought that Müller would probably make for Sumatra.

The German flag was raised on the schooner's foremast, and the little ship, which had been named after the prophet Mohammed's favorite wife, now became the newest and smallest addition to the Kaiser's fleet, Seine Majestäts Schiff *Ayesha*.

When she left the wreck of the *Emden* at 1630, the *Sydney* had to stop twice to pick up German sailors who had jumped off the cruiser and were keeping themselves afloat with pieces of wreckage. By the time she reached Direction Island it was too dark to put men ashore. Glossop decided to lay off the mouth of the lagoon until morning. There didn't seem to be any great urgency in dealing with the landing party or checking on the condition of the cable station.

The landing party set out from Port Refuge to board the *Ayesha*. (*Wilhelm Heyne Verlag*)

He sent an armed landing party ashore on the morning of November 10, with one of the *Emden*'s crew to act as interpreter. The station manager told them the birds had flown. When Glossop heard this, he "borrowed a Doctor [Dr. Ollerhead] and two assistants and proceeded as fast as possible to *Emden*'s assistance," according to his official report.

This cannot be quite correct because the *Emden* was just eighteen miles away, yet the *Sydney* didn't return to the wreck until 1300, according to Lieutenant von Hohenzollern. Lt. C. R. Garsia of the *Sydney* wrote that his ship arrived back at North Keeling just after 1030, but another British report gave the time as about noon. Since by all reports it became dark only four hours after the *Sydney* reached the wreck, it seems that Hohenzollern's recollection is the most accurate.

It is likely that Captain Glossop spent a good part of the morning in a futile search around the islands for signs of the *Ayesha* before he went back to the wreck. With a twelve-hour start, Mücke and his men were well out of reach of the *Sydney,* even in a slow sailing ship. In any case, Glossop had no idea which direction they had finally taken.

When the *Sydney* did arrive back at North Keeling, Lieutenant Garsia went over to the *Emden* in a cutter under a white flag. He told Müller that his men would be taken off the wreck and that the wounded would be given all possible medical attention, on condition that he gave his word that his crew would not interfere in any way with the operation of the *Sydney.* It is not certain whether Garsia also handed Müller his captain's remarkable letter asking the German to surrender. Neither Glossop nor Müller mentions this in their official reports.

In any event, the letter was irrelevant by this time. Müller had no choice but to agree to Glossop's conditions. His men had spent a miserable night on the wreck. A brief rainfall had brought some relief to the thirst of the wounded, but most of the crew were badly in need of medical attention, whether wounded or not. They were all thirsty and ravenous. They had not had a proper meal for more than thirty-six hours. Some of them were suffering from severe exhaustion.

After he went on board, Lieutenant Garsia commented, "She was nothing but a shambles and the whole thing was most shocking." Glossop also made a visit to the *Emden,* and in his official report he called the conditions on board "indescribable." He was more expansive in his later comments to a war correspondent. "Everybody on board was demented—that's all you could call it, just fairly demented—by shock, fumes and the roar of shells bursting among them. . . . One of our shells had landed behind a gun shield, and had blown the whole gun-crew into pulp. You couldn't even tell how many men there had been."

The crew of the *Sydney* spent four hours taking the wounded off the *Emden*. The surf pounding on the reefs made it a slow business to handle the injured men as gently as possible as they were passed down to the plunging and tossing boats. By the time they had finished, it was too dark to go ashore for the rest of the survivors. The *Sydney's* decks were crowded with casualties laid on makeshift cots. Dr. Ollerhead and his assistants worked through the night to help the *Sydney's* medical officers carry out operations on the most seriously wounded and bandage and care for the rest. Dr. Luther was so traumatized by his experiences that he couldn't offer them any help. The German sailors were given water, and then food, which they ate voraciously. Later on they were provided with clean clothes, soap, and tobacco.

Captain von Müller was the last to leave his ship. While he waited to be taken off, he surreptitiously ordered Fikentscher to go below decks and set fires to destroy anything useful that remained intact. Glossop sent over the captain's gig with several officers on board to escort Müller from his ship with full honors, even though he had requested that he be given no special treatment. In an unusual gesture, his captors allowed the German to keep his officer's sword.

The following morning at first light Glossop sent men across to the island to rescue those of the *Emden's* crew who had made it to shore. Several of them had died during the night, including Dr. Schwabe. Only the living were taken back to the *Sydney*. All of the *Emden's* dead were left where they were, whether on the wreck or on the beach. Two weeks later, the sloop HMS *Cadmus* was assigned the grisly task of recovering the decomposing bodies and giving them a proper burial. For now, the need was to get the wounded to a hospital as quickly as possible. After Glossop had taken Dr. Ollerhead and his helpers back to Direction Island, he set out at full speed to catch up with the convoy, which was then about six hundred miles to the north.

Captain Glossop showed great sensitivity by telegraphing Colombo to request that there be no cheering or any of the traditional celebrations when the victorious *Sydney* arrived in the harbor with her prisoners. This was in deference to the large number of the Germans' shipmates who had been killed or wounded at Cocos. Lieutenant Garsia wrote, "It quite shook them when they found out that the captain had asked that there be no cheering on entering Colombo, but we certainly did not want cheering with rows of badly wounded men laid out in cots on the quarterdeck."

Of the *Emden's* crew, 131 officers and men had been killed during the battle and 65 wounded. Four of the wounded later died of their injuries.

The *Emden*'s survivors wait on the blackened afterdeck for the first of the *Sydney*'s boats. *(Wilhelm Heyne Verlag)*

This meant that nearly two out of every three crew members were dead or wounded.

By contrast, the *Sydney* suffered extremely light casualties. Only three men were killed and eight wounded out of a crew of four hundred. All of these casualties occurred during the first few minutes of the battle when the *Emden*'s early salvoes found their mark. The Sydney had several shell holes in her upper works, but at first glance it was hard to tell that she had been in action, even though she had received sixteen direct hits from the *Emden*'s guns.

When news of the Battle of the Cocos Islands reached Britain, it was received with mixed feelings. Naturally, there was great satisfaction and pride in naval circles at the result, especially after Coronel. There was palpable relief in both Whitehall and in shipping offices that one of these "pests" had finally been "extirpated," to use Churchill's words. Lloyd's immediately cut its premiums in half. But there was also a tinge of sadness that the *Emden*'s adventure had come to such a bloody end. The British press mourned the loss of the gallant little cruiser and celebrated Müller's survival.

The editorial pages of the major London newspapers published glow-

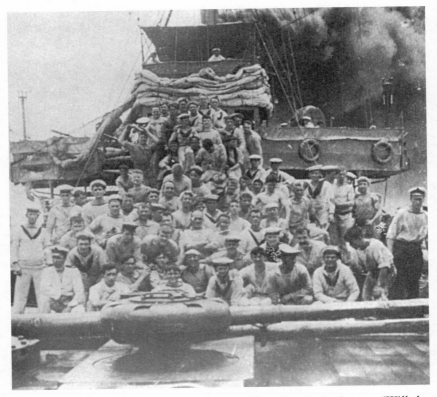

Crew members pose on the *Sydney's* forecastle after their victory. (*Wilhelm Heyne Verlag*)

ing tributes to the *Emden's* captain: he had "played the game . . . and . . . played it well." The *Daily Chronicle* wrote: "The Captain proved himself to be not only a brave and capable officer, but to possess chivalry in his treatment of the crews and passengers of captured ships. We can all take our hats off to the Captain."

Churchill said of him, "He did his duty," and personally ordered that full honors of war be accorded to Müller and his men after they were taken prisoner.

The Australians received the news with more unalloyed pleasure and pride, especially the citizens of Sydney. Of all the Allied ships that had hunted the *Emden,* it was their cruiser that had accomplished the destruction of this dangerous raider. Even though its captain and many of the officers and men were from the Royal Navy, most of the crew were Australians. The victory gave a tremendous boost to the morale and esprit de corps of the young Royal Australian Navy.

So ended the saga of the *Emden*. In three months she had steamed thirty thousand-odd miles and had intercepted thirty-two Allied and neutral merchant ships. She had sunk eighteen British ships with a total displacement of eighty thousand tons and almost as great a tonnage of cargo. She had captured three colliers with their valuable loads and had seized two other merchantmen and stripped them of their stores before releasing them to take prisoners ashore. Yet another captured vessel had been converted into an armed merchant cruiser.

All this had been achieved with no loss of life among the crews of unarmed merchant ships, who had been treated considerately and humanely. This was in stark contrast to what was to happen in the later stages of the war when the ruthless all-out U-boat campaign began.

The *Emden* had also carried out two daring raids on Allied seaports, inflicting considerable damage in one and sinking a cruiser and a destroyer in the other. All these losses in materiel are difficult to estimate in value and have been put at anywhere from £2 million to £12 million. As a Norwegian newspaper put it, "No one would have believed that a single cruiser could do so much damage in a modern war. . . ."

The *Emden* had also made a great impact of a less tangible kind. Shipping schedules in the Indian Ocean were disrupted; many vessels loaded with vital war supplies sat in harbors for long periods of time; sailings of troopships were frequently postponed. The most significant area where the *Emden* made an impact on the Allies' war effort was in the number of warships she diverted from other duties. The amount of time and energy expended by the Allies in a fruitless search for the *Emden* was enormous. At one time or another, no less than thirty-eight ships from five navies were occupied in trying to track down the German cruiser. Ironically, in the end it was almost by pure chance that one of them caught her.

Probably the greatest service that Karl von Müller performed for his country was also an intangible one. His combination of daring and sportsmanlike conduct, and his considerate and humane treatment of prisoners, led to his being called "the last gentleman-of-war." This was invaluable to the Germans as propaganda, for the German army had undoubtedly been guilty of excesses and atrocities during their march through Belgium. They had burned the city of Louvain and its ancient library, and they shot hundreds—if not thousands—of civilians in reprisal for the raids of the *francs-tireurs*. Their actions had given rise to an unenviable reputation in some countries and downright hatred of Germans in others. This, in turn, had helped to lend credence to lurid tales of German soldiers bayonetting newborn babies and raping nuns.

Germany was only too glad to have Müller's shining example to offset the stereotyping of its military as a horde of barbaric huns. Müller and his men showed the world that these were not universal German traits and led many people to doubt the horror stories they had heard. A French naval officer who was at Penang on October 28 told a war correspondent just one day after the raid that had cost so many of his countrymen their lives, "[H]e has made me, for one, feel extremely doubtful whether the much talked of German 'atrocities' are true, except where the exigencies of war have made them unavoidable."

The Kaiser later bestowed on Müller Germany's highest award for gallantry, the "Pour le Mérite." No recipient deserved it more.

The sinking of the *Emden* gave the Royal Navy a much needed boost in morale, coming on the heels of the humiliating defeat at Coronel. Now it could concentrate on the Graf Spee squadron and try to avenge Cradock and his men.

10

The Pursuit of Graf Spee

Tortoises were apportioned to **catch hares. Millions of tortoises can't catch a**
hare! *The Almighty arranged the greyhound to catch the hare. . . .*

—Adm. Sir John Fisher, First Sea Lord

O n the day that the first news of Coronel reached the Admiralty,
the initial reaction was shocked disbelief. The British consul-
general in Valparaíso sent a report that arrived in London on
November 4, but because the details came entirely from German sources,
it was not accepted as accurate. German accounts of the battle had made
no mention whatever of the *Canopus,* and Churchill could not believe
that Cradock had gone into action without his "citadel."

Nonetheless, the Admiralty realized that something had gone tragically
wrong off the coast of Chile. Two days later, Whitehall's worst fears were
confirmed.

The fleeing *Glasgow* reached the eastern end of the Strait of Magellan on
November 6. She caught up with the lumbering *Canopus* and learned that
the *Otranto* had passed safely by her into the Atlantic. Now that he was clear
of interference from the mountains of southern Chile, Captain Luce was able
to send a brief but sufficiently detailed message to London via the Falklands
wireless station. It removed all doubts about the extent of the fiasco.

Coronel was the first defeat suffered by a Royal Navy squadron in
more than a hundred years, and the way it had come about made it, in
Churchill's words, "the saddest naval action of the entire war."

The news only added to the turmoil that had been going on in the
Admiralty for the past week. Admiral Battenberg had resigned as First Sea
Lord, largely as a result of a campaign of vicious and unfounded attacks

173

on his loyalty carried out by the popular press. There was also a stream of letters to the editors from citizens disillusioned by setbacks the Royal Navy had already suffered in European waters. Both the editors and the letter writers held Battenberg responsible.

His German ancestry, titles, property, and even his accent made him an obvious target for such jingoistic publications as the weekly *John Bull*. Its editor, Horatio Bottomley, was looking for a scapegoat for the navy's conspicuous lack of success up to this point in the war and pilloried Battenberg mercilessly. The First Sea Lord's wife was, after all, the sister-in-law of Prince Heinrich of Prussia, the Kaiser's brother and grand admiral in the German navy.

This was evidence enough for the superpatriot Bottomley. As he put it in his magazine on October 24: "Blood is said to be thicker than water; and we doubt whether all the water in the North Sea could obliterate the blood-ties between the Battenbergs and the Hohenzollerns when it comes to a question of a life and death struggle between Germany and ourselves."

Battenberg was strongly supported by editorials in the more reputable London papers. King George V publicly proclaimed, "There is no more loyal man in the country," but it was generally recognized in government circles that it would bolster public confidence in the navy if Battenberg left the Admiralty.

The scurrilous attacks in the press finally became too much for him to bear. He wrote Churchill: "I beg of you to release me. I am on the verge of breaking down & I cannot use my brain for anything."

On top of his heavy responsibilities as First Sea Lord, Battenberg was under the daily strain of dealing with the much younger and more dynamic Churchill, who, nonetheless, as Battenberg said, "up to the end stood by me." On October 28 he sent in his resignation, writing: "I have lately been driven to the painful conclusion that at this juncture my birth and parentage have the effect of impairing . . . my usefulness to the Board of Admiralty. I feel it my duty to resign."

It was a sad end to a distinguished career. Although he later gave up his German titles on the advice of his cousin King George V, who appointed him Marquess of Milford Haven, and he changed the family name to Mountbatten, Battenberg died a broken and all but forgotten man in 1921. He was not even invited to the official victory celebrations when the German fleet surrendered at the end of the war.

Churchill knew the resignation had been inevitable and accepted it with a mixture of regret and relief: personal regret for the unpleasant circumstances that had caused it, relief that he would now be able to appoint a more forceful and effective partner in the Admiralty. He turned to Admiral of the Fleet Sir John Arbuthnot Fisher, the "living legend" who had already been First Sea Lord for six years until he was forced out of office in 1910.

Churchill achieved Fisher's reappointment in spite of serious reservations in both the Admiralty and the cabinet. Fisher had made many enemies because of his arrogant and overbearing personality. The appointment was made over the strong objections of the king, who neither liked nor trusted Fisher and did everything within his limited power to block it. Churchill threatened to resign if he did not get Fisher. Prime Minister Herbert Asquith finally prevailed upon the king to sign the appointment, which he did "with some reluctance and misgivings."

Fisher, universally known as "Jacky," was sometimes referred to by his admirers as "the old Malay" and by his enemies as "the Mulatto" because of his swarthy complexion and somewhat oriental features. He was a truly remarkable figure and in every way Britain's counterpart to Admiral von Tirpitz in terms of naval development.

In the years before the war, Fisher had drastically reformed and modernized a navy long convinced of its ineffable superiority over all others. He took the Royal Navy out of the dangerous state of complacent lethargy it had sunk into in the last half of the nineteenth century. Largely due to Fisher's untiring and ruthless efforts, Britain had (despite some remaining flaws) the finest fleet in the world in 1914.

Although he was seventy-three years of age—a "septuagenarian seadog" as Asquith called him—Fisher was physically fit and still brimming with energy and ideas. He soon made the Admiralty "quiver like one of his great ships at its highest speed." Churchill described him as "a veritable dynamo."

The thirty-nine-year-old First Lord was confident that they could work well together in spite of their differences in age and experience. Although sparks would undoubtedly fly from time to time, they could get things done. And indeed they did.

Within six hours of the initial report of Cradock's defeat, Churchill and Fisher had worked out a detailed plan to deal with Graf Spee once and for all.

Churchill at first proposed sending one of the new battle cruisers, which alone would be capable of destroying both the *Scharnhorst* and *Gneisenau* with her eight 12-inch guns. But, as he wrote: "I found Lord Fisher in a bolder mood. He would take two of these powerful ships [to deal with Graf Spee's squadron]." What Fisher had in mind was not merely victory but complete annihilation.

Churchill and Fisher leaving Whitehall *(Radio Times Hulton Picture Library)*

Since Coronel the German squadron had become more than a distant menace to troop convoys. It was now the most serious challenge to Britain's command of the far seas. Although Graf Spee had not yet attacked any merchant ships, his arrival off the coast of South America all but paralyzed the important British trade with Peru and Chile. If he entered the Atlantic, the interruption of trade with the Argentines would be far more damaging.

To Fisher, it was intolerable that the nation with the most powerful navy in the world couldn't guarantee the safety of its merchant fleet against the threat of a small group of German cruisers. He proposed strengthening Stoddart's squadron to protect the vital Argentine trade routes until the battle cruisers were ready to begin their search for Graf Spee, and he arranged for yet another battle cruiser to go to the Caribbean in case Graf Spee tried to use the Panama Canal route into the Atlantic.

On November 4, the day that the first report of Coronel reached the Admiralty, the signals began to fly. The first, marked "Urgent," went to Stoddart. "*Carnarvon, Cornwall* should join *Defence* off Montevideo. *Canopus, Glasgow, Otranto* have been ordered, if possible, to join you there. *Kent* from Sierra Leone has also been ordered to join your flag via Abrolhos. . . . Enemy will most likely come on to the Rio trade route. Reinforcements will meet you shortly from England." For security reasons, the message did not tell Stoddart what these reinforcements were.

A second signal was sent to the governor of the Falkland Islands. "German cruiser raid may take place. All Admiralty colliers should be concealed in unfrequented harbours. Be ready to destroy supplies useful to enemy and hide codes effectively on ships being sighted."

Churchill and Fisher expected Graf Spee to break in to the Atlantic by way of Cape Horn, not through the Panama Canal. The possibility that he might go west from Valparaíso was not seriously considered because of Patey's squadron in the South Pacific and the strong Japanese forces in the north.

The third and most dramatic signal went to Admiral Jellicoe, Commander in Chief of the Grand Fleet. "Order *Invincible* and *Inflexible* to fill up with coal and proceed to Berehaven with all dispatch. They are urgently needed for foreign service. Admiral and flag captain *Invincible* to transfer to *New Zealand*."

The last sentence showed that a new admiral was to be appointed to command this force, but Jellicoe was not told why these ships were "urgently needed."

Both Jellicoe and Adm. Sir David Beatty, commander of his battle cruiser squadrons, were just as unhappy about the removal of these two ships as they had been two months earlier. They protested again that this would mean the loss of their numerical edge over the High Seas Fleet in this class of capital ship. It took a personal message from Churchill explaining the urgent need to avenge Cradock's defeat to convince them to yield gracefully. When he read the message, "Sir John Jellicoe rose to the occasion and parted with his two battle cruisers without a word."

The battle cruiser was a completely new class of ship in 1914. Its creation had been Fisher's brainchild when he was First Sea Lord before the war. These vessels were as heavily gunned as battleships but much faster. The *Invincible* was designed to have a top speed of twenty-five knots, but with her new turbine engines she had reached twenty-eight knots on several occasions. This was a remarkable speed for a twenty-thousand-ton warship. Armor had been sacrificed for speed, and though this was to prove their eventual undoing as members of a battle fleet, their introduction spelled the end of the armored cruiser class.

To Fisher, they were his beloved "greyhounds of the sea." As he remarked of previous attempts to catch Graf Spee: "Tortoises were apportioned to *catch hares. Millions of tortoises can't catch a hare.* The Almighty arranged the greyhound to catch the hare—the greyhound so largely bigger than the hare as to annihilate it!"

The two "greyhounds" left the naval base at Invergordon on November 5 and arrived three days later at Devonport, where they had been rerouted to make it easier for the new admiral to take command. It was necessary for them to coal, repair a few mechanical defects, and load enough stores and ammunition for a three-month cruise. They were also to take stores for Admiral Stoddart's ships, as well as ammunition for the *Glasgow,* which had used nearly half of her shells at Coronel.

Rear-Adm. Godfrey Mundy, Admiral-Superintendent of the Devonport dockyard, was not told the purpose of these new arrivals, and he signaled the Admiralty, "The earliest possible date of completion . . . is midnight 13th November."

When Fisher saw this signal he retorted: "Friday, the 13th. What a day to choose!" He insisted that they must sail earlier. Churchill agreed and sent a terse reply, written in his own hand. This message went to Mundy's superior, Adm. Sir George Egerton.

> *Admiralty to C-in-C Devonport.* Ships are to sail on Wednesday 11th. They are needed for war service and arrangements must be made to conform. If necessary, dockyard men should be sent away in the ships to return as opportunity may offer.
>
> You are held responsible for the speedy dispatch of these ships in a thoroughly efficient condition.
>
> Acknowledge. *W.S.C.*

The admiral took the train to London to protest to Fisher in person that the deadline could not possibly be met. The First Sea Lord would not listen to his arguments and told him that as far as he was concerned, the workmen could be thrown overboard later if they had not finished their repairs by the time the ships left harbor. In the end, the two ships were ready to sail on the eleventh. A few skilled dockyard men were still working on board the *Invincible* when the battle cruisers left Devonport.

In the meantime, the burning question in Whitehall was who was to be put in command, not only of this powerful force but all the other ships searching for Graf Spee? It called for a senior and experienced admiral to take up the appointment as commander in chief South Atlantic and South Pacific. The new command was of greater latitude than that given to any admiral since Nelson.

Adm. Sir Doveton Sturdee, as chief of naval staff, would normally have been responsible for making such an appointment, but he knew his days at the Admiralty were numbered once Fisher had returned as First Sea Lord. Sturdee was anathema to Fisher, who regarded him as a "pedantic ass" whose "criminal ineptitude" had led to Cradock's defeat at Coronel. This was unjust. Churchill and Battenberg had been equally if not more responsible for the disaster.

Sturdee was a capable sea admiral and a respected tactician. He had not proved a brilliant success as chief of naval staff, but the real source of Fisher's deep animosity had nothing to do with Coronel. Sturdee had supported Fisher's sworn enemy, Adm. Sir Charles Beresford, in the enquiry which had led to Fisher's downfall in 1910. To make matters worse, when Fisher now proposed sending the two battle cruisers to the South Atlantic, Sturdee remarked that he had himself previously recommended sending battle cruisers to reinforce Cradock but had been overruled. This tactless comment enraged Fisher, and he stormed off to tell Churchill that he could not work with that "d——d fool" for another day as his chief of staff.

Churchill was in a terribly difficult position. He knew that Sturdee would not go easily, and since he was always loyal to his subordinates he could not bring himself to dismiss the admiral. He realized that if Fisher forced Sturdee out at this stage, it would reflect badly on his own role as First Lord in the events leading up to Coronel. In a matter of minutes, Churchill hit upon the brilliant solution of offering the new command to Sturdee. He wrote to him, "The destruction of the German squadron concentrated on the west coast of South America is an object of high and immediate importance and I propose to entrust this duty to you."

Sturdee accepted without hesitation. This was a master stroke by Churchill because it solved the two problems at once.

Those in naval circles appreciated the nice irony of the new appointment. Sturdee had undoubtedly been partly responsible for sending Cradock to his doom with an inadequate force, and it was only right that he be given the job of retrieving the situation. It has been claimed that

Fisher remarked at the time, "Sturdee is responsible for this bloody mess—now he can go and clean it up."

The admiral left for Devonport the next day and hoisted his flag in the *Invincible* on November 9. Two days later he set out on the long voyage to the South Atlantic to search for the German squadron.

A week earlier a triumphant Graf Spee had entered Valparaíso harbor. By international law he could take only three warships at a time into the neutral port. Besides the flagship, he chose the *Gneisenau* and *Nürnberg*. This gave him the opportunity to see his sons Otto and Heinrich, if only for a short time. He sent the *Leipzig* and *Dresden* to Más Afuera to guard the train of colliers and supply ships after their search for the *Glasgow* and *Otranto* had proved fruitless.

The victors were greeted at the harbor entrance by a Chilean torpedo boat, which led the ships to their assigned anchorages in the roadstead. The *Scharnhorst* fired a salute to the Chilean flag, then another to Chilean Vice Adm. Francisco Nef. Nef's cruisers *Esmeralda, O'Higgins,* and *Blanco Encalada* were in the harbor at the time, and they all enthusiastically returned the German salute.

The Germans were determined to make as much of the victory as possible to impress the already pro-German Chileans with their invincibility. Consul-general Gumprecht came out to the flagship in a pinnace and brought Graf Spee and his flag captain Felix Schultz ashore, where they were greeted formally by the German ambassador, Eckerdt, who had come down from Santiago for the great occasion. Both Graf Spee and Schultz were attired in full dress uniform, with cocked hats, epaulettes, and a profusion of gold braid.

Graf Spee wrote to his wife: "When I landed there were crowds at the landing stage and here and there small groups raised cheers. Cameras clicked everywhere."

Once ashore, he strode through the main square until he was so surrounded by throngs of admiring Chileans and cheering German emigrés that he had difficulty reaching the German consulate. The British consul protested the visit and the public display, but to no avail.

In spite of the occasion, Graf Spee was not in a particularly celebratory mood. He spent most of the day in talks with Gumprecht and Eckerdt about the war situation, especially Allied naval dispositions. They also discussed the difficulties of arranging coal supplies if he entered the Atlantic. Graf Spee knew perfectly well that once the Admiralty received a full report of the crushing defeat at Coronel, they would waste no time in sending powerful forces to hunt him down. There had to be celebrations,

Graf Spee is greeted at Valparaíso by the German ambassador and consul-general. (*Suddeutscher Verlag*)

of course, but Graf Spee insisted that these be limited to a brief dinner at the German Club for his captains, senior staff officers, and his two sons. Toasts would be allowed, but no formal speeches.

That evening, Graf Spee and his officers responded in style to the many patriotic toasts from the German colony. But when one overenthusiastic and inebriated club member proposed they drink the toast "Damnation to the British Navy!" the admiral had had enough. He rose and lifted his glass to his old friend Cradock. "I drink to the memory of a gallant and honourable foe." Then, according to an observer, "without waiting for support or even compliance he drained his glass, threw it on one side, picked up his cocked hat and made for the door—brushing aside the awed and silenced civilians."

By contrast, those officers and men who were lucky enough to have shore leave had a wonderful time in Valparaíso. They were showered with gifts and found no shortage of hosts willing to show them around the city and provide hospitality. One officer wrote, "Our friendly guide took us into a real café, something to which we were quite unaccustomed, something long forgotten."

Some of the officers found it hard to grasp that less than forty-eight hours after the miserably cold and uncomfortable conditions at sea off Coronel, here they were "in a café, seated on cushions, listening to music and looking at pretty black-eyed women."

The enlisted men were feted by the crews of German merchant ships, no less than thirty-two of them in port at the time. Many enthusiastic seamen from these ships volunteered for service in the three cruisers, which took 127 of them on board when they left.

The next day Graf Spee received a signal from Berlin. "You are advised to try and break through with all your ships and return home."

This message had been sent before the Admiralstab had received any news of Coronel. They were merely advising Graf Spee and characteristically did not order him to take any specific action. That morning he decided to leave Valparaíso within the prescribed twenty-four hours and join the rest of his ships at Más Afuera, to ponder his next move.

His prospects were uncertain, and he was filled with a deep sense of foreboding. As the Germans embarked in the boats taking them back to their ships, they were loaded with gifts of flowers and early strawberries. One lady on the quayside presented Graf Spee with a bouquet of roses and arum lilies as he prepared to step into his pinnace. "Thank you," he said solemnly. "They will do very nicely for my grave."

Graf Spee arrived back at Más Afuera on November 5. Although the island was Chilean territory, it was so isolated and sparsely populated that he could afford to ignore Chilean neutrality while he considered the squadron's options. There seemed to be only one real option. It was far too dangerous to go north or west because of Patey and the Japanese. The Germans could, of course, stay where they were and continue to block all Allied trade with the west coast of South America, but this idea didn't appeal to Graf Spee. In any event, his ships would soon need refits, which they could get only in a German port. In the end he concluded that it would be best to take the advice of the Admiralstab and break for home. He could attack the River Plate traffic on the way, then head for the mid-Atlantic, keeping away from regular sea-lanes. It took the admiral a long time, however, to arrive at this conclusion.

The constant strain of the past three months in his ever isolated and vulnerable position had eroded Graf Spee's ability to make incisive decisions. On the long voyage across the Pacific he had kept moving steadily and spent the minimum amount of time stopping to coal. Now he made no significant move for ten days. The longer he waited, the more opportunity he gave the Allies to react to Coronel and send a powerful force to hunt him down, and the further it lessened his chances of reaching Germany.

He had received a telegram from Berlin while he was at Valparaíso which informed him, "Lines of rendezvous [with German colliers] in the Atlantic are all compromised, and all trade routes are being strongly patrolled." This may have contributed to his indecision. He was well supplied with coal for the moment, but his supplies were certainly not enough for all five ships to reach Germany. Equally serious was the fact that the squadron had used almost half of its ammunition at Coronel. There was no prospect of resupply.

The squadron's morale was not helped by the delay. The feelings of elation after Coronel were dampened by the news that Tsingtao had fallen to the Japanese and that the *Emden* had been destroyed by the *Sydney*.

Graf Spee sent the *Leipzig* and *Dresden* for a brief visit to Valparaíso on November 13. He wanted to counter rumors that these two ships had been sunk at Coronel and to give their crews a chance to share in the adulation enjoyed by the rest of the squadron, to build their morale. But this move also informed the Allies that the German cruisers had not left Chilean waters.

Finally, on November 15, Graf Spee gave the order to raise anchor. The *Scharnhorst, Gneisenau,* and *Nürnberg* left Más Afuera with their colliers *Baden* and *Santa Isabel*. The pretty little *Titania,* which had lived up to her name and served them well, was emptied of supplies and scuttled. Graf Spee didn't believe she could survive the ordeal of a voyage around the Horn. The men of the cruisers watched glumly as their favorite capsized and sank.

The *Prinz Eitel Friedrich* was left behind, with orders to transmit false wireless messages for as long as she could (to try to convince the Allies that Graf Spee's ships were still somewhere off the Chilean coast). This ruse worked, because the Admiralty later miscalculated the earliest date that Graf Spee could possibly reach the Atlantic.

Because of the slow colliers the squadron was forced to steam at less than its usual ten knots. The *Leipzig* and *Dresden* met them at sea on November 18 and reported that they had captured and sunk the large British sailing vessel *North Wales* shortly after leaving port. They also brought Graf Spee a long message from Berlin, sent via the consulate in Valparaíso. This advised him to abandon the Pacific and carry out cruiser warfare in the Atlantic, keeping his ships in "groups strong enough to meet the enemy if he interferes." The Naval Staff warned him again that coal supplies in the Atlantic would be uncertain and left it to his "discretion to break off cruiser warfare as soon as you think it advisable and make your way home with all the forces you can concentrate." The Admiralstab concluded that this would require "careful preparations . . . accompanied by good luck." Graf Spee knew this better than anybody.

Berlin did, however, offer the prospect that the High Seas Fleet might send some battle cruisers to break through the Allied blockade and protect Graf Spee's ships in their final run toward Germany.

The message also contained the ominous sentence, "The *Invincible, Inflexible,* and *Indomitable* have probably been withdrawn from the Mediterranean."

Although the report was inaccurate, it should have warned Graf Spee that he might have to face battle cruisers when he reached the Atlantic. The information was apparently either ignored or discounted as an Allied bluff. Graf Spee did not believe for a moment that the Royal Navy would send such powerful units to track him down. He expected to meet nothing more formidable than armored cruisers of the type he had easily dealt with at Coronel.

While the German squadron was heading south toward Cape Horn, Sturdee and his battle cruisers were well on their way to their first coaling point at St. Vincent, in the Cape Verde Islands. Sturdee's orders were: "On leaving Devonport . . . proceed to . . . South American waters. Your main and most important duty is to search for the German armoured cruisers *Scharnhorst* and *Gneisenau*. All other considerations are to be subordinated to this end. . . ."

His orders gave him full authority over Stoddart and his squadron, indeed over all overseas commanders, in his search for Graf Spee. The Admiralty proposed that he rendezvous with Stoddart at the Abrolhos rocks off the coast of Brazil, then proceed in force to the Falkland Islands.

Surprisingly, there was nothing in Sturdee's orders about the need for dispatch or secrecy. The *Invincible* and *Inflexible* were six years old and thus quite capable of steaming at twenty-five knots for days, but Sturdee kept to an economical fifteen knots in order to conserve coal and to avoid overtaxing his engines and stokers. He knew he would need a sudden burst of speed if he sighted the Germans and didn't want to jeopardize any chance of catching them.

On the way south, no attempt was made to maintain W/T silence, and Sturdee even stopped several neutral merchantmen to look for contraband, thereby advertising his position and direction. When he left Devonport, it had been common knowledge in the dockside pubs that the men of the battle cruisers had been issued tropical uniforms and that dockyard work on the ships was a rush job. It was obvious to everyone, including German agents, that they were being sent to the South Atlantic. What else could their purpose be after Coronel but to pursue Graf Spee? But Sturdee needn't have given the Germans progress reports.

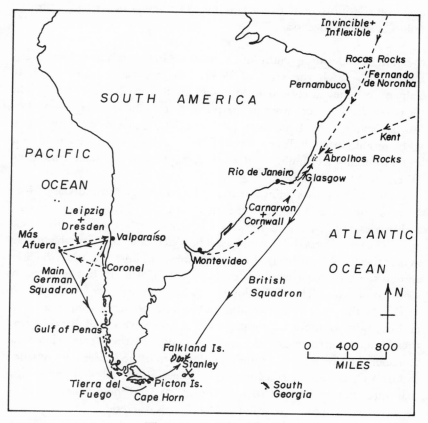

The pursuit of Graf Spee

It took six days to cover the twenty-five hundred miles to Cape Verde. On November 17 the two battle cruisers docked at St. Vincent, where they spent twenty-four hours coaling. Portugal was still neutral at the time, and several German merchant ships were in the harbor. They were all equipped with long-range transmitters, and they wasted no time in reporting to Berlin that Sturdee had arrived. The operators of the Western Telegraph Company also transmitted the interesting news to their offices in Rio de Janeiro and Montevideo, where German agents were plentiful.

Sturdee finally realized the need for secrecy when he heard that West African wireless stations were using his ships' call signs. After one station passed the less than momentous news to the flagship that one of her officers had just become a father, he signaled: "The utmost harm may be done by the indiscreet use of wireless. The key is never to be pressed unless absolutely necessary."

Steaming at a leisurely eight knots, it took Graf Spee's squadron nearly six days to reach the Gulf of Penas, one thousand miles south of Valparaíso. They anchored in St. Quentin Bay on November 21. The bleak conditions there were in sharp contrast to those being enjoyed by Sturdee's men in the tropical mid-Atlantic. The Germans were surrounded by mountainous cliffs and huge glaciers—solid walls of ice a mile wide and a thousand feet high. Sudden squalls and icy winds made conditions miserably wet and cold.

Coaling and provisioning for the arduous voyage around Cape Horn went on for five days. Some of the men went ashore to gather evergreens and berries and to cut pine trees for Christmas, which was just five weeks away. The crews hoped they would still be together to celebrate the holiday as best they could, probably at some remote spot in the Atlantic. Graf Spee and his son Otto went ashore to explore the local wildlife, but as the count wrote to his wife, "The only living things I met were pretty little birds."

During their stay in St. Quentin Bay, another collier arrived from Chile and brought some fresh newspapers. The crews were delighted to read the accounts of their exploits and the praise for their great victory at Coronel. The vessel also brought the news that the Kaiser had awarded the Iron Cross, First Class and Second Class, to the admiral and no less than three hundred Iron Crosses, Second Class, to the officers and men. The medals were to be awarded at Graf Spee's discretion.

With more than three thousand crew members in the squadron, this was no easy task. Graf Spee decided to rely on his captains to recommend those who had particularly distinguished themselves during the battle. He was embarrassed to learn that both of his sons' names were on the recommended list, particularly that of Heinrich, who was a very junior lieutenant on board the *Gneisenau*. Graf Spee was solemnly assured by both Maerker and Schönberg that they had chosen his sons with total objectivity. Their father gave the two boys the good news personally. As he wrote to the countess: "It was very nice to see how happy they were. Heinrich was especially glad as he had not thought it possible that he would qualify for an award."

It took a whole day to give out the medals, for the admiral was ferried from ship to ship to make the presentations. The cheers of the crews echoed round the desolate bay—surely a strange setting for such a ceremony, surrounded by wild and mountainous terrain that was only accustomed to the cries of seabirds.

*   *   *

Vice-Adm. Sir Doveton Sturdee *(Imperial War Museum)*

When Sturdee left St. Vincent, he decided to carry out a battle practice, but unfortunately a towing cable to one of the targets became entangled in the *Invincible*'s propellers. This caused a further delay of twelve hours, and the two ships didn't get under way to join Stoddart until November 19.

The ships that had escaped destruction at Coronel were also ordered to meet Stoddart at Abrolhos, but the *Glasgow* had to put into Rio de Janeiro first, to repair her battle damage. The Brazilian authorities had become so exasperated by German infringements of their neutrality that they allowed the *Glasgow* to spend five days in a government dockyard to complete her repairs. When she left, the authorities waived all charges, a remarkable gesture from a country where German influence had been so strong.

When Captain Grant informed London that the *Canopus* would also need five days to repair her engines at the Falklands before she could join Stoddart's forces, the Admiralty decided on a new role for the elderly battleship. Fisher had arrived at a more realistic assessment of her fighting value than Churchill, who once described her as "inexpugnable." Fisher signaled Captain Grant to stay at Port Stanley. "Moor the ship so that the entrance is commanded by your guns. Extemporize mines outside entrance . . . be prepared for bombardment from outside harbour. Governor to organize all local forces and make determined defence. Arrange observation station on shore, by which your fire on ships outside can be directed. . . . No objection to your grounding ship to obtain a good berth."

Grant carried out these instructions to the letter, and the grounded *Canopus* finally became the "citadel" that Churchill had always envisaged.

On the other side of the continent, preparations for the voyage around the Horn went on at a leisurely pace. On November 26 the German cruisers moved out into the Pacific, their decks piled high with coal to give them greater steaming range. They were accompanied by the *Baden, Santa Isabel,* and *Seydlitz,* which carried seventeen thousand tons of coal between them. Several more colliers were waiting in Montevideo, and these had been ordered to rendezvous with Graf Spee on December 5 near Punta Santa Elena on the Argentine coast. They would keep the squadron supplied with coal on its long voyage to Germany.

For Graf Spee to delay his departure from St. Quentin Bay for so long was another error of judgment. The German naval attaché in San Francisco had already warned him in a signal sent on November 11: "If the Cruiser Squadron decides to return home it appears advisable for it to leave immediately. In my opinion it is dangerously situated."

Graf Spee had also received intelligence from Punta Arenas that the *Defence, Cornwall, Carnarvon, Bristol, Glasgow,* and *Canopus* were all at the Falkland Islands. This was not true, but Graf Spee had no way of knowing it.

Typically, the Admiralstab kept to their principle of not interfering with the judgment of their man on the spot. The Chief of Naval Staff, Adm. Hugo von Pohl, believed it was "unwise to encroach on the freedom of action of the Count," whom he thought "would be better informed of the strength of the English force than we were." He signaled Graf Spee, but contented himself with asking: "What are your plans? How much ammunition have you?" Graf Spee simply replied, "The Cruiser Squadron intends to break through for home." He added that the two armored cruisers had roughly half their ammunition left and the three light cruisers somewhat more than half.

Churchill and Fisher expected the German squadron to attack the Falklands first, then move up the South American coast. They planned to forestall this by sending Sturdee's forces south from Abrolhos, but they had not overlooked other possibilities. Every foreseeable move by Graf Spee had been countered by deploying additional forces in the Pacific, at the Cape of Good Hope, off West Africa, and in the Caribbean.

As Churchill wrote later: "[T]o compass the destruction of five warships, only two of which were armoured, it was necessary to employ nearly thirty, including twenty-one armoured ships, for the most part of superior metal, and this took no account of powerful Japanese squadrons . . . French ships or of armed merchant cruisers. . . ."

Graf Spee's error in delaying his entry into the Atlantic was compounded by further, but this time unavoidable, delays when the squadron reached Tierra del Fuego. He decided to go around Cape Horn rather than through the Strait of Magellan, which would certainly be calmer water, but this route would be much more dangerous. His ships would not be able to move very fast in the narrow channels, and if his presence was detected by the enemy, there would be plenty of time for them to prepare an ambush before he could reach the Atlantic side.

The usually bad weather off Tierra del Fuego became even worse on November 27. The sea was so rough that the light cruisers were in serious danger of capsizing because of their high deck loads. Graf Spee gave them permission to jettison all deck coal, while the two armored cruisers stood by in case of emergency. The perilous situation of the light cruisers was described by one of the *Leipzig*'s officers. "The storm and sea grew steadily more violent. We steered out of the line because [our] position was beginning to get dangerous. The heavy seas had shifted the deck cargo and all the scuppers . . . got stopped up with coal so that water could no longer escape. At times there were three feet of water on deck and we were in imminent danger of capsizing. All hands had to turn to and shovel coal overboard. The men were standing all the time waist deep in water . . . which was very cold."

For two days they rode out the storm. According to the diary of an officer on the *Gneisenau:* "Impossible to lay the tables. Broken up furniture thrown overboard. All crockery was smashed. Impossible to be on deck. Necessary to secure oneself with ropes. We are about off entrance to Magellan Straits."

Just as slowly, Sturdee was making his way across the Atlantic to join Stoddart. He was still stopping neutral merchant ships to check for contraband and even sent an open signal to one of the cruisers waiting for him off the coast of Brazil. He also diverted his ships to the Rocas reefs area in search of the *Karlsruhe,* which had been at the bottom of the sea for three weeks. With this lack of secrecy or urgency it is not surprising that he didn't arrive at the Abrolhos rocks until November 26. By this time German agents in Rio and Montevideo were well aware of the presence of two British battle cruisers off the Brazilian coast.

Astonishingly, they did not inform Berlin immediately. They couldn't contact Graf Spee directly by wireless because he was on the other side of the southern Andes, and recent storms in Tierra del Fuego had even made communication with Punta Arenas unreliable. German agents may have reached Punta Arenas with the news, but if they did, and it was relayed to Graf Spee, it must have been discounted as an Allied bluff. It seemed very unlikely that the Royal Navy would send badly needed capital ships to the South Atlantic.

In the end, the German agents in Montevideo decided to send this vital piece of news to Graf Spee by means of a letter. This curious decision ensured that Graf Spee would be kept ignorant of the battle cruisers' arrival in South American waters for at least another nine days, because the letter was carried by one of the slow colliers going to the rendezvous at Santa Elena, which Graf Spee was not supposed to reach until December 5. This incredible breakdown in the normally efficient German intelligence network needlessly left Graf Spee in the dark about the Admiralty's plans.

The Admiralty sent Sturdee fresh information and instructions while he was at the Abrolhos rocks. "*Scharnhorst*'s squadron was at Mas a Fuera on [November] 15th; later evidence points to their presence at St. Quentin on 21st. Proceed south with whole squadron. Use Falkland Islands as main base for colliers. After coaling proceed to Chilean coast, avoiding letting your large ships be seen in Magellan Straits. Search the Straits' inlets and channels."

The signal finally pointed out the need for secrecy, but it made no mention of any need for haste. Partly because they had been taken in by the *Prinz Eitel Friedrich*'s signaling from Más Afuera, the Admiralty believed that the German squadron could not get to the Strait of Magellan before the end of November at the earliest, and it confidently expected Sturdee to reach Port Stanley by December 3. It thought he was steaming at the eighteen knots or better that the squadron was quite capable of maintaining.

By this time the German squadron was nearing Cape Horn. An officer wrote: "[The] weather began to get better on the 28th, the wind gradually falling and the sea getting more calm. . . . We had the dreaded Cape Horn on our beam on the night of 1 December."

To everyone's relief the passage around the Horn was uneventful because the sea remained relatively calm. The only danger came from huge icebergs, some of them a hundred feet high or more.

The next day they came upon the unusual sight of a four-masted barque, tacking against the wind under full sail. Graf Spee sent the *Leipzig* to stop her. She was the British *Drummuir,* bound for San Francisco with twenty-eight hundred tons of good Welsh anthracite. This was more coal than the light cruisers had thrown overboard during the storm. The *Leipzig* towed the barque into the mouth of the Beagle Channel, and all the ships anchored off Picton Island. The *Drummuir*'s cargo was transferred to the *Baden* and *Santa Isabel* and her crew to the *Seydlitz.* The barque was then towed out to sea and sunk. The *Dresden* had lost so much coal during the storm that Lüdecke reported he no longer had enough to make it to the rendezvous at Santa Elena, so her bunkers were filled from the *Seydlitz.*

Graf Spee decided to stay at Picton Island for three days to give his men a well-deserved break after the strain of their voyage around the Horn and the hard work of coaling. His decision was understandable, but after all the other delays, this one was to prove the most crucial. While they were at Picton Island, the men decorated their ships for Christmas. The officers went ashore duck hunting but managed to shoot only a few inedible seabirds. The admiral went over to the *Gneisenau* in the evenings to play bridge with Captain Maerker and his officers and to spend some time with Heinrich.

By now Sturdee had taken command of Stoddart's squadron. This consisted of the armored cruisers *Carnarvon, Cornwall,* and *Kent*—the last two being sister ships of the unfortunate *Monmouth*—and the light cruisers *Bristol* and *Glasgow.* There were also the armed merchant cruisers *Orama* and *Edinburgh Castle.* Stoddart had transferred his flag to the *Carnarvon* when the Admiralty decided to send the peripatetic *Defence* to the Cape of Good Hope.

Sturdee called a conference of all his captains on board the *Invincible.* He explained that he planned to go to the Falklands to coal before searching the Magellan area for Graf Spee. When he told them that he intended to stay at Abrolhos for seventy-two hours before starting out, Captain Luce of the *Glasgow* was appalled. He was convinced that the Germans would soon be in the Atlantic and that their first move would be to attack the Falklands. As a junior captain, he dared not say anything at the meeting, but after it had adjourned he went back to the flagship and "in some trepidation" asked to see the admiral.

When he was received by Sturdee, he said, "I hope you don't mind me coming over, sir, and please don't imagine I am questioning your orders, but thinking it over I do feel we should sail as soon as possible."

Sturdee replied, "But dammit Luce, we're sailing the day after tomorrow, isn't that good enough for you?"

Luce explained his conviction that it was vital to reach Port Stanley before Graf Spee could get there, and Sturdee reluctantly gave in with, "Very well, Luce, if you believe that's important, we'll sail tomorrow."

The squadron set sail from Abrolhos on November 28 at a speed of ten knots. The cruisers were in the van, fanned out in a broad line of search, followed by the two battle cruisers, with the *Orama* escorting the colliers in the rear. By now, Sturdee had been convinced of the need for secrecy, and on the way down to Port Stanley he gave the order that all W/T messages were to be sent and received by the *Bristol* and *Glasgow*. The Germans already knew that these two ships were stationed in South American waters.

In a week's time the weather began to turn cold, and the men changed from their tropical whites back into blue serge. They knew that every day brought them closer to a possible showdown with Graf Spee's squadron; surely Sturdee would not let the Germans slip by them. There was a keen air of expectation, especially on board the *Glasgow*.

Before the German squadron left Picton Island on December 6, Graf Spee had a meeting with his captains and staff officers on board the flagship to discuss what to do next.

Maerker of the *Gneisenau*, Haun of the *Leipzig*, Lüdecke of the *Dresden*, and most of the staff officers wanted to give the Falklands a wide berth. It seemed very risky to them to spend any time there, even if the success of an attack on Port Stanley was assured. They were eager to head for Germany without delay. They suggested raiding the River Plate traffic on the way, then making for the middle of the Atlantic, which would keep them well away from regular sea-lanes. These officers proposed a coaling stop in the Cape Verde or Canary Islands before making a final dash to Germany.

Graf Spee's subordinates expected the squadron to be supported by powerful units from the High Seas Fleet when it reached European waters. They felt confident that they would not be neglected after their great achievement at Coronel. They were not to know that Admiral von Pohl had changed his mind about running the North Sea blockade and had sent a signal to the German naval attaché in San Francisco, "Impossible to dispatch a large cruiser from home to the North Atlantic."

The news never reached Graf Spee.

The admiral didn't agree with Maerker and the others. Inspired by his triumph at Coronel, he was eager to see further action before trying to break for home. His attitude was shared by Captain Fielitz, his aggressive chief of staff, and by Schönberg of the *Nürnberg*. Graf Spee especially wanted to attack the Falkland Islands. He planned to destroy the wireless station and harbor installations—the Allies' only coaling station in the South Atlantic—and to sink any ships he found there. He also had the quixotic notion of taking the governor prisoner in retaliation for the humiliating capture of the governor of Samoa.

Graf Spee was encouraged by a report from the German agent in Punta Arenas who had just signaled that no Allied warships were anchored at Port Stanley. Except for the grounded *Canopus,* this report was correct as of December 6. Even if some of Stoddart's cruisers were there, Graf Spee may have felt that he would have to fight sometime, and it would be better to do so on his own terms. He meant to cause as much damage as he could, then rather than later, when he might be short of both coal and ammunition.

Captain Maerker remained strongly opposed to a raid on the Falklands, but naturally the admiral's view prevailed in the end. The attack was planned for the morning of December 8, and it was to be carried out by the *Gneisenau* and *Nürnberg,* with the rest of the squadron held back in reserve in case any British warships were at Port Stanley.

On the morning of December 7, the day after Graf Spee left Picton Island, lookouts in the Falklands sighted the smoke of several ships in the distance. The arrival of a German squadron had been anxiously expected daily ever since the Admiralty's signal to Captain Grant. As the ships drew near, there was a tremendous sense of relief when the lookouts identified the distinctive tripod masts of the two battle cruisers. These and battleships were the only ships that carried such masts, and they realized that the Royal Navy had come in time to save them.

The islanders had been as prepared as they could be. They had the grounded *Canopus* as a fortress, and some of her smaller guns had been taken off and set up as shore batteries. They had laid electrically operated homemade mines at the harbor entrance, and Captain Grant had set up a system of lookouts, signalers, and spotters on the hills around Port Stanley. The captain of marines of the *Canopus* had even drilled a local defense force made up of shepherds and fishermen. But they had been under no illusions about their chances against Graf Spee. Now they felt secure.

The armored cruisers and battle cruisers anchored in the outer harbor of Port William, and the light cruisers went to the inner harbor of Port Stanley, next to the beached *Canopus*. The armed merchant cruiser *Macedonia*, which had joined the squadron from Sierra Leone on the way down, was left outside the harbor mouth to act as guard ship.

All Sturdee's ships needed coal after their twenty-seven-hundred-mile voyage. The British didn't enjoy coaling any more than the Germans did. As an officer on the *Cornwall* wrote sarcastically in his diary, "The ever recurring delight of coaling ship is looked forward to directly anchorage is reached." The ships could not all be coaled at the same time because the *Orama* and the slower colliers had not arrived yet, and there were only three colliers in port. Sturdee gave orders for the *Carnarvon, Bristol,* and *Glasgow* to coal first. The rest of the squadron was to coal the next morning.

All ships were ordered to have steam up at two hours' notice, except for the guard ships *Macedonia* and *Kent,* which were to be ready to move at thirty minutes' notice.

In the evening, Sturdee had another meeting with his captains on board the *Invincible*. He explained that he intended to split the squadron into two divisions. The battle cruisers were to sail on the evening of December 8 and the rest of the ships on the ninth. His plan was to search through the Strait of Magellan with the smaller ships, which would meet up with the battle cruisers at the far end after they had searched around Cape Horn. Sturdee was determined to catch Graf Spee whichever route he took.

As Sturdee talked, the German squadron was less than eight hours' steaming distance from the Falklands.

11

The Battle of
the Falklands

The enemy fought splendidly, but were quite outclassed.

—R. H. Dixon, Surgeon-Lieutenant, HMS *Kent*

T he late spring night of December 7–8 was unusually clear for the
Falklands region. By 0230 the lookouts in the German cruisers
could make out the dark mass of the islands in the distance. Graf
Spee signaled Captain Maerker at 0530 and told him to detach the
Gneisenau and *Nürnberg* and to carry out his orders.

The attack was timed for daybreak. Maerker's first target was the wireless station at Cape Pembroke. Shortly afterwards, the *Gneisenau* reported back that due to an error in taking bearings, they were farther from
Cape Pembroke than had been estimated and couldn't reach it until 0930
at the earliest. They had lost the advantage of a surprise attack at dawn.

Graf Spee wasn't worried. He didn't expect Maerker to meet any serious opposition because he knew that the Falklands were lightly defended.
The islands had no shore batteries. There had been conflicting intelligence reports about the presence of some of Stoddart's ships in Port
Stanley, but the last signal from the German consul in Punta Arenas had
assured him they had left for West Africa. Even if this proved to be wrong,
the worst the squadron would have to face would be old armored cruisers. After their experiences against the *Good Hope* and *Monmouth* at
Coronel, Graf Spee was confident that his two big ships could easily take
care of such opponents.

By 0830 the lookouts on the *Gneisenau* and *Nürnberg* could see the
masts of the wireless station near Hooker's Point and the smoke of a ship
apparently entering the harbor. (This was the *Macedonia,* which was

being relieved of guard duty by the *Kent*.) The Germans also saw clouds of dark yellowish smoke rising over the port area. They thought their approach had been seen from shore and believed the smoke was coming from fires set by the islanders to destroy stores and coal supplies, as the French had done during the raid on Papeeté. The lookouts couldn't tell yet whether there were any ships in the harbor because their view was blocked by the low hills around Port Stanley. The Germans steamed on unperturbed.

Captain Maerker's instructions were to take his ships to a point five miles off Cape Pembroke and destroy the masts of the wireless station by gunfire. It was now too late to do this before any alarm could be sent out, but that couldn't be helped. Maerker was then supposed to reconnoiter the harbor mouth and, if no warships were seen, to put landing parties ashore to destroy the port installations and scuttle any merchant ships in the harbor.

The rest of the squadron was to stay in reserve about fifteen miles off the islands. If he found any warships in Port Stanley, Maerker was to draw them out onto the main squadron—and a second Coronel.

A Swedish civilian made the first sighting of the German ships. He was on Sapper Hill, manning one of the gunnery observation posts set up by Captain Grant. The post had a telephone line to the *Canopus*. At 0750 his first message to Grant reported "two strange warships" to the south, then a few minutes later, "a four funnel and a two funnel man-of-war in sight SE steering northwards." Because two of the *Nürnberg*'s three funnels were close together this was an understandable mistake. Soon afterwards, another lookout sighted the smoke of three more ships, much farther away than the first two. There could be no doubt that Graf Spee's whole squadron was approaching the islands.

The *Canopus* couldn't signal the flagship directly from where she lay on the mud bank, so she ran up a flag signal to the *Glasgow*, which was anchored a short distance away, "Enemy in sight."

The *Glasgow* tried to pass the message on to the *Invincible* by signal lamp, but there was no acknowledgment. The two battle cruisers were in the midst of coaling and were so wrapped in clouds of black dust that the *Glasgow*'s frantic signaling went unnoticed.

When the officer of the watch reported to his captain that he couldn't raise the flagship, Luce retorted, "Well, for God's sake do something about it—fire a gun, send a boat, don't stand there like a stuffed dummy."

The officer fired a saluting gun to attract the *Invincible*'s attention, then used a twenty-four-inch searchlight to penetrate the dust cloud and send the message to the flagship's bridge.

A flag-lieutenant raced down to the admiral's cabin to tell Sturdee, who had just finished dressing and was in the middle of shaving. He realized that he was in an extremely vulnerable position. If the Germans attacked immediately, they could rake his stationary ships while they were raising steam and could concentrate their fire on any ship that tried to leave the harbor. If one of them was sunk in the harbor mouth, the rest might be trapped. This would give Graf Spee plenty of time to complete his bombardment and steam away unscathed. Sturdee gave orders for all coaling to stop, then finished his shave.

The colliers were cast off to allow the cruisers' guns to be trained free of interference. Sturdee signaled all ships, "Raise steam for full speed, report when ready."

He also told his captains to clear for action and to be prepared to open fire at a minute's notice, using the island's observation posts to guide their aim.

It was going to take at least two hours for the battle cruisers to raise enough steam to push their huge hulls through the water to the harbor entrance. Fortunately, the men of the *Glasgow* and *Carnarvon* had worked through the night and finished coaling by 0600. These two ships were well on their way to raising full steam. The *Kent* was on guard duty and already had steam up. The *Bristol* and *Cornwall* reported they would need more than two hours because their fires were drawn and their engines opened up for minor repairs.

Sturdee was never one to panic. A fellow officer said of him, "[N]o man ever saw him rattled." The admiral wrote later, "I gave orders to raise steam for full speed and go down for a good breakfast."

Outwardly unperturbed, he displayed the Francis Drake touch and went down for his own breakfast—porridge, kippers, and tea. He could do absolutely nothing about Graf Spee for the next two hours, or so it seemed at the time.

Some time after the first sighting reports came in, the Falklands wireless station sent a message to the Admiralty. "Admiral Spee arrived in daylight with all his ships and is now in action with Admiral Sturdee's whole squadron, which was coaling."

Because the message had to be relayed, it didn't reach Churchill's desk until 1700. As he wrote later: "We had had so many unpleasant surprises that these last words sent a shiver up my spine. Had we been taken by surprise and in spite of all our superiority, mauled, unready at anchor?"

He turned to Vice-Adm. Henry Oliver, who had replaced Sturdee as

Sturdee's flagship, HMS *Invincible (Imperial War Museum)*

his chief of staff, and asked, "Can it mean that?" All a gloomy Oliver could find to say was, "I hope not."

By 0900 the *Gneisenau* and *Nürnberg* were near enough to Port Stanley that their lookouts could make out the masts of several warships above the low neck of land between Sapper Hill and Cape Pembroke. They reported that they could definitely see three armored cruisers and a light cruiser.

The *Gneisenau*'s gunnery officer, Lt. Comdr. Johann Busche, was in the gunnery control top high up the foremast. When his ship rounded the cape at 0930, he reported that he thought he could also see four tripod masts in the outer harbor. This meant that two bigger ships were present, either battleships or the dreaded battle cruisers. Busche believed they were the latter. Captain Maerker told him sharply that he must be mistaken—the nearest battle cruisers were far away in the Mediterranean.

Maerker signaled Graf Spee that there were probably three "County"-class cruisers and one light cruiser in Port Stanley and perhaps two larger ships of the *Canopus* type. The Germans knew the *Canopus* was in the Falklands area, and it seemed reasonable to them that two of the old predreadnoughts might be in the harbor. Maerker kept on toward Port Stanley. When he saw the *Kent* outside the harbor mouth, he increased speed to try to cut her off.

By now, the two German ships were so close to land that the watchers on shore could tell that their guns were trained on the wireless station. They could also make out the landing parties lined up on deck in their white and khaki uniforms. There was no mistaking the Germans' intent. When Maerker kept heading toward the *Kent*, Sturdee ordered her captain to turn back into Port Stanley before she was cut off.

It was time for the *Canopus* to take action. The old battleship was resting firmly on the mud flats behind the hills, and Captain Grant had wanted to demonstrate the accuracy of his spotting system to Sturdee, even though the *Canopus* had no view of the sea. A practice shoot had been scheduled for 0900 that morning. Grant asked the admiral if he could go ahead with the shoot using a real target.

Sturdee gave permission, and the *Canopus* opened fire on the *Gneisenau* at a range of thirteen thousand yards. The first shots were fired by the forward turret, which was using live ammunition. Even though the old guns were at maximum elevation, the shells fell into the sea well short of the target. The Germans were utterly astonished when towering splashes appeared in front of them as the huge 12-inch shells exploded on impact with the water. No enemy warship was in sight, and they had been assured there were no shore batteries at Port Stanley.

A worse shock was still to come. According to one of the officers on the *Canopus:* "The after turret's crew, in order to get one up on their deadly rivals in the fore turret, crept out privily by night and loaded with practice shell. Next morning they found it was a real battle and there was no time to unload. The result of this naughtiness was very interesting. . . ."

When the second turret fired, the dummy shells ricocheted instead of exploding. One of them hit the aftermost funnel of the *Gneisenau.* Although the freak hit caused no significant damage, Maerker immediately gave the order to turn away. He signaled the news to Graf Spee, who replied: "Do not accept action. Concentrate on course E. by N. and proceed at full speed."

The *Canopus* didn't fire again, but she had saved the day. Once he believed that predreadnought battleships were in Port Stanley, Graf Spee decided on discretion rather than action. "County"-class cruisers were not a serious threat, but he dared not let his ships get within range of the big guns of old battleships like the *Canopus.* Graf Spee was confident that he could easily outrun these slow ships, and he turned away from the islands, heading east at twenty-two knots. He signaled Maerker again, "Rejoin the flag at best speed."

Sturdee's ships now had plenty of time to raise steam and leave the harbor safely.

By 0945, less than two hours after the first sighting of Graf Spee's squadron, all of Sturdee's ships except the *Bristol* had full steam up. The stokers and engine room staff of every ship had worked like trojans. Fittingly enough, the *Glasgow* was the first to leave the harbor. Emotions ran high among her crew. They could well remember the explosion of the *Good Hope* and the blazing fires in the *Monmouth* as their ship fled from Graf Spee's squadron at Coronel. They raced ahead, with orders from Sturdee to maintain contact with Graf Spee but to stay out of range until the two battle cruisers caught up.

Fifteen minutes later the *Invincible, Inflexible, Kent,* and *Carnarvon* steamed out after them. Hundreds of civilians cheered them on from their vantage points on the hills around Port Stanley. Last to leave was the *Cornwall*. The *Bristol* and *Macedonia* stayed behind. Sturdee gave the order to hoist the exhilarating flag signal "General chase."

Eyewitnesses have written of the unforgettable sight of the two sleek battle cruisers cutting through the sea, creating huge bow waves and leaving masses of boiling white water in their wakes as they worked up to full speed. Because they were using oil as well as coal to fire their boilers they were belching thick clouds of black smoke from all three funnels. Every few minutes, the *Glasgow* reported Graf Spee's position and course to the *Invincible*.

The weather was remarkably fine for the Falklands in December, when it normally rains three days out of four. (According to the locals the climate was "nine months of winter and three months' bad weather.") Instead of the usual mists and rain squalls, the sky was clear and blue. A slight but cold breeze was blowing from the northwest, but the sea was calm. Visibility was limited only by the earth's curvature.

The five German ships were hull down on the horizon, about fifteen to twenty miles away. Sturdee knew that with his five-knot advantage it was only a matter of two or perhaps three hours before he overhauled them enough to bring them within range of his 12-inch guns. There were still over eight hours of daylight left. If the fine weather held, he would have Graf Spee in his sights long before the sun went down.

The lookouts high up the masts of the German cruisers could see the dense clouds of smoke as the British squadron steamed out of Port Stanley. Within a few minutes they were able to make out the shapes of

HMS *Inflexible* making smoke as she leaves Port Stanley at full steam *(Imperial War Museum)*

two larger vessels as they separated from the rest. To the Germans they seemed "much faster and bigger than the others, as their smoke was thicker, wider and more massive. All glasses were turned upon their hulls, which were almost completely enveloped by the smoke."

It wasn't long before the eyes straining through every available telescope and pair of binoculars were able to tell that these ships carried tripod masts. There could be no doubt from the masts and the three unequally spaced funnels that these were modern battle cruisers, not old predreadnoughts of the *Canopus* type. Lieutenant Commander Busche had been right.

Some of the lookouts were so dismayed by the sight of the dreaded tripod masts that, as one of them said after the battle, "They tried not to believe it."

When the shocking news was reported to the bridge of the *Gneisenau,* the first officer, Comdr. Hans Pochhammer, remembered that it came as: "a very bitter pill for us to swallow. We choked a little at the neck, the throat contracted and stiffened, for this meant a life and death struggle, or rather a fight ending in honourable death. . . . It would have been senseless to harbour any illusions, for the sky remained clear; there was not the smallest cloud to be seen, nor a wisp of fog to throw over us its friendly mantle."

It was a particularly bitter pill for Maerker and the other captains who had argued that the Falklands should be avoided.

When he heard the depressing news, Graf Spee immediately ordered a change of course to southeast in the hope of finding rain squalls or patches of Antarctic fog. If he couldn't lose his pursuers, all a German naval officer could do was "bear in mind that his chief duty is to damage the enemy as severely as possible . . . the situation will sometimes appear hopeless, but he must never show weakness. . . ."

Graf Spee was not going to give in easily in spite of the heavy odds against him.

By now, the German squadron was strung out in two ragged wings, with the armored cruisers in one line and the light cruisers to starboard in the other. Although Graf Spee had ordered his ships to steam at twenty-two knots, the squadron's best speed was barely twenty knots because several of the cruisers badly needed a refit after their long voyage to Easter Island. He knew the battle cruisers were capable of at least twenty-five knots and that they would soon catch his squadron unless the weather changed for the worse.

On the British side, the battle cruisers had reached twenty-five knots and had almost caught up with the *Glasgow*. The three armored cruisers were beginning to lag behind, especially the *Carnarvon*. Admiral Stoddart signaled that his ship could do no better than eighteen knots. At this time, the German squadron was fine on Sturdee's port bow, heading southeast.

The wind was coming from the northwest so that the smoke from the battle cruisers' funnels was blowing ahead of them, completely masking the gunners' view of the Germans. Graf Spee's lee position meant that his smoke was blowing away from the enemy, giving his own men a clear view. The *Invincible* and *Inflexible* were using a mixture of coal and oil in their furnaces to give them maximum steam pressure, and the smoke problem would continue to hamper their gun-layers unless Sturdee was able to maneuver into a lee position.

After an hour's chase, the lookouts in the foretops of the leading British ships could easily make out the funnels and upper works of the

German cruisers through their binoculars. It seemed certain that they would catch the enemy before very long. At 1130 Sturdee gave the order for the crews to go down to the mess decks for an early lunch. (It was generally believed that men would fight better on a full stomach.)

Many of the men were so intent on watching the exciting chase from the upper decks that they simply snatched a piece of bread and meat from the galley to make a sandwich and returned to their ringside seats. The officers had picnic lunches in the wardroom. As he went for lunch, one of them recalled, "Enemy visible as five little spots with five small streams of smoke right down on the horizon."

Sturdee twice ordered the battle cruisers to reduce speed, first to twenty-four knots, then to nineteen. He wanted to keep the squadron more concentrated since his ships were now strung out in a long line, with the *Carnarvon* struggling along six miles behind the flagship. Why he gave these orders is not clear, because he certainly didn't need the support of his armored cruisers to deal with the German squadron. The men on the *Glasgow* couldn't understand what their admiral had in mind—could it be that he was afraid of tackling Graf Spee on his own?

After forty-five minutes Sturdee realized that he risked losing his quarry by trying to keep all his ships together, and he ordered the two battle cruisers to resume speed at twenty-six knots. One of the *Inflexible*'s officers recalled that: "[A]t about 1220 the skipper came aft and said that the Admiral had decided to get along with the work. The men on deck cheered."

By 1247 the *Invincible* and *Inflexible* had the tail end of the German squadron within their maximum range of 16,500 yards. Sturdee gave the order to open fire. The *Invincible*'s gunnery officer, Lt. Edward Dannreuther, had calibrated his 12-inch guns at twelve thousand yards. He had never contemplated firing at a target well over nine miles away. Not surprisingly, the first salvoes were both wide and short. Even though they were gaining steadily on the German ships, things didn't improve.

According to Lt. Harold Hickling on board the *Glasgow:* "We were all dismayed at the battlecruisers' gunnery, the large spread, the slow and ragged fire. . . . An occasional shot would fall close to the target while others would be far short or over. . . ."

A fellow officer commented, "It's certainly damn bad shooting."

But by 1315 the range had fallen to thirteen thousand yards, or a little more than seven miles, and the battle cruisers began to straddle the *Leipzig*. She was the last ship in the German line. One salvo caused shell splashes so high and close to the little cruiser that both sides briefly lost sight of her and thought she had been hit. Graf Spee couldn't do much to help her, even though the battle cruisers were now nearly within range of his 8.2-inch guns. He had to conserve ammunition until he could be sure of doing some damage. But at the same time he realized that just one hit from Sturdee's 850-pound shells could cripple the *Leipzig*. A full salvo would rip her apart.

Graf Spee made the gallant and selfless decision to turn and fight Sturdee with his two big ships and thus give his light cruisers a chance to survive. At 1320 he signaled the *Leipzig, Nürnberg,* and *Dresden,* "Leave the line and try to escape."

As they pulled away to starboard, he ordered the *Scharnhorst* and *Gneisenau* to turn almost ninety degrees to port, to try to draw the British squadron onto himself.

Sturdee had foreseen such a move. In his battle instructions he had ordered his armored cruisers and light cruisers to break away in pursuit if the Germans split their forces. Without any signal from the flagship being needed, the *Glasgow, Kent,* and *Cornwall* turned south as soon as they saw the three German light cruisers leave the line. The *Carnarvon* was so slow that it would have been futile for her to join them, and Stoddart had no choice but to plod on after the battle cruisers.

Sturdee made a sharp turn to port to bring his two big ships onto a course roughly parallel to Graf Spee's armored cruisers. He was now about fourteen thousand yards away on the Germans' port quarter. From this point on, the battle developed into a series of separate actions.

The *Invincible* and *Inflexible* were now able to use full broadsides instead of just their forward turrets. They fired sporadically at the *Scharnhorst* and *Gneisenau* without scoring any apparent hits. The British gunners were still having trouble with the smoke, which was now blowing diagonally away from the enemy. The men of the *Inflexible* were having the greatest difficulty because their flagship's smoke was blowing across their line of sight.

At 1330, when the range had dropped to less than thirteen thousand yards, Graf Spee gave the order to return fire. Both German ships concentrated their attack on the British flagship. This left the *Inflexible*'s gunners free to carry out target practice undisturbed, except for the smoke. Graf Spee's first few salvoes fell short, but as the gap between the two lines narrowed, the experienced German gunners found the range. An officer on the *Invincible* wrote: "The German firing was magnificent to watch, perfect ripple salvoes all along their sides. A brown coloured puff with a centre of flame marking each gun as it fired. . . . Their shooting was excellent; they straddled us time after time."

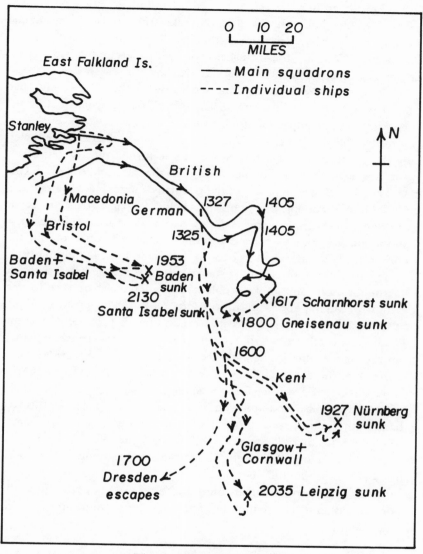

The Battle of the Falklands

Within fifteen minutes the *Scharnhorst* had hit the *Invincible* several times. Two hits on her superstructure wrecked the *Invincible*'s piano and burst a money chest, scattering gold coins all over the place. But at this distance the Germans' 8.2-inch shells couldn't penetrate the battle cruiser's main armored belt and do any vital damage.

Unknown to the British gunners because of the smoke, they had scored two damaging hits on the *Gneisenau,* one of them below the waterline, and one hit on the *Scharnhorst.*

Sturdee had allowed himself to be put at a tactical disadvantage by letting the German ships get too close, and he turned twenty degrees to port. This opened up the distance enough so that he could still reach Graf Spee yet take his own ships out of the Germans' range. He was afraid that a lucky hit might cripple one of his ships before he had a chance to get an unimpeded view of the enemy. London had made it abundantly clear to him that he was not only expected to sink Graf Spee's squadron but also to bring Beatty's battle cruisers back to the Grand Fleet in fighting trim.

The battle was approaching a stalemate. Sturdee knew he had to do something to solve the smoke problem. He ordered a sharp turn to starboard, toward Graf Spee's stern, to try to get into a lee position. While he was inside his own smoke screen, he didn't see that the German admiral had immediately turned due south. When the battle cruisers emerged from the smoke, they could only see the sterns of the *Scharnhorst* and *Gneisenau* in the distance. They were now well out of range. Graf Spee had outmaneuvered Sturdee up to this point.

The sky was still clear, but it would have been very unusual for this area if bad weather didn't come up from the south some time before sunset. The *Gneisenau*'s first officer recalled thinking hopefully: "Every minute we gained before nightfall might decide our fate. The engines were still intact and were doing their best. . . ."

But the afternoon remained sunny and bright, and after a lull in the action that lasted forty-five minutes, Sturdee's ships caught up with their fleeing enemy.

The second phase of the main action began at 1450, when Sturdee had once again brought the enemy ships within range. Less than four hours of daylight remained, and he knew he had to do something to slow the Germans down. Because he was now dead astern of them, he could only train his forward turrets on the enemy, so he ordered a turn to port to bring full broadsides to bear. The *Invincible* opened fire on the *Scharnhorst* at fourteen thousand yards, while the *Inflexible* took on the *Gneisenau.*

The Germans couldn't hope to repeat their earlier maneuver and out-run the British ships; Sturdee would not be tricked a second time. Graf Spee knew he would have to fight to the end. The enemy now had him within range, and they had the great advantage of a main armament broadside in excess of ten thousand pounds to his own thirty-five hundred. His only chance was to close the range to bring his secondary 5.9-inch armament to bear. These were effective weapons at shorter range, unlike the battle cruisers' secondary battery of 4-inch guns, which their detractors called "wretched peashooters."

The German ships turned ninety degrees to port to bring them onto a converging course, and when the range came down to ten thousand yards, they opened fire with their 5.9-inch batteries as well as their main armament.

But with the change of direction, the British gun-layers and range find-ers were less troubled by the smoke, and the battle cruisers' fire was much more effective at this shorter range. They began to score frequent hits on both the *Scharnhorst* and the *Gneisenau*. When the British fired, they could now see bright orange-red flashes appear on the sides of the enemy ships, instead of only the tall fountains of water they had seen earlier.

The bigger British guns were at lower elevation, and their 850-pound shells tore through the 6-inch armor plate of Graf Spee's ships. This was just as thick as the battle cruisers' armor, but it couldn't withstand the impact of 12-inch missiles. The British shells were loaded with lyddite, and its effect was devastating. This was the first time the new picric acid explosive had been used in a full-scale naval battle. The shells caused tremendous damage and many casualties in the heart of the German ships. The lighter German shells had a steeper trajectory and plunged onto the armored decks of the battle cruisers and broke up, resulting in little damage and few casualties.

Both of Graf Spee's ships—especially the *Scharnhorst*—were suffering dreadful blows from the battle cruisers' heavy guns. Smoke from the *Invincible* was again hampering the gunners on the *Inflexible,* and the *Gneisenau* received fewer hits as a consequence. Still the German ships kept up a steady rate of fire. According to one of their gunnery officers: "Every casemate presented the same picture. The men with their powder blackened faces and arms, calmly doing their duty in a cloud of smoke that grew denser as the firing continued; the rattling of the guns in their mountings; the cries of encouragement from the officers; the monoto-nous note of the order transmitters, and the tinkling of the salvo bells. Unrecognizable corpses were thrust aside, and when there was a moment, covered with a flag. . . ."

At the height of the action, both sides were astonished to see a large sailing ship come onto the battle scene from the east and pass between the two lines "with all sail set, including stunsails." In the words of a British officer, "A truly lovely sight she was with every stitch of canvas drawing as she ran free in the light breeze, for all the world like a herald of peace bidding the two lines of grim warships cease the senseless destruction."

It was the Norwegian vessel *Fairport*. Her captain realized he was in great danger from a stray shell and turned back the way he had come, tacking his way to safety as the battle went on.

In desperation, Graf Spee ordered a sharp turn toward the enemy to try to cross his "T." This classical maneuver would allow both his ships to use their full broadsides on the leading British ship, which would be able to reply solely with her one forward turret. The second ship would not be able to fire at all without endangering her leader.

Sturdee countered this move by wheeling his ships through a 360-degree turn away from the Germans. This temporarily opened up the range to fourteen thousand yards. When they came out of their turn, the *Inflexible* was leading the flagship, and as they closed to twelve thousand yards with their superior speed, she began to fire at the *Scharnhorst*.

By 1530 the German flagship had been hit at least forty times. Three of her four funnels had been knocked over, and she was on fire and listing to port. The ship was drawing three feet of water more than normal. Her speed slackened, but not her rate of firing.

It must have been unnerving for the German gun-layers and range finders to watch the flashes and puffs of smoke from the British guns several miles away, then to endure the fearful wait for the huge shells to arrive. They never knew whether they would be covered with harmless spray from a near miss or feel the sickening impact as another shell burst below their decks, mangling or maiming still more of their fellow crew members. In spite of this, they managed to keep up a steady rate of fire, which amazed the British with its discipline and accuracy.

At 1540 Captain Maerker on the *Gneisenau* anxiously signaled the flagship: "Why is the Admiral's flag at half mast? Is he dead?"

But it was only a shell splinter that had severed one of the halyards holding up the flag. The reply came back: "I am all right so far. Have you hit anything?"

Maerker could only tell him, "The smoke prevents all observation."

At this point in the battle Graf Spee made a typically gracious gesture. He acknowledged that his old friend and bridge partner had been quite right when he advised him to stay clear of the Falklands. He signaled Maerker, *"Sie haben doch recht gehabt."*

By 1545 the range had fallen to less than ten thousand yards. At this distance the battle cruisers' guns were at very low elevation, and their shells had a pulverizing effect on the two armored cruisers. The *Scharnhorst*'s firing slackened—most of her port side guns were out of action. Graf Spee swung the ship around to bring his starboard battery to bear. As he did so, Sturdee cut across his stern and finally gained the lee position, completely free from smoke.

The *Inflexible*'s gunnery officer wrote: "For the first time I experienced the luxury of complete immunity from every form of interference. I was now in a position to enjoy the control officer's paradise: a good target, no alteration of course and no next aheads or own smoke to worry me."

The *Inflexible* kept on hammering the severely damaged *Scharnhorst*. Soon "her upper works seemed to be but a shambles of torn and twisted steel and iron, and through the holes in her side, even at the great distance we were from her, could be seen the dull red glow as the flames gradually gained the mastery between her decks."

At 1600 the German flagship turned directly toward her tormentors in a last desperate attack, just as the *Good Hope* had done at Coronel. Graf Spee made his final signal to Maerker. "Endeavour to escape if your engines are still intact."

Because the *Scharnhorst* was still firing, the *Inflexible* turned to meet her and poured in a withering hail of fire at almost point-blank range, but the battered German flagship kept firing back even though she was hit time after time. Her funnels were leaning drunkenly against each other, and both masts were down. A jury mast had been rigged aft, where her battle flag was flying defiantly.

The *Invincible*'s gunnery officer was watching the onslaught. "She was being torn apart and was blazing and it seemed impossible that anyone could still be alive." He recalled saying to a fellow officer, "What the devil can we do?" Then the *Scharnhorst* "suddenly shut up as when a light is blown out." The British ships halted their devastating attack on the blazing hulk.

According to Sturdee: "At 1604, the *Scharnhorst*, whose flag remained flying to the last, suddenly listed heavily to port, and within a minute it became clear that she was a doomed ship; for the list increased very rapidly until she lay on her beam ends, and at 1617 she disappeared."

One of those watching Graf Spee's Götterdämmerung was Lieutenant Dannreuther, son of a well-known musical family and, in an oddly appropriate way, a godson of Richard Wagner.

No one from the *Scharnhorst* survived. She took with her the courageous admiral and almost eight hundred of his officers and men.

Sturdee's ships couldn't stop to lower boats because they were still under heavy fire from the *Gneisenau*.

The *Carnarvon* had just joined the battle, and when she steamed over the spot where the German flagship had gone down fifteen minutes before, all that could be seen was some floating wreckage. Any of her crew who had not been sucked down with the ship must have died quickly in the near freezing water.

As the *Gneisenau* limped away at barely sixteen knots, her first officer was watching the death throes of his stricken flagship. He wrote: "[W]ith her screws still turning, she slid swiftly into the abyss, a few thousand yards astern of us. A thick cloud of smoke from her boilers shot up above her grave as high as her masts. It seemed to be telling us, '*Scharnhorst* awaits *Gneisenau*.' A feeling of utter loneliness, as if one had lost one's best friend, came over everyone who witnessed the end."

Ironically, the fine weather was now beginning to break up, with mist and rain squalls blowing up from the south, but they came too late to help the *Gneisenau*. Maerker kept her on a southwesterly course in the hope of reaching safety, but with all three British ships on his heels, he had no chance. Incredibly, the wounded *Gneisenau* kept up the unequal struggle for nearly two more hours, continually zigzagging to try to avoid being hit.

It is an impressive tribute to German naval construction, and the remarkable discipline and courage of her crew, that the *Gneisenau* kept on firing as she was being pounded mercilessly by the two battle cruisers and the *Carnarvon* at a range of less than ten thousand yards. It was estimated that she must have suffered at least fifty direct hits from 12-inch shells, many of them from close range in the final stages of the battle.

The *Gneisenau*'s first officer later described the results of some of these hits. "[A] shell fell into the after-dressing station, and freed some of the wounded from their sufferings. The doctor was killed there, and the squadron chaplain ended his life of duty. . . . Another shell exploded on the upper deck. . . . It swept the men away as if they had been bundles of clothes. . . . Our ship's resistance capacity was slowly diminishing. . . . Debris and corpses were accumulating, icy water dripped in one place and in another gushed in streams through shell-holes."

But there was no thought of surrender. "Wherever it was possible to do so efforts were made to man the guns." Sturdee had no choice but to keep firing until the *Gneisenau* either surrendered or sank. She scored her last defiant hit on the *Invincible* at 1715. Finally, the *Gneisenau*'s ammunition ran out, even the practice shells the Germans were reduced to using at the end. Sturdee gave the order to cease fire.

As her boilers lost steam, the German cruiser stopped dead in the water, a blazing hulk. What was left of her superstructure was a mass of twisted steel. With about six hundred of his crew killed or wounded, Maerker ordered all hands on deck. Those who could do so fell in and gave three cheers for the Kaiser. Finally the sea-cocks were opened, and Maerker gave the order, "All men overboard."

The *Gneisenau* slowly rolled over at 1800, showing her red-painted underside. The British could see men scrambling down her sides to get away from the ship before she took her final plunge. The *Invincible* and *Inflexible* immediately lowered all boats to pick up survivors, but by a cruel twist of fate, the weather had changed for the worse. A choppy sea and a bitterly cold wind made lifesaving a slow and difficult process. "The Germans in the water were all waving their arms and shouting—not because they wanted to be saved any quicker, but because they had been told to, so as to keep them warm."

The shock of being plunged into the bone-chilling thirty-nine-degree water killed many of the wounded before they could be picked up. The

The *Inflexible* picking up survivors from the *Gneisenau* (*Imperial War Museum*)

rescuers had to beat off skuas and albatrosses that attacked the men in the water relentlessly.

The only time that day that anyone saw Sturdee lose his unruffled air of calm was when the *Carnarvon* was slow to lower her boats to pick up survivors. He became quite angry and twice signaled sharply to Stoddart, "Lower all boats immediately." By a strange coincidence one of the Germans picked up by the *Carnarvon* had the same name as her commander. When he came on board the cruiser, he said to his rescuers: "I believe I have a first cousin in one of your ships. His name is Stoddart."

When the boats returned to the British ships loaded with survivors, the waves battered them against the cruisers' sides. One of the *Carnarvon*'s boats was smashed to pieces. A midshipman wrote: "One of our cutters was near and managed to rescue all our men, but some of the Germans floated away calling for help which we could not give them. It was shocking to see the look on their faces as they drifted away and we could do nothing to save them. A great many were drowned. . . . We could see them floating past, a horrible sight."

In the end, only 190 men out of a crew of 765 were pulled from the water alive. Many of them later died of their wounds or from shock and exposure. Captain Maerker and young Heinrich von Spee were not among the survivors.

In stark contrast to the more than thirteen hundred men lost when the two German armored cruisers sank, casualties on the British side were incredibly light. The *Invincible* had suffered the most punishment, but in spite of being hit twenty-two times, she had no casualties at all. The *Inflexible* was hit just three times, but she had one killed and two wounded. The *Carnarvon* was completely unscathed, because the Germans had concentrated their fire on their most dangerous foes.

An officer on the *Inflexible* recalled that after the main cruiser action was over:

> We were very busy getting out clothes . . . for [the survivors], and by dinner-time we had several dining in the mess, and very nice fellows they are, too. Most of them could not sleep that night, the scenes in their ship were so terrible. To see one's best friend suddenly torn to bits, or rush on deck one huge wound covered with blood and just have time to send his love home, is terrible. But we were all good friends after the fight, and both agreed that we did not want to fight at all, but had to.

He added, "But they fought magnificently, and their discipline must have been superb."

* * *

Earlier in the afternoon, when the three light cruisers broke away from the *Scharnhorst* and *Gneisenau,* they were about ten to twelve miles ahead of their pursuers. The *Dresden* was leading, followed by the *Nürnberg* and then the *Leipzig*, which was still lagging behind. They were badly out-gunned, especially by the *Cornwall* and *Kent*. Their only chance of escape was to keep on toward the south, hoping for fog or heavy rain squalls, then to turn toward safety in the inlets of Tierra del Fuego.

There was little difference between the designed speeds of the German and British ships. With their head start, it seemed doubtful whether any of Graf Spee's light cruisers would be caught. But after their long service without a refit, the boilers and engines of the *Nürnberg* and *Leipzig* were in no condition to reach their rated twenty-four knots. The freshly repaired *Glasgow* was capable of twenty-five knots or better, and she pulled ahead of the two armored cruisers. After an hour's chase she had almost caught up with the *Leipzig*.

Captain Luce's first idea was to chase the fastest German cruiser, the *Dresden,* and leave the other two to the slower armored cruisers. But he soon realized that if the *Dresden* kept to her present speed and position four miles ahead of the *Nürnberg,* he might not be able to catch her before nightfall and thus ran the risk of letting the other two escape as well.

By 1445 Luce had the *Leipzig* within range, and a few minutes later he opened fire with his forward 6-inch gun, hoping to slow down the German formation. He thought they would stick together if one of them was attacked, but the *Leipzig* immediately turned sharply to starboard and returned his fire with full broadsides from her five 4.1-inch guns. The other two ships kept on to the south at full speed.

The *Leipzig*'s gunnery was accurate, as she had already shown at Coronel. Within a few minutes she had scored two direct hits on the *Glasgow*. Luce was obliged to make a turn to starboard so he could bring both of his 6-inch guns to bear. Although some of the *Leipzig*'s 4.1-inch shells were actually passing over the *Glasgow*, Luce still couldn't reach the German ship with his bigger guns, which were supposedly of longer range. After the *Glasgow* turned away, the *Leipzig* resumed her original course, following the *Dresden* and *Nürnberg*.

Capt. Walter Ellerton of the *Cornwall* made a signal to Luce and Capt. John Allen of the *Kent*. "I will take centre target (*Leipzig*) if *Kent* take left (*Nürnberg*) and *Glasgow* right (*Dresden*)."

Luce was senior officer, and he rejected Ellerton's proposal. He signaled back: "I fear I am gaining very slowly on *Dresden*. Having already engaged *Leipzig* I feel I must stand by you."

Luce decided that he probably could not catch the *Dresden* before dark and tried another attack on the *Leipzig*. He hoped to delay the Germans until the *Cornwall* and *Kent* were able to get them within range.

The *Leipzig* once again turned to engage the *Glasgow* with her full broadside, but the Germans realized what Luce was trying to do and scattered their formation. The *Dresden* made off to the southwest and the *Nürnberg* to the southeast, while the *Leipzig* kept on alternately firing broadsides at the *Glasgow* and turning due south.

Luce's tactics paid off, because every time the *Leipzig* turned to fire broadsides at the *Glasgow,* she lost another mile or so of her lead. By 1617 the *Cornwall* had the *Leipzig* within range and opened fire on her port side. For a while the *Glasgow* kept firing at her starboard side, then moved across her stern to join the *Cornwall* and concentrate on one side of the German cruiser. This restricted the *Leipzig* to using only the five guns of her port battery. She soon switched her target to the more dangerous *Cornwall,* leaving the *Glasgow* free to fire undisturbed. After the two early hits by the *Leipzig,* she suffered no further damage.

Meanwhile, the *Kent* had turned to port to pursue the *Nürnberg,* and the plucky *Leipzig* fired on her as she went past. By now, Lüdecke had managed to get the *Dresden* up to a remarkable twenty-seven knots, and she was gradually disappearing into the mist and rain that were coming up from the south.

The *Leipzig*'s fire remained disciplined and accurate, but she was locked in an unequal struggle with two ships that outgunned her, particularly the *Cornwall,* with her broadside of nine 6-inch guns. The British ships kept altering the range to make spotting difficult for the German gunners. By 1800 the mist and rain were coming closer. The *Leipzig* was still gamely firing back with regular salvoes and hitting the *Cornwall,* but her light shells were doing little damage against two-inch armor plate.

Luce signaled Ellerton to close the range to eight thousand yards. The *Cornwall* began using lyddite, and she hit the *Leipzig* repeatedly with terrible effect. According to one of the *Leipzig*'s officers: "The lyddite would burst in the middle of a group and strip them of their arms and legs—men would rush about with exposed bones, crazy from the effects of the shell . . . each explosion would account for about forty men."

To make things even worse, the German cruiser was on fire in several places. Ellerton signaled her: "Am anxious to save life. Do you surrender?"

The only reply was another broadside. Then the *Leipzig*'s rate of firing slackened and became irregular. After another quarter of an hour most of her guns were silent. She was nearly out of ammunition.

By 1900, four hours had passed since the *Glasgow* had first opened fire. The *Leipzig*'s desperate struggle was almost over. Her mainmast and two funnels were down, and she was ablaze from stem to stern. When all his shells had been used up, Captain Haun told his torpedo officer, Ensign Schwig, "Go ahead, it's your turn now. . . ." Schwig fired three torpedoes at the *Cornwall*, but she was too far away for them to have any chance of a hit.

Finally, Haun ordered the sea-cocks to be opened. He told his remaining crew to gather amidships where the fires were less intense. "The survivors . . . assembled on the afterpart of the forecastle . . . practically the only unencumbered deck space. Everywhere else lay heaps of ruins with the bodies of dead and dying upon them."

Luce closed in with the *Glasgow* and circled slowly around the *Leipzig* to see if she had surrendered. The crippled ship had almost stopped, but her flag was still flying, and there was always the danger of another torpedo attack. The British cruiser opened fire at close range to finish her off. According to one of the *Leipzig*'s officers: "[This] played havoc among the crowded groups of men and caused frightful slaughter. Many men sought shelter behind the gun shields but were mown down by shell splinters that ricocheted from the conning tower."

Haun gave permission for his men to jump over the lee side to protect themselves. Those who did soon perished in the freezing-cold sea. Others "decided . . . to swim towards the enemy . . . but the cold water numbed them. None of them were saved. . . . The survivors stood by the Captain on the forecastle."

The *Leipzig* fired two green flares, which Luce took to be a sign of surrender, and he gave the order to cease fire. At 2100 he signaled the German ship, "I am sending boats to save life." Twenty minutes later the *Leipzig* rolled over and sank, her courageous struggle against overwhelming odds finally over. The British cruisers lowered all their boats, but the choppy sea and the darkness made lifesaving difficult. An officer recalled, "[O]ur searchlights poked hither and thither to assist the cutters in their search for survivors—our guns' crews leaning silently against their guns. . . ."

Only eighteen men were rescued out of a crew of more than three hundred. Although he had been alive and uninjured to the end, Captain Haun was not among the survivors. When the *Cornwall*'s captain was told, he replied, "I deeply regret that so gallant an officer was not saved."

Casualties on the British ships were amazingly light. The *Cornwall* had been hit eighteen times, but not a single man was wounded. Her only serious damage was a hole below the waterline that had flooded two bunkers and caused a list. The *Glasgow* was hit just twice, at the beginning of the action, and she had one killed and four wounded. One of her boilers had been holed, and this reduced her speed.

There was now no question of going after the *Dresden*. Luce had no idea which direction she had finally taken, and anyway, both his ships were low on ammunition.

When Sturdee signaled him for news of the light cruiser action, Luce told him they had caught the *Leipzig* but the *Dresden* had got away. This was more unfortunate for the admiral than it was for Luce, because Sturdee had been expected to achieve complete annihilation of Graf Spee's squadron. When he asked about the *Nürnberg*, Luce could tell him nothing. He had neither seen nor heard from the *Kent* for several hours.

When the *Kent* turned away from the other ships and went in pursuit of the *Nürnberg*, the situation didn't look at all promising to Captain Allen. His ship was the oldest of the "County" class, vintage 1901, and had the reputation of being a poor steamer. It seemed doubtful whether she could reach her rated speed of twenty-three knots. Another problem was that due to the hasty departure from Port Stanley that morning, she had barely enough coal for a day's steaming at full speed.

The *Nürnberg* was now about ten miles ahead, but despite her two-knot advantage on paper, she wasn't able to pull away from the *Kent*. Her engines were badly in need of an overhaul after steaming more than twenty thousand miles in three months.

Throughout the bright sunny afternoon the *Kent*'s stokers and engineers made herculean efforts to respond to Allen's order for "utmost speed." At one point they managed to develop five thousand horsepower beyond the ship's designed maximum—the pressure gauges reached into the red danger zone.

The rest of the crew helped by bringing down to the boiler rooms every scrap of available wood to add to the fires: ladders, targets, lockers, and capstan bars were burned to increase the heat in the furnaces. Even the chaplain's lectern and some of the ship's furniture were chopped up and burned.

The old cruiser eventually reached an unprecedented twenty-five knots. At this speed her engines were causing the ship to vibrate so much that the range finders couldn't be focused.

By late afternoon it began to drizzle, and patches of mist were forming. The *Kent* was clearly gaining ground. By 1700 she was within twelve thousand yards of her prey. The *Nürnberg* opened fire at this great range with her stern battery. As expected from one of Graf Spee's ships, her shooting was accurate; she soon began to score hits on the *Kent*. Incredibly, some of her shells passed over the *Kent*, but when Allen responded ten minutes later with his supposedly longer-range 6-inch guns, he still couldn't reach the target.

The *Nürnberg*'s speed dropped to nineteen knots, and when the range had closed to seven thousand yards, both ships began making direct hits. Captain von Schönberg knew he could no longer hope to outrun his pursuer before dark and made a sharp turn to port to bring his full broadside to bear. Allen made a similar turn and brought his ship onto a converging course. By 1730 the range had come down to three thousand yards.

The *Kent* changed from ordinary shell to lyddite, and at this short distance she inflicted many punishing hits on the light cruiser. These started fires that could easily be seen from the *Kent*, nearly two miles away. The *Nürnberg* was still firing regularly and hitting the *Kent* frequently, but the lighter German shells were breaking up against her armor plate with little effect. Schönberg turned around to bring his undamaged starboard battery to bear, but the *Kent* swung away onto a parallel course and opened the range to four thousand yards.

The *Nürnberg* was undoubtedly the unluckiest of all the German cruisers that day. Around 1830, when the visibility had become so poor that she might still have made it to safety in the mist, two of her overstrained boilers blew up. Her speed dropped rapidly. There was no longer any hope of escape.

The *Kent* was now able to pass her easily and cut across her bow to pour murderous broadsides of lyddite into her at close range. By an odd quirk of fate, it had fallen to the *Monmouth*'s sister ship to avenge her by sinking the cruiser that had been her nemesis at Coronel. The *Nürnberg* could expect no mercy. An observer wrote that she was soon "riddled like a watchman's bucket."

In less than thirty minutes the *Nürnberg* was quite still in the water. All her guns had stopped firing; she was down by the stern and listing to starboard, with her foremast gone and bridge shattered. Her flag was still flying from the after mast, and as Allen closed in to see if she would surrender, one of her guns fired and hit the *Kent*. Allen had no choice but to open fire again. A few minutes later the *Nürnberg*'s flag was hauled down. Allen gave orders to cease fire and lower all boats.

At 1926 the crippled *Nürnberg* heeled over to starboard and began to sink slowly by the stern. Her end was witnessed by the barque *Fairport*, which had once more chanced upon the battle area. According to one observer, she seemed like "a great ghost ship. . . . Slowly, majestically, she sailed by and vanished into the night."

Surgeon-Lt. T. B. Dixon of the *Kent* was also watching the final throes of the *Nürnberg* and later wrote in his diary, "The enemy fought splendidly, but were quite outclassed."

All but two of the *Kent*'s boats had been badly damaged during the battle. It took the ship's carpenters twenty agonizing minutes to patch these two enough to make them reasonably seaworthy. The men in the *Kent*'s leaking boats eventually managed to pull twelve officers and men from the bone-chilling water. They were the only survivors out of a crew of more than three hundred. But according to one observer: "A few men were found floating lashed to hammocks, but many of these were dead from the cold, and albatrosses were attacking even the living. In the end only seven men were saved alive."

One of the survivors recalled that: "[The albatrosses] surveyed the field of the dead and avidly sought prey. It was just as well to have a spar in the hand to defend oneself. One of our officers, noticing a bird swoop down on a man, shouted to the latter: 'Hit him on the paws.'"

Captain von Schönberg and Otto von Spee were not among those rescued. Otto had outlived his father and younger brother by merely a few hours.

The *Kent* spent the next hour and a half looking for more survivors until it became too dark to see, then turned back toward the Falklands at 2100. She had been hit thirty-eight times, but only four of her crew were killed and twelve were injured, although some of them later died of their wounds.

She was extremely fortunate to escape with so few casualties. During the height of the battle, one of the *Nürnberg*'s shells had caused a fire that ignited some cordite charges in an ammunition passage. Sgt. Charles Mayes of the Royal Marines had the presence of mind to throw the burning cordite away from the other ammunition before flooding the compartment. He received the Conspicuous Gallantry Medal for his brave action and was later awarded an annuity of £20 by Parliament. If he had not acted so promptly the fire would have spread quickly to the *Kent*'s magazines and blown the ship sky high, as happened to several British ships later in the war, with heavy loss of life.

By this time the *Invincible, Inflexible,* and *Carnarvon* had finished picking up survivors from the *Gneisenau,* and Sturdee signaled his other captains for news of the rest of Graf Spee's squadron. "*Scharnhorst* and *Gneisenau* sunk: where are the others?"

The first to reply was Capt. B. H. Fanshawe of the *Bristol,* who had been left behind when the squadron set off in pursuit of Graf Spee. He reported that in company with the *Macedonia* he had pursued, captured, and sunk two of Graf Spee's supply ships, but the third ship reported off the Falklands had escaped.

After the first reports of the German squadron came in on the morning of the battle, a Mrs. Felton, the wife of a sheep farmer in Port Darwin, had stationed herself and her maid on Mount Pleasant to watch for more ships. They saw the smoke of three ships about twenty-five miles to the west of Port Stanley. Leaving her maid to keep watch, Mrs. Felton dashed back to her house to telephone the governor, who passed the news on to Sturdee at 1127. There had been rumors that the Germans planned to put an occupation force on the islands, and Sturdee believed that the new arrivals were troop transports. He immediately signaled Fanshawe to take the *Bristol* and *Macedonia* out of the harbor as soon as they had steam up and "destroy transports."

In fact, the three ships were the colliers *Baden, Santa Isabel,* and *Seydlitz.* The first two had orders to move in close to shore and await the outcome of the raid, while the *Seydlitz* was to stay close to Graf Spee's cruisers in case she was needed as a hospital ship. By the time the *Bristol* and *Macedonia* arrived off Point Pleasant, the *Baden* and *Santa Isabel* had headed out to sea after they had seen Graf Spee turn away from the islands, but Mrs. Felton was able to report their direction. After a long chase they were caught at 1500.

When Fanshawe captured these ships, he interpreted Sturdee's signal to "destroy transports" quite literally and overlooked the sentence in the admiral's instructions, "The opportunity might occur to capture the enemy's colliers." The *Bristol* sank the two ships by gunfire after their crews had been taken off, wasting their valuable stores and coal supplies.

Fanshawe went to look for the third German supply ship, but the captain of the *Seydlitz* had made off to the southwest at high speed as soon as it became clear that his squadron was doomed. The collier escaped into the darkness before Fanshawe could get close enough to open fire on her. (This was fortunate for the British crew of the *Drummuir,* who were prisoners on board the *Seydlitz* and might have been killed by their fellow countrymen.) After making for the relative safety of the icebergs and rocks of Tierra del Fuego, her captain tried to contact the *Dresden,* which he had seen escaping, but without success. In the end, the *Seydlitz* headed for Argentine waters and internment in San Antonio.

The next captain to reply to Sturdee's signal was Luce. He confirmed that he had sunk the *Leipzig* but that the *Dresden* had got away.

Allen never replied, even after repeated wireless signals. From the ominous silence, the admiral was worried that the *Kent* might have been badly damaged or sunk. It was not until twenty-four hours later that the cruiser arrived back in Port Stanley, having been forced to steam slowly to conserve her dwindling coal stocks. Allen reported that his wireless transmitter had been knocked out by a direct hit early in the action but that they had sunk the *Nürnberg*.

The British were delighted with the day's results. They had destroyed four of Graf Spee's five cruisers and two of his three supply ships. When the news reached London, the Admiralty was jubilant. Even if it wasn't the complete annihilation that Fisher had envisaged, it was, as Admiral Beatty said, "The most decisive battle of the war." Indeed, the Falklands was one of the most decisive actions in the Royal Navy's long history.

Fisher and his beloved battle cruisers, which his critics had called "monstrous cruisers," were vindicated. They had obliterated the menace of Graf Spee's big ships. The First Sea Lord gleefully reminded his critics that they had thought him "mad for denuding the Grand Fleet of our fastest battlecruisers to send them 14,000 miles on a supposed wild-goose chase. . . . And how I was execrated for inventing the battlecruisers!"

In the end it had turned out exactly as Churchill once remarked of Graf Spee and his squadron: "He was a cut flower in a vase. Fair to see yet bound to die."

The loss of four cruisers and more than two thousand trained men didn't have a major impact on German naval strength, but the gain to the Allies was far more significant. In Churchill's words the results of Sturdee's victory were:

> far-reaching and affected simultaneously our position in every part of the globe. The strain was everywhere relaxed. All our enterprises, whether of war or commerce, proceeded without the slightest hindrance. Within 24 hours orders were sent . . . to a score of British ships to return to home waters. For the first time we saw ourselves possessed of immense surpluses of ships . . . of trained men and of naval supplies of all kinds. . . . The public, though gratified by the annihilating character of the victory, was quite unconscious of its immense importance to the whole naval situation.

The victory had a profound effect on morale. The deep sense of humiliation after Coronel had been wiped away. Cradock was avenged, the prestige of the Royal Navy was restored, and its total command of the seas was regained. The people were happy in the knowledge that Britannia once again ruled the waves.

The British representative in the South Atlantic was showered with praise and congratulations. The king signaled him, "I heartily congratulate you and your officers and men on your most opportune victory." The Admiralty sent him a telegram. "Our thanks are due to yourself and to your officers and men for the brilliant victory you have reported." Similar messages of praise came from Jellicoe, Beatty, fellow admirals, and old shipmates. The French and Russian admiralties also sent Sturdee their congratulations.

Sturdee enjoyed his moment of glory, but he didn't forget that the victory was just as much that of his captains, officers, and men. He commended them all for their actions "in attaining this great result" and for their "zeal and steadiness under fire."

One who perhaps did not receive full credit for his contribution to the victory was Captain Luce. Sturdee made no mention in his reports that Luce had urged him to leave Abrolhos earlier than he had planned, which had led to his timely arrival in Port Stanley. When Luce later brought up the subject of their discussion at Abrolhos, he met with a frigid reception from his admiral. Sturdee didn't want to be reminded of how near he had come to missing Graf Spee.

Even though the *Dresden* had escaped, Sturdee had done what was expected of him. Within six weeks of leaving Devonport he had sunk Graf Spee's two big ships and destroyed the famous cruiser squadron. He had achieved this with minimal casualties and negligible damage to his own ships. As expected of him, he was able to return their precious battle cruisers intact to Jellicoe and Beatty.

Although his tactics and the large amounts of time and ammunition he had needed to dispatch an inferior enemy formation were subsequently criticized, Sturdee had refused to panic in the difficult situation he found himself in on the morning of December 8. He had acted calmly and deliberately throughout the day of the battle.

While he had clear superiority of firepower, just as Graf Spee had had at Coronel, the positions facing the two admirals were quite different. Cradock had run headlong into his enemy with largely obsolescent ships and untrained crews and had made no attempt to evade action. This made Graf Spee's task simply one of close-range destruction. But at the Falklands, Sturdee had to pursue a tricky and experienced foe who had at least a fifteen-mile head start, with modern ships and battle-hardened crews.

Sturdee had been outmaneuvered by Graf Spee at first, but he had used his twin advantages of speed and gunpower wisely and had not hazarded his ships or his men unnecessarily. What did it matter how many shells he had used when measured against the lives of trained seamen?

It was just as Sturdee remarked to his flag captain on the *Invincible* on the evening of December 8. "Well, Beamish, we were sacked from the Admiralty, but we've done pretty well."

But one ship of Graf Spee's once proud squadron was still intact. As long as she remained afloat, she would be a threat to Allied shipping wherever she might show up.

12

The Hunt for the *Dresden*

Object is destruction not internment. . . . Press your chase.

—Admiralty instruction to Sturdee's cruiser captains

As soon as Luce informed him that the *Dresden* had escaped, Sturdee took the *Invincible, Inflexible,* and *Bristol* on a sweep toward the tip of Tierra del Fuego. He thought it probable that Lüdecke would head for the Germans' previous rendezvous at Picton Island to meet one of his colliers, and he hoped to catch the *Dresden* while she was coaling. But after searching the area around the entrance to the Beagle Channel for twenty-four hours, the British ships were forced by the thick fog to return empty-handed to the Falklands. They arrived on the morning of December 11, the day after the missing *Kent* showed up.

Sturdee sent a memorandum to each of his captains and ordered them to read it aloud to the assembled ships' companies. He congratulated the officers and men on their outstanding performance but reminded them that "the victory will not be complete until the remaining cruiser is accounted for. . . . directly the squadron is coaled a further organized search will be made. . . ."

By late evening on the day of the battle, Lüdecke knew the worst. He intercepted wireless messages between the British ships, which in the first flush of victory didn't bother to encode their signals. These told him that his ship was probably the only survivor of Graf Spee's squadron. He didn't hold out much hope that the *Nürnberg* had been able to outrun the *Kent*.

The *Dresden* was badly in need of coal after her high-speed escape, but Lüdecke doubted that any of the colliers would make it to Picton Island, where they had been ordered to rendezvous. He had heard transmissions from the *Bristol* that she was pursuing the *Baden* and *Santa Isabel*; he had heard nothing from the *Seydlitz*. Even if the *Seydlitz* had managed to escape, it would be risky for the *Dresden* to go anywhere near the Beagle Channel. By now, the Allies would surely have been informed that it had been used as a German coaling point.

Instead, Lüdecke kept well to the south of Cape Horn. On the day after the battle, he took the *Dresden* into the tortuous and partly uncharted Cockburn Channel and anchored in the isolated Sholl Bay. With only 160 tons of coal left, he was obliged to send landing parties ashore to cut green timber. He hoped this would burn when it was combined with his remaining coal supply. But before the men ashore could finish their work, the Chilean destroyer *Almirante Condell* showed up on December 11 to remind Lüdecke of the twenty-four-hour rule.

Rather than spend any more time in Sholl Bay, Lüdecke decided to go to Punta Arenas, which was only about eighty miles away. He told the captain of the Chilean destroyer that he needed both coal and provisions and asked him to wireless his superiors to see if they would grant him permission to obtain these in Punta Arenas. Admiral Cuevas wirelessed back that the Germans could stay in port for twenty-four hours. The Chilean port commandant could hardly refuse Lüdecke's request— he had recently allowed HMS *Otranto* to coal there for much longer than this.

In 1914 Punta Arenas was still a busy seaport, for the full impact of the Panama Canal opening on the Cape Horn trade route had not yet been felt. When Lüdecke arrived there on December 12, however, he had difficulty at first in purchasing coal and other necessities. The captain of the U.S. collier *Minnesota* refused to sell him any coal or supplies. (The Germans claimed he had been bribed by the British not to supply the *Dresden*.) Lüdecke was eventually able to get some coal from a German ship, the *Turpin*, but had to settle for her low-grade briquettes.

Lüdecke's timing was indeed fortunate because the next day instructions arrived from Santiago that Admiral Cuevas was not to permit German warships to coal there at all. The Chilean government had finally lost patience with the Germans' repeated infringements of their neutrality.

Lüdecke knew that the British consul would have immediately informed Port Stanley of his arrival, and he left Punta Arenas as soon as his bunkers were filled. His next hiding place was the desolate Hewett Bay, near the mouth of the Gonzalez Channel. From here he could easily flee into the Pacific at the first sign of an enemy warship.

* * *

When Sturdee heard the news that the *Dresden* had put in to Punta Arenas, he immediately sent the *Bristol* there to investigate, followed soon after by the *Inflexible* and *Glasgow*. He also dispatched the *Carnarvon* and *Cornwall* to search the Argentine coast north of the Strait of Magellan in case Lüdecke had doubled back into the Atlantic. But by the time the searchers arrived on the scene, the report from Punta Arenas was thirty-six hours old. There was no sign of the *Dresden* in either location.

In London the Admiralty learned that the *Dresden* had not only escaped from the battle area but also had eluded Sturdee's attempts to catch her off Tierra del Fuego. They ordered him to return to Britain with the two battle cruisers as soon as possible and told him to leave Stoddart in charge of the other cruisers to carry on with the search.

When the first report came in that the *Dresden* had docked at Punta Arenas, the Admiralty optimistically concluded that Lüdecke had gone

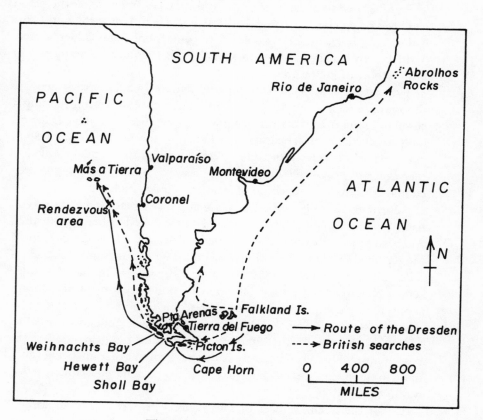

The hunt for the *Dresden*

there to seek internment. But after Sturdee signaled that she had left immediately after coaling, it changed its previous orders and left it to his discretion as to how to proceed with the hunt.

The Admiralty wirelessed him: "Object is destruction not internment. . . . Press your chase."

This instruction was passed on to all the ships' captains. Sturdee replied that he would start out for Devonport with the *Invincible* on December 16 and leave the *Inflexible* behind for two more weeks before turning the search over to Stoddart and his armored cruisers.

By December 18 Fisher was seething with rage over Sturdee's failure to sink the *Dresden* and achieve the total annihilation of Graf Spee's squadron that he and Churchill had planned. He signaled the admiral, "Report fully reason for course you have followed since action. . . ."

This was only the first of a series of increasingly sharp telegrams between the First Sea Lord and his bête noire.

Sturdee tried to explain, calmly at first, that his actions after the battle had been based on the best information available to him at the time. This had indicated that Lüdecke would try to contact one of his colliers secretly off Picton Island, rather than advertise his presence by going to the busy seaport of Punta Arenas.

Fisher was not satisfied with this explanation. In a letter to Jellicoe he venomously referred to "Sturdee's criminal ineptitude in not sending a vessel to Punta Arenas after the action on December 8. . . ." He made no reply to Sturdee until January 3, by which time the *Invincible* was well on her way back to Devonport. He called upon him to, "Explain why neither *Inflexible, Invincible* nor any other vessel of your command proceeded immediately on completion of action to Punta Arenas. . . ."

An irritated Sturdee replied tersely that the "reasons for actions taken" had been given in his previous signal. This infuriated Fisher even further, and he shot back that Sturdee's response "does not answer the question." He repeated in full his previous demand for an explanation of the admiral's actions immediately after the battle. A by-now exasperated Sturdee sent back a long and reasonable point-by-point account of his actions, supported by the intelligence reports available to him. He concluded his signal by stating: "Their Lordships selected me as Commander-in-Chief to destroy the two hostile armoured cruisers and I endeavoured to the best of my ability to carry out these orders. I submit that my being called upon in three separate telegrams to give reasons for my subsequent action was unexpected."

Under the circumstances this was a mild protest. Many an admiral would have made a less temperate response. Nonetheless, Fisher sharply rebuked him. "Last paragraph of . . . your signal . . . is improper and such observations must not be repeated." Fisher concluded the acrimonious exchange with the ominous remark, "Their Lordships await your written report and dispatches before coming to any conclusion."

When Sturdee reached Gibraltar, the *Invincible* had to go into dock for minor repairs. While he waited he wrote the Admiralty a long official account of the battle and his subsequent actions. Fisher did not respond. That seemed to be the end of the unsavory affair.

But Fisher petulantly proposed that Sturdee be transferred to one of the armored cruisers and that he be left in the South Atlantic for as long as it took until the *Dresden* was caught and destroyed. Churchill overruled him. Such an assignment would have been both an insult and a demotion, and as he remarked, "scarcely suited to his rank and standing, and woefully out of harmony with his recent achievement."

When Churchill read Sturdee's dispatch from Gibraltar, he knew that Fisher's harsh criticism was unjustified, and he offered Sturdee a new appointment upon his return to Britain. This was command of the Fourth Battle Squadron. It was a definite promotion since it meant the admiral would have four battleships under his command. Sturdee gratefully accepted.

Churchill didn't want the acrimony between his First Sea Lord and his admiral to escalate until it became public knowledge. Nothing must be allowed to tarnish the glorious victory that had restored the people's "absolute confidence in the supremacy of the Navy." As far as Churchill was concerned the important thing was that, apart from a few armed auxiliaries, the seas were now practically clear of German raiders. The only regular warship on the loose was the *Dresden*. The *Königsberg* was intact, but she was bottled up in an African river and therefore was not an immediate threat. The *Karlsruhe* had not been heard from for over a month. In Churchill's view the search for the *Dresden* could safely be left to Stoddart and his armored cruisers. His sensible decision led to strained relations with Fisher, who in happier times had referred to his superior as "a genius without doubt."

Fisher's vindictiveness was not exhausted, even though he had been forced to yield to Churchill. When Sturdee arrived back in Devonport he received widespread public acclaim. He learned that he was to be recommended for the baronetcy traditionally awarded for a victory at sea—the first time this had happened in more than a hundred years. But Fisher was determined to take the shine off Sturdee's glory and did everything he could to make things unpleasant for the admiral, whom he regarded as both incompetent and insubordinate.

When Sturdee passed through London on his way to take up his new command, he reported officially to the Admiralty. Fisher made the admiral cool his heels for several hours outside his office before admitting him. During a frosty five-minute interview, Fisher castigated the admiral for allowing the *Dresden* to escape. At this meeting, neither Churchill nor Fisher "evinced the slightest interest in the engagement," according to an indignant Sturdee.

Then the First Sea Lord found out that the admiral was to have an audience at Buckingham Palace to give a personal account of the battle to the king and queen. He tried to prevent this by ordering Sturdee to leave London immediately to take up his new appointment at Scapa Flow. But the admiral refused to go until he had seen their Majesties.

Fisher's venom even extended to the officers and men of the victorious squadron. He excised many names from Sturdee's list of those mentioned in dispatches for possible honors and medals. He also drastically curtailed Sturdee's official report of the battle and doctored it to reduce the credit due to the admiral and his captains before he would allow it to be published in the *London Gazette*. This thoroughly unedifying performance by the First Sea Lord did not become widely known until after the war.

Meanwhile in the South Atlantic, Stoddart and his six ships were left with the unenviable task of trying to track down a solitary cruiser in the countless bays and channels of the rocky Patagonian coast. Many of the areas to be searched were poorly charted waters. Captain Milward, the British consul in Punta Arenas, did his best to help the hunters by gathering intelligence about the *Dresden*'s movements, but this was countered by the German consul, Herr Stubenrauch, and his agents. They spread so many false leads and rumors that Milward's advice was usually ignored by the Admiralty.

Stoddart deployed his ships to search the Atlantic coast as far north as the Abrolhos rocks, as well as the areas around the Falklands and Tierra del Fuego. The Admiralty ordered him to send the *Kent* and *Orama* up the coast of Chile to meet the *Newcastle, Idzumo,* and *Asama* coming down from the north.

Milward was convinced that the *Dresden* was still somewhere in Tierra del Fuego because there were many possible hiding places in that area, and the consul had obtained information that small vessels were being chartered by German agents in Punta Arenas, presumably to supply the *Dresden* with provisions. This strongly suggested that she had not left.

*   *   *

When Lüdecke coaled at Punta Arenas on December 12, he rejected Consul Stubenrauch's advice that he seek internment there. But when he left for his hiding place in Hewett Bay, he didn't have a firm idea of what to do next. He knew that coaling would be difficult whatever he decided. Unlike Müller, he was content to sit and wait for supply ships to be sent to him rather than go out to sea and try to capture Allied colliers.

After two weeks in Hewett Bay, the *Dresden* was seen by a passing schooner. As soon as the vessel was out of sight, Lüdecke gave the order to raise anchor, knowing that the schooner would report his position, and he moved the ship to a new hiding place in Weihnachts Bay, (so-called by the *Dresden*'s crew because they spent Christmas there). This was about eighty miles farther up the coast of Chile.

After three uneventful weeks, the North German Lloyd freighter *Sierra Cordoba* joined him there on January 19. She had been dispatched by the Etappe in La Plata. The Germans were lucky; the *Sierra Cordoba* had been spotted by the *Cornwall* on December 26, but the freighter was inside territorial waters at the time, and the British cruiser was being watched by a Chilean destroyer. It was broad daylight, and Captain Ellerton had no choice but to leave her alone. The *Sierra Cordoba* eluded him after dark.

Unfortunately for Lüdecke, the *Sierra Cordoba* didn't have much coal on board, although she carried plenty of supplies and provisions. He waited in vain for the other colliers that had been instructed to rendezvous with him off Tierra del Fuego. One was captured near the Falklands by the *Carnarvon;* another was sunk in the Pacific by HMAS *Australia;* and yet another was prevented from sailing when her crew mutinied at Pernambuco.

In early January Milward received information that the *Dresden* was hiding in Weihnachts Bay. He signaled the news to Stoddart and to the Admiralty, but they didn't believe it. The Admiralty thought it was another German plant, meant to send British ships on a wild-goose chase into rocky inlets where they might be wrecked. Rumors about the *Dresden*'s location were so rampant that the Admiralty's scepticism was understandable. It was even rumored that the *Dresden*'s officers were going to Punta Arenas on leave every weekend.

Although it refused to accept Milward's information, the Admiralty signaled Stoddart to send the *Glasgow, Kent,* and *Cornwall* to search the fjords in the uncharted Smyth Channel area. They were ordered to proceed inland as far as Last Hope Inlet, well over a hundred miles from the open sea. This order was based on false rumors spread by German agents. Once again the Admiralty exercised its penchant for interfering with local judgments. In this case it was particularly dangerous since some charts showed several of the areas to be searched to be shallows, or even dry land.

Milward remained convinced that the *Dresden* was still hiding in Weihnachts Bay. He heard persistent reports that supply vessels were leaving Punta Arenas to take provisions to her. He couldn't sway the Admiralty, which ordered yet another futile search of Last Hope Inlet. During this operation the *Bristol* damaged her rudder so badly on the rocks that she had to go into dry dock.

It was a frustrating and hazardous time for the crews of the British cruisers. In the diary of one of the *Kent*'s officers there is the frequent entry, "No news of *Dresden*."

To relieve their boredom and the monotony of their diet, the crews engaged in fishing expeditions. Most of the time they were unsuccessful using fishing lines, and so they resorted to throwing guncotton charges into the sea. They did manage to hook a few sharks, which they shot with revolvers before hauling them on board. Shark fin soup was a welcome change. Occasionally, the tedium was interrupted by the sight of smoke on the horizon, and the ships set off in hot pursuit, only to discover a harmless merchantman. In one instance they found they were chasing HMS *Orama*.

On January 21 Lüdecke received a signal from Berlin, relayed by the Punta Arenas consulate, advising him to return to Germany via "the sailing vessel route." A merchant ship had recently succeeded in getting back to Germany using this route, which was far off the usual steamer tracks. Lüdecke rejected the Admiralstab's advice. He made excuses about the uncertainty of coal supplies and the state of his engines, which he claimed could not maintain the high speed needed to run the Allied blockade. He informed Berlin that he had decided to "try to break through the west coast of South America on February 3. Intend to carry on commerce warfare in East Indies if sufficient coal is procurable."

This was exactly what the Allies feared he might do. At about this time, Fisher acidly remarked to his chief of staff, "If the *Dresden* gets into the Bay of Bengal by means of colliers arranged with Berlin, we shall owe a lot to Sturdee."

Berlin signaled Lüdecke again on February 10 and told him, "Further coal supplies for Pacific or Indian Oceans impossible."

Once again they advised him to "return home" via the Atlantic and told him that they had arranged for a collier to meet him near the equator. But Lüdecke had made up his mind. On February 14 he set out in a driving snowstorm with the *Dresden* and *Sierra Cordoba* and headed up the coast of Chile, keeping about two hundred miles offshore.

In the next three weeks he sighted only one British ship, which was the sailing vessel *Conway Castle,* bound from Australia to Valparaíso with a load of barley. She was captured and sunk. The Germans transferred her crew to a passing Peruvian sailing vessel, the *Loston,* whose captain was sympathetic to the German side.

Lüdecke's cautious approach in staying so far off the coast kept him away from the usual steamer routes and led to his conspicuous lack of success as a commerce raider. But his very inactivity made it difficult for Stoddart's ships to track him down. They had heard no reports of the *Dresden,* true or false, for several weeks.

By February 19 Lüdecke had taken the last of the *Sierra Cordoba's* coal, and he sent her to Valparaíso to get more. Her captain was able to purchase the coal by falsely registering his destination as Callao. While he waited for the collier to return, Lüdecke kept on toward the Juan Fernández Islands, steaming slowly to conserve the cruiser's dwindling coal stocks.

The weary and fruitless game of hide-and-seek in Tierra del Fuego was prolonged by further Admiralty instructions. These were again largely based on false information supplied by Consul Stubenrauch and his agents. During one of these futile searches, Stoddart's flagship, the *Carnarvon,* struck a submerged rock on February 22. She was so badly holed that she had to be beached to avoid sinking while temporary repairs were made.

But early in March 1915 two developments shifted the scene of the hunt to the Pacific. The British had chartered a small steamer named *Galileo* to help the *Glasgow* and *Kent* search the many inlets of southern Patagonia. On March 4 she put into Weihnachts Bay because of persistent rumors that the *Dresden* was hiding there. When the *Galileo* reported to Captain Luce that the bay was empty, he concluded that Lüdecke must have moved north toward the Pacific.

The next day, the Admiralty wirelessed Stoddart saying that it had intercepted a coded telegram to Lüdecke from a German agent in Chile. The deciphered message contained instructions for the collier *Gotha* to meet the *Dresden* at a point three hundred miles west of Coronel on March 5.

By the time the news reached Luce it was several days old, but he immediately dispatched the *Kent* to the rendezvous position. She reached it on the morning of March 7. Captain Allen hoped that he might at least trap the collier, even though he had arrived two days late. When he got there the area was thick with fog.

The sun had burned off the fog by mid-afternoon, and the lookouts on the *Kent* were amazed to find not the expected collier, but the *Dresden!* She was lying twelve miles to the west of them, motionless. Her hull was high out of the water because her bunkers were nearly empty, and, according to an observer on the *Kent*, "she looked huge." It was obvious that her collier had failed to make the rendezvous.

As soon as she sighted the *Kent*, the *Dresden* moved off quickly to the north. The *Kent* set off in pursuit, and her stokers worked like trojans, just as they had at the Falklands. Soon there were flames and sparks shooting high out of her funnels. Although the old cruiser managed to work up to twenty-one knots, the *Dresden* proved that she was still capable of steaming faster than the *Nürnberg*, in spite of Lüdecke's excuses to Berlin. Allen couldn't get her within range before nightfall. He wrote: "By 2000 [the *Dresden*] was hull down and only her masts and tops of funnels showed. Our funnels were glowing red hot and sparks were flying astern. . . . At 2100 it was nearly an hour since I had seen anything."

By now, the *Kent* was getting low on coal herself, and she returned to the rendezvous area. Allen managed to signal the news to Luce in the *Glasgow*, despite the *Dresden*'s furious efforts to jam his transmissions. Time was running out on the *Dresden*. If she didn't meet her collier in the next few days, she would find herself out of coal in the middle of the ocean. Luce and Allen were well aware of her plight.

Lüdecke had no choice but to make for the nearest anchorage, which was at Más a Tierra. If he was spotted in the open sea, he didn't have enough coal left to run away a second time. His only alternatives were to wait at anchor for the *Gotha* or to seek internment. He had already received a wireless message from Berlin, "His Majesty the Kaiser leaves it to your discretion to lay up." This meant he had permission to intern his ship if necessary.

When the *Dresden* anchored in Cumberland Bay on March 19, Natalio Sánchez, governor of the Juan Fernández Islands, came on board to tell Lüdecke that he must leave within twenty-four hours. The German replied that he now had only eighty tons of coal left and couldn't possibly leave until he got more fuel. Also, his engines were badly in need of repair. The next day, however, he informed the governor that he had decided to intern his ship, but he refused to immobilize his engines or lower the German naval ensign, as requested by the Chilean.

He told Sánchez that he would prefer to wait for a Chilean warship before he formally gave up his ship to the authorities, knowing that it would take some time for such a Chilean vessel to arrive. If his collier showed up first, he doubtlessly would have changed his mind about internment and left Cumberland Bay in a hurry. If a Chilean ship did get there before his collier, he could then intern the *Dresden,* knowing that the British would not dare fire on him while he was being escorted by a neutral warship.

When Luce received the news of the *Dresden*'s escape from the *Kent* he had to wait until the following morning to navigate safely out of the narrow fjords he had been searching before speeding north with the *Glasgow.* The *Kent* had gone into Coronel to coal, and Luce signaled her to meet him south of Más a Tierra as soon as possible. He also ordered the *Orama* to escort the squadron's colliers from Vallenar and join up with the other two cruisers.

Luce had already decided to search the Juan Fernández archipelago because he guessed that the *Dresden* would have to go there to wait for coal. His idea was confirmed the next day when he received an intercepted German signal: "I am at Más a Tierra. Meet me there."

It wasn't clear whether the signal came from the *Dresden* or from her collier, but Luce immediately wirelessed the *Kent* and *Orama* to meet him at Más a Tierra on March 13. He planned to sink any German ships he found there.

The following morning the British ships steamed into Cumberland Bay at daybreak, cleared for action. The *Glasgow* and *Orama* came in from the west and the *Kent* from the east. They found the *Dresden* anchored five hundred yards offshore, with huge cliffs towering above her.

Luce had eluded the *Dresden* at Coronel, and she had eluded him at the Falklands. He had spent three frustrating months searching for her, and he was not about to concern himself with the niceties of international law. The Germans had already been at Más a Tierra for well over the prescribed twenty-four hours, and Luce knew they must have violated Chilean neutrality many times while the British ships were searching for them. In any case, no Chilean warship was present to enforce the rules. The Admiralty instruction was "destruction not internment."

Luce gave orders to close to an eight-thousand-yard range. He told the gunnery officers to make sure the buildings on shore were out of their line of sight before they opened fire, which they did at 0850. The first two salvoes from the *Glasgow* struck the *Dresden*. The *Kent* opened fire on her two minutes later and also scored several hits. The Germans fired back, but they were heavily outgunned and in a hopeless position, tactically, while they were at anchor.

The *Dresden* at Más a Tierra, flying the white flag from her foremast *(Imperial War Museum)*

After five minutes the *Dresden* had suffered so much damage that Lüdecke hoisted a white flag to avoid further senseless casualties. Luce gave the order to cease fire. The Germans flew the signal, "We want to negotiate."

The message was not understood because the flags were hoisted in the wrong order—perhaps deliberately.

Lüdecke sent a cutter across to the *Glasgow* under a flag of truce. The boat was commanded by the wily Lt. Wilhelm Canaris, who was Lüdecke's adjutant and intelligence officer. He protested to Luce that he had fired on the *Dresden* while she was inside neutral waters. Luce told him that questions of neutrality and international law were for the Chilean and British governments to decide; he was sorry, but he had his orders. Canaris then claimed that his ship had already been interned. Luce pointed out that this was patently untrue because the German naval ensign was still flying. Canaris finally tried to negotiate terms of surrender. Luce told him he would accept no conditions. If the *Dresden* did not surrender immediately, she would be sunk where she lay.

All these arguments by Canaris were stalling tactics to give Lüdecke enough time to plant timed explosive charges in the cruiser's magazine and get his men ashore. He didn't dare risk the British capturing his defenseless ship, but it wasn't enough merely to open the sea-cocks, because the ship was in shallow water. Lüdecke was determined to make the *Dresden* unsalvageable.

Another boat came out to the *Glasgow*, this one bearing Natalio Sánchez. The Chilean protested vigorously to Luce about his flagrant infringement of Chilean neutrality. He complained of damage done to civilian property by the British bombardment. Luce parried these protests as best he could and paid the governor £500 in gold as compensation for any damage done ashore.

While all this was taking place, the Germans had completed their preparations to blow up the *Dresden*. Lüdecke and his men were now heading for shore in boats. The British ships moved in closer to the *Dresden* to find out what the Germans were up to.

An officer on the *Kent* recalled seeing a seaman run up on the *Dresden*'s deck and wave off the last boat before diving into the sea. At 1045, just after the man had been picked up, two dull explosions were heard as the charges went off and a split second later a thunderous roar as the *Dresden*'s magazine exploded. As the echoes rumbled across the bay, flames and yellow smoke poured out of the stricken ship.

According to an observer, the British ships "closed to within a mile and watched; at first she sank very slowly, going down by the bows. Then more quickly she listed and sank. The ship's company were fallen in on the shore and, as the ship went down, they cheered. Our crews cheered too. It was an extraordinarily interesting sight, the sinking ship with the ensign and white flag together, the Germans on the shore and our decks crowded with men."

Eight crewmen were killed and sixteen wounded on the *Dresden* during the brief but fierce bombardment. Because there was no hospital in the Juan Fernández Islands, Luce chivalrously offered to take the injured men to Valparaíso in the *Orama* without requiring them to be interned in either neutral territories or in prisoner of war camps. The offer was gratefully accepted, and the three British cruisers left the next day with the *Dresden*'s wounded.

Lüdecke and the rest of his crew waited for a Chilean warship to take them to the mainland. They were eventually interned at a camp on Quiriquina Island, a few miles north of the scene of their victory at Coronel.

When news of the sinking reached Santiago, the Chilean government protested to London about the violation of its sovereignty. The British pointed out that the *Dresden* had so often abused Chilean neutrality with impunity that they were justified in sinking her wherever they caught her. Whitehall sent profuse apologies to Santiago. It had been most regrettable for Captain Luce to have to act as he did. The Chileans were mollified by the prompt and diplomatic response to their protest and by generous offers of compensation, and that was the end of the affair.

The destruction of the *Dresden* closed the book on Graf Spee's squadron, but one of the eight cruisers still remained to be hunted down before the far seas were swept clear of German raiders. London had learned about the explosion on board the *Karslruhe* by this point, thus leaving the *Königsberg* as the only serious threat to British overseas trade.

13

The Last of
the Raiders

Proceed with all despatch . . . destroy the Königsberg at all costs.
                        —Admiralty order to Capt. Sidney Drury-Lowe, HMS *Chatham*

The hunt for the last of the German cruisers proved to be a long and often frustrating task for the Royal Navy. But as long as this one raider remained afloat, she was a threat to Allied shipping wherever she might show up. The Admiralty had already seen how much damage and disruption a single cruiser could cause in the Indian Ocean. Churchill was determined that the last of these "pests" must be "extirpated."

The pursuit of the other seven German raiders took place on the open sea and ended in ship-to-ship slogging matches where the more heavily gunned vessels inevitably triumphed. By contrast, the Royal Navy had to use a bizarre partnership of newfangled and outmoded weapons against the *Königsberg,* which fought her last battle miles away from the sea.

Before 1914 Germany had sent out nothing more formidable than a few old gunboats to defend the entire coastline of its four African colonies. The East African colonists felt that they had been neglected by the Admiralstab and the Reichsmarineamt. They thought their colony was the most important in the empire, yet they had been assigned only the ancient gunboats *Eber, Geier,* and *Möwe*—unimposing ships in both appearance and armament.

Berlin corrected its oversight in April 1914. Commander Max Looff was given command of the cruiser *Königsberg* with orders—from the Kaiser no less—to prepare her for the long voyage to Dar es Salaam. She was to replace the *Geier* on the East Africa Station. The cruiser was less than ten years old and a sister ship of the *Nürnberg*. With her ten modern guns and top speed of twenty-four knots, she would be a match for any of the old Royal Navy ships based at Zanzibar.

The *Königsberg* left Kiel on April 25 with a handpicked and highly trained crew, chosen as much for their stamina as for their seamanship because of the unhealthy climate they would have to endure in the mosquito-infested coastal waters of equatorial East Africa.

After a voyage of more than seven thousand miles through the Mediterranean, Suez Canal, and Red Sea, the *Königsberg* arrived at the capital of German East Africa on June 6. As she steamed into the harbor at Dar es Salaam, she was greeted by ringing church bells and booming salutes from the guns of the fort and the *Geier*. Cheering crowds thronged the dockside. After she had docked, hundreds of colonists came on board to tour the ship. Among the many Europeans who visited the *Königsberg* were Governor Heinrich Schnee and his colonial officials and the redoubtable Colonel Paul Emil von Lettow-Vorbeck, commander of all the land forces in German East Africa. Thousands of natives came out of the bush to look at the new *manowari,* with her sleek silver-gray hull and her decks bristling with guns. They were most impressed by the three tall funnels, which they called "fire-tubes" and judged to be the true measure of a ship's strength.

The *Geier* left the harbor soon after the *Königsberg* had docked, bound for Singapore and the East Asia Station. Since the *Eber* had recently been sent to the Atlantic coast, the only other German warship left on the east coast was the *Möwe*. This gunboat had been converted into a survey ship, and for the past few months she had been charting the coastal waters and river deltas of the colony. Her surveys were to give Captain Looff a tremendous advantage over his enemies, who had scant knowledge of the inshore waters they would have to patrol.

Looff spent the rest of June visiting other German settlements to show the flag and to fulfill his social obligations to the colony's dignitaries. He also went on side trips into the bush to look for big game with his newly purchased 9-millimeter hunting rifle. All these activities ceased on June 28 with the news from Sarajevo and the "possibility of international complications."

Looff used most of July for a war-training cruise. While at sea he received messages almost daily from the wireless stations at Dar es Salaam and Mafia Island, which relayed instructions from Berlin and gave him information about coal supplies and provisions. He was ordered to be ready to carry out hit-and-run attacks on the Cape-Durban-Suez trade route and to tie up as many Royal Navy ships as he could off the East African coast.

* * *

The *Königsberg* in the harbor at Dar es Salaam *(Verlag Ullstein)*

The British naval forces in East Africa were part of the weak Cape of Good Hope squadron based on Simonstown and commanded by Rear-Adm. Herbert King-Hall. Toward the end of July the admiral happened to be on a routine visit to Mauritius with the old cruisers *Hyacinth*, *Astraea*, and *Pegasus*. When the political situation in Europe worsened, he left Port Louis on July 27 to look for the *Königsberg*, which, according to the last report he had received, was at Dar es Salaam.

The three British cruisers together might have been a match for the modern *Königsberg*, but the *Astraea* and *Pegasus* carried twenty-year-old weapons that the newer German guns could easily outrange. King-Hall's flagship, the *Hyacinth*, was the only serious threat to Captain Looff. Even though her battery of eleven 6-inch guns made her more formidable on paper, she would find it difficult to get the *Königsberg* within range because of the German ship's superior speed.

The British squadron approached Dar es Salaam in the late afternoon of July 31. A lookout spotted the German cruiser coming out of the harbor. Looff wasn't going to be trapped and spend the war blockaded in port. King-Hall immediately gave the order for his ships to converge on the *Königsberg*. He was determined to shadow her until war was declared. The

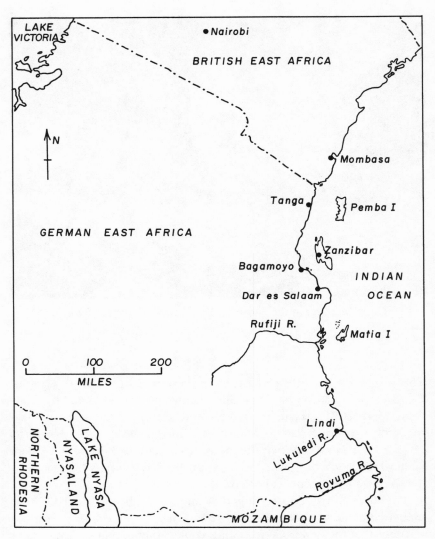

The area of the *Königsberg* campaign

Astraea and *Pegasus* kept on parallel courses to the north of the German ship, while the *Hyacinth* headed directly toward her from the south.

Looff had other ideas. He knew that the British cruisers had been in service since the 1890s and were probably capable of twenty knots at best. He ordered his chief engineer to raise enough steam to give him twenty-two knots when called for, warning him not to give the game away by making too much smoke while he was about it. The four ships steamed on at a leisurely ten knots, with the British about three thousand yards away on either beam of the *Königsberg*.

Just before nightfall, after his engine room had reported steam up, Looff gave the order for full ahead on both engines. He turned sharply to starboard, away from the *Astraea* and *Pegasus,* then suddenly wheeled his ship to the south, in the direction opposite to the *Hyacinth*'s approach. Before the British captains were able to react, the *Königsberg* had steamed past the *Hyacinth* and disappeared into the quickly gathering dusk. King-Hall knew it would be futile to go chasing after the Germans in darkness, so he stayed on patrol off Dar es Salaam in case they returned. This was the last clear view of the *Königsberg* that the Royal Navy was to have for several weeks.

Looff expected the British ships to stay in the Dar es Salaam area, knowing they would blockade the port as soon as war was declared because it had the best harbor facilities in the German colony. So he headed for Mafia Island as a temporary refuge. This small island off the delta of the Rufiji River was well to the south of Dar es Salaam and the nearby British naval base at Zanzibar.

Looff's collier *Somali* was docked at Dar es Salaam with twelve hundred tons of good quality coal on board and so were his supply ships *König, Feldmarschall,* and *Tabora*. But it was too risky to go back for them. After staying at Mafia for a few days, he decided it was safer to leave the area completely for the time being. He signaled the captain of the *Somali* to try to evade the British blockade and meet him at a rendezvous off the Horn of Africa.

Looff planned to raid the rich Suez Canal traffic at its focal point near the mouth of the Red Sea as soon as war was declared. On August 5, as she steamed north toward Aden, the *Königsberg* received a wireless message relayed from Berlin. It consisted of only the code word "Egima." This told Looff that Germany was now at war with Britain, France, and Russia.

In the first two days of the war Looff sighted only a Japanese steamer, which he let pass without signaling. On August 6 a British merchant ship was spotted. The Germans signaled, "What ship?" but received no reply. The wireless operators heard the merchantman trying to contact Aden to report that she was being challenged by a German cruiser, but they succeeded in jamming her transmissions. It was two weeks before the Allies learned that she had been captured.

The 6,601-ton passenger-freighter *City of Winchester* was carrying the bulk of the Ceylon tea crop of 1913–14. Her crew and passengers were transferred to the German freighter *Zieten;* she was kept with the cruiser until all her coal and provisions had been stripped, then she was scuttled. The *City of Winchester* was the first British merchant ship to be captured in the war. (The loss of her cargo and that of the *Diplomat,* sunk by the *Emden,* made tea a scarce commodity in Britain in the autumn of 1914.)

Meanwhile, King-Hall had taken the *Hyacinth* to Simonstown to reinforce the Cape of Good Hope Station. This left only the *Astraea* and *Pegasus* to patrol the East African coast in search of the *Königsberg*. On August 8 the *Astraea* went to Dar es Salaam and destroyed the wireless station by gunfire. She also bombarded the harbor installations and damaged the *Feldmarschall* and *König*. The harbormaster panicked and sank a floating dock across the harbor entrance to prevent the *Astraea* from steaming in to capture the weakly defended port.

This was bad news for Looff because it denied him access to the only good harbor in the colony and prevented his supply ships from coming out to meet him. If he returned to East Africa, the loss of both the port facilities and supplies would restrict his options severely. No other Etappen were located in the Indian Ocean.

On August 12 Looff received a wireless message from Lieutenant Herm of the *Somali* saying that he had managed to slip out of Dar es Salaam before the harbor was blocked. He was waiting for the *Königsberg* at Al Hallaniya Island, off the south coast of Arabia.

Looff thought it was too risky to transfer coal anywhere near the Gulf of Aden, because frequent interceptions of coded W/T messages indicated the area was being heavily patrolled by Allied warships. He signaled the *Somali* to meet him in a sheltered bay near Cape Ras Hafoun on the Somali coast. After filling the cruiser's near empty bunkers at this rendezvous, the two ships headed south to the isolated Aldabra Islands, which lie at the western end of the Seychelles chain.

Looff decided to hide there and prey on French merchant ships coming north from Madagascar, but it turned out that ever since the report of the sinking of the *City of Winchester,* French shipping had been held up in Diego Suarez. After the *Königsberg* had taken all but 250 tons of the *Somali*'s coal supply, Looff realized that they couldn't stay where they were for much longer. They were burning up precious fuel to no purpose.

Captain Herm knew the East African coast thoroughly and proposed that the *Königsberg* head for temporary shelter in the Rufiji River. The *Möwe*'s recent soundings had shown that the river delta was unexpectedly deep in places. There were at least two channels of entry and escape and six more where ships could maneuver, especially at high tide. Even if the British discovered that the Germans were hiding in the Rufiji, it wouldn't be easy for them to blockade the whole delta.

Looff agreed with Herm's suggestion. Keeping well clear of Zanzibar and Dar es Salaam, he took the *Königsberg* and *Somali* into the Rufiji delta. The ships anchored off the customs and forestry station at Salale, five miles upstream from the Simba Uranga entrance. The dense growth of mangrove trees along the riverbanks made it practically impossible for them to be seen from offshore.

The British knew they had prevented the *Königsberg* from using her best harbor at Dar es Salaam, so the *Astraea* and *Pegasus* cruised along the coast to see if she had gone to one of the other German harbors at Tanga, Lindi, or Bagamoyo. There was no sign of the cruiser at any of these settlements. Then they spent several fruitless weeks searching every likely bay and island where she might be hiding.

Fortunately for them, they didn't find her. Neither of these old ships would have stood much of a chance against the *Königsberg*.

There had been no definite news of the raider since the capture of the *City of Winchester* almost a month earlier. Rumors abounded: she was still somewhere off Aden; she was operating off the Horn of Africa; she had moved across the Indian Ocean; she had been seen off Sumatra. Later on these rumors were fueled by news of the *Emden*'s exploits in the Bay of Bengal. At one time the British feared that Looff had gone to join forces with Müller.

By the beginning of September the Admiralty had become convinced that the German cruiser had abandoned the African coast for good, and it decided to assign the *Astraea* to convoy escort duties. Admiral King-Hall objected strenuously to this decision, pointing out that it would leave only the obsolescent *Pegasus* to guard the whole of the East African coastline, and it would be terribly dangerous if the *Königsberg* came back. But once again the Admiralty preferred its long-range judgment to that of its local commander. They told him that in their opinion the risk was small and worth taking.

The *Pegasus* had been steaming up and down the coast for several weeks without a break, and she finally had to put in to Zanzibar for an engine overhaul and boiler cleaning. King-Hall instructed her captain,

Comdr. John Ingles, to keep steam up in one engine at all times while repairs were being carried out on the other, even though the *Königsberg* was believed to be hundreds if not thousands of miles away. To guard against a surprise attack, the armed tug *Helmuth* (recently captured from the Germans) was left on patrol outside the harbor mouth.

Looff soon learned from German spies that the *Pegasus* was undergoing a refit at Zanzibar. In the early hours of September 20 he took the *Königsberg* out of her hiding place in the Rufiji. Within two hours he was at Zanzibar, and the completely blacked-out ship steamed slowly into the southern channel of the port. She was spotted in the moonlight by the *Helmuth* at 0530.

This channel had been forbidden to merchant shipping, so the captain of the *Helmuth* suspected something was amiss and went to tell the stranger to turn back. The *Königsberg* fired two rounds of blank shell at the tug to scare her off, but before the tug's captain could warn the *Pegasus* of the danger, Looff gave the order to open fire. The British cruiser was anchored broadside to the *Königsberg* at a range of eleven thousand yards. The first shots fell short, but within ten minutes the German cruiser had got to within seven thousand yards of her target. At this distance the *Königsberg* simply overwhelmed the *Pegasus* with rapid salvoes from five of her 4.1-inch guns. Altogether, she fired three hundred shells at the luckless British ship.

The rudely awakened crew of the *Pegasus* had no chance to get the ship under way and escape the onslaught, but they did manage to return the *Königsberg*'s fire after her third salvo. Not surprisingly, their aim was wild. They hit the German cruiser only once, causing no significant damage.

By 0600 it was all over. The *Pegasus* was a floating ruin, with smoke and steam pouring out of gaping holes in her hull. All her guns were out of action, and she was slowly settling in the water. Casualties were heavy: 31 dead and 55 wounded out of a crew of 234. Nine of them later died of their wounds.

The Germans thought they could see a white flag being hoisted on board the crippled ship, but Looff was in a great hurry to leave the narrow channel and didn't stop to find out whether the *Pegasus* had really surrendered. He doubted it, because he knew that British captains traditionally didn't haul down their colors under any circumstances. He put the incident down to the action of an individual crew member.

Captain Ingles had, in fact, given the order to surrender to avoid further loss of life on board his now defenseless vessel. Because of Looff's haste to get away from the scene, Ingles was spared the disgrace of having his ship captured.

Fortunately for the crew of the *Pegasus,* the collier *Banffshire* was anchored only a few hundred yards away. Her boats managed to rescue the survivors of the brief but devastating attack and take the wounded to a hospital in Zanzibar. The steamer *Kilwa* towed the crippled ship to a sandbar and tried to ground her, but the shore was too steep, and the *Pegasus* slid back into deeper water. It was not until 1400 that afternoon that the old cruiser finally rolled over and sank, leaving only her broken masts sticking above the surface.

The sinking of the *Pegasus* came as a severe blow to British prestige in East Africa, but the consequences of the raid might have been much more serious. The Germans could easily have captured the *Banffshire,* loaded with coal, and put landing parties ashore to destroy the wireless station and cut the underwater telegraph cables.

But Looff was keen on getting far away from Zanzibar before he could be shadowed by an Allied patrol vessel. He wanted to keep his course a secret because he had just received fresh orders from Berlin instructing him to head for the Atlantic and raid shipping while on his way around the Cape of Good Hope. He was then supposed to run the Allied blockade and get back to Germany. Unfortunately for Looff, fate intervened.

The *Königsberg* had been steaming steadily for two months, often at high speed, and as she raced away from her one-sided victory at Zanzibar, her engines developed serious faults. Boiler pipes had burst and high pressure valves and gauges had collapsed under the strain. Looff had no choice but to limp back to his hiding place in the Rufiji. Because no spares were available anywhere in East Africa, he needed a foundry and machine shop to repair his engine parts. Several pieces of heavy machinery had to be lugged through miles of mosquito-ridden mangrove swamps to get to the highway leading to Dar es Salaam, where the nearest foundry was located. This required the backbreaking labor of hundreds of natives and German civilians (who were all pressed into service).

It was going to take several weeks before the repairs could be completed and the *Königsberg*'s engines were back in normal operation. By that time the Royal Navy was certain to send strong reinforcements to avenge the *Pegasus.* Looff and his crew were in an unenviable position. If the British discovered their anchorage before repairs were finished, they might be trapped in the Rufiji.

While they waited for their engine parts, the Germans set up an elaborate signaling system. They installed spotters with heliographs high in the trees and signaling stations equipped with telephone or telegraph lines on the shoreline. Any British ship appearing off the coast could be reported to

Looff immediately, thus giving him the advantage of knowing his enemy's exact movements while his own whereabouts remained a mystery.

The Germans fortified the shoreline around the Kikunja and Simba Uranga entrances to the delta—the two main streams leading into the Rufiji River proper. They dug trenches and built up gun emplacements, using 2-inch guns and heavy maxim machine guns from the cruiser. The fortifications were intended to repel landings or small boat attacks if the British should discover where the *Königsberg* was hiding.

Looff was also able to communicate with the powerful wireless station at Windhoek in German Southwest Africa and hence directly with Berlin. He soon found out from intelligence reports what the Admiralty intended to do about the sinking of the *Pegasus*.

Apart from the loss of prestige was the danger that the *Königsberg* might become another *Emden*. The morning after they heard the news of the Zanzibar raid, the Admiralty sent an urgent message to HMS *Chatham*, which was escorting transports in the Red Sea. She was the nearest Royal Navy cruiser to Zanzibar now that the *Hyacinth* had been transferred to the Cape of Good Hope. Her captain, Sidney Drury-Lowe, was told to put into Aden immediately to take on coal. He was ordered to "proceed with all despatch . . . destroy the *Königsberg* at all costs."

The *Chatham* was a sister ship of HMAS *Sydney*. She was just as capable of dealing with the *Königsberg* as her sister was to deal with the *Emden*, but one ship wasn't enough to track down an elusive German cruiser. The Admiralty ordered the modern *Weymouth* and *Dartmouth* and the old cruiser *Fox* to join Drury-Lowe in the search. These ships were as far away as Bombay and Port Said when they received the signal, and it was going to take them two weeks to reach Zanzibar.

The *Weymouth* and *Dartmouth* were similar in armament to the *Chatham*. Each of them carried eight 6-inch guns to the *Königsberg*'s ten 4.1-inch. They were also two knots faster than Looff's ship, so it would be no contest if any of the three caught up with her.

Captain Drury-Lowe was appointed senior naval officer on the East Africa Station. (By an odd coincidence, he had served as a midshipman on the corvette *Calliope* with Frank Brandt of the *Monmouth* and John Glossop of the *Sydney*. The three had been involved in a famous international incident at Apia in 1889, when the *Calliope* had distinguished herself by being the only ship able to keep her station during a hurricane.) The Admiralty had given Drury-Lowe more than adequate forces to destroy the *Königsberg*, but his task was not going to be an easy one.

He didn't even know what to expect as he headed south from Aden because the maximum range of the wireless stations in British East Africa was only a few hundred miles. For all he knew, both Mombasa and Zanzibar might already be in German hands. These ports were weakly defended in 1914, as Looff had already shown by steaming in and out of Zanzibar unmolested. The Germans might have put armed landing parties ashore and occupied the only safe harbors available to the *Chatham*. Mombasa had only a small garrison, and its shore batteries consisted of antiquated muzzle loaders that were just as likely to blow up in their gunners' faces as they were to damage the *Königsberg*.

The captain of the *Chatham* was greatly relieved to see the Union Jack still flying when he reached Mombasa on September 27, but he was appalled to find German civilians moving freely about the town. He immediately telegraphed the governor of British East Africa to have all Germans in the colony rounded up and sent to an internment camp in Nairobi. He stayed at Mombasa for a day to shore up the defenses by landing machine guns and setting up barbed wire emplacements. He also mined the harbor entrance in case the *Königsberg* tried to repeat her success at Zanzibar.

The *Chatham* arrived in Zanzibar on September 28 to learn that there was no definite information on the whereabouts of the German cruiser. Captain Ingles of the ill-fated *Pegasus* had been busy fortifying the harbor against another raid. He had managed to salvage the cruiser's 4-inch guns, which luckily had fallen free of the ship when she capsized. Ingles had also been gathering intelligence, but despite his best efforts, rumors and vague reports about the *Königsberg* were so numerous and conflicting that little he could tell Drury-Lowe was reliable.

Unconfirmed reports had Looff turning south after leaving Zanzibar, so Drury-Lowe decided to search the coast as far south as Mafia Island to see what he could find out for himself.

As the *Chatham* cruised along the coastline, her lookouts often saw groups of natives on the beach and sometimes in the trees. They were watching the cruiser and furiously waving white flags. This puzzled Drury-Lowe, since he had not made any threatening gestures. At night, the British lookouts could see signal bonfires being lit every time the *Chatham* came close to the shoreline.

A lucky break came on September 30 when the *Chatham* was near the small offshore island of Koma. Her lookouts spotted several white men in khaki uniforms carrying rifles, accompanied by a group of armed natives. Drury-Lowe turned in toward land and anchored. A few rounds from the cruiser's three-pounder guns caused a general panic on shore, and everyone fled into the bush. An armed landing party went ashore without meeting any opposition. They destroyed wireless masts and a signaling station and captured several dhows and catamarans that were being used to supply the German defenders.

They also found one German who had not run away. He was dressed in civilian clothes and claimed to be a planter, but his papers showed him to be an army reserve officer, one of several who had been recalled to active service to help with the *Königsberg*'s intelligence system. He was fortunate not to be shot as a spy. The other reservists on the island had left their personal effects behind in their haste to get away from the *Chatham*'s shells. Among these was a diary that provided Drury-Lowe with two valuable pieces of information.

One entry gave the details of an elaborate signaling system based on the use of white flags. The British were incensed over the misuse of white flags to signal information to the *Königsberg*. Drury-Lowe telegraphed Governor Schnee at Dar es Salaam to inform him that in the future any white flags seen along the coast would be fired on without warning.

Another diary entry was a reference to the *Königsberg* being anchored at a certain location, but the British officer doing the translation had great difficulty deciphering the German script. All he could say for sure was that the *Königsberg* was anchored at a place whose name was six letters long and might be Falalo, Galalo, or Salalo. The British were unfamiliar with the name of the obscure village of Salale where the *Königsberg* was hiding, but they were soon to connect the name in the diary with other intelligence.

Drury-Lowe was now confident that his quarry had not left East Africa. The *Königsberg* had not been seen offshore, and no sinkings had been reported since the *Pegasus*. There was a strong possibility she was hiding in one of the rivers along the coast. When the *Dartmouth, Weymouth,* and *Fox* arrived on October 6, Drury-Lowe divided the coast into four search areas stretching from Zanzibar in the north to Lourenço Marques in the south, a distance of more than fifteen hundred miles.

To try to foil the German intelligence network, which had shown how efficient it was in the *Pegasus* incident, Drury-Lowe ordered all four cruisers to have their distinguishing marks—names, numbers, and funnel rings, for example—painted out. To an untrained observer, the three bigger ships would appear identical. Even though they were spotted from shore, it wouldn't be easy for the Germans to track their movements.

The *Chatham* concentrated on the area immediately south of Dar es Salaam because of persistent rumors that the *Königsberg* was hiding somewhere near Mafia Island. All four cruisers kept in constant W/T contact, not only with each other but with the coastal wireless stations from Durban to Diego Suarez, so that any sightings of the German cruiser could be reported to Drury-Lowe right away. But there was nothing to report.

Looff was still anchored at Salale waiting for his engine parts. He knew that he was now in a tight spot: reports had come in that no less than four British cruisers were patrolling the coast. Even when his engines were working again, he would need a great deal of luck to sneak out of the Rufiji and dodge all four of them.

His only chance was to move downriver in broad daylight, because it was too dangerous to navigate the winding channels at night. If his ship ran aground on one of the many shoals, it would be disastrous. But if he could reach the river mouth without being spotted, he would make a dash to the open sea as soon as it became dark.

After he had combed the group of small islands off the coast near Mafia Island, Drury-Lowe received a report that German ships had been seen at the settlement of Lindi. On October 19 he steamed into the mouth of the Lukuledi River, cleared for action, but the only vessel he found moored there was the merchant ship *Präsident*. She was flying the flag of the International Red Cross, and a large white cross was painted on her red hull. The governor of Lindi ordered a white flag of truce to be flown over the fort, and Drury-Lowe accepted this temporarily by hoisting a similar flag at the *Chatham*'s masthead.

Notes were politely exchanged between the captain and the governor. These were taken back and forth by cutter. The German tried to convince Drury-Lowe that the *Präsident* was being used exclusively as a hospital ship. Because her markings didn't conform to the Hague Convention, and there had been no prior notification that the ship was to be used for this purpose, Drury-Lowe was sceptical.

He sent his first officer, Cmdr. R. Fitzmaurice, to board the *Präsident* with an armed party of seamen. They found no evidence whatever of hospital facilities or any sign of doctors or patients. Fitzmaurice told his men to disable the ship's engines so that the *Präsident* couldn't be used by the Germans for any purpose. The governor feigned great indignation over this action, but he could do nothing about it while the *Chatham*'s guns were trained on his fort.

More important, Fitzmaurice discovered documents that showed that the *Präsident* had been supplying the *Königsberg* with both intelligence and provisions at a place called Salale. The mystery of the name of the *Königsberg*'s hiding place was cleared up, but not its location, for the obscure village wasn't shown on any of the British maps.

Fitzmaurice also found charts of a recent hydrographic survey of the waters off the Rufiji delta, which strongly suggested that the *Präsident* had been in the Rufiji River lately. The problem was that the Admiralty charts showed the entrance to its delta as too shallow for it to be navigable by a cruiser drawing sixteen feet of water, except possibly at the highest spring tides.

What the British did not know was that the *Möwe*'s survey had found a channel leading into the delta that was more than twenty feet deep, even at ordinary high tides. Several branches of the river were navigable, with care, for ten to fifteen miles inland. But the *Chatham* had recently run aground off Koma Island, and even though no serious damage was found after she floated off, the British captains had grown extremely cautious about taking their ships close inshore. Nevertheless, Drury-Lowe decided to investigate the Rufiji delta and to send armed landing parties ashore to take prisoners for interrogation.

The problem was that the delta was more than twenty miles wide, and eight main watercourses led into the Rufiji itself. The two principal channels, the Kikunja and Simba Uranga, were connected to each other and to the other streams by a maze of cross channels. To make matters worse, the Germans had removed all buoys and channel markers and set traps for unwary navigators. One well-known landmark used by river boatmen to avoid the shoals was a white customhouse. The Germans had smashed it to the ground, and a similarly shaped building some distance away was painted white to lure enemy ships directly onto the shoals.

From his limited knowledge of the delta, Drury-Lowe believed that the Germans were most likely to have used the Simba Uranga entrance, if indeed the *Königsberg* had gone into the Rufiji. Not only was it the widest channel, but it also seemed to have more lookouts and fortifications around its mouth than the other entrances.

Then the British were fortunate enough to find an out-of-date copy of the *Handbuch der Ostküste Afrikas* in which the village of Salale was mentioned as being on the Rufiji, although it didn't give its precise location. This was good enough for Drury-Lowe.

On the morning of October 30 he took the *Chatham* to the northernmost mouth of the delta and anchored his ship four miles offshore in plain view. From this distance all that could be seen on land, even from the crow's nest, were the mangrove swamps and occasional palm trees. But Drury-Lowe knew natives were watching in the trees who would report his arrival to the Germans.

Having established the *Chatham*'s position off the northern channel,

Drury-Lowe waited until dark, then quietly moved his ship ten miles to the south, just off the Kiomboni peninsula. At daybreak he sent the *Chatham*'s steam cutter into shore, towing another cutter loaded with armed seamen. The men of the landing party were not fired on as they dashed to Kiomboni village. They learned from the natives that the German guards had just left to go back to their base for breakfast. The raiding party seized the village headman and two other men and hustled them back to the cutters before the Germans found out what was happening.

The three natives were at first bewildered and frightened by the turn of events, but once they realized they had been captured merely for questioning, they became quite cheerful. When asked if they wished to return to the mainland after the interrogation, all three declined. Even though they had left their wives and families and all their possessions behind, they were clearly afraid of the Germans, who had beaten them and forced them to dig trenches.

The British interrogated the natives separately, starting with the headman, Ali Bin Turemi. He told them that he had seen a man-of-war with three funnels and two masts pass by his village at the beginning of September, heading up the Simba Uranga. (Bin Turemi worked for the Royal Navy as a scout for a long time afterwards and became very popular with the British sailors, who nicknamed him "Boombi.") The second prisoner not only corroborated the headman's statement but also told the interrogators that he had been to market at Salale village three days previously and had seen six ships lying there, two of which were much larger than the others. One of the big vessels was a warship with three funnels and two masts, and the other was a steamer with one funnel and two masts. The third man confirmed his story. When shown a photograph of the *Königsberg*, they both said it was just like one of the ships they had seen anchored in mid-channel at Salale. The interrogators concluded that the other big ship must be the *Somali*.

The natives estimated that Salale was five miles upriver from the Simba Uranga mouth. Drury-Lowe moved the *Chatham* up the coast to a position about four miles off this entrance. Although there was up to twenty feet of water there at high tide, the tide was receding, and he didn't want to take a chance on running aground. At this distance nothing could be seen at first from the crow's nest except the tall mangrove and palm trees. Then one of the lookouts spotted mastheads above the treetops, unmistakably the masts of a warship. The *Königsberg*'s hiding place was a mystery no longer—but what was to be done next?

Drury-Lowe signaled the *Weymouth* and *Dartmouth* to leave their patrol areas and join him off the Rufiji delta. While he waited for them, he shelled the German wireless station at Mafia Island, hoping to disrupt Looff's communications. Then on November 1, the day that Graf Spee and Cradock were locked in battle at Coronel, Drury-Lowe returned to the spot where they had seen the *Königsberg*'s masts and waited for high tide.

He took his ship in as close to shore as he dared. The range finders estimated the distance to the German masts at 14,500 yards, more than the supposed maximum range of the *Chatham*'s 6-inch guns. They fired several rounds, but the shells landed well short of the *Somali* and even farther from the *Königsberg,* which was anchored about a mile beyond her. Drury-Lowe ordered some of the *Chatham*'s tanks to be flooded to give the ship a five-degree list, to increase the elevation of the guns, but this still wasn't enough to reach the German ships. The only result of the bombardment was that the cautious Looff raised anchor and moved the *Königsberg* another two miles upstream.

When the other two cruisers arrived on November 3, the *Dartmouth*'s bunkers were nearly empty, and she was drawing much less water than usual. She was able to move in two miles closer to shore than the *Chatham,* but she couldn't reach the *Königsberg*'s new anchorage, even with her guns at maximum elevation.

It was obvious that unless Looff decided to make a run for it, the Royal Navy's great superiority in firepower wasn't much use.

Drury-Lowe decided that all he could do for the moment was try to bottle up the *Königsberg* while he made other plans to destroy her. He sent Boombi ashore one night to check on the cruiser's location. The headman came back safely from this dangerous mission the next day with the news that the German cruiser was anchored in the Suninga channel, about seven miles from the river mouth. Since Looff had gone into this channel, Drury-Lowe concluded that it must be the safest one to navigate, and he was determined to block it. Even if there was another way out, it would mean one less entrance for his ships to blockade.

The Admiralty collier *Newbridge* was brought down from Mombasa to Zanzibar to get her ready as a block ship. This vessel was 350 feet long, and her flat bottom made her ideal for going upriver. The problem was that to anchor a vessel of this size in a precise location normally required the calm, undivided attention of the crew. This was going to be far from the case once the Germans in the shore batteries and machine-gun emplacements spotted them.

Steel plating was fixed to the bridge and wheelhouse to give extra protection to the crew, but some of the men would have to move out on deck to let go the anchors when the ship was in position to be scuttled.

The best that could be done for them was to pile sandbags in the poop and forecastle areas, but the anchor parties would still be in a dangerously exposed position. Drury-Lowe wrote of the *Newbridge*'s crew, "I hardly expected to see them again."

The men were all volunteers, drawn from the *Chatham*'s complement. So many volunteered that in the end Drury-Lowe had to pick the three officers, seven seamen, and four engine-room ratings himself. He put Commander Fitzmaurice in command of the *Newbridge* operation.

The plan was for the block ship to be escorted as far as the river mouth by the *Chatham, Dartmouth,* and *Weymouth,* which would then lie offshore and pound the shore defenses with 6-inch shell. But once the collier turned left into the Suninga channel, she would be out of sight of the cruisers. The rest of the way she would have only the armed steamer *Duplex* to protect her. The biggest guns she carried were two three-pounders.

A steam picket, sent from the battleship *Goliath* at Zanzibar, and the steam cutters from the three cruisers were to go with the *Duplex.* Their role was to take off the crew of the *Newbridge* after she had been sunk. These small boats were protected as much as possible by adding steel plates and sandbags. The *Goliath*'s picket boat carried two 14-inch torpedoes to sink the *Newbridge* if explosive charges failed to do the trick.

The three cutters were armed only with rifles and machine guns. Since the Germans on shore had four-pounder guns and heavy maxim machine guns, it would be no picnic.

The little armada arrived off the Simba Uranga entrance just before dawn on November 10. Surprise was essential if the *Newbridge* was to get safely past the heavy fortifications at the river mouth and into the Suninga channel before she could be sunk by the Germans, who would quickly realize what the British were up to. The *Chatham* moved inshore as far as she could, taking careful soundings. She was ready to provide covering fire, but only along the right bank of the river.

Shortly after 0500 the *Newbridge* moved quietly upstream in the darkness, followed by the *Duplex* and picket boats. They turned into the Suninga branch. When dawn broke twenty minutes later, the Germans on both banks opened up a furious barrage with their four-pounder guns, concentrating their fire on the *Newbridge.* The *Duplex* fired back with her three-pounders. The gunfire was punctuated by the rattle of maxim guns, which were aimed mainly at the cutters. The heavier boom of the *Chatham*'s big guns could now be heard in the distance.

By 0540 Fitzmaurice had maneuvered the collier into position in the deepest part of the channel, and he gave orders to let go the bow anchor.

When the current had swung the ship across the channel, the men on deck let go the two stern anchors. The anchor parties were under heavy rifle and machine-gun fire the whole time the *Newbridge* was being maneuvered into position. Miraculously, none of them was killed, although several were wounded. As soon as the ship was firmly anchored, the crew opened her scuttles.

The *Chatham*'s cutter came alongside to take off the crew and pick up the spool of wire connected to the guncotton charges that had been placed inside the collier and under the ship's bottom. When the cutter had pulled away to a safe distance, the charges were detonated. After two dull explosions the collier began to settle by the head. She had been loaded with rock and gravel at Zanzibar, and she was soon resting firmly on the muddy river bottom. Only her upper works showed above the surface. The river current had been stronger than expected, and she wasn't exactly at right angles to the shore, but her position would make it exceedingly hazardous for the *Königsberg* to try to pass by her, even at high tide.

Mission accomplished, the little flotilla steamed back to the mouth of the delta at high speed, still under heavy fire from the riverbanks. Luckily for them, one of the *Chatham*'s 6-inch guns knocked out the main German gun emplacement, causing heavy casualties. After this, the firing from shore slackened noticeably.

In spite of running the gauntlet again, this time in broad daylight, British casualties were surprisingly light. Only two men had been killed and nine wounded. Most of the casualties were suffered by the men in the cutters. Both officers and men had shown remarkable coolness in navigating and anchoring the *Newbridge* and removing her crew safely.

The operation had an unexpected bonus. By moving so close in to shore to give covering fire, the *Chatham* had managed to get to within thirteen thousand yards of the *Somali*. The cruiser shelled her and set her on fire. The *Königsberg*'s supply ship was loaded with coal, wood, and stores, and she burned furiously for two days before she was gutted. The loss of the coal supply was critical for Looff. He had to have another collier if he was ever going to escape from the Rufiji.

Overall, the *Newbridge* operation was considered a huge success, and the Admiralty in London was jubilant. They announced to the world that the *Königsberg* was "now imprisoned and unable to do any further harm."

This wasn't strictly true, but Looff's position had certainly become desperate. His engines were soon working again, but he had lost his main supply ship. Because of the block ship, he could now get out of the Rufiji only by way of the Kikunja entrance, where Drury-Lowe was waiting for him with the *Chatham* and *Fox*.

Once the Admiralty was convinced that the *Königsberg* was penned in, they sent the *Dartmouth* and *Weymouth* to Cape Town to reinforce King-Hall's weak squadron. (The British feared that Graf Spee might decide to cross the Atlantic after his victory at Coronel.) Even if Looff did manage to get out of the Rufiji at high tide, which it doubted he could, the Admiralty thought the *Chatham* and *Fox* would be quite sufficient to destroy the *Königsberg*.

After nearly three months in the mangrove swamps, the men of the *Königsberg* were suffering terribly from the incessant heat and the myriad insects. Many of them came down with malaria, dysentery, or typhus. At one stage, two out of every five crew members were in the sick bay, mostly with malaria.

To make matters even worse, Looff had been forced to moor the cruiser even farther upriver after the *Chatham*'s shells had reached the *Somali*. The *Königsberg* was now ten miles from the open sea. To the crew this was as good as an admission that their captain was resigned to staying in the Rufiji indefinitely, which didn't improve their morale.

Looff had a sports ground built on the riverbank to give his men some exercise. The chance to go ashore gave the crew a change from repeated drilling and long periods of boring inactivity. Now that they were at anchor, many of their normal day-to-day duties were no longer required, and there was little for them to do. The only break in their daily routine came when they moved the ship to a new anchorage. To relieve the deadly monotony, some of the officers went on boat trips to hunt for hippopotamus. Others went into the bush to look for rhinoceros.

The Germans stopped using their diminishing coal stocks, holding them in reserve for a possible breakout. They were reduced to burning wood to keep up enough steam to generate electricity for the ship's machinery and gun turrets, which produced dense black smoke from the funnels. The British, seeing the wood smoke rising above the treetops, knew that their enemy must be in dire straits as far as fuel was concerned. Things looked grim indeed for the *Königsberg*'s crew as they waited for the Royal Navy's next move.

The British seamen were almost as fed up, endlessly patrolling off the delta. Once they realized that they were never going to destroy the *Königsberg* unless she came out of the river, the only relief from the monotony of the blockade was an occasional trip to Zanzibar to get coal.

Drury-Lowe realized that he would have to use different tactics if he was going to sink the *Königsberg,* or at least damage her so badly that she would cease to be a threat to Allied shipping. As long as she remained intact, there was always a chance she might sneak out of the Rufiji some dark night and slip past him to become another *Emden.*

It was absolutely out of the question to send one of his cruisers upriver where she might run aground and be at the mercy of the German shore batteries; and if the efficient German spotting system directed the *Königsberg's* fire onto his grounded ship, she would be powerless against her unseen enemy. What Drury-Lowe needed were shallow-draft warships that could go far enough upriver to get the *Königsberg* within range.

Just as important, he had to have an observation system to give directions to the gunners, who would never be able to get a clear view of their target because of the bends in the river and the tall mangrove trees.

The tactics called for were both echoes of operations used for the first time in the American Civil War. When the federal ship *Monitor* fought the Confederate ironclad *Merrimack* to a standstill in Hampton Roads in 1862, her surprising success gave rise to a new class of warship that took her name. Many navies used shallow-draft monitors in the late nineteenth century, mainly for river patrols or coastal defense. Later developments in naval warfare stressed attack, not defense. This made monitors all but obsolete by 1914.

The Royal Navy had no monitors left in service when war broke out, but luckily three of these vessels had been completed in Vickers' shipyards in February 1914 as part of an order for the Brazilian navy. When the Brazilian government couldn't afford to pay for them, they were laid up in Barrow dockyard awaiting another buyer. As soon as war was declared, the Admiralty purchased all three to prevent any hostile country from getting them.

Commissioned for the Royal Navy and renamed the *Humber, Severn,* and *Mersey,* they were armed with two 6-inch guns and two 4.7-inch howitzers, big enough weapons to sink any light cruiser. Best of all, the monitors drew less than six feet of water, and so they would have no difficulty navigating up the Rufiji delta.

The Admiralty decided to send the *Severn* and *Mersey* to East Africa to deal with the *Königsberg* once and for all, but it took a long time to get the monitors ready for service. The ships needed new guns because they had worn out their gun barrels bombarding German army positions on the Belgian coast. But now that the Admiralty believed the *Königsberg* was locked in the Rufiji for good, there seemed to be little reason for haste in getting the monitors refitted. They weren't even ready to leave the dockyard until the end of February.

Monitors were slow and ungainly vessels—essentially floating gun platforms. They looked more like ferryboats than warships. According to one naval authority, "They were totally unsuited to operate in the open sea, as their shallow draft permitted them to be blown sideways."

The *Severn* and *Mersey* had to be towed the entire seven thousand miles from Chatham to Zanzibar, using two oceangoing tugs for each monitor. They were accompanied by a collier and the armed merchant cruiser *Trent*. The average speed of this motley group was about six knots, and consequently, the long voyage took almost two months.

While he waited for these reinforcements, Drury-Lowe made plans to pinpoint the monitors' target from the air. The first time aerial observation was used to direct artillery fire was during the American Civil War, when both sides employed observation balloons. This tactic had never been used to guide naval gunnery, but the Admiralty had foreseen the need for reconnaissance aircraft when it formed the Royal Naval Air Service in 1912. Unfortunately for Drury-Lowe, not a single naval aircraft was stationed anywhere in Africa, and the fledgling service claimed it couldn't spare him any from Europe.

The nearest civilian aircraft was an old Curtiss flying boat that was being used to give exhibition flights to a curious public in Durban. The Admiralty bought this plane and gave its pilot, a Mr. Dennis Cutler, a temporary commission as a sub-lieutenant in the Royal Naval Reserve. Aircraft at the time were of unproven military value and noted for their mechanical unreliability. This one was no exception. Cutler did his best to overhaul it and get it ready for shipment to Niororo Island. This lay just to the north of Mafia Island, which was still in German hands.

The Union Castle liner *Kinfauns Castle* went to Durban to pick up Cutler and his seaplane. When the plane arrived at Niororo on November 15, Cutler had to spend several days tuning the engine and repairing its leaky radiator. There were no aircraft spares or mechanics anywhere in East Africa, but a midshipman on the *Kinfauns Castle* named Gallehawk was an aircraft enthusiast. He did an excellent job as Cutler's mechanic.

When the flying boat was ready for service, it had to be taken to a sheltered bay because it wouldn't take off unless the water was perfectly calm. Even then it refused to lift off with a passenger on board. The totally inexperienced Cutler would have to act as his own observer. The plane's flying time was limited to fifty minutes. This would give Cutler just enough time to fly to the mainland, carry out a quick search of the delta, and get back safely to Niororo.

On November 19 the great day arrived, and the brand-new Lieutenant Cutler took off on his first reconnaissance mission. The *Chatham* anchored off the mouth of the Simba Uranga to provide him with a reference point. Her crew watched him fly past at four thousand feet, heading inland. After an hour had passed, there was no sign of Cutler's plane. The lookouts on the *Chatham* began to worry. Several more hours went by, and still no sign of the plane. By now, everyone was convinced that Cutler had either crashed or been shot down and captured by the Germans.

Happily, the plane was discovered a few hours later on the beach at Okusa Island, eighteen miles south of Mafia. Cutler was found "placidly bathing, under the impression that it was the same place he had started from." He had lost his bearings in the clouds over the mainland and had mistaken Okusa for Niororo. He hadn't been able to see the *Königsberg* through the clouds and had been forced to make an emergency landing because of a persistent leak in his radiator. The rough landing resulted in damage to the seaplane's hull. The hull was easily patched, but where on earth were they to get a new seaplane radiator?

The situation didn't look very promising until someone recalled seeing a Ford car in Mombasa with a radiator of about the right size. Drury-Lowe sent the *Fox* there to commandeer it. This meant that one of His Majesty's cruisers had to steam more than five hundred miles to transport a car radiator, which might or might not be usable.

Luckily, the Ford radiator worked like a charm, and on November 22 Cutler took off on his second reconnaissance. This time he sighted the *Königsberg*. The cruiser had been moved a mile upriver from where she had been reported three weeks previously.

When they saw Cutler's plane overhead, the Germans realized that their situation had changed dramatically for the worse. They could no longer hope to conceal their anchorage, and any attempt to sneak out of the delta would almost certainly be spotted from the air before they reached the river mouth.

Drury-Lowe, on the other hand, was delighted. It was now clear that the combination of plane and monitor was a feasible way of destroying the *Königsberg*. But his plans received a setback when Cutler had to make a crash landing on his next return to base. This time the plane's hull was damaged beyond repair.

By now, another civilian seaplane had arrived at Durban, and the *Kinfauns Castle* went to get it. It may seem strange nowadays to send a huge liner nearly two thousand miles to fetch a mere seaplane, but this ship was the fastest one available to Drury-Lowe. No expense was to be spared in destroying the *Königsberg*. After all, the Admiralty had told him to destroy the cruiser "at all costs."

The liner returned with her precious cargo on December 3. The new seaplane proved to be capable of taking off with a passenger on board. That same day Cutler, with Commander Fitzmaurice as his observer, flew over the delta and discovered that the *Königsberg* had been moved yet again. Cutler made four more flights during the next week; it was now possible for Drury-Lowe to get almost daily reports of the cruiser's location. The seaplane was fairly safe from the *Königsberg*'s small arms fire at three thousand feet, and the cruiser's big guns couldn't be elevated enough to act as an antiaircraft battery.

The latest reconnaissance flights revealed two significant changes. The *Königsberg* had turned into a cross channel between the Suninga and Simba Uranga branches. She was therefore in a position to make a move toward the sea in either of two directions. Cutler also noticed that all her 2-inch guns had been taken off the ship and mounted on shore. It looked as if the Germans were ready to fight to the end, on land or on water.

On December 10 Cutler had to make his reconnaissance without the extra weight of an observer because the plane's engine wasn't running properly. When he arrived over the *Königsberg*, observers on the *Chatham* could tell that he was having trouble maintaining his altitude. They saw his plane come down somewhere to the north of the German cruiser. They didn't know whether Cutler's engine had failed or if he had been hit by gunfire, as the Germans later claimed. In any event, he had to make a forced landing.

When Cutler was reported missing, the adventurous Gallehawk took an armed party of seamen in a steam launch, escorted by the tug *Helmuth,* and made a dash upriver to try to rescue his friend. He found the seaplane alright, but there was no sign of Cutler. Gallehawk was afraid that he had either drowned or been eaten by crocodiles. Much later it was discovered that he had swum ashore and been captured by the Germans.

Gallehawk succeeded in towing the seaplane back to the river mouth under heavy fire, but by the time he reached the *Chatham,* the machine was so badly shot up that it would never fly again. The seaplane was sent back to Durban. (It now rests in the city museum, an honored relic of the pioneer days of naval aviation.)

Now that his squadron had been deprived of its eyes, Drury-Lowe pressed the Admiralty for a replacement seaplane. In the meantime, he kept up the blockade with the *Chatham, Fox, Kinfauns Castle, Duplex, Helmuth,* and the recently captured *Adjutant.* These ships intercepted every Arab dhow that the Germans sent from Tanga or Dar es Salaam with supplies for the *Königsberg* so that the cruiser's only line of supply was the overland route from the north of the colony. The British couldn't do anything about this as long as Lettow-Vorbeck's forces held out.

Boombi made several more dangerous scouting expeditions up the Simba Uranga and Suninga channels and kept Drury-Lowe informed of the *Königsberg*'s movements as best he could. He was absolutely convinced that the cruiser could reach the sea only by these two channels. In his opinion, the others had too many dangerous shoals. Doubtless, had the Germans caught Boombi he would have been shot as a spy, for they knew he had been taken from his village by the British.

Boombi was invaluable to the British as an intelligence agent, and they eventually rewarded him for his services with a grant of six hundred rupees. This made him a rich man. Drury-Lowe wrote, "I last saw him in Zanzibar, dressed in all the colours of the rainbow, the possessor of a fine dhow and a new wife."

In spite of Boombi's courageous efforts, what Drury-Lowe really needed was another plane to keep reporting the *Königsberg*'s movements, especially when the *Chatham* had to go to Zanzibar or Mombasa to coal. On these occasions the *Fox* was the only regular warship left on the blockade, and the watchers on shore were bound to report this to Looff. It was doubtful whether this old cruiser could stop the *Königsberg* if the Germans decided to make a run for it.

Drury-Lowe continued to press London for another aircraft. On December 14 the Admiralty informed him that it was sending a squadron—given the rather grandiose title of the RNAS Expeditionary Squadron No. 4.—of the new but untested Sopwith seaplanes. In fact, it consisted of just two aircraft.

Meanwhile, the stalemate on the Rufiji dragged on. The crews of the *Chatham* and the *Königsberg* had grown used to each other's presence, and a sort of long-range camaraderie had developed. Humorous Christmas greetings went back and forth by wireless. One message alluded to the British sailors' faded hopes of being back home in time for the holidays. "Kony we wish you the best of good cheer,/But blame you for stopping our Xmas beer."

On New Year's Day 1915, Drury-Lowe sent Looff a greeting, *"Wir wünschen Ihnen ein glückliches neues Jahr und hoffen, Sie bald zu sehen."*

Looff responded politely in English: "Thanks. Same to you. If you want to see me I am always at home."

* * *

The new flying squadron was commanded by Flight-Lt. J. T. Cull. It had a second pilot, H. E. Watkins, and eighteen men. These included a mechanic named Boggis, fresh from the Sopwith factory, who had volunteered his services. The new model seaplanes were equipped to carry bombs as well as an observer, and the Royal Navy hoped they could bomb the *Königsberg* into submission.

The squadron, with all its equipment and supplies, including a very useful motorboat, was loaded on board the SS *Persia*. It left Tilbury on January 16 bound for Bombay, where it docked on February 8. The now-experienced Gallehawk went to meet it on board the *Kinfauns Castle*, which was to take the squadron on the final leg of its journey to Niororo. The planes were uncrated, reassembled, and flight-tested at Bombay, and the entourage left for East Africa two days later.

The squadron arrived at Niororo on February 20, and the planes were made ready for their first reconnaissance and bombing raid on the *Königsberg*. Unfortunately, when they were loaded with pilot, observer, enough fuel for one hour's flying, and two sixteen-pound and two fifty-pound bombs, they stubbornly refused to leave the water. The aircrews made determined efforts to vary the fuel by mixing different ratios of gasoline and aviation spirit and to improve the air-intakes of the Gnome engines, which had not been designed for the high temperatures of East Africa.

After much trial and error the planes finally managed to lift off, but only when there was neither an observer nor bombs on board. Even then they could reach an altitude of but fifteen hundred feet, a height suitable for observing the *Königsberg* but one that made the planes extremely vulnerable to ground fire.

Then, after a week of testing, one of the planes crashed. It was a total wreck. The heat not only affected engine performance, but under the blazing sun the planes' floats sprang leaks after the air pressure built up inside them. The one surviving plane sank in shallow water. After it was salvaged, the problem was overcome by putting air vents in the floats.

After long days of frustration, Flight-Lieutenant Cull finally took off on his first reconnaissance flight. He spotted the *Königsberg* still lying at her last reported anchorage, with a group of small supply ships nearby.

Early in March Admiral King-Hall arrived off the Rufiji in the *Goliath* (a sister ship of the *Canopus*). He had come to take charge of the *Königsberg* campaign, and he hoped that the battleship's 12-inch guns could reach her and destroy her. It was not to be. The *Goliath*'s huge draft of twenty-six feet made it impossible for her to get close enough inshore. Someone remarked at the time, "[T]he *Goliath* was as much use as a Percheron at Epsom Downs."

A disappointed King-Hall shifted his flag back to the *Hyacinth* and sent the *Goliath* to the Dardanelles campaign, where she was promptly torpedoed and sunk by a Turkish destroyer. He also detached the *Chatham* from the blockade and sent her to Aden for a much needed refit. Although Drury-Lowe was to return briefly with the *Chatham* in April, he was not present to see the results of all his efforts.

The Air Department at the Admiralty eventually decided that the Sopwiths were unsatisfactory. This had been patently obvious to everyone at Niororo for some time. They informed Cull that they were sending him three new seaplanes. The RNAS men greatly rejoiced when they heard they were getting new aircraft. The planes were sent out on the Cunard liner *Laconia* and arrived at Durban in mid-April.

The RNAS men went there in the *Kinfauns Castle* to meet them. They helped to uncrate the planes and reassemble them on the docks so that cranes could lift them back onto the *Laconia*'s deck, ready for use. But the men were bitterly disappointed when the crates were unpacked to reveal three old Short seaplanes. They were a type that the RNAS had been using for more than a year, and their engines were badly in need of overhaul. Nevertheless, when the planes were repaired and taken to Mafia Island, they turned out to be a great improvement over the Sopwiths.

By now, the Allies had captured this island, which gave them a more sheltered seaplane anchorage. Work was also under way to build an airstrip on the island for future land-based aircraft. The British hoped that conventional planes would have less trouble than seaplanes in taking off with a bomb load on board.

While the Admiralty was arranging to send Cull and his squadron to keep track of the *Königsberg*, the Admiralstab were making their own plans to free her. They assumed that Looff could navigate to the mouth of the Rufiji in daylight without being seen, because there had been no reports of reconnaissance flights since Cutler's plane had crashed. Then, at night, the *Königsberg* might be able to make a dash to the open sea and dodge the blockade in the darkness. Looff had saved just enough coal to do this. With his knowledge of the river, the spring tides, and which Allied ships were on patrol, he could time his escape for a day when the blockading flotilla was at its weakest. This would be futile, however, if he didn't have enough coal to get away from the coast quickly and outrun the inevitable pursuit. He needed to rendezvous with a supply ship as soon as possible after he left the Rufiji if he was to have any hope of surviving, let alone of resuming his career as a raider.

The Admiralstab designated the captured British steamer *Rubens* to act as a blockade-runner, and they planned to have her rendezvous with the *Königsberg* near Tanga. This 3,850-ton ship was loaded with sixteen hundred tons of coal, as well as ammunition, provisions, medical supplies, and new uniforms. Even beer for the *Königsberg*'s crew was packed on board. The *Rubens* also carried fifteen hundred rifles and ammunition for Lettow-Vorbeck's hard-pressed land forces.

She was repainted to look like a Danish merchant ship and given the name *Kronborg*. The real *Kronborg* was in Copenhagen at the time, and German coastal patrols were to make sure she stayed there. The commander of the blockade runner was Lt. Carl Christiansen who came from one of the North Friesian Islands just off Denmark and spoke the language well enough to pass as a Dane.

He was ordered to go to East Africa and arrange a rendezvous with Looff after he had broken out of the Rufiji. This was no small order because Christiansen needed to penetrate the tight British blockade in the North Sea, steam ten thousand miles via the Cape of Good Hope, and reach Tanga without being detected by Allied patrols. If they stopped his ship, he would have to convince them of her new identity.

The *Rubens* left the Jade River on February 18, flying the Danish flag, and headed north under cover of darkness toward the Norwegian coast. After hugging the coast as far as Alesund, Christiansen cut across the North Sea toward Iceland, keeping to the north of the Faeroes. When he had succeeded in getting through the most heavily patrolled area, he headed out into the mid-Atlantic and gave the Azores and Cape Verde Islands a wide berth. He stayed well clear of Cape Town before turning north into the Mozambique channel. After a voyage of almost two months, he made his first landfall at Aldabra Island on April 9.

Even though he had completely eluded Allied patrols, his wireless signals to the *Königsberg* and to Tanga were intercepted by British and French stations as he passed by Madagascar. He had been forced to use his wireless to arrange a rendezvous with Looff now that the spring tides were at their highest. One of the *Königsberg*'s responses asked if he had brought the beer as well as the coal.

The Allies easily decoded these signals because they had obtained a copy of the German naval code. The cruiser *Magdeburg* had run aground in the Gulf of Finland in August 1914 and was destroyed by Russian artillery. When the Russians boarded the ship, they found an intact codebook on the body of a German signalman. Since that time, the Allies had been able to decipher German naval signals without too much difficulty. In this case, they had only to determine which cipher rotation Christiansen and Looff were using on a given day.

When King-Hall learned that the relief ship was making for Tanga to wait for the *Königsberg,* he took the *Hyacinth* and *Duplex* there on April 13 to patrol the harbor approaches. The *Rubens* managed to steam undetected past the *Duplex* during the night, but at dawn on the fourteenth she was spotted by the *Hyacinth* as she headed toward Tanga.

King-Hall gave orders for full speed ahead, to try to cut her off before she could reach the harbor. As he got close to the freighter one of his engines broke down with a tremendous crash. The linkages between the pistons and connecting rods had snapped. The *Rubens* took advantage of the *Hyacinth*'s sudden drop in speed to turn away and head into the shallow Manza Bay. King-Hall couldn't follow her there and was forced to lie off the coast.

The *Hyacinth* opened fire on the *Rubens* across the headland protecting the bay. The British gunners didn't have a clear view of the steamer, but they succeeded in damaging her so badly that the unfortunate Christiansen had to beach her to avoid sinking.

Their plans had been frustrated, but the Germans managed to take the rifles and ammunition for Lettow-Vorbeck from the wreck, as well as some of the supplies for Looff, but none of the precious coal or beer. By this time Cull and his fresh seaplanes had arrived at Mafia Island. Looff had lost his best chance to escape from the Rufiji.

On April 25 Cull and his mechanic Boggis, who also acted as his observer, took off in one of the new Short seaplanes and headed for the delta. These planes were more reliable than the Sopwiths, but they climbed poorly. Cull wasn't able to reach any greater altitude than twelve hundred feet. When he arrived over land, downdrafts forced him back to eight hundred feet, where the plane was vulnerable to the continual rifle and machine-gun fire from the riverbanks. As the plane approached the *Königsberg*'s anchorage, the enemy fire intensified, and the cruiser's 2-inch guns joined in the barrage. Cull and his passenger could now see menacing puffs of smoke below them from the bursting shrapnel.

They found the cruiser lying in the same bend of the river where she had last been reported. She was not camouflaged by tree branches, as had been rumored earlier. On the contrary, it seemed that the *Königsberg* was far from resigned to staying in the river. According to Cull: "She looked as though she had been newly painted. Her side-screens and awnings were spread, smoke was issuing from her funnels and in general she was looking very spick-and-span."

In spite of the heavy ground fire, Cull managed to take some remarkable photographs of the scene from seven hundred feet using an ordinary camera—aerial cameras didn't exist in 1915. The *Königsberg* was lying in mid-channel near the western end of the Simba Uranga, with several small supply ships and dhows close by.

When Cull was still a mile away from the cruiser, his engine began to sputter, and he was forced to turn back because he was losing height rapidly. After he had passed the burned-out wreck of the *Somali* and the partly submerged *Newbridge,* the seaplane's engine failed altogether. He was still about six miles from his anchorage alongside the *Laconia,* but with great skill he managed to glide and make a safe landing on the water a few hundred yards from the liner. The wings and fuselage were riddled with numerous bullet holes. One bullet had hit the air-intake and another had severed the main oil pipe, which had caused the engine to overheat and stall.

After this close shave the pilots kept several miles between themselves and the *Königsberg.* It was still possible at this distance to tell whether she had been moved. Even with this precaution, Watkins's plane was hit in the rudder on one trip, and he had to make a crash landing in the sea on his way back to base. The plane was a total wreck, but Watkins survived.

The weeks dragged on as the *Königsberg* was kept under constant surveillance using the one surviving seaplane. Frustration was mounting on board King-Hall's ships. The constant strain of blockading the *Königsberg* and not being able to do anything about it was beginning to depress everyone. The *Rubens* had shown that the North Atlantic blockade was not leak proof, and the unexpectedly trim condition of the *Königsberg* raised fears that the Germans might try to organize another breakout. No matter how closely the British ships patrolled the mouths of the river, there was always a chance she might get by them some dark night.

The RNAS pilots were even more frustrated. They could actually see the *Königsberg* every day yet were powerless to damage her. Their seaplane absolutely refused to lift off with a bomb load aboard. Finally, Cull, Watkins, Bridgeman, and Gallehawk devised a reckless—not to say suicidal—scheme to use their motorboat to go upriver and torpedo the German cruiser. They made a silencer out of a 6-inch cartridge case and attached it to the boat's noisy engine. They also fitted homemade torpedo dropping gear on the side of the boat. The four men were highly enthusiastic about their chances of slipping quietly into the delta at night and getting close enough to the *Königsberg* to release their 14-inch torpedo. But they knew that if they were spotted, they faced almost certain death at the hands of the cruiser's gunners and the shore defenses.

They gave a successful trial demonstration of the operation for Admiral King-Hall. He watched silently, then wirelessed the Admiralty to tell them what was being planned. The Admiralty immediately vetoed this or any other scheme to use small boats in the delta for the very good reason that the monitors were now on their way to East Africa. They were expected to arrive at the beginning of June.

Cull and his men needn't have worried about the *Königsberg* breaking out. On May 1 Looff was ordered to send 7 officers and 111 men of his crew to reinforce Lettow-Vorbeck's beleaguered land forces. He protested to Governor Schnee that his men were trained for naval operations, not soldiering, and the governor supported him against Lettow-Vorbeck. Looff had been promoted to captain after he sank the *Pegasus,* so technically, he outranked Lettow-Vorbeck. In the end, he was overruled by Berlin.

After the failure of the *Rubens* operation, the Admiralstab had given up on further attempts to extricate the *Königsberg*. They were content simply to have Looff tie up British warships indefinitely on blockade duty.

With his crew so drastically reduced, Looff no longer had enough men to run the ship as well as man the guns. He could do nothing but prepare to fight from where he lay.

14

Assault on the *Königsberg*

S.M.S. Königsberg is destroyed but not conquered.

—Capt. Max Looff

After its long, slow voyage from Europe, the odd convoy of monitors, colliers, and escort vessels arrived at Mafia Island on June 2.
Because of their low freeboard and unseaworthy nature, the
Severn and *Mersey* had been battened down against heavy seas and their
crews carried on board HMS *Trent*. But they had made it to East Africa
without mishap.

A lot of work would have to be done before they could go up against
the *Königsberg*. Steel plates had to be fitted on deck above the magazines
and around the bridge and wheelhouse. The ships were stripped of all
inflammable gear. Free space inside the hulls was filled with four thousand
empty kerosene tins, to give extra buoyancy in case of a hit below the
waterline. The ships' rudders were lengthened to give them better steering in the narrow channels of the delta.

Last, but not least, there was target practice. A dhow was anchored as
a target eight thousand yards away from the monitors on the far side of a
small island, out of sight of the ships. The seaplanes had no wireless, and
a flag code was devised for the planes to signal the monitors about their
fall of shot. The system was rehearsed over and over by the monitors'
gunners and the seaplane pilots.

These preparations took four weeks of hard work. Before they were
complete, four more welcome aircraft arrived on board HMS *Laurentic,*
with three pilots and several aircrew and mechanics. The new arrivals
were conventional land-based aircraft: two Henri Farman and two

Caudron biplanes. These had been urgently requested after all the problems experienced with the seaplanes. The landing strip on Mafia was ready, and closer reconnaissance was now possible because these planes could easily climb to four thousand feet, where they were relatively safe from ground fire. Better still, they were equipped with a two-way wireless. In spite of these improvements to the aerial spotting system, one Caudron crashed on its first trial flight, and a Farman later suffered engine failure and also crashed. Both were total wrecks, but the pilots were unharmed.

Tuesday, July 6, was chosen as the big day for the assault on the *Königsberg*. The monitors' crews were quietly confident of success, although their consensus was, "We're in for a pretty hot time."

On the evening before the attack, everything was ready at Mafia Island. The monitors' topmasts had been taken down to reduce the possibility of their being seen, and zigzag camouflage stripes were painted on the hulls and upper works. Captains Fullerton and Wilson assembled their men on the quarterdecks to compliment them on all their hard work and to wish them good luck for the next day.

Just before 1900 the *Severn* and *Mersey* cast off from the side of the *Trent*, which was to follow later as a hospital ship. They made their way slowly across the strait separating Mafia from the mainland, thirty miles away. The expedition was commanded by Capt. Eric Fullerton (who later became Admiral Fisher's son-in-law).

The plan was to steam into the northern, or Kikunja, entrance to the delta just before dawn and try to get within eight thousand yards of the *Königsberg* before beginning the bombardment. The British hoped that at this distance, the monitors' 6-inch guns would be able to knock out the *Königsberg* before she found the range on them. (Reports had come in from Coronel and the Falklands about the remarkable range of the German 4.1-inch guns.) The key to a successful operation was whether the planes would be able to guide the monitors' fire more accurately than the German spotters could direct Looff's counterattack.

The northern entrance to the delta was chosen for the monitors' attack to avoid any interference from the sunken *Newbridge*. King-Hall planned to mount a diversionary attack on the southern entrance so he transferred his flag to the *Weymouth* because of her shallower draft. During the night he moved his flagship to the Simba Uranga entrance, along with the *Hyacinth* and the newly arrived *Pyramus* and *Pioneer* (sister ships of the unfortunate *Pegasus*). At daybreak the Germans would see that this channel was being heavily blockaded, and the cruisers' bombardment would

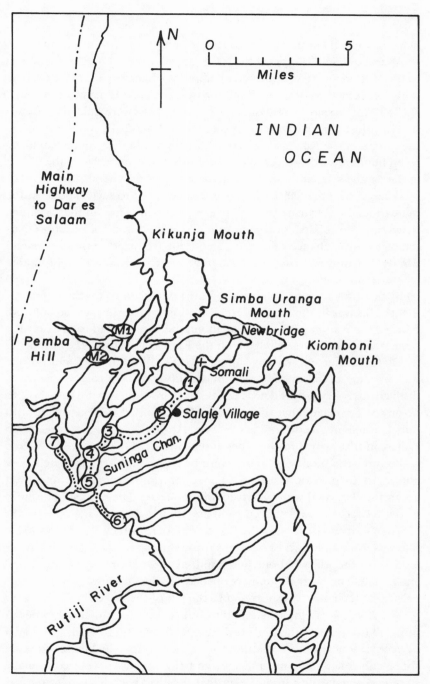

The Rufiji delta (Legend: Circled numbers=the *Königsberg*'s anchorages; M1 and M2=the monitors' positions during the first and second bombardments)

help convince them that the attack was coming from this direction.

After the monitors crossed the straits, they lay several miles off the delta to give the crews a few hours' rest before the attack began. Most of them were too excited to sleep. At 0300 the order came, "All hands, turn out." By 0400 the monitors were under way again. They were guided in toward shore by the lights of navy whalers stationed off the coast, and they reached the mouth of the Kikunja at 0520. Although this branch of the Rufiji was seven hundred yards wide, the *Severn* slowly and cautiously led the *Mersey* in the darkness, taking soundings all the way to avoid the shoals.

When dawn broke at 0540 they increased speed to seven knots. At the same time, the Germans on both riverbanks opened fire on the monitors, shattering the stillness of the morning. The light guns of the shore batteries had little chance of causing any serious damage to the *Severn* and *Mersey*. The only real effect of the barrage was to warn the *Königsberg* that an attack was under way.

By 0623 the monitors had reached the point planned for the bombardment. This was in the lee of a large island in midstream, whose tall trees blocked the *Königsberg*'s view. The monitors' gunners had to fire over the same trees, but they were relying on the RNAS pilots to be their eyes.

Flight-Lieutenant Watkins had taken off at 0500 in the Caudron. He was carrying several small bombs, but no observer. His role was to try to distract the *Königsberg*'s defenders, because his bombs were too small to do any real damage. Half an hour later, Cull took off in the Farman, with Sub-Lieutenant Arnold as his observer. At 0617 he wirelessed Captain Fullerton that he was ready to begin spotting.

By now, the monitors' crews were busy anchoring their vessels bow and stern to provide stationary gun platforms. The *Severn* anchored about four hundred yards upstream of the *Mersey*. The estimated distance to the *Königsberg* was between eight and nine thousand yards.

The German cruiser was the first to open fire, which she did at 0643. She was using only two of her guns for ranging purposes. The first shots landed on the island, about five hundred yards short of the monitors' anchorage. The *Severn*'s gunners opened fire five minutes later. Cull signaled that their aim was short and to the left of the target.

The *Königsberg*'s gunners found the range very quickly, and they began using all five guns of the starboard battery. According to Cull, who had a perfect view of the whole battle scene, "Her firing, which was obviously shore controlled, was magnificent, and the monitors were continually straddled, it appearing from the air that they had been hit many times, as the splash of the salvoes often hid the two ships from observation."

In reality, neither monitor received a direct hit for nearly an hour. At

0740 the *Mersey*'s forward 6-inch gun was knocked out by a shell that killed all of the gun's crew and wounded several other men. This hit started a dangerous fire near the magazine, which badly burned several more men before it was put out.

Captain Wilson informed Fullerton that he was moving his anchorage several hundred yards farther back to avoid more serious damage, now that the *Königsberg*'s gunners had zeroed in on his ship. This was a wise decision. No sooner had the *Mersey* raised anchor and got under way when a perfect salvo of five shells landed twenty yards astern of the monitor. If these had found their target, the British forces would have been cut in half in an instant.

For the first hour of the battle the monitors' fire was ragged and inaccurate, most of their shells landing on shore. Shells falling in the trees or on the muddy riverbanks made it very hard for Arnold to spot them accurately. But at 0755 the *Severn* scored her first hit: the shell knocked out the *Königsberg*'s forward gun. In the next fifteen minutes she hit the cruiser six more times. The spotting system was working as planned, and it seemed only a matter of time before the *Königsberg* was put out of action. Inexplicably, the monitors' gunners suddenly lost their aim.

The *Königsberg,* now firing with only four guns, began to straddle the *Severn.* Fullerton decided to shift his position to throw the Germans off their aim, just as Wilson had done. This was another fortunate decision, because as soon as the *Severn* had started moving, a full salvo landed in the exact spot where she had been anchored. The splashes from the near misses drenched the anchor party and flooded the monitor's quarterdeck.

From their new position the *Severn*'s lookouts were able to see several men in khaki uniforms on a platform high in the trees, less than a mile away. They were obviously directing the fire of the cruiser.

Fullerton wrote later: "[A]s we swung around I fired three 6-inch lyddite shells into the position. This was undoubtedly a prearranged spotting position, and shows that the enemy must have somehow got hold of the very day of the attack, and of the exact anchorage."

After this, the *Königsberg*'s shooting became less accurate, and her rate of fire slackened. Now that he had lost his best observation post, Looff decided to conserve his ammunition.

The monitors' aim was no better. The pilots were confused in reporting the fall of shot for two different ships, which often fired their guns simultaneously. It was discouraging for the gunners on one monitor to be signaled to alter their direction and range by a certain amount and, after doing so, to be given exactly the same correction as before, meaning their aim was not improving.

Also, the pilots and observers were continually changing as the planes went back to Mafia to refuel. This didn't help matters. Finally, Cull's plane developed engine problems, and the spotting for both ships had to be done by Watkins's plane. This led to an interruption every time Watkins left to refuel.

The battle had reached a deadlock. No further direct hits were made by either side during the next two hours, although there were many near misses. By mid-afternoon the tide began to run out of the delta, and Fullerton decided it was time to call it a day before his ships were in danger of running aground. The crews had been on duty for twelve straight hours, and they were exhausted. The signaling system clearly wasn't working as planned. As they steamed back down the river, the monitors came under small arms fire all the way to the river mouth, where the shore batteries were situated. These opened up a fierce barrage with four-pounders, but they did little damage to either ship.

The monitors arrived at Koma Island where the rest of the blockade squadron was waiting for them. The men of King-Hall's cruisers greeted them with rousing cheers, but on the whole it had been a discouraging day for the crews of the *Severn* and *Mersey*. They had fired more than six hundred shells at the *Königsberg*, yet they had only registered about a dozen definite hits. They had certainly wounded her, but not mortally.

The monitors had also received some damage, none of it serious. They had been quite fortunate to escape so lightly, especially in the first few hours before the *Königsberg's* best observation post was knocked out. According to the captain of the *Severn*, "[I]n my opinion it was sheer good luck that kept the ship from being sunk, as shells were continually falling ten yards short or over."

Casualties were also surprisingly light, the only fatalities being the gun crew of the *Mersey*. Several crewmen on each monitor were wounded. These men were transferred to the hospital on board the *Trent*.

On the positive side, the *Königsberg's* security had been breached after long months of immunity. The morale of her crew had been lowered by the sound of shells screaming at them from an unseen enemy and by the certain knowledge that this wasn't the last assault they would have to endure. Four of their shipmates had been killed and eleven more seriously wounded. They knew there was no longer any hope of escape from the trap they were in.

It was clear to the British that at least one more assault was needed to finish the job. The operation had exposed serious flaws in the spotting system that had to be corrected. Aerial observation was in its infancy in

1915, but valuable lessons had been learned in the Rufiji delta. During the next attack the two monitors would never fire simultaneously, and one plane was to be assigned to spot exclusively for each ship. Greater secrecy was vital. The date of the attack would not be announced until the evening before it was to take place.

The crews spent the next few days repairing the monitors, especially their bulkheads, which had been strained by the long bombardment. They piled extra sandbags around the gun positions; ammunition stocks were replenished; and new crew members were transferred from the *Hyacinth* to replace those killed and wounded in the first raid. By July 10 everything was ready for a second assault on the *Königsberg*.

That evening King-Hall gave the order for the operation to begin at 0800 the following morning. The fortunate coincidence of daybreak and turn of the tide that had occurred on July 6 wouldn't happen again for several months, so he decided to send the monitors into the river in broad daylight, at flood tide. This meant that they could reach their firing positions more quickly than they had during the first raid, but it also meant that the bombardment couldn't start until mid-afternoon, when the heat of the sun would be at its worst. With all the crews under cover, the conditions would be sweltering, especially for the men in the engine rooms, where the temperature was expected to reach 135 degrees Fahrenheit.

The earlier mood of enthusiastic anticipation among the monitors' crews had been replaced by one of grim determination. They had failed to destroy the *Königsberg* once, and they were resolved not to fail again.

The navy tugs *Blackcock* and *Revenger* towed the *Severn* and *Mersey* from Mafia Island to the mainland. Towing wasn't really necessary, but it was an attempt by King-Hall to confuse the observers on shore as to where the monitors were going. The rest of the squadron set out ostentatiously from Mafia Island, heading in the opposite direction, toward Zanzibar.

At 1040 the monitors cast off their tows and steamed across the sandbar into the Kikunja entrance. By this time King-Hall's cruisers had swung back and lay offshore, ready to bombard Pemba Hill, just north of the Kikunja, where the main German observation post was now located.

By 1130 the two monitors reached the all too familiar riverbanks and came under heavy fire from German field guns and small arms. The monitors replied with their three-pounders and raked both banks with machine-gun fire. The *Mersey* suffered one hit from a field gun, which wounded several men but did no serious damage.

This time the plan was to have the *Mersey* stay in the same place as in the previous raid, to try to draw the *Königsberg*'s fire. She was to move about slowly in midstream to present a tempting target. The *Severn* would anchor a thousand yards farther upriver. King-Hall hoped that she would be free to concentrate on the *Königsberg,* undisturbed by the cruiser's counterattack.

The Germans refused to cooperate. The *Königsberg* opened fire just after noon, and she did aim at the *Mersey* at first, but her opening salvoes were either well over or well short. As soon as the German spotters reported that one of the monitors was moving farther upstream, the cruiser shifted her target to the *Severn.* A few minutes later, while the *Severn's* crew were busy maneuvering the ship into a broadside position ready to drop anchor, the *Königsberg's* shells started landing all around them. Some were as close as fifty yards away.

It took the *Severn's* perspiring crew fifteen minutes to position and anchor the ship. During this time the anchor party was in great danger—far greater than when the *Newbridge* had been anchored. It is a tribute to their coolness under fire that the crew managed to do their job successfully under such trying conditions. If they had fouled the anchor or run aground, it would have been disastrous.

At 1230 the *Severn* was firmly anchored, and she opened fire on the *Königsberg* from a distance of about seven thousand yards. At the same time, the first spotter plane appeared overhead. This was the Farman, once again carrying Cull and Arnold. They had taken off from the Mafia airstrip at 1150 and climbed to two thousand feet over the delta. By now, the *Weymouth* and *Pyramus* were close in shore, and they began their bombardment of Pemba Hill. What with the planes, monitors, and cruisers, the German gunners were kept busy with a variety of targets.

The *Königsberg's* shells were still falling all around the monitors but miraculously doing nothing worse than soaking the gun crews from the near misses. The *Severn* fired salvo after salvo in the direction of the cruiser. The first four salvos missed. The shells landed in the bush beyond the *Königsberg's* position, which made it hard for Cull and Arnold to spot them accurately. They wirelessed corrections to the *Severn* to shorten the range by four hundred yards at a time, until the monitors' shells began to land near the cruiser. The next correction was only one hundred yards down. After one more minor correction the *Severn's* eighth salvo crashed into the *Königsberg.* This happened at 1242, only twelve minutes after the monitor had opened fire.

Cull and Arnold saw two shells explode on the cruiser's forecastle, one of them destroying a gun turret. The *Königsberg* had already lost one of her starboard guns in the first attack, and her broadside was down to three. Once the *Severn* found the range, the spotter aircraft needed to signal only minor alterations.

This was the critical point in the action. If the Germans couldn't score some direct hits on the *Severn* immediately and disable her, they were finished. But the German gunners were at a great disadvantage because they were aiming at a much smaller target, due to the monitor's shorter hull and low freeboard.

During the next ten minutes the *Severn* hit the *Königsberg* repeatedly with 6-inch lyddite shells. Cull and Arnold were even able to shift the monitor's aim from the cruiser's forecastle to her midship section, and then onto her stern. At 1250 they saw a large explosion on board the battered cruiser, and by 1253 the *Königsberg* had only one gun still firing.

At the climax of the battle the Farman's engine began to sputter. Just after Arnold had wirelessed his last correction to the *Severn*'s gunners, the plane began to lose height. Cull signaled: "We are hit. Send boat for us." Ironically, one of the *Königsberg*'s shrapnel shells had burst directly underneath the spotter plane just as it had finished its deadly work. The explosion blew off one of the engine's cylinders, the engine stopped altogether, and Cull lost control of the plane for a few moments before he was able to put it into a glide. He then headed toward where the *Mersey* was lying.

With considerable skill Cull managed to avoid hitting the mangrove trees and landed the plane in the river less than two hundred yards from the *Mersey*. As he wrote later: "Our landing on the water was very slow but the machine, on touching, at once turned a somersault. My Observer shot over my head well clear. I, however, had foolishly forgotten to unstrap my belt, and I went down with the machine. . . . I had the greatest difficulty in freeing myself. . . . When I came to the surface, my Observer was hunting in the wreckage for me, and we both started swimming for the *Mersey*, whose motor-boat picked us up."

The two aviators were lucky there were no snipers in the vicinity, or crocodiles, which must have been scared off by the din from exploding shells.

During the next hour the *Severn* fired forty-two more salvoes at the *Königsberg*. Then her gun barrels became so hot that she had to cease firing. With minor corrections from her spotters, she had been able to rake the cruiser from end to end. The monitor's crew heard at least eight more large explosions, followed by the sight of clouds of yellowish lyddite smoke rising over the trees.

At 1340 Fullerton ordered the *Mersey* to move past him, until the second monitor was less than seven thousand yards from her target. With Lieutenants Watkins and Bishop spotting from the newly arrived Caudron, the *Mersey* fired another twenty-eight salvoes. She began hitting the *Königsberg* after the third. Fullerton's orders were that the German cruiser was to be totally destroyed before they left the Rufiji. After this final bombardment, he commented: "I personally went to the topmast head and saw the enemy on fire fore and aft. . . . It is estimated that she must have been struck with some fifty to seventy 6-inch lyddite."

Finally, at 1420, there came the long-awaited signal from Watkins's aircraft: "Target destroyed."

Conditions on board the *Königsberg* were appalling. Of the 220 crew remaining on board, 22 more had been killed in the latest attack and 48 wounded. Looff himself had been wounded early on in the *Severn*'s onslaught. He was wounded again, this time seriously, during the *Mersey*'s final barrage.

The guns of the starboard battery were all out of action, but there was no question of turning the ship around to use the port battery. The *Königsberg* had been so badly holed that she would surely have foundered in midstream if she had left her anchorage. At that point she was probably resting on the mud and couldn't have moved anyway.

The ship was a ruined hulk. One funnel was down, her masts were shattered, and the deck was a scene of devastation. All that could be seen were masses of tangled metal and gaping holes. Fires were blazing out of control in the forecastle and stern sections. Looff told his men to flood the magazines to prevent the ship from blowing up.

He had no choice but to order his crew to abandon ship. When the dead and wounded had been carried off, the rest of the men lined up on shore at a safe distance to watch the end of the *Königsberg*. Looff told his first lieutenant to go below and set a timer to detonate two of the torpedo warheads. When they exploded, they tore the bottom out of the ship. The battered cruiser listed sharply to starboard and settled firmly onto the Rufiji mud, with the water lapping over her decks.

At sunset the *Königsberg*'s battle flag was hauled down for the last time. The exhausted men on shore gave three cheers for the Kaiser, then marched off into the bush.

The dead were buried and the wounded were taken to a nearby field hospital. Some of the surviving crew members went on to fight on land with Lettow-Vorbeck's forces. Others served on gunboats in the naval campaigns against the British on Lake Victoria and Lake Tanganyika. Most of the cruiser's guns were salvaged and became part of Lettow-Vorbeck's field batteries.

The Kaiser recognized the heroism of the *Königsberg*'s crew during the long siege by awarding the Iron Cross, First Class, to Captain Looff, and

The wreck of the *Königsberg* before she was scuttled *(Verlag Ullstein)*

the Iron Cross, Second Class, to 150 of his men. When Looff wrote his official report of the final battle, he ended it with the statement, "S.M.S. *Königsberg* is destroyed but not conquered."

It is hard to quarrel with this conclusion.

Meanwhile, the victorious monitors had steamed out of the Rufiji. After exchanging fire with the shore defenses for the last time, they met the two tugs waiting to tow them back to Mafia Island. The *Weymouth* came across to the mainland to escort them. Admiral King-Hall was on her bridge, decked out in his white dress uniform, and he called for three cheers for the monitors' crews.

After they arrived at Mafia Island, celebrations were held on board ship and at the RNAS airfield. The beer, rum, and champagne flowed freely. Later on there was a grand victory reception at the capital of the British colony, hosted by the Sultan of Zanzibar.

The Admiralty was greatly satisfied when it received the news that the *Königsberg* had been destroyed. It was the first air-sea operation in history, and it had been a highly successful one. After a long campaign the last of the eight German raiders was accounted for. It had taken almost a year to sweep the seas clear of the menace to Allied shipping. Merchant ships were now able to supply Britain with vital food and war materials without much interference.

The respite didn't last long, however. Ironically, the Royal Navy's success against the eight cruisers led to a much graver danger to Allied merchant ships. The Germans knew full well that they would never bring Britain to its knees by preying on its commerce with a handful of surface raiders. For the rest of the war they concentrated their efforts on the untested but potentially more deadly U-boats. But that is another story.

Epilogue

The overseas cruiser actions of 1914–15 did not, in purely material terms, have a major effect on the course of the war. The loss of eight cruisers and twenty-four hundred trained men was a severe but hardly a crippling blow to the German navy; nor did the loss of six warships and forty-two merchantmen amount to a serious drain on Allied maritime resources. Nonetheless, Graf Spee's ships were responsible for sinking nearly 250,000 tons of valuable ships (and their equally precious cargoes) in less than six months. It is notable that over the same period, German U-boats managed to sink only three British merchant ships.

The losses caused by the surface raiders were small, however, in comparison to the enormous tonnage sunk by the German U-boats from 1916 to 1918. In 1916 alone—the first year of unrestricted submarine warfare—the U-boats sent more than a million tons of Allied merchant ships to the bottom, and they eventually brought Britain to the brink of starvation.

What was more serious in the first years of the war was the dislocation of troop movements caused by Graf Spee's menacing presence and the frequent paralysis of Allied shipping by lone raiders such as the *Emden* and *Karlsruhe*. Just as important was their tying up large numbers of badly needed warships on endless patrols and searches. But the most significant result the cruisers achieved was their effect on morale and prestige—for both sides.

The German navy was barely forty years old in 1914, and because of its lack of tradition and war experience it had come to feel deeply inferior to the Royal Navy, with its long and glorious history. This was overcome by the smashing victory at Coronel and the brilliant success of the *Emden*. Even the defeat at the Falklands helped build morale in the German navy, because its men and ships had battled courageously for hours before succumbing to greatly superior Royal Navy forces. The news of Graf Spee's victory at Coronel and Müller's daring raids on Madras and Penang also gave heart to German soldiers fighting in the mud of Flanders and the snows of the eastern front.

In Britain, the long-held conviction that its Royal Navy was invincible was shattered. Confidence in the navy had been badly shaken in the first few months of the war by a series of setbacks: the daring escape of the *Goeben* and *Breslau* from the Mediterranean fleet; the loss of the armored cruisers *Hogue*, *Aboukir*, and *Cressy*, sunk by a lone U-boat in the space of forty-seven minutes; the sinking of the brand-new battleship *Audacious*, which foundered after she had struck but a single mine.

And then, in the navy's first major sea battle since Trafalgar, it suffered a crushing defeat at Coronel. Confidence was to some extent restored by Sturdee's one-sided victory off Port Stanley, but things were never quite the same again.

The Germans were encouraged to send ships of their battle fleet out of their safe harbors into the North Sea. (They were also taking advantage of the absence of the *Invincible* and the *Inflexible* from Beatty's battle cruiser force.) Only two days after Coronel, Adm. Franz von Hipper's battle cruisers began a series of daring raids on towns on the east coast of England, which they bombarded in broad daylight, causing many civilian casualties. For several weeks the Royal Navy was seemingly unable to do anything about these hit-and-run attacks in its own backyard, until Beatty's battle cruisers caught Hipper's squadron off the Dogger Bank. Even then, faulty communications allowed the German force to escape the trap largely intact.

But could Graf Spee have accomplished more than he did? His tactics at Coronel were sound, even if he did let the *Glasgow* get away almost unscathed, and his maneuvers at the Falklands were nearly flawless. Graf Spee cannot be faulted for turning away from Port Stanley once he learned that ships with much bigger guns than his own ships carried were anchored in the harbor. (There is some dispute in various accounts of the battle as to when the Germans actually realized they were up against battle cruisers. Since Graf Spee did not give the order to turn southeast at full speed until well after the *Canopus* opened fire, it seems reasonable to accept the eyewitness acccounts of the *Gneisenau*'s survivors as being the most reliable.)

In any event, Graf Spee had no idea the enemy squadron was in the midst of coaling and therefore so vulnerable. If the weather that day had changed a bit sooner, his clever maneuvering might have allowed more of his ships to escape destruction.

But some of Graf Spee's strategic decisions are open to serious criticism. It was unquestionably a mistake to delay his entry into the Atlantic for so long after Coronel and an even worse one to attack the Falklands instead of breaking directly for home. But probably his most serious strategic error was in deciding to keep all his ships together as a squadron.

With the advantage of hindsight, it would have been much better if he had split his forces at the beginning of the war. He could have kept the *Scharnhorst* and *Gneisenau* together as a powerful unit and still have been the same threat to British control of the far seas that so worried the Admiralty. Graf Spee's decision to use his strength to attack enemy warships and shore installations, rather than merchant ships, would not have been greatly hampered if he had detached all his light cruisers to act as commerce raiders, for their presence didn't materially strengthen the two armored cruisers as a fighting force.

The light cruisers played only a minor role at Coronel and were no help to Graf Spee at all in the Falklands. In fact, he would have been better off if he had not had these vulnerable units to worry about. His big ships may have been no faster than his light cruisers, but with a twenty-mile head start, the *Scharnhorst* and *Gneisenau* might just have escaped into the mist if Graf Spee had not had to sacrifice them by turning to fight a delaying action with Sturdee's battle cruisers.

When Graf Spee was at Pagan he should have been more intent on causing the Allies' commerce as much disruption as possible, especially after he had listened to Müller's proposal. If he had detached the *Nürnberg* as well as the *Emden,* and then when he reached Easter Island had ordered the *Leipzig* and *Dresden* to continue as independent raiders, there is no telling how much more damage he would have caused. By keeping the squadron together he simplified the Admiralty's task of hunting it down and destroying it, even though it took them a long time to send a force that was adequate for the job.

It is not hard to imagine the havoc that might have resulted if three more light cruisers, in addition to the *Emden, Karlsruhe,* and *Königsberg,* had been let loose to prey on Britain's lifelines. The Allies' defenses in the Indian Ocean and South Atlantic were woefully weak, and the Germans knew this. With a combination of good luck and determination, each of the light cruisers might have achieved as much destruction as the *Emden* or *Karlsruhe.* It was, after all, ill fortune that shortened the careers of two of the raiders. The *Königsberg*'s engine breakdown and the explosion on board the *Karlsruhe* were not the result of enemy action.

Coaling so many raiders would have been a problem, of course, but Müller and Köhler managed quite well by capturing Allied colliers whenever the Etappen let them down. There is no reason to suppose that Schönberg and Haun would not have had as much success if given the opportunity. It is true that Lüdecke was a disappointment as a raider, but he had not been selected for this role. Even he caused the Allies serious concern.

With so many lone raiders to track down, the Royal Navy's communications would have been tested to the limit. The hunters would never have known from reports of sinkings or attacks on shore installations which raider they were chasing at any given time. It would have forced the Admiralty to send out many more ships to hunt down six lone raiders, as well as the dangerous *Scharnhorst* and *Gneisenau*. This could have had a crucial effect on the balance of naval forces in European waters, especially if more of the speedy battle cruisers had been needed to do the job.

The other light cruisers might not have lasted any longer than the *Emden* did, but they would surely have done more damage than they did at Coronel and the Falklands. One of the Admiralty's persistent fears was that the *Königsberg* or the *Dresden* might become another *Emden*. Imagine their problems if there had been six *Emden*s to worry about.

Postscripts

GRAF MAXIMILIAN VON SPEE

Although Graf Spee and his only sons perished at the Falklands, the Germans wanted the name of the gallant count to live on. Less than a year after his death, they laid down the keel of a thirty-thousand-ton battle cruiser at the Schichau works in Danzig. When the ship was launched in 1917, they named her *Graf Spee*. Designed to be a match for the newest British battle cruisers of the *Repulse* class, she was much more powerful than any of the ships that sank Graf Spee's flagship off Port Stanley. But the *Graf Spee* was never completed. Work was suspended in the last year of the war, and the hull lay neglected on the slips until 1921, when it was broken up for scrap. At least it was spared the indignity of surrendering with the rest of the High Seas Fleet in 1918.

A replacement for the *Graf Spee* was launched in 1934. When she was commissioned for service in Hitler's Kriegsmarine in 1936, the ship was given the full name *Admiral Graf Spee*. She was one of a series of ships designed specifically to serve as long-range commerce raiders. They were supposedly heavy cruisers, but the Washington Naval Treaty of 1922 limited this type of warship to a maximum displacement of ten thousand tons. By the time the new *Graf Spee* was ready for service, she was well over twelve thousand tons. The Germans classified these vessels as *Panzerschiffe* (armored ships), but their flouting of the treaty rules led them to be known as "pocket battleships." In reality, they were heavy cruisers with battleship-type gun turrets.

At the time she was launched, the Kriegsmarine decided "[T]he motto of the battleship's complement, like that of Admiral Graf Spee and his men, would be now and for all time: 'Faithful unto Death.'"

On August 21, 1939, the *Graf Spee* left Wilhelmshaven without any publicity or fanfare and stationed herself off the Cape Verde Islands to wait there until war was declared. Her commander, Capt. Hans Langsdorff, had orders to disrupt Allied sea traffic by attacking merchant ships in the Atlantic and Indian Oceans. In the first two months of the war he had captured and sunk only nine merchant ships—with no loss of life among their crews—but he had tied up no less than twenty major Royal Navy units hunting for him.

Then, almost twenty-five years to the day after Graf Spee's final battle, the ship named after him was also cruising in the South Atlantic. Her captain had decided to raid the rich sea traffic going in and out of Montevideo and Buenos Aires, just as Graf Spee had planned to do in 1914 after he had dealt with the Falklands.

As she approached the mouth of the River Plate, the raider was sighted at daybreak on December 13, 1939, by three ships of Force G. This was probably the weakest of the eight Royal Navy hunting groups that had been assigned to seek out and destroy the pocket battleships *Graf Spee* and *Deutschland*. It consisted of the cruiser *Exeter,* the light cruiser *Ajax,* and her sister ship from the Royal New Zealand Navy, the *Achilles.* As luck would have it, the fourth and strongest member of Force G, HMS *Cumberland,* had just left the squadron to undergo minor repairs in the Falklands.

The *Graf Spee* heavily outgunned the British ships with her six 11-inch and eight 5.9-inch guns. The *Exeter* carried 8-inch weapons, the light cruisers solely 6-inch guns. The weight of a full broadside from the pocket battleship was nearly three times that of the whole British squadron.

In spite of this, Commo. Henry Harwood of the *Ajax* immediately launched a determined assault on the *Graf Spee.* He split his forces into two divisions, with the *Exeter* in one and the light cruisers in the other. They began shelling the German ship from two directions. Langsdorff had trouble at first trying to direct his fire at three targets simultaneously, and he soon concentrated on his most dangerous opponent, the *Exeter.* This freed the two light cruisers to fire undisturbed, but their 6-inch shells couldn't penetrate the *Graf Spee*'s armor plate and do any vital damage.

During a running battle that lasted for an hour and a half, the *Exeter* was badly mauled by hits from the 670-pound shells of the pocket battleship's 11-inch guns. She had scored several hits on the *Graf Spee,* but with heavy casualties and only one gun still firing, Harwood told her captain to pull out of range under cover of a smoke screen.

The two light cruisers continued to harry the slower pocket battleship with gunfire and torpedo attacks. This was very risky for such thinly armored ships, but their captains were so skillful at altering the range frequently that they were not heavily damaged. By this time the *Graf Spee* had suffered more than twenty direct hits, but although her damage was extensive, none of it was critical.

The British ships broke off the action because they were having little effect on Langsdorff's ship now that the 8-inch guns of the *Exeter* were silent. They didn't dare get close enough to the *Graf Spee* to launch a successful torpedo attack.

Commodore Harwood decided to shadow her until strong reinforcements could be brought up. At this point the crews of the British ships were amazed to see the pocket battleship turn away from them and head for shelter in Montevideo. The battered and leaking *Exeter* struggled to Port Stanley for repairs, while the *Ajax* and *Achilles* stayed on guard off the mouth of the River Plate.

The port authorities in Montevideo sent a naval commission on board the *Graf Spee* to examine the damage; they judged that only minor repairs were needed to make her seaworthy. Despite Langsdorff's request for a fourteen-day stay to allow him to repair all damage, the Uruguayans informed him that his ship could stay in port just seventy-two hours longer. The deadline was December 17.

The British Embassy tried delaying tactics to prolong his stay, in order to give the Royal Navy more time to reinforce the ships waiting off the mouth of the Plate. Only the *Cumberland* had arrived on the scene by December 14; it was going to take another five days before the battle cruiser *Renown* and the aircraft carrier *Ark Royal* could get there. Langsdorff didn't know this and thought he had no chance of fighting his way past the blockade and reaching Germany. British agents did everything they could to foster the impression that the Royal Navy was waiting in great strength off Montevideo.

Langsdorff believed that his options were strictly internment, scuttling, or making a dash upriver to Buenos Aires. He hoped the Argentine authorities would be more sympathetic than the Uruguayans and allow him a fourteen-day stay to carry out full repairs. They weren't. In the end, he decided to scuttle his ship. (Adm. Erich Raeder had already authorized him to take this step if he felt it was unavoidable.) Contrary to newspaper reports and rumors that Hitler sent him a direct order to scuttle the ship, the decision was Langsdorff's.

On the evening of December 17 the *Graf Spee* set sail for the last time. She steamed out of the harbor into Montevideo Roads with only a skeleton crew aboard, including Langsdorff. A crowd estimated at more than 250,000 people watched from shore, as the world's radio, press, and news cameramen reported her every move. None of them knew for certain what Langsdorff was going to do—fight or scuttle.

As the sun began to set, the skeleton crew were taken off in Uruguayan tugboats. A few minutes later the *Graf Spee* was ripped open by a series of rumbling explosions as timed charges went off deep inside the ship. Clouds of black smoke erupted from her bowels, and her superstructure crumbled into a mass of twisted steel. Finally, her forward magazine exploded. Shortly afterwards, the torn and ravaged hull of the once handsome ship sank into the mud of the River Plate.

Captain Langsdorff asked to be taken to the German Embassy in Buenos Aires. A few days later he wrote a final report to Admiral Raeder and a letter to his wife. Then, perhaps unable to face the disgrace of having destroyed his fine ship, or possibly feeling that he should share her fate, he draped himself in the German naval ensign and put a bullet through his head. There have been no more *Graf Spee*s in the German navy.

KARL VON MÜLLER

After the Battle of Cocos, Müller was taken to Colombo on board the *Sydney*. While he was there, Captain Grant of the *Hampshire* asked to see the man he had hunted for so long. He was given permission to visit the prisoner, and the two captains had a long private conversation. What they talked about is not recorded, but it must have been a fascinating exchange of their experiences in the Indian Ocean.

On November 17 Müller was transferred to the SS *Orvieto*, which took him and the uninjured *Emden* prisoners to a prisoner of war camp in Malta. (When he arrived at Valletta he learned that the Kaiser had awarded him the Iron Cross, First and Second Class.) The prisoners were kept at Fort Verdala and closely guarded by a hundred Australian troops. The Allies had had enough trouble with the men of the *Emden*, but Lt. Erich Fikentscher did manage to escape, reaching Sicily in a small boat in April 1916. Unfortunately for him, Italy had by then joined the Allies, and he was soon recaptured.

Müller's stay at Fort Verdala was uneventful and reasonably comfortable, although he did suffer from occasional spells of malaria. Things changed in October 1916 when he was brusquely taken aboard HMS *London,* which was in Valetta harbor under full steam, ready to sail for England. He was given no explanation.

The old battleship arrived in Plymouth on October 16, and Müller was sent to a prison camp at Sutton Bonington in Derbyshire, where he was kept under maximum security. He was even under close guard when he used the toilet. He protested that his treatment was not in accord with either the Hague Convention or that due to a senior officer, but to no avail. He was the most distinguished German officer in captivity, and the Allies didn't want to take any chance of his getting back to Germany to achieve a propaganda triumph. He was asked to give his word that he would not try to escape, but he refused on principle. He did escape once, but was recaptured the next day. This resulted in fifty-six days' solitary confinement.

By January 1918 Müller's malaria attacks had become worse, and as part of a humanitarian exchange of prisoners, he was transferred to an internment camp in Holland for medical treatment. He was repatriated in poor health in October 1918, less than a month before the Armistice. The *Emden*'s skipper was promoted to captain and given an administrative post in the Reichsmarineamt in Berlin, but he served there for just a few months. He retired in January 1919 in failing health and lived quietly at the family home in Blankenberg thereafter. Müller refused all invitations to speak in public or to write about his experiences. He believed he had done no more than his duty and that any attempt to capitalize on his experiences would be to profit from the deaths of his comrades.

He did leave behind a long and detailed official report on the *Emden*'s activities, however, but this was written only at the direct order of the Admiralstab. An unseemly row occurred at the time Müller was recommended for the order Pour le Mérite in March 1918. The Kaiser's aide-de-camp, Adm. Georg von Müller (no relation), questioned Müller's actions in wrecking his ship and demanded the fullest explanation before passing the recommendation on to his master. The Admiralstab were incensed, but Adm. Henning von Holtzendorff ordered Karl von Müller to write a complete report.

When he read it, the Kaiser wrote on the report, "He is fully justified." He sent a long telegram to Müller awarding him the order. In it he wrote, "You have conferred high honour on the name of your ship for all time, giving the entire world a brilliant example of the most decisive and chivalrous conduct of cruiser warfare."

After the war Müller refused all offers to take part in any quasi-political associations that promoted the interests of the military or the nobility, although he was elected and served briefly in the Braunschweig Parliament as a deputy for the liberal German National Party. He continued to live a quiet life, mainly at home in Blankenberg, until 1923. Physically drained by malaria attacks and worn out by his wartime experiences, he died suddenly at Braunschweig on March 11, two months before his fiftieth birthday.

FRITZ EMIL LÜDECKE

After he had scuttled the *Dresden* at Más Afuera, Fritz Lüdecke, along with his uninjured crew members, was taken in a Chilean warship to the naval base at Talcahuano on the mainland and thence to Valparaíso. They were initially housed on board the interned German freighter *Yorck,* which had been one of Graf Spee's supply ships. The British ambassador protested vigorously that this was obviously risky from a security standpoint, and the Chileans agreed. The prisoners were transferred to a camp on Quiriquina Island, just north of Coronel, where most of them stayed until the end of the war. Not all, because several enterprising souls escaped and managed to find their way back to Germany.

Lüdecke was repatriated in 1919 and appointed to an administrative position in the Baltic command. His main tasks for the next year were to wind up the affairs of the cruiser squadron and to supervise the paying off and decommissioning of the highly successful merchant raider *Seeadler.* He had been promoted to captain after Coronel and stayed at this rank until March 8, 1920, when he was given the titular rank of rear admiral. He was pensioned off the following day and vanished into a well-deserved obscurity.

MAX LOOFF

When Max Looff had recovered from the wounds he received during the monitors' bombardment, Lettow-Vorbeck put him in charge of the defenses in the Lindi area. His forces were a mixture of the cruiser's crew members and native Askari troops, known as the *Königsberg-Abteilung* (detachment). Greatly outnumbered, they fought bravely on at Lindi against British and Portuguese troops until 1917, when they were forced to retreat to the southern border of the protectorate.

By late 1917 they were in bad shape. Some had been killed, and many were wounded or sick with influenza or malaria. Their supplies and ammunition were all but exhausted, and they had become a liability to Lettow-Vorbeck. As a diversion to cover his other moves, the colonel ordered Looff to surrender to the King's African Rifles, which he did on November 26, 1917.

The tattered remnants of the Königsberg-Abteilung were taken to Dar es Salaam to wait for a ship to transport them to prisoner of war camps in Egypt. The men went to Cairo and the officers to Alexandria. Looff was eventually sent to England and spent the rest of the war in a camp at Hull.

After the Armistice he arrived in Rotterdam, where he rejoined some of his old shipmates. Only two officers and twelve men were left out of the original Königsberg-Abteilung. Other crew members who had fought on land with Lettow-Vorbeck's forces had also been repatriated, and some who had been captured by the British had managed to escape and get back to Germany via Arabia and Turkey. They were all reunited in Berlin in 1919. On March 2 a parade was held to commemorate the *Königsberg,* and they marched through the Brandenburg Gate, where they were saluted by Admiral Rogge, the chief of naval staff.

In the postwar years Looff served under the chief of the Baltic Station, in charge of mine, blockade, and demolition systems. In 1922 he was given command of the Kiel naval garrison and later became town-major of Kiel. He returned to the Baltic Station in 1920 as inspector of torpedoes and mines. During this period he was promoted to rear admiral.

Looff was discharged from the navy in 1922 at the age of forty-eight and given the honorary rank of vice admiral. He remained on the navy reserve list until May 1939 but was never recalled to active service. He survived World War II and died in Berlin on September 20, 1954, at the age of eighty.

HELLMUTH VON MÜCKE

After Hellmuth von Mücke and his men escaped from Direction Island in the *Ayesha,* they successfully navigated the leaking schooner to Sumatra. This was a remarkable feat, considering the state of the ship's pumps and the primitive instruments and charts on board. They arrived at Padang, nine hundred miles due north of Cocos, on November 27. Here they had arguments with the Dutch naval authorities, who wanted to intern the ship as a prize. Mücke insisted the *Ayesha* was now a regular warship and was as entitled to a twenty-four-hour stay to take on supplies as any other warship.

Finally, with the help of the local German consul, Herr Schild, Mücke was allowed to leave Padang on November 29. Schild also arranged for a rendezvous with a more suitable vessel to take the *Emden*'s landing party on its way. This was the *Choising,* the same freighter that had failed to rendezvous with the *Emden* at Angaur at the beginning of her war cruise.

Meanwhile, the Royal Navy had been searching for the *Ayesha* ever since Admiral Jerram learned that Mücke had eluded the *Sydney.* In Jerram's opinion she was "a menace to trade until captured."

In reality, the leaking *Ayesha* was more of a menace to her own crew than she was to even the slowest merchant ship. The crew's only concern was to reach Germany, and they knew the little schooner would never get them there.

They met the *Choising* as arranged at a point two hundred miles south-southwest of Padang on December 15, and they proceeded to the Pagai Islands to make the transfer. (This was where the *Emden* coaled from the *Buresk* for the last time.) After they had taken their remaining provisions to the *Choising,* they bored holes in the hull of the schooner and watched as she settled in the water. Mücke's men gave her three rousing cheers as she went to the bottom. SMS *Ayesha* had logged nearly two thousand miles in her brief career as a warship.

They soon found that the freighter was no great improvement as a transport. She couldn't make the ten knots she was supposed to, and worse still, she had a persistent coal fire in one of her bunkers. Instead of pumping water out of their vessel, the crew now had to let water in to put out the fire, thus reducing their speed even further. Even so, they managed to steam more than five thousand miles across the Indian Ocean with the help of Captain Minkwitz and the civilian crew of the freighter.

They disguised the *Choising* either as a Dutch or an Italian vessel and kept clear of regular sea-lanes. Every time they saw smoke on the horizon, they turned away from it. Undetected by Allied patrols, they kept well away from Aden as they steamed past Perim Island through the Bab-al-Mandab Strait into the Red Sea. They arrived safely at Hodeida on the coast of Yemen on January 9, 1915. Since this was a Turkish possession—the territory of Germany's staunch ally—they felt they would have no trouble.

What happened over the next five months was a remarkable trek of more than two thousand miles as the *Emden*'s detachment made its way north to Constantinople, at that time the capital of Turkey. Mücke and his men showed great courage and amazing resourcefulness as they made use of every form of transport available in their determination to get back to Germany. They marched through the desert, sailed along the coast in dhows and motor launches, rode camels, and finally reached Jiddah, where they boarded a train on the famed Hejaz railway.

Aftermath: The *Emden*'s landing party at Constantinople *(The Robert Hunt Picture Library)*

The territory they passed through on the way to the railhead was largely unknown to Europeans. They had to contend with armed assaults by Bedouin tribesmen (who demanded impossible ransoms for their safe passage), duplicitous Arab sheiks, and equivocal Turkish officials. There was also the constant and ferocious heat, frequent shortages of food and water, and sickness. They lost one man to typhus and three to wounds from Bedouin bullets. But they made it, due in large measure to Mücke's inspired leadership and his unrelenting efforts to take care of his men.

The men arrived in Constantinople in May 1915, the only members of Graf Spee's squadron not dead or in captivity. They were dressed in brand-new uniforms that had been sent on to them by train from German naval stores in Turkey. On May 23, Hellmuth von Mücke, in full dress uniform, marched his men to a reviewing stand where they were greeted by Adm. Wilhelm Souchon (the man who had eluded the Mediterranean fleet with the *Goeben* and *Breslau* and had helped bring Turkey into the war).

Lieutenant Commander von Mücke dipped his sword in respect and said to Admiral Souchon, "Beg to report, landing party from S.M.S. *Emden* numbering five officers, seven petty officers and thirty-seven men, present and correct."

JULIUS LAUTERBACH

When the captured collier *Exford* parted from the *Emden* on the day before the raid on Cocos, she had on board the reserve lieutenant Julius Lauterbach as captain, sixteen sailors from the cruiser, and the Chinese members of her original crew. Müller's orders to Lauterbach were to take the *Exford* to the mouth of the Gulf of Aden and wait for him off the island of Socotra. If the *Emden* didn't show up by the end of November, Lauterbach was supposed to head for a neutral port and seek internment.

He managed to reach Socotra without running into Allied patrols, and for two boring weeks the men of the *Exford* waited. All they could do was steam monotonously in circles and keep a sharp eye open for the cruiser, as well as for enemy ships. By December 1 their food supplies were getting desperately low, and Lauterbach decided he couldn't wait for the *Emden* any longer. He didn't dare try to buy fresh supplies because of the risk of giving away his position to the Allies.

The men on the *Exford* had heard no news of the *Emden,* but they realized by now that the attack on the Cocos Islands had not gone according to plan. They set out for Sumatra and arrived off Padang on December 11, two days after their comrades in the *Ayesha* had left harbor.

Jerram had dispatched two armed merchant cruisers to the Padang area to search for the schooner after reports came in that she had docked there. These were the *Himalaya* and the *Empress of Japan.* They arrived too late to trap the *Ayesha,* but the *Empress of Japan* did catch the *Exford.*

Capt. M. B. Baillie-Hamilton sent over an armed boarding party that seized the collier before she could be scuttled. Lauterbach could only protest that his ship was inside Dutch territorial waters. Since the *Exford* was clearly at least twenty-five miles offshore, Baillie-Hamilton ignored the protest. The Germans on board were taken prisoner, and the *Empress of Japan* escorted the ship and her Chinese crew to Singapore.

On December 15 Lauterbach and his men were taken to Tanglin Barracks, where they were guarded by Punjabi troops of the Fifth Light Infantry, Indian army. As the only officer prisoner, Lauterbach was offered more comfortable accommodation in a hotel if he would give his word not to try to escape. He refused the offer; he had other plans. On the Kaiser's birthday, January 27, 1915, he and Lt. Johann Merckl, the second officer of the *Markomannia,* along with two interned civilians, began to tunnel their way out.

They need not have bothered, because on February 15, long before the tunnel was finished, the Indian garrison mutinied during a bloody uprising in which most of the British officers and noncommissioned officers were killed. Lauterbach and the *Exford*'s prisoners escaped amid the general confusion. Although six of them were recaptured by fresh troops sent in to put down the mutiny, Lauterbach and the rest managed to get to Sumatra by dugout and sampan. They then took a train to Padang, where they arrived on March 15, 1915.

Lauterbach reported to the Dutch authorities and was detained. The rest of his group were interned because they were regular navy men. A Dutch court ruled, however, that as a merchant marine officer Lauterbach was a civilian and free to go, providing he remained in Sumatra. The British requested that he be turned over to them, but the Dutch were waiting for a ruling from the Netherlands before deciding his fate.

Lauterbach had no intention of waiting; he was absolutely determined to get back to Germany. He left Padang and embarked on a remarkable odyssey. Even without embellishment the story of his journey reads more like a piece of adventure fiction.

When Lauterbach reached Batavia, the German consul-general provided him with money and travel documents and gave him dispatches to take to the consulate in Shanghai. Lauterbach then took a boat from Sumatra to Cebu in the Philippines, where he boarded the train to Manila. He was traveling alone at this point. The British put a price on his head that at one time reached £1000.

With the help of friends and consular officials who provided him with false passports, he made his way to Shanghai via Tientsin and Nanking. He traveled sometimes under the guise of an Arab merchant, at other times as a Dutch or Belgian businessman. After reporting to the German consulate in Shanghai, he boarded a U.S. ship bound for Nagasaki and Yokohama.

By that point he had acquired a U.S. passport, stolen for him by friends in Shanghai, and booked his passage as a Mr. W. Johnson. He stayed on this ship, which was going next to Honolulu. (When he arrived there he saw his old command, the *Staatssekretär Krätke*, lying in Pearl Harbor, where she had been interned.)

Another American ship took him to San Francisco, where he now became a Danish businessman. After taking the train to New York, he bribed the captain of a Danish freighter to sign him on as a stoker. He set sail across the Atlantic but didn't do any stoking.

When the freighter arrived in European waters she was stopped off the Orkneys by a British patrol vessel, which escorted the ship into Kirkwall for further scrutiny as a suspected blockade-runner. The port authorities detained her for five days, but they didn't discover Lauterbach's real identity. When the freighter was released she went to Oslo and finally docked in Copenhagen. Lauterbach called on the German naval attaché, who provided him with papers to travel through Denmark and across the German border.

On October 10, 1915, seven months after leaving Singapore, he arrived at Warnemünde, site of the family home. He was given a tumultuous reception in his hometown from the townspeople and the band of the local regiment, who all turned out to welcome their returning hero. After a short visit with his family, he went to Berlin and reported to the Reichsmarineamt.

Lauterbach received an equally warm welcome in Berlin because his adventures had been widely publicized. It was great propaganda. He was granted an audience with Admiral von Tirpitz and another with the Kaiser, no less. They were both keen to hear Lauterbach's saga firsthand. The Admiralstab soon promoted him to lieutenant commander in the reserve and found him a new job on the Baltic Station.

He was given command of a converted merchantman that was engaged in protecting shipping against Allied submarine attacks. Lauterbach again distinguished himself by sinking one Russian and two British submarines.

In January 1918 he was put in command of the *Möwe*. This had been one of the most famous German surface raiders when she was under the command of Graf zu Dohna-Schlodien in the early part of the war. Disguised as an unarmed merchant ship, she had certainly been the most successful raider in terms of tonnage of Allied shipping sunk. Now she was being used as a minelayer. Lauterbach continued to excel, capturing a Russian gunboat and the eight merchant ships she was escorting in the Gulf of Finland.

The end of the war found Lauterbach at Kiel, trying to keep order on his ship during the German naval mutiny of November 1918. Not surprisingly, he was successful in controlling his men, just as he was in all his other ventures. He was a truly amazing character.

WILHELM CANARIS

Captain Lüdecke made a speech to the men of the *Dresden* after they reached the internment camp on Quiriquina Island, telling them: "The Chilean government has assigned us this island as a place of residence. The Chilean sentries are only here to prevent attempts to escape, which I would strongly caution you against."

But, according to a fellow prisoner, "It was not long before Wilhelm

Canaris began to chafe at wasting his time on this godforsaken island, and he began making plans to escape."

On the night of August 3–4, 1915, Canaris sneaked out of his hut and made his way down the cliffs to the shore, where he met a Chilean fisherman. He had arranged to pay this man twenty-five pesos to ferry him to the mainland. Once ashore at Concepcion he found no shortage of German settlers willing to help him on his way with money, railway tickets, and letters of introduction to friends in Argentina.

Traveling on foot or on horseback, Canaris made his way south to Osorno before crossing the lower part of the Andes. He was completely fluent in both Spanish and English and stayed at out-of-the-way inns using a false Chilean passport. Inside of two weeks he was across the border into Argentina and reached the estate of a Herr von Bülow, where he stayed briefly to rest. The Bülows helped him get to Neuquén, where he took a train to Buenos Aires, arriving on August 21, 1915.

At the German Embassy the naval attaché provided him with a new passport and identity. He was now to be a half-British Chilean subject named Reed Rosas, on his way to Europe to claim an inheritance in the Netherlands. He boarded the Dutch steamer *Frisia,* which sailed for Europe a few days later. Her first stop was at Plymouth. Canaris not only passed the naval inspection but also helped his interrogators question a suspected illegal immigrant by acting as interpreter. When the *Frisia* was released, she sailed to Rotterdam. Canaris had no difficulty using his Chilean passport to travel to Germany.

At that point he was thoroughly exhausted, and he spent a short time resting at his aunt's house in Hamburg before reporting to the Reichsmarineamt in Berlin. He was granted a well-deserved leave and promoted to lieutenant commander. For the rest of the war he served in the newly formed naval intelligence service, which was looking for men like Canaris. After the war he returned to regular naval duties and eventually rose to command—in the rank of captain—the battleship *Schlesien.*

In 1936 Canaris was appointed head of the *Abwehr,* the German military intelligence organization devoted mainly to counterespionage. He was soon promoted to admiral and became a highly successful director of the Abwehr during World War II. Toward the end of the war he allowed (or encouraged) it to become a center of anti-Nazi activity.

Canaris was implicated in the plot to assassinate Hitler in July 1944, although he was not directly involved. At first he was merely placed under house arrest at Fürstenberg castle, but he was eventually taken to Flössenburg concentration camp where he was kept in manacles, hand and foot. Prolonged and often brutal Gestapo interrogation couldn't break down his defense that he had not known about the assassination plot.

Finally, in April 1945, the accidental discovery of his diaries sealed his fate. Hitler was in his bunker at the time, with Russian shells falling all around him. He was in a fit of rage after reading the diaries and ordered Canaris's execution.

After a speedy mock trial, the Gestapo took Admiral Canaris from his cell at dawn on April 9, 1945, and told him to strip. Then they hanged him with their favorite noose material, piano wire.

SIR CHRISTOPHER CRADOCK

Unlike his adversary Graf Spee, Cradock was not commemorated by having a ship named after him. It was not the practice in the Royal Navy to name ships after admirals, victorious or otherwise, until they had been dead for a hundred years. Nelson was the only exception to the unwritten rule. But Cradock was suitably remembered for his gallant, if headstrong, action off Coronel.

At a memorial service in York Minster in 1916, the First Lord of the Admiralty gave the address (perhaps fittingly, it was not given by Churchill, who had been forced to resign in the wake of the fiasco at Gallipoli). Arthur Balfour unveiled the memorial and said:

> Why did he attack, deliberately, a force which he could not have hoped to destroy or put to flight? The German Admiral was far from any port where he could have refitted. If, therefore, he suffered damage, even though he inflicted greater damage than he received, his power might suddenly be destroyed. He would be a great peril as long as his squadron remained efficient, and if Admiral Cradock judged that he himself, and those under him, were well sacrificed if they destroyed the power of this hostile fleet, then there is no man but would say that such a judgement showed the highest courage in the interests of his country. We shall never know his thoughts when it became clear that, out-gunned and outranged, success was an impossibility. He and his gallant comrades lie far from the pleasant homes of England. Yet they have their reward; theirs is an immortal place in the great roll of naval heroes.

It would be hard to find a more fitting epitaph to Cradock than that taken from the Book of Maccabees and inscribed on his memorial in York Minster.

> *"God forbid that I should do this thing, To flee away from them; If our time be come, let us die manfully for our brethren, And let us not stain our honor."*

SIR DOVETON STURDEE

After his triumph over Graf Spee, Sir Doveton Sturdee was showered with honors and praise. He had already been knighted in 1913 and in 1916 was raised to the peerage. He was given the baronetcy traditionally awarded to admirals for winning a victory at sea. Parliament voted him a grant of £10,000—a great deal of money in 1916—which made him financially independent for the rest of his life.

In 1916, when Fisher resigned in a rage over the conduct of the Dardanelles campaign, Sturdee was an obvious choice to succeed his old enemy as First Sea Lord. Churchill thought this was inevitable, or at least so he told Fisher in an attempt to get him to withdraw his resignation. But Sturdee was passed over in favor of Adm. Sir Henry Jackson. (It would have been a delicious irony, though, if Fisher had been replaced by his bête noire.)

Sturdee continued to command the Fourth Battle Squadron and led it into action at Jutland in his flagship *Benbow.* (Jerram was on his flank, commanding the Second Battle Squadron.) After the disappointing escape of the German fleet from destruction at the hands of superior British forces, it was decided that a new commander in chief was needed for the Grand Fleet. Sturdee was one of the senior vice-admirals, the victor at Port Stanley, and again an obvious choice. But he was passed over once more, much to his chagrin, this time by the dashing young Admiral Beatty, seen by many as the hero of Jutland.

Sturdee was promoted to admiral in 1917, and at the end of the war he was given the important post of commander in chief of the Nore. He received the ultimate naval accolade when he was made admiral-of-the-fleet in 1921, the year after Fisher's death. After his retirement, he devoted himself to supervising the restoration of Nelson's flagship *Victory* at Portsmouth dockyard. He died in 1925, at the age of sixty-six.

JOHN GLOSSOP

Following his victory over the *Emden,* Captain Glossop continued his naval career without further notable incident. Although he reached the rank of vice-admiral in 1926, for some reason he was not granted the knighthood that normally went with such promotions. He retired in 1931 and lived a quiet life in Dorset, where he died in 1933 at the age of sixty-three.

World War II saw an eerie coda to the story of HMAS *Sydney.* This time the captain of the *Sydney* was not as fortunate as Glossop had been. By a strange coincidence, the second *Sydney* was on convoy escort duty in November 1941 in the same stretch of ocean where her predecessor had been twenty-seven years earlier. A German surface raider was also in the vicinity, and by yet another coincidence, she was named after the *Emden*'s first war prize. The two ships were involved in a battle to the death only thirteen hundred miles from the scene of the Cocos action.

The German raider *Kormoran* was an auxiliary cruiser disguised as an unarmed merchantman. When she approached the convoy on November 19, 1941, the captain of the *Sydney* went to investigate. Not suspecting any danger, he came too close to the other ship, and the *Kormoran* opened fire at point-blank range. The devastating surprise attack severely damaged the Australian cruiser and started several fires. In a short but savage engagement the wounded *Sydney* fought back and, in turn, damaged the *Kormoran* so badly that she had to be scuttled.

The crippled and blazing *Sydney* drifted away from the battle area and was never seen again. Whether she sank after exploding when the fires reached her magazine, or whether she was torpedoed by the German raider or a Japanese submarine has never been established. The only wreckage found consisted of two empty lifejackets and a Carley float. There was no trace of her 645 crew members.

The Australian prime minister concluded in an official announcement: "Her actual fate, in the absence of other evidence, must remain a mystery. All we know is that she fought gallantly and successfully achieved her aim—the destruction of the enemy."

EDWARD DANNREUTHER

Several of Sturdee's officers went on to have distinguished naval careers and eventually reached flag rank, among them Luce and Hickling of the *Glasgow* and Dannreuther of the *Invincible*. Edward Dannreuther was still serving as her gunnery officer when she went into action at Jutland in May 1916 as the flagship of the Third Battlecruiser Squadron.

She disabled two German cruisers and heavily damaged Admiral Hipper's flagship, the *Lützow*, in the early part of the action, but Hipper's ships badly mauled Beatty's lightly armored and vulnerable battle cruiser squadrons. Two of his ships were destroyed by magazine explosions, which led to the loss of nearly all their complements—more than two thousand men.

Later on, the *Invincible* was herself hit by a full salvo from one of

Hipper's squadron, the *Derfflinger.* The resulting magazine explosion broke the huge ship cleanly in half. Because they were in shallow water the two halves of the sunken ship could be seen sticking above the surface, with the survivors clinging to the wreckage. Only 6 men out of a crew of 1,032 were left alive.

One of the six was Dannreuther. He had been in the gunnery control position high in the foretop when the ship blew up, and he was flung clear—miraculously unhurt. He recalled later: "I just waited for the water to come up and meet me. Then I stepped out and started swimming. The water was quite warm and there was no shortage of wreckage to hold on to."

He was picked up by the destroyer *Badger,* whose captain remarked that Dannreuther came on board as coolly as if he was on a courtesy visit to a sister ship.

THE GERMAN CRUISERS

The Germans wanted to perpetuate the names of the ships that had fought so gallantly against heavy odds. Before the war ended, they had launched replacements for all six of the light cruisers. They didn't waste much time replacing the *Königsberg;* her successor was launched on December 18, 1915, only five months after Looff's ship was destroyed in the Rufiji River. She was soon followed by the *Emden II,* the *Karlsruhe II,* and the *Nürnberg II,* which were all launched in early 1916. The *Dresden II* and the *Leipzig II* were not launched until later in the war, and the latter had not been completed by the time of the Armistice.

The new ships were improved versions of the originals: they were both oil and coal fired and had a much longer cruising range. They were also bigger and more heavily armed, each carrying eight 5.9-inch guns. The Germans had learned the hard lesson that 4.1-inch guns could not stand up to the 6-inch batteries of British light cruisers. They went into active service (except for the *Leipzig*) with the scouting groups of the High Seas Fleet, and they all survived the war.

The *Emden II* was distinguished by having a large Iron Cross fixed to each side of her bow, an honor never bestowed on any German warship before or since (except for her successor, the *Emden III*). The heroic crew of the first *Emden* were honored in another unusual way. After the war a decree was passed that entitled her survivors to add the name "Emden" to their family name. More than a hundred families took advantage of this distinction. Karl von Müller was not one of them, but the erstwhile captain of the *Exford* became known as Julius Lauterbach-Emden. Even the cruiser's regal torpedo officer adopted the title and became Prince Franz Josef von Hohenzollern-Emden.

When the German fleet surrendered in November 1918, the problem for the Allies was what to do with this formidable force until the terms of the Treaty of Versailles had been agreed upon. It was decided that the ships should go to Scapa Flow and turn themselves over to the Royal Navy, to be interned until the treaty was settled.

The senior officers of the German navy had other ideas. They had no wish to see their ships taken over by their former (and possibly future) enemies as part of war reparations, so they secretly made plans to scuttle the fleet after it reached Scapa Flow. Ironically, Adm. Ludwig von Reuter, who was in command of the German fleet, transferred his flag to the *Emden II* because he couldn't rely on the near mutinous crew of the flagship *Friedrich der Grosse*. It was from this specially honored ship that he finally gave the less than heroic order to scuttle his fleet.

No less than fifty-two proud warships went down in Scapa Flow in an unprecedented act of self-destruction. They ranged from lumbering battleships to frail destroyers. Another twenty-two ships were run aground before they could sink, once the British realized what the Germans were up to.

Fittingly, the *Emden II* was not one of the suicides. She and her sister ship the *Nürnberg II* drifted ashore in sinking condition and beached themselves. The *Dresden II* and the *Karlsruhe II* both sank. (The *Königsberg II* was not at Scapa Flow and was spared the ignominy of being scuttled, only to be turned over to the French navy, where she became the *Metz.*) The two beached cruisers were salvaged, but they were too badly damaged for active service. They had to suffer the final indignity of being used as target ships by the French and British navies.

The Germans launched third editions of the light cruisers in the late 1920s and early 1930s (interestingly, there was no *Dresden III*). They saw action in World War II, but fate was not much kinder to them than to their predecessors.

The *Nürnberg III* and *Leipzig III* were torpedoed by the submarine HMS *Salmon* in December 1939, and although heavily damaged, they managed to get back to port. They were both out of action for a long time but survived the war. At the end of the war the *Nürnberg III* was turned over to the Russians and became the *Admiral Makarov.* The *Karlsruhe III* was not as fortunate. She was torpedoed and sunk by HMS *Truant* off Kristiansand in April 1940. In the same month the *Königsberg III* was sunk off Bergen in a historic dive-bombing attack by Skuas from

HMS *Sparrowhawk* in the Orkneys. (This was the first time dive-bombers had ever been used to sink a major warship.)

The *Emden III,* still bearing the Iron Crosses on her bow, almost made it to the end of the war. She was too slow for active service and thus served mainly as a training ship. She was caught and sunk by RAF dive-bombers near Kiel at the beginning of May 1945.

There was a fourth *Emden:* not a light cruiser this time but a modern antiaircraft frigate. She was launched at Hamburg in 1959 and completed in 1961 for the West German navy. The *Emden IV* saw twenty-two years of peacetime duty in the *Bundesmarine* before she was decommissioned in 1983.

To ensure that the tradition was carried on, a new *Emden* was launched in 1981, appropriately at the Emden shipyards. She came into service in the West German (now German) navy in the same month that the *Emden IV* was paid off. The *Emden V,* a Type 122 frigate, is still in service today. One of her sister ships is the *Karlsruhe.* And so the tradition of the Kreuzergeschwader lives on.

The Germans also planned to replace Graf Spee's two big ships before the end of the war, but after the Falklands battle it was clear that the day of the armored cruiser was over. In 1915 they ordered the shipyards at Kiel and Hamburg to build an *Ersatz Scharnhorst* and an *Ersatz Gneisenau.* These were designed to be thirty-three-thousand-ton battle cruisers armed with eight 15-inch guns, but as a result of the experiences at Jutland, the ships were redesigned in 1917 to make them less vulnerable to magazine explosions. This delayed the work, and the hulls had not been laid down by the end of the war. Consequently, the orders were canceled.

After the war a near bankrupt Weimar Republic could not afford such luxuries as battleships, and it was nearly twenty years before a new *Scharnhorst* and *Gneisenau* were built by the Third Reich. They were based on the earlier design, but their main armament was changed to nine 11-inch guns. They were called battleships, but they were under gunned for this class and were more properly described as battle cruisers. This change was to prove their eventual undoing. They were launched in 1936 and commissioned in late 1938 and early 1939, just in time for World War II.

The Kriegsmarine's new ships had short but spectacular careers. Their first sortie in November 1939 was to be a raid on Atlantic shipping, but they encountered the armed merchant cruiser *Rawalpindi* off Iceland before they reached the North Atlantic shipping lanes. The *Rawalpindi* put up a courageous fight with her four 6-inch guns, but she was easily overwhelmed and sunk. She had served her purpose, because the Germans had given away their presence too early, and they returned to base without sinking any merchant ships.

Next, they were used in support of the German invasion of Norway. During this campaign they were surprised by HMS *Renown* off Vesterfjord in May 1940. Although the British battle cruiser was thirty-four years old (she first came into service two months after Jutland) and outnumbered, her 15-inch guns were too much for Admiral Lütjens in the *Gneisenau*. After his flagship had been badly damaged by several direct hits, he broke off the action. The two German ships fled for safety. They suffered further damage by steaming at high speed in heavy seas, but they managed to elude Allied patrols and reach Kiel.

Two months later they met a less dangerous foe in the shape of the aircraft carrier *Glorious*. The lightly armed and vulnerable carrier was escorted by merely two destroyers, and she was severely battered before her planes could fly off. Although the destroyer *Acasta* managed to hit the *Gneisenau* with a torpedo, the German ships easily sank the *Glorious* and both of her escorts.

They made a second sortie into the Atlantic in February 1941. This one was much more successful than the first. They sank twenty-two Allied ships for a total of 115,000 tons, and they seriously disrupted the Allied convoy system. The *Scharnhorst* and *Gneisenau* usually operated as a unit and seemed so inseparable to the crews of the British ships chasing them that they became known as the twins, "Salmon and Gluckstein."

After their second foray into the Atlantic they returned to port, this time at Brest, where they were pinned down for almost a year by repeated heavy bombing raids by the RAF. They were both damaged, although not seriously. It would be only a matter of time before they would be put out of action permanently, so it was important to get them to a safer harbor in Germany.

Although Hitler was no naval genius, he conceived a daring plan to run the Allied blockade in the English Channel. This was Operation Cerberus. On February 14, 1942, the two battle cruisers, accompanied by the heavy cruiser *Prinz Eugen,* left Brest at daybreak and made a high-speed dash up the Channel in broad daylight. They were escorted by six destroyers and given heavy air cover by fighter planes based on airfields in France and Holland. The Royal Navy and the RAF were caught napping, and the German ships sailed undetected until they reached the Straits of Dover. Here they easily brushed aside hastily mounted attacks by destroyers, motor torpedo boats, and ancient Swordfish planes. Although both the *Scharnhorst* and *Gneisenau* hit mines off the coast of Holland, they reached Wilhelmshaven safely.

Operation Cerberus was both a successful naval operation and a huge propaganda triumph for the Germans. It was an equally huge embarrassment for the British, especially the Royal Navy.

Despite their daring escape, the *Scharnhorst* and *Gneisenau* were never again a threat to Allied shipping. In December 1943 Admiral Bey was in command of the *Scharnhorst*, this time without the *Gneisenau* as company, and he made the mistake of attacking the Russian convoy JW-55B on its way to Murmansk.

Although the convoy was closely escorted only by the cruisers *Belfast*, *Sheffield*, and *Norfolk* and several destroyers, the battleship *Duke of York* and the cruiser *Jamaica* were less than two hundred miles away. The three cruisers with the convoy managed to beat off the *Scharnhorst*'s attack with their 8-inch guns until the *Duke of York* could get there. They also knocked out the German radar with a direct hit on the *Scharnhorst*'s conning tower so that Bey was unable to detect the approach of the *Duke of York*.

The British tracked the *Scharnhorst*, using radar, until they finally spotted her through the mist off the North Cape. The roar of the battleship's 14-inch guns and the huge splashes of her shells caught Admiral Bey completely by surprise. The *Duke of York*'s gunners found the range very quickly. Bey had no chance because his 11-inch guns were ineffectual against the battleship's armor plate. He tried to escape, but several punishing hits from the *Duke of York*'s sixteen-hundred-pound shells reduced his speed, and he was trapped between the two British squadrons.

After a severe battering and four hits by torpedoes from British destroyers, the crippled *Scharnhorst* limped away into the mist. Admiral Fraser sent the *Jamaica* after her to finish her off with torpedoes. Before she went down, the *Scharnhorst* had taken an incredible thirteen hits from 14-inch shells and fourteen or fifteen hits by 21-inch torpedoes. This was yet another amazing testimonial to German naval construction.

As with the *Good Hope* at Coronel, none of her enemies actually saw her sink, but the *Jamaica* was able to save thirty-six men who were found desperately clinging to wreckage in the near freezing water. They were the only survivors from a crew of just under two thousand.

The *Gneisenau* didn't outlive her sister ship for very long. She never went to sea again after Operation Cerberus, and she was so badly damaged in an RAF raid on Kiel in November 1942 that attempts to repair her were abandoned. Her guns were taken off and used for coastal artillery batteries in Holland and Norway, and the hull was towed to

Gdynia. In 1945 she was sunk as a harbor block ship. After the war a Polish company broke up the hull for scrap.

There have been no more *Scharnhorst*s or *Gneisenau*s in the German navy—at least up to now.

THE BRITISH CRUISERS

In contrast to the German naval practice of naming ships after their Great War admirals, there has been no HMS *Sturdee* in the Royal Navy, let alone an HMS *Cradock*. But the names of some of the cruisers involved in the Battles of Coronel and the Falklands have been carried on. Although there has never been another *Good Hope,* there have been other ships named *Cornwall, Kent, Monmouth,* and *Glasgow.* Also, the name of Sturdee's flagship lives on in the Royal Navy.

By an odd quirk of history, the latest HMS *Invincible* also saw action off the Falklands, sixty-four years after Sturdee's victory over Graf Spee. The twenty-thousand-ton aircraft carrier *Invincible* was one of the two major units of Adm. John "Sandy" Woodward's task force in the 1982 Falklands conflict. She played an important role in clearing the area of Argentine warships before the landings that led to the recapture of the islands.

During the action off Port Stanley, the *Invincible* narrowly missed being hit by an Exocet missile. She escaped destruction by firing clouds of tinsellike "chaff," which decoyed the missile's radar. This was extremely fortunate for the British forces. Had she been crippled or destroyed by one of these deadly new weapons, as three smaller British ships were, it would have been disastrous from both a military and a political standpoint.

By one more remarkable coincidence, another of Admiral Woodward's ships was HMS *Glasgow,* a Type 42 destroyer, which, at forty-one-hundred tons, was nearly as big as Luce's cruiser had been. The *Glasgow* was not as lucky as the *Invincible.* She was attacked by Skyhawks of the Argentine air force and suffered a direct hit from one of their bombs. Fortunately, it passed through the hull without exploding, but the *Glasgow* was so badly holed that she had to make temporary repairs to enable her to limp back to a British dockyard.

ENVOI

There is one final, poignant postscript to add. In the summer of 1916, fishermen off the coast of Schleswig found a waterlogged twelve-foot boat drifting not far from the naval base at Cuxhaven. They were barely able to make out the faded letters painted on the side, but they spelled the name *Nürnberg*. The boat's journey of eight thousand miles had taken eighteen months, but she had finally found her way home to Germany.

One of Graf Spee's few surviving officers described the "little water-worn dinghy" as "this fragment of a once fine cruiser, all that was left of a splendid squadron."

Appendix 1

A NOTE ON NAVAL GUNNERY IN 1914

During the days of sail, most sea battles were fought at a range of several hundred yards, frequently between ships moving on parallel courses at more or less the same speed. Once the enemy's range and deflection had been established, they didn't vary significantly. Since the gun-layers could see their target clearly with the naked eye, all they had to do was train their guns on it and fire. Their main difficulty was allowing for the roll of the ship during the time delay between pulling the lanyard and the actual detonation of the charge.

Because the trajectory of the projectiles was virtually flat and their time of flight negligible, only small corrections in aim were required—by spotting the fall of shot—until the gunners began hitting their target. The percentage of hits expected was high—generally well over 50 percent; it could approach 100 percent if the range was shortened by an aggressive captain until it became virtually point blank.

In the early days of steam, ranges were not as short: usually of the order of one thousand yards or perhaps two, as in the naval battles of the Spanish-American and Sino-Japanese Wars. Trajectories were still nearly horizontal and the time of flight only one or two seconds. Range taking and deflection settings did not pose major problems, and the rate of change of range and deflection was slow. The expected percentage of hits to shells fired was lower than 50 percent, probably on the order of 10 percent.

As naval guns increased in caliber and weight of shell, and breech loading and rifling replaced muzzle loading and smooth bore, both range and accuracy increased. In the first modern naval battle between ironclads, the Russian and Japanese fleets engaged each other at Tsushima in 1905 at ranges of up to eighteen thousand yards, although most of the battle was fought between three and five thousand yards. The percentage of hits was still reasonably high, especially from the well-trained Japanese gun-layers.

Due to advances in weaponry between 1900 and 1914—particularly the development of larger caliber guns, and the resulting great increases in weight of shell—future battle ranges were expected to be anywhere from eight thousand to fifteen thousand yards. This presented new and troublesome problems for range takers and gun-layers. Although the new weapons were much more accurate at long range, crews experienced great difficulties in training them on board their rolling and pitching gun platforms to aim at a distant target whose range, speed, and course were initially unknown. Then, after they were first estimated by range taking and observing the fall of shot, they might be continuously and rapidly changing.

The full extent of the problem was not appreciated at first. Practice shoots were carried out in calm weather, using either a stationary target or having one towed at a constant and predetermined speed. These were not an adequate preparation for gun-laying and range finding under real battle conditions.

Naval personnel soon realized the urgent need for both accurate range finders and methods of calculating changes of rate and deflection and for making adjustments for the changes in these quantities during the time of flight of the shells—no longer the negligible factor it had been in earlier sea battles.

The most pressing need was for an accurate method of determining the initial range. Without this, no corrections could be made for changes in the relative speeds and courses of the firing ship and her target. The British developed optical range finders of the "coincidence" type. These employed prisms and mirrors and two independent focuses on the target at a fixed distance apart, which allowed trigonometric calculation of the range. The Germans concentrated their efforts on the development of stereoscopic range finders.

Both types had their merits. The stereoscopic devices allowed for a quicker initial determination of the range, with the result that the German guns were likely to be on target first. The coincidence type, although slower to get on target, was better at holding onto it once the initial range had been established. Consequently, German warships had the advantage in the early stages of a battle, but as it progressed the advantage shifted in favor of the British gun-layers.

The next need was for a method of rapid and continuous correction of range and deflection, changes in rate, and allowance for these changes during the time of flight, which could be twenty seconds or more. This would permit gun-layers to make adjustments before they fired their next shot. Such methods became known as fire control. The British were ahead of the Germans in this area, largely due to the competitive efforts of two ingenious inventors, Arthur Pollen, a civilian, and Frederic Dreyer, a naval officer. They developed sophisticated mechanical devices, employing clockwork motors, gyroscopes, trigonometric calculators, and plotters.

These devices, or gunnery control "tables" as they were known, could give continuous plots of the relative course and speed of the enemy ship once the initial range had been estimated, so that the necessary information could be transmitted to the gunners. The so-called fire control tables were, in effect, forerunners of the modern computer, since they involved calculation and integration of several different types of input data, the most important of which was the initial range setting. Spotting the fall of shot was still important for feeding corrections to the table.

In the end, the Admiralty adopted the Dreyer Table over the Pollen device. The latter was probably intrinsically superior in a scientific sense, but for various extrinsic reasons, including the personality of the inventor and the fact that Dreyer was a naval officer, the decision was made to use the system that had been developed in-house.

The battle cruisers at the Falklands were both equipped with the Dreyer Mark I Table, although by 1914 it was already obsolete. One of its deficiencies was that it couldn't account properly for turns made by its own ship. In the early part of the Falklands engagement, however, the opposing ships were moving on nearly parallel courses. This meant the rate was changing slowly and steadily. In the later stages the range was so short that the shortcomings of the Dreyer Mark I weren't that serious either. None of the other British ships at either the Falklands or Coronel had any fire-control devices installed.

The problem of accurate gun-laying was far from solved by the time of the battle. Although the two battle cruisers had fire-control tables, these ships had a tendency to roll excessively. Equally serious was the combined effect of pitch and roll, or yaw, especially when the guns were trained in a forward direction, as they were during the long pursuit of the *Scharnhorst* and *Gneisenau*. This was known as cross-roll error. It meant that spotting corrections were made to the fire-control table calculations on the assumption that these were responsible for the error when, in fact, it was the gun-laying. This partly explains the large number of shells the *Invincible* and *Inflexible* fired unsuccessfully before they caught up with Graf Spee's armored cruisers.

The British gunners' difficulties were compounded by the Germans' zigzagging. The British suspected they were making small changes in course every three or four minutes. Nonetheless, the overall percentage of hits they achieved was about 7 percent, which was not bad in light of the later experience at the Dogger Bank and Jutland actions, where the success rate for various German and British squadrons was at best 3 to 4 percent and for some British units, much lower than this.

The Germans, working more or less independently, had developed their own method of directing their gunnery, the *Richtungsweiser*, which was believed to be technically inferior to the British system, although it performed adequately at Jutland. In any event, neither the *Scharnhorst* nor the *Gneisenau* was equipped with fire control and, like the other German cruisers, had to rely on the accuracy of their range finders and their highly trained gun crews.

Another important problem in naval gunnery that had been worked out before the war was the question of independent versus centralized firing of the guns of the main armament—so-called "local" versus "director" control. Most gunnery officers were naturally opposed to director control because it diminished their responsibilities and skills, but a convincing demonstration of its superiority in a practice shoot in 1912 led to its adoption. It was not until just before the war, however, that the electrically controlled and simultaneous firing of all main armament guns began to be installed in major units. None of the ships at Coronel or the Falklands had such an automatic system.

Director control meant that guns were trained on the target with a master sight that was electrically connected to each gunsight and fired on command from a director situated high in the foretop, whose view was less likely to be obscured by smoke or spray than that of a gunnery officer in one of the main deck turrets. In some cases the so-called principal control officer could fire all the guns of the main battery simultaneously by pressing a single key. Where fully automatic director control equipment had not yet been installed, he would have to signal the gunnery officer in each turret when to fire his guns. He did this either by sounding a bell or by giving the order through a voice pipe. In this way a salvo could be fired nearly simultaneously (i.e., ripple fire), which was more effective in terms of the tightness of the group of shells arriving at or near the target. This made spotting easier than when the guns fired independently (local control), as well as making the result more telling when a salvo was on target.

Except for the two British battle cruisers, none of the ships at the Falklands battle had any system of director control installed and had to rely on local control.

Such technical matters were not the only problems the gun-layers at the Falklands had to deal with. Most serious of these was the smoke from their own funnels and guns, which obscured their view of the enemy and made range taking and deflection setting extremely difficult. Seaspray and spray from near misses also caused the lenses of the range finders to become encrusted with salt, which had to be scraped off before they could be used again. This was a hazardous task because the men involved were exposed to flying shrapnel. Range finding was also hampered by the vibration of the ship's engines during the high-speed chase.

The noise and shock of their own guns firing often deafened or stunned the gunners, so that commands were missed and the next firing delayed. This was particularly true of the middle "P" and "Q" turrets of the battle cruisers when they fired across the deck. Also, as Sturdee's reports of the action make clear, the battle cruisers' gunners were bedeviled by minor mechanical problems with the gun mounts and the opening and closing of the breeches. These led to more delays in firing some of the guns, which in turn meant ragged or scattered fire, rather than tight salvoes.

Whether the German gunners experienced similar mechanical problems at the Falklands is not known, but it seems unlikely judging from the discipline, accuracy, and rapidness of their fire. Certainly they were less hampered by funnel- and gunsmoke than Sturdee's men because of the direction of the wind during most of the battle.

As far as ammunition was concerned, when the British changed from common shell to armor-piercing or high-explosive shell using lyddite, their fire had a devastating effect. Some of the German survivors reported that they believed the British ships had suddenly started using larger caliber guns. Even so, there were serious problems with the British armor-piercing shell. Many of these either failed to pierce the German armor, or their fuses malfunctioned. The problem was that these shells had been tested and their fuses set for essentially perpendicular impact, but at the long ranges involved in the earlier stages, the oblique impact meant they often failed to penetrate before exploding.

These problems were less serious in the final stages, when the battle cruisers severely battered Graf Spee's armored cruisers at close range. The German armor-piercing shells appear not to have had such problems, judging by the holes torn in the sides of the British armored cruisers at Coronel. But at the Falklands, their 8.2-inch shells were simply incapable of penetrating the thicker armor of the battle cruisers.

Overall, the final judgment must be that, given the many technical and other problems facing the gunners on Sturdee's ships, their performance at the Falklands was fairly creditable. Despite the unfavorable criticism Sturdee received after the battle, his men did far better than the gunners on Beatty's battle cruisers did at Jutland. On the other hand, the performance of Cradock's gunners at Coronel was extremely bad, even allowing for the poor light and weather conditions.

During both battles the accuracy of the German gunnery on both the armored cruisers and the light cruisers can only be described as truly remarkable.

Appendix 2

DETAILS OF PRINCIPAL GERMAN WARSHIPS

Scharnhorst
(Capt. F. Schultz)
(Flagship of Vice Adm. Graf von Spee)
Armored cruiser

Laid down 1904, completed 1907. Normal displacement: 11,600 tons (full load 12,781). Length 450 feet, beam 71 feet, draught 25 feet. Main armament: 8 8.2-inch, 6 5.9-inch. Broadside: 1,958 lbs. Maximum range: 13,500 yds. Main armor: 6–6.75 inches. Designed speed: 22.5 knots. Recent best speed: 21 knots. Complement: 765.

Gneisenau
(Capt. G. Maerker)
Armored cruiser

Details same as for *Scharnhorst,* with two exceptions. Laid down 1905; recent best speed, 24.8 knots.

Emden
(Capt. K. von Müller)
Light cruiser

Laid down 1906, completed 1909. Normal displacement: 3,364 tons (full load 4,268). Length 387 feet, beam 44 feet, draught 18 feet. Main armament: 10 4.1-inch. Maximum range: 10,500 yds. Broadside: 192 lbs. Main armor: 0.75–2 inches. Designed speed: 23.5 knots. Recent best speed: 24 knots. Complement: 361.

Nürnberg
(Capt. K. von Schönberg)
Light cruiser

Laid down 1906, completed 1908. Normal displacement: 3,469 tons (full load 4,002). Length 383 feet, beam 44 feet, draught 17 feet. Main armament and armor same as *Emden.* Designed speed: 23 knots. Recent best speed: 24.5 knots. Complement: 322.

Leipzig
(Capt. J. Haun)
Light cruiser

Laid down 1904, completed 1906. Normal displacement: 3,250 tons (full load 3,756). Length 363 feet, beam 43 feet, draught 17.5 feet. Main armament and armor same as *Emden.* Designed speed: 22 knots. Recent best speed: 21 knots. Complement: 303.

Dresden
(Capt. F. Lüdecke)
Light cruiser

Details same as for *Emden,* with three exceptions. Laid down 1907, completed 1908; designed speed, 24 knots; recent best speed, 24.5 knots.

Karlsruhe
(Capt. E. Köhler)
Light cruiser

Laid down 1911, completed 1914. Normal displacement: 4,900 tons (full load 6,191). Length 467 feet, beam 45 feet, draught 18 feet. Main armament: 12 4.1-inch. Broadside: 229 lbs. Main armor: 0.75–2.25 inches. Maximum range: 10,500 yds. Designed speed: 27 knots. Complement: 373.

Königsberg
(Capt. M. Looff)
Light cruiser

Laid down 1905, completed 1907. Normal displacement: 3,390 tons (full load 3,814). Length 377 feet, beam 43 feet, draught 17 feet. Main armament, armor, speed, and complement same as *Nürnberg.*

Maximum range refers to largest caliber guns carried.

Main armor refers to range of midships belt, turrets, barbettes, and casemates, not deck armor.

Appendix 3

DETAILS OF PRINCIPAL BRITISH WARSHIPS

Good Hope
(Capt. P. Francklin)
(Flagship of Rear-Adm. Sir Christopher Cradock)
Armored cruiser
Laid down 1899, completed 1902. Normal displacement: 14,100 tons. Length 530 feet, beam 71 feet, draught 28 feet. Main armament: 2 9.2-inch, 16 6-inch. Broadside: 1,560 lbs. Maximum range: 12,500 yds. Main armor: 5–6 inches. Designed speed: 23 knots. Recent best speed: 23.5 knots. Complement: 900.

Monmouth
(Capt. F. Brandt)
Armored cruiser
Laid down 1901, completed 1903. Normal displacement: 9,800 tons. Length 463 feet, beam 66 feet, draught 25.5 feet. Main armament: 14 6-inch. Broadside: 900 lbs. Maximum range: 11,200 yds. Main armor: 4–5 inches. Designed speed: 23 knots. Complement: 690.

Glasgow
(Capt. J. Luce)
Light cruiser
Laid down 1909, completed 1910. Normal displacement: 4,800

tons (full load 5,300). Length 453 feet, beam 47 feet, draught 15.5 feet. Main armament: 2 6-inch, 10 4-inch. Broadside: 425 lbs. Maximum range: 11,200 yds. Main armor: 0.75–2 inches. Designed speed: 25 knots. Recent best speed: 26 knots. Complement: 411.

Canopus
(Capt. H. S. Grant)
Battleship (predreadnought)
Laid down 1897, completed 1900. Normal displacement: 12,950 tons (full load 13,150). Length 418 feet, beam 74 feet, draught 26.5 feet. Main armament: 4 12-inch, 12 6-inch. Broadside: 4,000 lbs. Maximum range: 13,500 yds. Main armor: 6–12 inches. Designed speed: 18.25 knots. Recent best speed: 16.5 knots. Complement: 750.

Sydney
(Capt. J.C.T. Glossop)
Light cruiser
Laid down 1911, completed 1913. Normal displacement: 5,400 tons. Length 430 feet, beam 50 feet, draught 16 feet. Main armament: 8 6-inch. Broadside: 500 lbs. Maximum range: 11,200 yds. Main armor: 2 inches. Designed speed: 25 knots. Recent best speed: 25.7 knots. Complement: 392.

Invincible
(Capt. T.H.P. Beamish)
(Flagship of Vice-Adm. Sir Doveton Sturdee)
Battle cruiser
Laid down 1906, completed 1908. Normal displacement: 17,250 tons (full load 20,000). Length: 567 feet, beam 79 feet, draught 26 feet. Main armament: 8 12-inch, 14 6-inch. Broadside: 6,800 lbs. Maximum range: 16,400 yds. Main armor: 6–10 inches. Designed speed: 25 knots. Recent best speed: 28.6 knots. Complement: 837.

Inflexible
(Capt. R. F. Phillimore)
Battle cruiser
Details same as for *Invincible,* with one exception. Recent best speed, 28.4 knots.

Carnarvon
(Capt. H.L.d'E. Skipwith)
(Flagship of Rear-Adm. A. P. Stoddart)
Armored cruiser
Laid down 1902, completed 1905. Normal displacement: 10,850 tons.

Length 473.5 feet, beam 68.5 feet, draught 25.5 feet. Main armament 4 7.5-inch, 6 6-inch. Broadside: 1,100 lbs. Maximum range 12,000 yds. Main armor: 4.5–6 inches. Designed speed: 22.5 knots. Recent best speed: 22.1 knots. Complement: 653.

Cornwall
(Capt. W. M. Ellerton)
Armored cruiser
   Laid down 1901, completed 1904. Normal displacement 9,800 tons. Length 463.5 feet, beam 66 feet, draught 25.5 feet. Main armament 14 6-inch. Broadside: 900 lbs. Maximum range 11,200 yds. Main armor: 4–5 inches. Designed speed: 23 knots. Recent best speed: 24 knots. Complement: 690.

Kent
(Capt. J. D. Allen)
Armored cruiser
   Details same as for *Cornwall,* with one exception. Laid down 1900, completed 1903.

Pegasus
(Capt. J. A. Ingles)
Light cruiser
   Laid down 1896, completed 1898. Normal displacement: 2,135 tons. Length 300 feet, beam 36.5 feet, draught 17 feet. Main armament: 8 4-inch. Broadside: 155 lbs. Maximum range: 9,800 yds. Main armor: 2 inches. Designed speed: 20 knots. Recent best speed: 16 knots. Complement: 224.

Chatham
(Capt. S. R. Drury-Lowe)
Light cruiser
   Laid down 1911, completed 1912. Details same as for *Sydney,* with three exceptions. Main armor, 2–3 inches; recent best speed, 25.7 knots; complement, 429.

Severn
(Capt. E. L. Fullerton)
Monitor
   Laid down 1912, completed 1914. Normal displacement: 1,260 tons (full load 1,520). Length: 267 feet, beam 49 feet, draught 5.75 feet. Main armament: 2 6-inch, 2 4.7-inch. Broadside: 290 lbs. Maximum range: 11,200 yds. Main armor: 1.5–3.5 inches. Designed speed: 12 knots. Recent best speed: 9.5 knots. Complement: 140.

Mersey
(Capt. R. A. Wilson)
Monitor

Details same as for *Severn,* with one exception. Laid down 1912, completed 1913.

Maximum range refers to largest caliber guns carried.

Weight of broadside given assumes all guns workable.

Main armor refers to range of midships, turrets, barbettes, and casemates, not deck armor.

Selected
Bibliography

Bassett, Ronald. *Battlecruisers: A History, 1908–1948.* London: Macmillan, 1981.

Bennett, Geoffrey M. *Naval Battles of the First World War.* London: Pan Books, 1974.

————. *Coronel and the Falklands.* London: Pan Books, 1967.

Bingham, Barry. *Falklands, Jutland and the Bight.* London: John Murray, 1919.

Breyer, Siegfried and Gerhard Koop. *Von der 'Emden' zur 'Tirpitz.'* Bonn: Wehr & Wissen, 1981.

Brissaud, Andre. *Canaris: The Biography of Admiral Canaris, Chief of German Military Intelligence.* London: Military Book Society, 1973.

Bromby, Robin. *German Raiders of the South Seas.* Sydney: Doubleday, 1985.

Buchan, John. *Naval Episodes of the Great War.* London: Nelson, 1938.

Buley, Ernest Charles. *Glorious Deeds of the Australasians in the Great War.* London: Melrose, 1916.

Burdick, Charles B. *The Japanese Siege of Tsingtau.* Hamden, CT: Archon Books, 1976.

Busch, Fritz Otto and Gerhard Ramlow. *Admiral Graf Spees Sieg und Untergang. Deutsche Seekriegsgeschichte, Fahrten und Taten in Zwei Jahrtausenden.* Berlin: Bertelsmann Gutersloh, no date.

Chack, P. and J.-L. Antier. *Histoire Maritime de la Premiere Guerre Mondiale.* 3 vols. Paris: Edition France-Empire, 1969.

Chatterton, E. Keble. *The 'Königsberg' Adventure.* London: Hurst & Blackett, 1932.

Christiansen Carl. *Die Kapitäne Christiansen nach Logbüchern erzählt.* Berlin: E. S. Mittler, 1939.

Churchill, Winston. *The World Crisis.* London: Butterworth, 1923.

Corbett, Julian Stafford. *Naval Operations.* Vols.1–5. London: Longmans Green, 1920–1931.

Corse, Carl D., Jr. *Introduction to Shipboard Weapons.* Annapolis, MD: Naval Institute Press, 1975.

Creswell, John. *The War on Sea.* London: Benn, 1929.

Cruttwell, C.R.M.F. *A History of the Great War, 1914–1918.* London: Grafton, 1982.

Dixon, T. B. *The Enemy Fought Splendidly.* Poole: Blandford, 1983.

Falls, Cyril Bentham. *The First World War.* London: Longmans, 1960.

Farrere, C. and P. Chack. *Combats et Batailles sur mer.* Paris: Librairie de la Revue Francaise, 1925.

Fayle, C. E. *Seaborne Trade.* Vols. 1–3. London: Murray, 1924.

Fisher, John Arbuthnot. *Fear God and Dread Nought.* London: Cape, 1952.

―――. *Memories.* London: Hodder & Stoughton, 1919.

―――. *Records.* London: Hodder & Stoughton, 1919.

Frothingham, T. G. *The Naval History of the World War: Vol. 1. (1914–1915).* Freeport, NY: Books for Libraries Press, 1924.

Gilbert, Martin. *The Challenge of War. Winston S. Churchill, 1914–1916.* London: Minerva, 1971.

Goebel, Julius. *The Struggle for the Falkland Islands.* New Haven, CT: Yale University Press, 1927.

Gröner, Erich. *Die Deutschen Kriegsschiffe, 1815–1945.* Band 1. Munich: Bernard & Graefe, 1982.

Hansen, Hans Jürgen. *The Ships of the German Fleets, 1848–1945.* London: Hamlyn, 1974.

Hase, Georg Oskar von. *Kiel and Jutland.* London: Skeffington, 1921.

Heydecker, Joe Julius. *Der Grosse Krieg 1914–1918.* Frankfurt/Main: Ullstein, 1988.

Hezlet, Arthur Richard. *The Electron and Sea-Power.* London: P. Davies, 1975.

Hildebrand, Hans Jürgen, Albert Röhr, and Otto Steinmetz. *Die deutschen Kriegsschiffe: Biographien.* Herford: Koehler, 1979.

―――― and Ernest Henriot. *Deutschlands Admirale 1849–1945.* Osnabrück: Biblio, 1988.

Hirst, Lloyd. *Coronel and After.* London: Peter Davies, 1934.

Hoehling, A. A. *The Great War at Sea.* New York: Crowell, 1965.

Hohenzollern, Franz Josef, Fürst von. *L'Emden.* Paris: Payot, 1929.

―――. *Emden: The Last Cruise of the Chivalrous Raider, 1914.* Lyon: Brighton, 1989.

Höhne, Heinz. *Canaris.* London: Secker and Warburg, 1979.

Hough, Richard. *Former Naval Person: Churchill and the Wars at Sea.* London: Weidenfeld & Nicholson, 1985.

―――. *The Pursuit of Admiral Graf Spee.* London: Allen & Unwin, 1969.

―――. *The Great War at Sea, 1914–1918.* Oxford: Oxford University Press, 1983.

―――. *First Sea Lord: An Authorized Biography of Admiral Lord Fisher.* London: Allen & Unwin, 1969.

Hoyt, Edwin Palmer. *The Germans Who Never Lost. The Story of the 'Königsberg.'* New York: Funk and Wagnalls, 1968.

―――. *The Last Cruise of the 'Emden.'* New York: MacMillan, 1966.

―――. *Kreuzerkrieg.* Cleveland: World Publishing Co., 1968.

―――. *The Karlsruhe Affair.* London: Arthur Barker Ltd., 1976.

Hurd, Archibald. *The Fleets at War.* London: Hodder, 1914.

———. *German Sea Power: Its Rise and Progress, and Economic Basis.* London: Murray, 1914.

——— and Hector Charles Bywater. *From Heligoland to Keeling Island: One Hundred Days of Naval War.* London: Hodder, 1914.

Irving, John. *Coronel and the Falklands.* London: A. M. Philpot, 1927.

Jane, Fred T. *Jane's Fighting Ships.* London: S. Low, Marston, 1906–07, 1914.

Jung, Dieter. *Tanker und Versorger der deutschen Flotte. 1900–1980.* Stuttgart: Motorbuch Verlag, 1981.

Keegan, John. *The Price of Admiralty: War at Sea from Man of War to Submarine.* London: Hutchinson, 1988.

King-Hall, Stephen. *The War on Sea.* London: E. Benn, 1929.

Kirchhoff, Wilhelm. *Der Weltkrieg zur See.* Berlin: Askanischer Verlag, 1916.

Kroschel, Günter. *Die deutsche Flotte, 1848–1945.* Wilhelmshaven: Lohse-Eissing, 1963.

Langmaid, Kenneth J. R. *Clear for Action. The Royal Navy in Defence and Attack.* London: Jarrold's, 1970.

Lehman, John. *Command of the Seas.* New York: Scribner's Sons, 1988.

Lettow-Vorbeck, Paul Emil von. *East African Campaigns.* New York: Speller, 1957.

Lochner, R. K. *The Last Gentleman of War: The Raider Exploits of the 'Emden.'* Annapolis, MD: Naval Institute Press, 1988.

———. *Kampf im Rufiji-Delta: das Ende des Kleinen Kreuzers 'Königsberg.'* Munich: W. Heyne, 1987.

———. *Kaperfahrten des Kleinen Kreuzers 'Emden.'* Munich: Heyne, 1982.

Lockhart, J. G. "Of the Company of Privateers" in *Great Sea Stories of All Nations.* Harrap, 1932.

Marder, Arthur. "Naval Warfare in the Twentieth Century, 1900–1945" in *Essays in Honour of Arthur Marder.* Gerald Jordan, editor. London: Croom-Helm, 1977.

———. *From the Dreadnought to Scapa Flow: Vol.1: The Royal Navy in the Fisher Era, 1904–1919.* Oxford: Oxford University Press, 1978.

McClement, Fred. *Guns in Paradise: The Saga of the Cruiser 'Emden.'* Toronto: McClelland & Stewart, 1968.

Middlemas, Keith. *Command of the Far Seas.* London: Hutchinson, 1961.

Mirow, Jürgen. *Der Seekrieg 1914–18 in Umrissen.* Göttingen: Musterschmidt, 1976.

Montgomery, Michael. *Who Sank the* Sydney? N. Ryde, NSW: Cassell, 1981.

Morton, Frederic. *Thunder at Twilight.* New York: Scribner, 1989.

Mücke, Hellmuth von. *The 'Ayesha.'* Boston: Ritter, 1917.

———. *The 'Emden.'* Boston: Ritter, 1917.

Newbolt, Henry. *A Naval History of the War 1914–1918.* London: Hodder & Stoughton, 1921.

No primary author. *British Ships Lost at Sea, 1914–18.* Cambridge: Patrick Stevens, 1977.

———. *Conway's All the World's Fighting Ships, 1906–1921.* Annapolis, MD: Naval Institute Press, 1986.

———. *Die Kämpfe der Kaiserliche Marine in den deutschen Kolonien.* Berlin: E. S. Mittler, 1935.

———. *Fighting Ships of World Wars One and Two*. London: Peerage Books, 1986.

———. *Jane's Fighting Ships*. New York: Arco Publishing Co., 1919.

———. *Jane's Fighting Ships of World War I*. London: Studio Editions, 1990.

———. *Jane's Fighting Ships of World War II*. London: Bracken Books, 1989.

———. *The World Almanac Book of World War II*. Peter Young, editor. Englewood, NJ: Prentice-Hall, 1981.

———. *Warships and Sea Battles of World War I*. London: Phoebus, 1973.

Parker de Bassi, Maria Teresa. *Tras las estela del Dresden*. Santiago: Ediciones Tusitala, 1987.

Persius, Lothar. *Der Seekrieg: die Seekämpfe der deutschen Flotte im Weltkrieg*. Charlottenburg: Verlag der Weltbühne, 1919.

Pitt, Barrie. *Revenge at Sea*. New York: Stein & Day, 1960.

Pochhammer, Erich. *Before Jutland: Admiral Spee's Last Voyage*. London: Jarrolds, 1931.

Pollen, Arthur Hungerford. *The Navy in Battle*. London: Chatto & Windus, 1918.

Preston, Antony. *Cruisers*. London: Arms and Armour Press, 1988.

Raeder, Erich. *Der Krieg zur See, 1914–1918*. Berlin: Verlag Mittler, 1923.

———. *Der Kreuzerkrieg in den ausländischen Gewässern*. Berlin: E. S. Mittler, 1922.

Roskill, Stephen. *Churchill and the Admirals*. London: Collins, 1977.

Saarlas, Maido. *Steam and Gas Turbines for Marine Propulsion*. Annapolis, MD: Naval Institute Press, 1987.

Scheer, Reinhard. *Germany's High Seas Fleet in the World War*. London: Cassell, 1920.

Schoen, Walter von. *Auf Vorposten für Deutschland: unsere Kolonien im Weltkrieg*. Berlin: Ullstein, 1935.

———. *Deutschlands Kolonialweg*. Berlin: Im Deutschen Verlag, 1939.

Smith, Myron J. *Battleships and Battlecruisers, 1884–1984: A Bibliography and Chronology*. New York: Garland, 1965.

Spencer-Cooper, Henry Edmund. *The Battle of the Falkland Islands*. London: Cassell, 1919.

Sumida, Jon Tetsuro. *In Defence of Naval Supremacy*. Boston: Unwin Hyman, 1989.

Tarrant, V. E. *Battlecruiser Invincible*. London: Arms & Armour Press, 1986.

Thomas, Lowell. *Lauterbach of the China Sea*. London: Hutchinson, 1939.

Thursfield, H.G. *Brassey's Naval Annual*. Vols. 1898–1948.

Tirpitz, Alfred von. *My Memoirs*. London: Hurst & Blackett, 1919.

Trotter, Wilfrid Pym. *The Royal Navy in Old Photographs*. London: Dent, 1975.

Tuchman, Barbara. *The Guns of August*. New York: Macmillan, 1962.

Van Der Vat, Dan. *The Last Corsair*. London: Granada, 1984.

———. *The Grand Scuttle*. London: Hodder & Stoughton, 1982.

———. *The Ship That Changed the World*. London: Hodder & Stoughton, 1985.

Verner, R. *The Battle-Cruisers in the Action off the Falkland Islands*. London: John Bale Sons & Danielsson, 1926.

Warner, Oliver. *Great Sea Battles*. London: Spring Books, 1968.

Wyllie, William Lionel. *Sea Fights of the Great War: Naval Incidents during the First Nine Months*. London: Cassell, 1918.

Young, Filson. *With the Battlecruisers*. London: Cassell, 1921.

Index

323

About the Author

A native of Preston, England, Keith Yates served in the Royal Navy from 1946 to 1948. Earning doctoral degrees at the University of British Columbia and Oxford University, he joined the faculty of the Department of Chemistry at the University of Toronto in 1961. He has been a professor emeritus since 1991. Among his many other appointments have been an associate professorship at the Université de Paris (1970–71) and visiting professorships at the University of Padua (1971), the University of Western Ontario (1976), the Université Paul Sabatier in Toulouse (1981), and the University of Bristol (1985–86).

Mr. Yates's other publications include *Hückel Molecular Orbital Theory* (Academic Press, 1978), papers in published conference proceedings, and nearly 160 articles and reviews in international journals.

Mr. Yates presently lives on Mayne Island, British Columbia, with his wife.

The **Naval Institute Press** is the book-publishing arm of the U.S. Naval Institute, a private, nonprofit society for sea service professionals and others who share an interest in naval and maritime affairs. Established in 1873 at the U.S. Naval Academy in Annapolis, Maryland, where its offices remain, today the Naval Institute has more than 100,000 members worldwide.

Members of the Naval Institute receive the influential monthly magazine *Proceedings* and discounts on fine nautical prints and on ship and aircraft photos. They also have access to the transcripts of the Institute's Oral History Program and get discounted admission to any of the Institute-sponsored seminars offered around the country.

The Naval Institute also publishes *Naval History* magazine. This colorful bimonthly is filled with entertaining and thought-provoking articles, first-person reminiscences, and dramatic art and photography. Members receive a discount on *Naval History* subscriptions.

The Naval Institute's book-publishing program, begun in 1898 with basic guides to naval practices, has broadened its scope in recent years to include books of more general interest. Now the Naval Institute Press publishes more than seventy titles each year, ranging from how-to books on boating and navigation to battle histories, biographies, ship and aircraft guides, and novels. Institute members receive discounts on the Press's nearly 400 books in print.

For a free catalog describing Naval Institute Press books currently available, and for further information about subscribing to *Naval History* magazine or about joining the U.S. Naval Institute, please write to:

Membership & Communications Department
U.S. Naval Institute
118 Maryland Avenue
Annapolis, Maryland 21402-5035

Or call, toll-free, (800) 233-USNI.